Earth's Final Days

Earth's Final Days

Bob Anderson • Phil Arms • John Barela
Dave Breese • Steve Butler • J.R. Church
Don S. McAlvany • D.A. Miller
Chuck Missler • Lester Sumrall
David F. Webber • John Wesley White
with William T. James

New Leaf Press

First printing, March 1995

Library of Congress Catalog Number: 94-69834
ISBN: 0-89221-279-9

Cover photo: Barry Blackman Studio, Inc., New York, NY 10010

The information and opinions contained in each chapter of this book reflect the views of the individual authors, and in no way are particularly endorsed by the essayists as a group.

For Jesus

Acknowledgments

All acknowledgments, in order to place credit and gratitude properly, must begin with the God of heaven, who makes all good things possible. There is none other like Him. He alone deserves all honor and glory and worship. I am confident that each of us who have been privileged to undertake this work on His behalf are humbly grateful to Him for the opportunity.

So many wonderful people were involved in the production of this book in one way or another that to try and name them all would do great disservice to those who would inadvertently, though inevitably, be overlooked. Suffice it to say, therefore, that I am deeply indebted to each and every person who had a part in bringing *Earth's Final Days* to publication.

My very special thanks to each contributing author, all of whom are dedicated to using their immense, God-given talents and anointing for the forth-telling of the marvelous truths within God's Holy Word, and for spreading the blessed gospel of the Lord Jesus Christ to the whole world.

To my friend and Christian brother, Tim Dudley, and to all of the outstanding associates at New Leaf Press who, as always, bring profound expertise and a very special and exciting flair to their book projects, my sincere appreciation.

To Angie Peters, whose superb editorial and research skills are indispensable, but who means so much more than that to us in that we consider her just another member of the James gang family, and to her husband, Kurt, and their terrific little folks, Nick and Lindsey, for so generously allowing her the considerable blocks of time required for working on this project, my appreciation and my thanks.

To Margaret, Terry, and Nathan, who mean everything to me, all my love.

Finally, on behalf of the family and many friends of Arbra Carman, perhaps the most dedicated Christian I have ever known, who left us at age 89 to be eternally useful in the presence of the Lord she loved so dearly and served so diligently, our heartfelt thankfulness for the blessing of having been touched by this extraordinary and enormously productive life. Her prayers of intercession are greatly missed, as is the inspiring example of how to live the Christian life she provided us each and every day she lived.

Contents

Introduction

by William T. James

Doomsday talk and speculation about the end of the world seems laughable to many people of our most privileged generation. Spectacular achievements and awesome sights in the heavens; brilliant prospects for the future through dynamic, emerging technologies; and a growing global effort to bring about world peace mark this generation as living during the most exciting time of recorded history. Man has, in less than one century, moved from traveling only as fast as a horse can run to speeding at many thousands of miles per hour, from crossing oceans in weeks or months to leaping them in a few hours, and, in the case of space travelers, in only a few minutes.

". . . Where is the promise of his coming? For ever since our ancestors died, all things continue as they were from the beginning of the creation" (2 Pet. 3:4;NRSV). This describes the attitude of most people today when they have occasion to consider the matter. But have all things indeed remained the same?

We have progressed at, literally, light speed in our ability to communicate with one another. Mankind has gone from being able to hear and be heard across expanses of no more than a few hundred yards to sending and receiving voice messages to the moon and back — instantaneously, and accompanied by pictures! Things truly have not remained the same as they were in those past generations when our ancestors lived and died.

Skeptics of the sort described in 2 Peter 3:4 hold these grand accomplishments of mankind up before the eyes of a humanistic world and proclaim them to be proof that any such doomsday predictions are foolishness accepted only by the lunatic fringe of religious society. Man is in control, they haughtily boast, and the shimmering by-products of ever-advancing science and technology make it clear that mankind will eventually master every problem it now faces or will ever face — whether in the arena of geopolitics, socio-economic, ecology, or whatever.

The Christian Bible, with its narrow-minded, bigoted, antiquated notions about God-given morality and final judgment for sin is totally out of step with the New Age that is dawning for this generation of earth's inhabitants. The Bible, they mockingly assert, is irrelevant. Really? *Earth's Final Days, Essays in Apocalypse III* is intended to examine this matter of just how relevant God's Holy Word is to this day in which we live.

The Bible, when studied in its overall context, points to a specific generation that will possess certain, unmistakable characteristics, and that will witness and participate in issues and events identifiable by their extraordinary nature. That generation, God's Word says, will suffer God's most severe judgment, and its remnants will see the literal triumphant return of Jesus Christ to earth, where He will first set foot on the Mount of Olives just outside of Jerusalem.

We are told by media and by utopian architects, however, that things are looking brighter every day. Mankind has now traveled far enough from the moment he first emerged from the primordial slime of his conception and birth and advanced to the point at which he can reach forth into the cosmos — both into physical space and into meditational trans-state spheres to become God-like. Every day, in every way, it is getting better and better for man.

God's Word, on the other hand, tells that God created man perfectly but that, because God gave man a free will, man could choose to obey God or rebel against him. Man chose rebellion. As God predicted that if man chose evil he would surely die, mankind has been in the process of dying — of degenerating, of spiraling downward, morally and in every other way, to our present generation. Man is not getting better and better but worse and worse.

The generation of Earth's final days will be the end product of the serpent-engendered fall in the Garden of Eden. That generation is the one referred to in Matthew 24:22: "And except those days should be shortened, there should no flesh be saved. . . ." If Christ did not return at that moment, man would self-destruct, so violent would be his murderous war-making.

That said, let us consider the truth of the matter. Are we, as a generation of human beings, getting better and better? Or are we entering the final stages, that would, if it were possible, lead to oblivion for the human race?

World Conditions Prophesied for the End of the Age

A serious study of God's Holy Scripture leaves no doubt that He intends to alert believers in Him — particularly believers who will be alive at the time when His Son, Jesus Christ, will return to planet earth to institute His righteous millennial kingdom — that apocalypse, Armageddon, and that glorious return are very near. We have only enough space to briefly look at a few passages of the tremendous body of text that God, in His omniscience, deemed good to share with us.

The Geopolitical Situation

Jesus said in Luke 21:25: "And there shall be signs in the sun, and in the moon, and in the stars; and upon the earth distress of nations, with perplexity; the sea and the waves roaring."

Although His words paint a broad picture in one majestic, sweeping sentence, we are able at this late date in human history to more clearly understand Christ's prophecy and can glean more specific details from this Scripture than could any previous generation. The Lord's words cut with surgical precision to the heart of today's global realities.

God's Word has much to say, particularly in the Book of Revelations, about geophysical and astrophysical occurrences of unusual sorts that will be witnessed by the generation alive during earth's final days. The sun and the moon, we are told, for example, will be darkened during the Great Tribulation, that last three-and-a-half-year period of the present age just prior to Jesus' physical, literal return.

Jesus speaks in general terms about the sun and the moon and the stars in the above Scripture. His prophecy, however, encompasses not only that last three and a half years of the Great Tribulation but "the last days" as a whole. Certainly, we have not witnessed a nova-type condition in our sun nor seen the moon darkened as a result of such an astrophysical calamity, nor have we seen stars literally fall from the heavens in such a dramatic fashion as described in the Revelation.

The description given by Jesus in this prophecy indicates, I believe, the admonition to the generation alive at the end of the age to take heed when they see things in the heavens begin to take place that are unlike occurrences witnessed by any other generation in recorded history. It seems to me also that Jesus tied the astrophysical signals together with the geophysical in a prophetic linkage that will mark that era of earth's history as unique from all others. The dynamics of the times, Jesus is saying here, will make for volatile, geopolitical interaction. ". . . And upon the earth distress of nations, with perplexity; the sea and the waves roaring."

Have we seen such signs in the heavens? Is there distress among earth's nations during our time? Are the diplomats, politicians, statesmen, and political scientists, not to mention the social engineers and economists of our day, perplexed as to what to do to change things for the better? Does the human sea of people rage and roar because of the disparities between the "have's" and "have-not's" during our own violent time on earth?

Scoffers and skeptics mockingly assert that such things have always been. But have they really? Has there ever been such a time when so many of earth's peoples have seen such fantastic signs in the heavens and on the earth — simultaneously? The answer has to be no.

Never before has there been such technology. As a nature catalyst for the storms of human rage around the world, technology sharply defines and gives stark contrast to the inequities and disparities between the "have's" and the "have-not's."

The same marvelous technology that let us watch Neil Armstrong take mankind's first steps on the moon, and more recently gave us a stunning impact-by-impact visual display of a comet slamming into Jupiter, is the same technology that made the leaderships of all nations acutely aware of who are the "have's" and who are the "have-not's." Thus the sea of humanity writhes and roars with the envious hatreds fed by deadly deprivations.

Starvation smothers life in Africa and other impoverished regions. Slaughter by brute beast warlords, in order to fulfill their desires for absolute control, causes the rivers of Rwanda to run red with the blood and bodies of innocent men, women, and children.

We in America, sitting in our oak-paneled dens, watch on our high-resolution television screens the ongoing massacres in Africa, the Middle East, the former Yugoslavia, and even our own inner cities, while our young murder and maim each other in a flood of violence, which, it seems, cannot be stemmed.

Perplexity certainly seems the word to most accurately reflect the frustration of presidents, potentates, priests, and parents while they attempt to deal with distress among nations.

Social, Economic, and Technological Conditions

Many Scriptures in God's Holy Word combine to give a scathing description of the almost insane pursuit of accumulating wealth that will drive mankind's lusts during the earth's final days.

The apostle Paul writes of that generation, which will be conducting social and economic affairs during that perilous time: "For men shall be lovers of their own selves, covetous, boasters, proud, blasphemers, disobedient to parents, unthankful, unholy, Without natural affection, trucebreakers, false accusers, incontinent, fierce, despisers of those that are good, Traitors, heady, highminded, lovers of pleasures more than lovers of God; Having a form of godliness, but denying the power thereof . . . (2 Tim. 3:2-5).

God's Word speaks His opinion about these greedy ones and their soul-consuming compulsion to gather to themselves all they can hoard even at the expense of their contemporaries. His judgment is awesome, and prophesied in terms that cannot be misunderstood. "Go to now, ye rich men, weep and howl for your miseries that shall come upon you. Your riches are corrupted, and your garments are motheaten. Your gold and silver is candered; and the rust of them shall be a witness against you, and shall eat your flesh as it were fire. Ye have heaped treasure together for the last days" (James 5:1-3).

A significant body of prophetic text predicts a generation just before the end of the age that will ultimately go into a materialistically mad frenzy where human love will be extinguished. At the same time, the appetite for money will become insatiable, and seducers and evildoers will grow worse and worse. Society, culture, and economics will become incorrigibly intertwined and a judgment-deserving generation will plunge into what God's Word describes as earth's darkest hour — the Great Tribulation.

The end product of this mad drive for luxuriant living and power over others will be a beastly kingdom of totalitarian control that will subjugate nearly everyone on the planet. Its strength will derive from its absolute control over all commercial activity, thus holding under its despotic rule the ability of all people to buy and sell.

The Bible vividly describes that hellish end-time beast-state and the most terrible of all dictators, the Antichrist, who will be its master. "And he causeth all, both small and great, rich and poor, free and bound, to receive a mark in their right hand, or in their foreheads: And that no man might buy or sell, except he that had the mark, or the name of the beast, or the number of his name" (Rev. 13:16-17).

The information age exploded upon our generation in a way that boggles the minds of even the most computer literate among us. Economics experts and monetary analysts seem inadequate to their tasks of making understandable their vital field of endeavor for the rest of us who, it seems, are becoming more and more enslaved to the economic realities of our time.

Internet, the fledgling global communications network that will apparently be the nucleus for what Vice President Al Gore has termed the "information superhighway" is maturing at an alarming pace, shrinking our world into a more manageable-sized sphere for the monetary power brokers. Talk of wedding national and international economies with fantastic new technologies is now almost routine. There looms on the horizon for America a national identity card, that, it is conjectured, will contain each citizen's record from birth to death in a single microchip.

New electronic funds-transfer technology is being implemented in Europe that will make traditional monetary systems obsolete and, thus, unnecessary. At the same time, it will draw the European Union (EU) together into the most powerful economic bloc ever to exist.

Plans are in the works, it has been reported on such shows as "Good Morning, America" and others, to develop a system of buying and selling that will eventually be done almost exclusively by in-home computer/television hookups using a single identification number for each person transacting business through a super high-tech process of electronic funds transfer. The prototype for such a system has been tested in the Columbus, Ohio, area for a number of years.

Revelation 13:16-17 approaches ever closer while the New World Order-builders tighten the noose around the neck of personal freedom. Technology is swamping humanity in a gigantic wave of liberty-crushing power to control.

Daniel the prophet gave God's word on what would be the social, economic, and technological conditions at the end of the age. ". . . Daniel, shut up the words, and seal the book, even to the time of the end: many shall run to and fro, and knowledge shall be increased" (Dan. 12:4). He also says that the last generation at the end of the age will be swamped by a massive wave of human conflicts. ". . . and the end thereof shall be with a flood . . ." (Dan. 9:26).

Religious Conditions

John the Apostle wrote that he himself was living in "the last time." His God-given prophecy minced no words in telling what will be mankind's rebellion come-to-fruition just before Jesus Christ's return. "Little children, it is the last time: and as ye have heard that antichrist shall come, even now are there many antichrists; whereby we know that it is the last time. . . . Who is a liar but he that denieth that Jesus is the Christ? He is antichrist, that denieth the Father and the Son" (1 John 2:18,22).

The spirit of Antichrist, then, is any spirit of rebellion that strains to pull away from the tugging of Christ's desire to reconcile all men, women, and children to God the Father. That Antichrist spirit is indelibly marked by God's own pen as being possessed by certain unmistakable characteristics that are manifested in fallen human nature. Those hell-destined characteristics will, the apostle Paul tells, drive the generation alive during earth's final days into a fury that will ultimately bring all the armies of the world together for the conflagration that will be Armageddon.

As satanically-inspired irony would have it, the self-willed destructiveness that will characterize that last generation just before Jesus returns will have woven throughout its fabric threads of pseudo-godly religious fervor. A devilish religious conglomerate in the form of a universal church that accepts basically all beliefs except the true Christian belief will sit haughtily astride the beast-state ruled by the world's last tyrant.

"This know also, that in the last days perilous times shall come. For men shall be lovers of their own selves, covetous, boasters, proud, blasphemers, disobedient to parents, unthankful, unholy, Without natural affection, trucebreakers, false accusers, incontinent, fierce, despisers of those that are good, Traitors, heady, high-minded, lovers of pleasures more than lovers of God; having a form of godliness, but denying the power thereof . . ." (2 Tim. 3:1-5).

John the Apostle wrote in the Revelation about this end-time religious system that will display characteristics in diametrical opposition to the holiness demanded by God — holiness obtainable only through a personal, redemptive relationship with Jesus Christ. Rejection of the only begotten Son of God by a sin-embracing world gone mad will produce a religious monstrosity described with symbolic language in Revelation 17:6: "And I saw the woman drunken with the blood of the saints, and with the blood of the martyrs of Jesus: and when I saw her, I wondered with great admiration."

John graphically portrayed the end-time religious amalgamation as a harlot who, in ancient Babylonian-like paganism, slavishly serves the Antichrist and his geopolitical and socioeconomic dictatorship. As the generation of earth's final days approaches, evidence of such a religious structure will surely be in view.

It is essential to ask at this point: Is there such an organization in sight during our troubling times — a religious structure that piously proposes to embark upon godly causes so that all mankind will benefit yet indignantly refuses to acknowledge that Jesus is the only one who can save man by reconciling him with God the Father, the Creator of all things? (Explore the fascinating answer to that question in Chapter 8.)

Mankind's March Toward Eternity

The hour is late.

Authors within *Earth's Final Days* examine in depth the often explosive, sometimes deadly issues and events of our time on this volatile planet, prayerfully considering just how near we are to that hour which will catapult billions of earth's inhabitants into the darkest time of human history.

Despite the terrifying prospects that we believe loom just ahead, it is not the intention of these essayists to point to a bottomless abyss out of which there is no escape. Rather, it is our passionate desire to project the Light of the World into the soul of every person who is willing to accept God's offer of redemption.

Jesus Christ is that eternal beam of effulgence who, alone, has the power to illuminate and regenerate the hearts and minds of men. He is the King of kings, that bright and morning star who will forever dispel the billowing blackness of evil with the brightness of His coming.

Section I

Jesus Describes the Last Days

by William T. James

"The end is near!" "Prepare to meet thy doom!" These and other gloomy slogans have long been the warnings scrawled across large picket signs held by scruffy cartoon characters clad in long white robes, beads, and sandals.

Just beneath the surface of that cynical humor, however, desire has always burned within most of humanity to know what awaits them in the murky future. The intense curiosity in that regard has just as long kept the soothsayers spinning out their very profitable though totally false prophecies. "When will the end of the world come?" That question has been around at least since man began recording his thoughts.

The end of the world has been predicted hundreds of times. This entire volume could, if one wished to fill space with failed end-of-the world predictions, devote chapters to such prophecies issuing forth from every literate or semi-literate society, culture, and era. Still, the question burns.

Rather, *many* questions burn. "When will the end of the world come?" "Will there be any warnings?" "Will it end with a bang, or with a whimper?" "Is the end near?" "Is there anyone or any group who can provide the answer to the matter of how, when, etc., this planet and its inhabitants will pass into cosmological history?"

These questions were foremost on the minds of the disciples

when they approached Jesus at a moment when He was not surrounded by the throngs of people, which His presence more and more drew as the time of His ministry on earth approached its end. "Tell us, when shall these things be? and what shall be the sign of thy coming, and of the end of the world?" (Matt. 24:3), they asked Jesus.

He answered them in very specific, literal terms backed up with parabolic analogies and examples to illustrate and make understandable His troubling prophecies. What a unique and astonishing moment in human history! Here was God himself, come to earth in fleshly form to not only provide the once and for all atoning sacrifice for the sin of man, but to teach the creation He loves His precepts for living life to its fullest. This was, and is today, Jesus Christ, the Living Word, giving a precise account of how the world as we know it will come to its end.

This section deals with matters involving Jesus' answers to the disciples' questions that day as He and they discoursed from their vantage overlooking the Temple Mount. "Is the end near?" "Are we living as part of the generation that will endure earth's final days?"

Careful analysis of Christ's words, taken together with the urgent issues and events of our time, provide much fascinating food for thought. Serious contemplation of these things should cause each of us who are privileged to draw breath during this exciting age to examine our own motives and intentions, and, most of all, our relationship to the One who gave us the answer to the burning question about the end of the world.

1

False Christs, False Prophets, Deceivers Arise

by Bob Anderson

The return of Jesus Christ, the "second coming," Armageddon, and the "end of the world" are topics discussed, argued, and debated among Christians and non-Christians alike at an escalating frequency. What has been termed by some as millennial madness will likely continue at an even more frenzied pace as we draw nearer to the end of this decade, century, and millennium.

Author Stanley J. Grenz, in his book, *The Millennial Maze: Sorting Out Evangelical Options,* observes:

> At the close of the twentieth century the message of the doomsday preachers — once the brunt of jokes and the laughing stock of "enlightened" citizens of the modern world — has become in the minds of many people a serious possibility and a genuine concern in a way unparalleled in prior decades. For the first time in recent history we sense that our civilization is tottering on the edge of a precipice peering into the abyss of self-destruction and chaos.[1]

Christians have been anxiously awaiting the Lord's return for nearly 2,000 years. But they are not the only ones sensing that something of an extraordinary nature could soon happen to the world.

Omni magazine featured a tongue-in-cheek article entitled "The End Is Nigh — Again." In this review, the authors quoted many religious and even non-religious people who believe in and are pointing to the year 2000 or thereabouts for some earthshaking event.

Among the sources *Omni* quoted were the prophecies of the sixteenth-century French philosopher Nostradamus and a seventeenth-century mystic called the Seeress of Prague. The authors also cited New Age prophecies from a modern group called the New Age Millennialists, as well as twentieth-century psychics Edgar Cayce, the "sleeping prophet," who saw 1998 as the beginning of a New Age, and Jean Dixon who "foresees an evil and charismatic Antichrist leading . . . the world astray in this decade."[2]

The *Omni* authors even quoted writings that dated back thousands of years to the Aztec and Mayan Indian cultures. Each source stated that a great cataclysmic event would happen sometime near the end of this decade or early in the twenty-first century, and that it would be followed by a millennial period of peace on earth.[3]

The Bible is exceedingly clear in its warning against putting stock in occult sources (Deut. 18:9-14). It is fascinating to note, however, that even the world believes something unique is about to happen — that we are headed for some staggering event in which the world will go through a great crisis followed by a period of 1,000 years of perfect peace.

The Most Distinct Sign

In theological terms, the study of Christ's return and the end times is called eschatology. In studying this subject, one cannot minimize the importance of Matthew 24. This section of Scripture paints a vivid picture of conditions on earth just prior to Christ's return.

In verse 4, Jesus begins to answer the questions posed to Him by His disciples concerning His advent, specifically, ". . . When shall these things be? and what shall be the sign of thy coming, and the end of the world?" Notice that the word "sign" is singular, not plural: "What shall be the sign of Your coming?"

A quick review of Matthew 24 reveals that Jesus does not immediately answer the initial part of the question, "When shall these things be?" He does, however, talk about the sign of His coming and the end of the world or end of the age. He begins with these words of warning: "Take heed that no man deceive you," then proceeds to caution that many will come in His name, saying "I am Christ" and deceiving multitudes.

The very first sign that Jesus mentions concerning His coming is that people will arise in (or on the strength and authority of) His name, stealing the title that belongs only to Him, and deceiving many. Three times in this chapter (verses 5, 11, and 24), Jesus warns that the end of the age, just prior to His return, will be characterized by the appearance of false Christs, false prophets, and false Messiahs who will not only deceive great multitudes, but ". . . if it were possible, they shall deceive the very elect" (Matt. 24:24).

Jesus also mentions other "signs" of His coming (verses 6 and 7). He refers, for example, to wars and rumors of wars, famines, pestilences, and earthquakes in diverse places.

In the past 50 years the world has experienced these "other" signs like no previous generation. However, it is interesting to note that Jesus is asked for the *one* sign that will distinguish His second coming — and three times He mentions the rise of spiritual deceivers! Notice that He mentions wars, famines, pestilences, and earthquakes only once. Apparently, there is something extremely significant about religious deceptions just prior to His return. Why else would the Son of God refer to it so often in this short series of verses?

Yes, Jesus obviously wanted His disciples to be keenly alert to the fact that the beguilers would come! He was so concerned about this problem that He called these false prophets ravenous (savage) wolves disguised as sheep (Matt. 7:15-23). From this analogy we derive the common expression, "a wolf in sheep's clothing." We are instructed to observe the "fruit" of these wolves.

The context of this series of verses obviously pertains to false prophets. It becomes quite apparent upon examination that the "fruit" of these wolves is false prophecy.

In the days immediately prior to Christ's return, many unbelievable things will no doubt occur. But the most distinct problem endured by that generation will be one of religious deception. Ours may well be that generation.

Spiritual Counterfeits

Fifty years ago had people been asked, "What will the world be like at the end of the age?" many would most likely have predicted a lack of religious beliefs — that atheism and agnosticism would be the prevailing sentiments. However, Matthew 24 indicates quite the opposite.

An explosion of interest in things religious and spiritual will develop at the end of the age, but a great deal of the attention will be directed toward the counterfeits. Likewise, in 2 Timothy 3:8, the apostle Paul warns that just as Jannes and Jambres (magicians in the pharaoh's court) had opposed Moses, men of corrupt minds would appear and present counterfeits of the true faith.

How did Jannes and Jambres oppose Moses? Was it by denying the miraculous? No, they also worked miracles through the power of Satan. Similarly, the end of the age will not be a time of atheism and skepticism. Rather, an outpouring of interest in religion and in the miraculous will occur, but deception and delusion will be rampant.

Today, in many nations of the world, a revival of "religion" is occurring. Unfortunately, in most of these nations the religion undergoing revival is not Christianity. Islam, second only to Christianity in size, is not only the dominant faith in the Middle East, but it is also the fastest-growing religion in the world.

Statistics from *The Church Around The World* (Tyndale House) show that over the past half-century Christianity's membership increased by 47 percent. During that same time, however, Buddhism's following increased by 63 percent and Hinduism's by 117 percent. The number of Islam (Muslim) devotees exploded with an astounding 500 percent growth, from 200 million to the present 1 billion members.[4]

According to Muslim expert Dr. Robert A. Morey, "In England, there are more Muslims than there are evangelical Christians. Abandoned Anglican churches are being bought and converted into mosques so rapidly that some Muslims claim that England will be the first Muslim European country."

Here in the United States, more than 500 Islamic centers have been built, with plans for significant expansion underway.[5] According to *USA Today,* Islam's membership in this country exceeds 4 million.

Carol Stone, whose demographic analysis is included in a research collection, *The Muslims in America,* estimates that 6 million Muslims will reside in the United States by the year 2000. Islam will replace Judaism as the nation's second-largest religion sometime within this decade.[6]

What Is a Cult?

America has always guaranteed her people the freedom of religion. Cults, likewise, are protected under the same rights granted by our constitution to every citizen.

By use of the term "cult," I do not mean to imply anything of a derogatory nature to any group named herein. The word "cult" (from the Latin word cultis) simply refers to a group of individuals. However, theologically speaking, when brought into the context of Christianity, which has produced most of the cults in the world today, a cult is a group of persons gathered around somebody's interpretation of the Bible.

Such groups generally claim to be in sympathy or in harmony with orthodox Christianity, but all members deny essential doctrines of the faith as defined by the creeds of the historic church and upheld through the ages. These doctrines include the deity of Christ, the Trinity, Christ's bodily resurrection, salvation by grace through faith alone, Christ's bodily return, the virgin birth of Christ, and eternal punishment for the unredeemed.

Cults and aberrant groups began to form here in America in the nineteenth century. Groups such as the Church of Jesus Christ of Latter Day Saints (Mormons), Seventh-Day Adventists, Theosophy, Christian Science, Unity, Jehovah's Witnesses, and others, all began to take shape during that period.

The twentieth century has seen a proliferation of cultic and occultic organizations. In addition to the older, well-established groups, the last 25 to 30 years in particular have produced Jim Jones, Charles Manson, Rev. Sun Myung Moon, Elizabeth Clare Prophet, "Moses" David Berg, Roy Masters, Jose Silva, Werner Erhard, and David Koresh, just to a name a few founders or leaders of relatively new aberrational religious movements in America. Additional deviant groups of every conceivable variety spring up almost daily.

America has also been besieged by occultic teachings from the East. Many of these teachings and/or techniques have come in under the guise of the latest "scientific" approaches to relaxation, meditation, health, medicine, and physical fitness. Under the banners of "New Age," "Human Potential," and "Holistic Health," many of these practices have become widely accepted in business and public education, and have even infiltrated Christian churches.

In short, the twentieth century has produced a cult explosion the likes of which our forefathers could never have imagined. According to the late Dr. Walter Martin, founder of the Christian Research Institute, in 1830 there were less than 1,000 cultists in the entire country.[7] Yet today, estimates by experts in countercult ministries place that figure in the tens of millions.[8]

Occult Invasion

Eastern occultism made its major debut here in America during the 1960s, 1970s, and 1980s, under the leadership of numerous Indian gurus. Most of these men not only claimed to be divine, but in many cases were worshipped by their followers. Among the more prominent gurus were Maharishi Mahesh Yogi, who founded colleges in Iowa and California where students study his Eastern philosophies; Thackar Sing, who enticed many young people to follow him back to India where they have become his devoted disciples; Maharaj Gi, who, at the tender age of 14, was worshipped as God by his ardent followers; and the late Bhagwan Shree Rajneesh, who built an occult empire in Oregon while separating many thousands of people from millions of their dollars before finally being deported by the U.S. government.[9]

In 1982, Benjamin Creme, a New Age counterfeit of "John the Baptist," helped the Tara Center in Los Angeles run a $500,000 newspaper ad campaign in more than 20 major cities of the world. These ads, including a 1987 full-page display in *USA Today,* proclaimed Lord Maitreya to be the Christ. According to Creme, Maitreya is the one awaited by all major religions. For the deceived Christians, he's the second coming of Christ; for the Buddhists, he's the fifth Buddha; for the Hindus, he's the Lord Krishna; for the Muslims, he's the Imammahdi; for the Jews, he's the long-awaited Messiah.

Maitreya's status and location are supposedly known to only a few. When the appointed time arrives, he is expected to make himself known to all of mankind. His task, according to the ads, is "to show us how to live together peacefully as brothers."[10]

The initial foray of gurus and messiahs from the East were followed by many teachings and seminars, including Transcendental Meditation, Erhard Seminars Training (EST), the Forum, Life Spring, Dianetics, biofeedback, Silva Mind Control, International Society for Krishna Consciousness, Eckankar, Nichiren Shoshu, and numerous others.

Psychics, not to be overshadowed, regularly buy prime time on independent TV stations and "fringe" time on network stations, airing programs like the "Psychic Friends Network" with Dionne Warwick. Jean Dixon, a long-time frequent feature of occult magazines and grocery store tabloids, now appears regularly in TV commercials promoting her astrology telephone service along with Mickey Dane and numerous others.

A poll conducted in 1981 by George Gallup Jr., and confirmed by a *USA Weekend* poll in 1986, shows that nearly one out of every four Americans — roughly 60 million people — have now accepted the occult doctrine of reincarnation, a belief that lies in direct opposition to the biblical teaching on resurrection.[11]

If one were to combine the previously mentioned tens of millions who are involved in the "mainline" cults with the 60 million involved in occultic activities, even allowing for some possible overlapping, one would arrive at the startling figure of at least 80 to 85 million people. That's about one out of every three Americans who are involved in some form of spiritual deception.

According to Gallup, "This is the most crucial decade in history. Designer à la carte religion flourishes as traditional Christianity is undermined by counterfeits."[12]

Terminology Twisters

Adding to the dilemma of the deception created by cults, the occult, and false religions worldwide are two other developing phenomena among the general populace: a deficiency in biblical knowledge and the rejection of absolute truth. A growing number of Americans, possibly as many as one-third, "do not believe in the God of the Bible, but have other notions of who (or what) God is or means."[13]

This problem seems to worsen annually — an inherent consequence of the declining percentage of people who read the Bible and/or attend Christian church services and Sunday school each year.[14] This decline in biblical knowledge renders the gullible, spiritually naive person easy prey for the cults and the occultists who twist Scripture to fit their own preconceived ideas and theology.

Consider the words of Jesus in Matthew 7:16 that we would know the false prophets "by their fruit." It is interesting that many cultists feel that their organizations are indeed the "true" church because of their "good works." By twisting Jesus' words, the cultist reasons that he is a genuine Christian due to his religious activities and ethical lifestyle.

It is indeed true that many cultists can and do live moral and ethical lives. In fact, many of them lead lives that exceed the ethics and morality of some Christians. Thus, the world looks at the virtuous life and reasons, "Well, that's good fruit; therefore, the tree must be good." The problem, of course, is that it is entirely possible to lead, at least on the surface, an ethical and a moral life, and at the same time be hostile toward God and antagonistic to His Word.

Atheists, agnostics, and skeptics, as well as members of multiple forms of world religions, are often capable of living lives that appear to comply with Christian ethics and morality. However, all of them share one common theological attribute: Every non-Christian religion and religious system will not only deny that Jesus Christ is the exclusive way to God but will reject His incarnate deity as well.

The lives that these people live may be acceptable, but their teachings and their doctrines are corrupt. Therefore, the tree must be judged not only by the fruit of the life that is lived, but more importantly by the fruit of the doctrine that is taught.[15]

Cult Litmus Test

The writers of the New Testament stress the need to guard against coming religious treachery. Paul alerts us in 2 Corinthians 11:4 that there would be those coming who "preacheth another Jesus, another spirit . . . another gospel. . . ." Paul again cautions the church about a different gospel in Galatians 1:6-9. John, Peter, and Jude warn us to beware of false prophets and teachers.

With all this New Testament caution of coming spiritual treachery, it is incumbent upon us to learn to recognize cults. Is there an acid test to determine a full-fledged cult?

Consider the words of Jesus in John 8:24, "I said therefore unto you, that ye shall die in your sins: for if you believe not that I am he, ye shall die in your sins." Jesus states categorically that a person must believe that He is the I AM.

What exactly does He mean by this statement? Jesus is quoting Exodus 3:14, where Jehovah (Yahweh) God, speaking to Moses through a burning bush, identifies himself as "I AM that I AM." In John 8, Jesus applies this title to himself and says one must believe that He is the I AM or he will perish.

Other references that verify that Jesus is the I AM of the Old Testament are found in John 8:58, 10:30-33, 13:19, and 18:5-6. Scripture confirms that Jesus is God incarnate, the second person of the Trinity. For anyone to deny this fact not only categorizes that person as a false prophet but condemns him to spiritual death as well, no matter how ethical and moral a life he may live.

Billion Dollar Cults

Due in part to biblical illiteracy in our society and compounded by a breakdown in morality, groups such as the Church of Jesus Christ of Latter Day Saints (Mormons), the Jehovah's Witnesses, and others who espouse virtue and family values are experiencing phenomenal growth.

The Witnesses, for example, while denying every basic doctrine of orthodox Christianity, have grown by more than 400 percent in the United States since 1960. In 1940 there were only slightly more than 58,000 active, baptized Witnesses in the U.S.; by 1950 there were more than 108,000; by 1960 the figure reached 205,900; there were 416,789 by 1970; 565,309 by 1980; 850,120 by 1990; and their numbers now approach 1 million.[16]

The Mormons are perhaps the most widely condoned cult (even among Christians), yet their highly unorthodox doctrine includes the teaching that God the Father was once a man who worked His way to godhood, and that we, too, can become gods.

Mormons, like the Witnesses, have experienced phenomenal growth in the last few decades. From around 200,000 members in 1890, the Latter Day Saints today claim a worldwide membership of more than 8 million.[17] It is estimated that the Mormon faith is growing at a rate of 1,500 members per day.

In addition to being one of the largest cults, it is also one of the wealthiest, with an estimated income of $4.7 billion per year. The Mormon church reportedly controls at least 100 companies or businesses (including a $300 million-a-year media conglomerate), and has an investment portfolio exceeding $1 billion.[18]

The New Age Hodgepodge

The New Age movement has made tremendous gains in the West over the past decade. A national opinion poll conducted by the University of Chicago shows that 67 percent of Americans "now profess a belief in the supernatural," and 42 percent "believe that they have been in contact with someone who died."[19] Two million Americans have reported having "out of body" or near-death experiences; another 20 million are "tuning in" to psychics and transchannelers; and at least two-thirds of these adults have experienced ESP.[20]

The term "New Age movement" is in itself a misleading euphemism. It is neither new, nor a movement. Actually, "New Age" is an umbrella term covering a hodgepodge of ideas ranging from reincarnation, evolution, and meditation to cosmic enlightenment through the aid of extraterrestrials. Its roots can be traced back thousands of years to the occult religions of the Babylonians and to India and Hinduism, which claims to be the world's oldest religion. The New Age movement would, therefore, be more correctly classified as a belief system, philosophy, or religion than a movement.

How widespread this "movement" is can only be guessed. *Guide to the American Occult,* 1988 edition, lists "over 3,500 Mystical, Metaphysical, Psychic, ESP, Spiritualist, Faith Healing, Astrological, Pagan, Wicca (sic) and other new and unconventional religions and 'occult' organizations, publishers, book dealers, newsletters, and journals in the United States and Canada."[21]

High-Tech Deception

Many New Age tenets are simply the practices of shamans and occultists of the past, packaged in Western terminology and disguised as the latest technology. The reason for this approach is simple. Hinduism and Eastern philosophies are not very palatable in the West due in part to our religious heritage. Both Christianity and Judaism, the dominant religions of America, believe in just one God — a belief known as monotheism. The New Age, by contrast, sees the entire universe as divine, a belief called pantheism.

Maharishi Mahesh Yogi realized that he faced problems peddling his ideas in the U.S. due to the great religious and cultural differences between East and West. He soon discovered, however, that Americans would accept his brand of occultism more eagerly if he could make it appear as the latest in "scientific" technology.

To appeal to America's fascination with technology, Maharishi began to utilize biofeedback machines, which monitor blood pressure, basic metabolic rates, brain wave patterns, etc. Once people were hooked up to the machine, Maharishi would then teach them his Eastern meditation techniques.

People discovered that during such sessions they would achieve lower blood pressure, lower basic metabolic rates, etc., and, thus convinced of the benefits, would eagerly embrace Maharishi's total "scientific" system of relaxation. In these meditation sessions, a person is taught and encouraged to cast out all thoughts. The problem with this type of meditation is that it can lead to altered states of consciousness and to possible demonic influence.[22]

By contrast, Christians are told in Isaiah 26:3, "Thou wilt keep him in perfect peace, whose mind is stayed on thee. . . ." Romans 12:2 states, "And be not conformed to this world: but be ye transformed by the renewing of your mind. . . ." In 2 Corinthians 10:5 we read, "Casting down imaginations, and every high thing that exalteth itself against the knowledge of God, and bringing into captivity every thought to the obedience of Christ." The Bible simply does not teach the practice of emptying the mind.

Making Your Own Way to God

Scripture not only warns of deceivers attacking the Church from without, but also of false prophets who will mislead people from within. For example, in 2 Peter 2:1, Peter is obviously addressing those in the church. "But there were false prophets also among the people, even as there shall be false teachers among you, who privily shall bring in damnable heresies, even denying the Lord that bought them, and bring upon themselves swift destruction."

We are told, ". . . in the latter times some shall depart from the faith, giving heed to seducing spirits, and doctrines of devils." (1 Tim. 4:1). Scripture teaches that the time will come when people will not endure sound doctrine, ". . . but after their own lusts shall they heap to themselves teachers, having itching ears; And they shall turn away their ears from the truth, and shall be turned unto fables" (2 Tim. 4:3-4). Some will be ". . . carried about with every wind of doctrine . . ." (Eph. 4:14).

About 100 years ago, a heresy called New Thought was rejected and expelled from the Church. It was the New Age movement of its day. From those who were banished from the Church came the founders of the mind science cults — Christian Science, Unity School of Christianity, Science of Mind, Religious Science, etc.[23]

This movement has been kept alive in the Christian church today largely through the writings of the late Dr. Norman Vincent Peale. Peale has managed, over the years, to maintain credibility among his millions of readers of *Guideposts* magazine despite regular features of the "spiritual stories" of non-Christians. The magazine has even, on occasion, spotlighted cultists.

Such was the case with former Atlanta Braves baseball star Dale Murphy, a devoted Mormon, who was featured in Peale's publication. That incident would not surprise those who recall that Peale went to the late Mormon president and prophet, Spencer W. Kimble, for the laying on of hands to receive the Holy Ghost. Peale said he had never felt the power of God so strongly as he did on that occasion. Moreover, when Peale, as a guest of the Phil Donahue program was asked if a person had to be "born again" to reach heaven, he replied, "Oh, no, you've got your way to God, I've got mine. I found eternal peace in a Shinto Shrine."[24]

Peale, a 33rd degree Mason, was featured on the covers of two masonic publications, *The New Age* (May 1986), and the *Scottish Rite Journal* (March 1991). Peale also delivered the eulogy at the funeral of his friend Earnest Holmes, founder of the cult known as Religious Science.

Peale's protégé, Robert Schuller, has one of the largest followings of any American preacher, with a weekly television audience of nearly 20 million people.[25] Yet, according to the late Dr. Walter Martin, Schuller denies several cardinal teachings of Christianity, including the doctrine of eternal punishment. Schuller teaches that hell is the loss of self-esteem, says Martin, and that Jesus suffered hell on the cross when He lost His self-esteem. Schuller believes that the greatest need of mankind today is to regain his self-esteem.[26]

Although Paul wrote that ". . . Christ Jesus came into the world to save sinners . . ." (1 Tim. 1:15), and Christ himself said that He came to call sinners to repentance (Luke 5:32), Schuller comments, "I don't think anything has been done in the name of Christ and under the banner of Christianity that has proven more destructive to human personality and, hence, counterproductive to the evangelism enterprise, than the often crude, uncouth, and un-Christian strategy of attempting to make people aware of their lost and sinful condition."[27]

Schuller, on the "Praise the Lord" television program, was asked by Trinity Broadcasting Network president Paul Crouch if he teaches repentance and redemption. Schuller replied, "Of course I do. But I do it so positively no one recognizes it."[28]

Date Setters

One current trend or "wind of doctrine" as we approach the year 2000 is the idea that we can somehow know the time of Christ's return. Of course, the practice of date-setting is certainly not confined to the twentieth century. Since the first century A.D., there have been hundreds, if not thousands, of prophecies predicting "the end."

The Jehovah's Witnesses have been setting dates for more than 100 years. The Witnesses first proclaimed Christ's presence in 1874. Subsequent dates heralding the end of the world were set for 1914, 1918, 1925, 1941, and 1975. Each time the *Watchtower,* a periodical publication of the Jehovah's Witnesses, sets a date, membership soars. When the prophesied event fails to materialize, the Witnesses' leadership suddenly develop amnesia, denying that they ever made such a claim or passing the blame for the failure on to "over-zealous" members.

In 1835, Mormon founder Joseph Smith declared "The coming of the Lord is nigh — even 56 years should wind up the scene."[29] This prophecy specifically dates the second coming of our Lord no later than 1891. Another of Smith's fantastic prophecies, given in 1832, reads: "Verily this is the word of the Lord, that the city — New Jerusalem [which they define as Independence, Missouri] — shall be built by the gathering of the saints, beginning at this place, even the place of the temple, which temple shall be reared in this generation."[30]

Another cult leader, William Miller, a second advent preacher of the nineteenth century, had a sizable following. Miller eagerly awaited Christ's second coming in the year 1843. After that prophecy failed, Miller changed the date to October 1844. When neither of these dates proved true, Miller denounced the movement and left.

James and Ellen G. White and Hiram Edson, who were among the hundreds of thousands influenced by Miller, saved the movement by instituting the "Sanctuary Doctrine," also known as the "Investigative Judgment," in which Jesus played a "new role" in heaven beginning in 1844. In effect, Jesus, according to them, moved from one compartment of heaven to another, where He was to "investigate" our works. This strange teaching is still accepted today among this group, now known as the Seventh Day Adventist Church.[31]

The late Herbert W. Armstrong, founder of the Worldwide Church of God, was another date setter with a list of failed prophecies. Space does not permit a comprehensive account of them all, but in 1968, Armstrong gave his followers this prophecy: "The 6,000 years are about up. We may have another 3, 5, or 10 years to go."[32] The great tribulation, which he prophesied would start in 1972, of course, failed to materialize.

Worldwide Rapture Fever

Many people have been prophesying "the end" for years. Most of those "prophecies," at least during the past few centuries, have come from aberrant teachers or groups considered cults or sects outside of orthodox Christianity. Few, if any, among orthodox Christians gave much credence to those who espoused "the end," much less set dates for the same.

More recently, however, the practice of setting dates for Christ's return by otherwise fundamental, conservative Christian teachers has become almost fashionable. Even more upsetting, perhaps, is the number of Christians who have fallen prey to these false prognosticators.

We have already witnessed several failed attempts at date setting during the late eighties and early nineties by Christian ministers. Probably the most notable, because of the sheer numbers of people affected, was the failed prophecy of Edgar Whisenant, author of a 92-page booklet, *88 Reasons Why the Rapture Will Be in 1988*.

The book was an overnight sensation circulating throughout America. As the title suggests, Whisenant claimed that Christ would return for His church in 1988, between September 11 and 13, during the feast of Trumpets (Rosh Hashanah), to be precise. According to Whisenant's publisher, the World Bible Society, more than 4.5 million copies were printed. The Society, apparently undisturbed by the failed prophecy, asserted that although Christ had not returned, many people had come to Christ and the book had inspired revival and renewal in the hearts of many Christians.[33]

The United States is by no means the only country affected by rapture fever. *USA Today* ran a full-page ad on October 20, 1991, paid for by the worldwide Hyoo-go ("rapture") or Jong Mal Ron ("end-time theory") movement based in Korea. The ad read "RAPTURE: OCTOBER 28, 1992 — JESUS IS COMING IN THE AIR." It went on to state that "50 million people will die in earthquakes, 50 million in traffic accidents, 50 million from fires, 50 million from collapsed buildings, 1.4 billion from World War III, and 1.4 billion from a separate Armageddon."[34]

Failed Prophecy

A more recent "failed prophecy" occurred on the Trinity Broadcasting Network. On Paul Crouch's "Praise the Lord" program, a Southern California Pastor, John Hinkle, proclaimed that God had told him that on June 9, 1994, "All evil will be ripped from the earth."

The prophecy received wide coverage, having been promoted by both Crouch and Christian Broadcasting Network president Pat Robertson. Crouch even admitted that if the prophecy did not come to pass, it would prove that Hinkle was a false prophet! Of course, June 9 came and went and, as we have seen and experienced, evil is still very much with us. As might have been predicted, the proclaimers quickly "spiritualized" the event, claiming that it was "accomplished in the spirit world" or something to that effect.

Anyone with a pittance of biblical knowledge should have realized the absurdity of such a prophecy. As long as man inhabits the earth there will be evil. Jeremiah 17:9 reads, "The heart is deceitful above all things, and desperately wicked: who can know it." Evil is in the human heart. How could evil be removed without man being removed? Does the apostle Paul see evil being ripped from the earth? No; quite the contrary. "But evil men and seducers shall wax worse and worse . . ."(2 Tim. 3:13). How could evil be ripped from the earth when the Antichrist is yet to come? (2 Thess. 2:4-10). Even during the thousand-year reign of Christ, man's heart will still be capable of evil, as evidenced by the attack against Christ in Jerusalem (Rev. 20:7-9).[35]

Another within the Christian church who issued forth a so-called prophecy that has proved false is Harold Camping. Although orthodox concerning essential doctrines, through a system of numerology, speculation, and private interpretations, Camping introduces some truly bizarre renditions of Scripture. In his book *1994?*, Camping proclaimed that the end of the world would occur between September 15 and 23. "When September 6, 1994 arrives, no one else can become saved. The end has come."[36]

Earlier in this chapter, I pointed to the fact that Jesus did not immediately answer the first part of the question His disciples posed in Matthew 24:3 as to when He would return for His church. In Matthew 24:36, Jesus tells us why: "But of that day and hour knoweth no man, no, not the angels of heaven, but my Father only."

One would think that this admonition by the Lord would make people fearful about precise date setting. If Jesus himself didn't know the day or the hour of His return, how can anyone else? Certainly it seems to many Christians that the time is short, but when will men ever learn to quit setting precise dates?

Back to the Basics

Deuteronomy 18:21-22 gives us the definition of a true prophet of God: "And if thou say in thine heart, How shall we know the word which the Lord hath not spoken? When a prophet speaketh in the name of the Lord, if the thing follow not, nor come to pass, that is the thing which the Lord hath not spoken, but the prophet hath spoken it presumptuously; thou shalt not be afraid of him."

In Old Testament times, a person proclaiming himself to be a prophet of God needed to fail in only one professed revelation from God to be labeled a false prophet. The penalty for such a performance was death by stoning. Today, many of the supporters of these false teachers simply develop a case of amnesia, and anxiously await the next serving of spiritual arsenic.

Believers in Jesus Christ are called to be the salt of the earth (Matt. 5:13). Salt is known as a preservative. We are to be preservers of the Christian faith. We are to affect the world for Christ. But how can we be salt if we don't even know the basics of that faith?

One of the most glaring problems within the church of Jesus

Christ today is that too many Christians don't know why they believe what they believe. How then can they ever hope to follow Peter's command to "... be ready always to give an answer to every man that asketh you a reason of the hope that is in you ..." (1 Pet. 3:15)?

That is exactly why more than 80 percent of the cults' membership consists of people who were once members of Christian churches.[37] They simply didn't know the real gospel message. Hosea 4:6 reveals the result of such a condition. "My people are destroyed for a lack of knowledge. . . ."

If we are ever to make a difference in our world, we must get back to the Bible. We would be wise indeed to consider the biblical admonition found in 2 Timothy 2:15: "Study to shew thyself approved unto God, a workman that needeth not to be ashamed, rightly dividing the word of truth."

2

Wars, Rumors of Wars, Raging Human Seas of Hatred

by William T. James

Wars have been at the core of human interaction since the moment in time when the first man, Adam, determined to agree with the serpent in Eden. By taking the forbidden fruit offered by Eve, man alienated himself from God, the author of the only true peace.

Never before in recorded history have rumors of war of such frightening scale more dominated the conduct of human affairs than the day in which we live. This fact should not surprise the believer in the true God. Throughout the millennia, He has demonstrated to His creation, through word and deed, that to rebel against Him is to short-circuit the marvelous peace He alone provides. To secede from that perfect union He established between himself and all His creation is to bring upon mankind the hellish turbulence which will culminate in that greatest of all conflagrations, Armageddon.

Jesus said in His Olivet discourse that the last days would be characterized by a marked increase in the number of wars and rumors of wars. Jesus warned that these increasingly vicious and terrifying wars will be generated by the violent, billowing storm clouds of ethnic hatreds and genocide.

Any honest observer of the human condition must admit that the similarities between the current world of armed conflicts — and prospects for war — reflect Christ's prophetic words: "And ye shall hear of wars and rumours of wars: see that ye be not troubled: for all these things must come to pass, but the end is not yet. For nation shall rise against nation, and kingdom against kingdom . . ." (Matt. 24:6-7). Anyone who would deny that we live in just such a time as Jesus described must be hopelessly ignorant of the unfolding events or deliberately unwilling or unable to realistically assess the glaring facts.

There would literally not be enough space in this entire volume to do justice to the examination of the wars and rumors of wars that have pockmarked the twentieth century. Thus, the balance of this chapter will highlight as many of the armed conflicts as possible and analyze whether those conflicts constitute a body of evidence sufficient to conclude that we live in a day of wars and rumors of wars suspiciously similar to that end-time period prophesied by Jesus Christ.

The Russian Malefactor

God's mighty prophet, Ezekiel, warned in chapters 38 and 39 of the book that bears his name that in the last days there would come together a bloc of nations north of Jerusalem intent upon invading Palestine and destroying Israel. That confederation, according to the prophet, will be called Magog, whose leader is given the name Gog.

Most scholars who study this future matter agree that the nation at the nucleus of that end-time invasion will be Russia, whose leadership will conceive the evil thought to go down and take for themselves the riches of all that region promised by God to the children of Israel.

"Thus saith the Lord God; It shall also come to pass, that at the same time shall things come into thy mind, and thou shalt think an evil thought: And thou shalt say, I will go up to the land of unwalled villages; I will go to them that are at rest, that dwell safely, all of them dwelling without walls, and having neither bars nor gates" (Ezek. 38:10-11).

The premise of *Earth's Final Days, Essays in Apocalypse III,* at least in part, is to examine whether our present generation bears resemblance to the prophesied end-time generation. It is relevant to ask: Can we now see such a bloc of nations configuring that might fulfill the invasion scenario prophesied by Ezekiel?

To understand current issues of war and peace, particularly in that powder keg called the Middle East, it makes sense to attempt to discern those actors upon the world stage — the humanly controlled forces and event-driven dynamics — that have been most central in bringing the world to its present level of conflict. Knowing the facts in this regard should provide a clearer view of the direction future issues of war and peace might be taking us.

Ezekiel, the prophet, under God-given inspiration, said plainly that building conflicts will ultimately produce an explosive invasion from a far-distant northern geographical area by probably the most powerful military juggernaut ever to exist. There can be no doubt that in the twentieth century, particularly from 1917 to the present (even taking into account the astounding dissolution of the USSR), the singular national entity capable of producing such a juggernaut is Russia.

Russia, at the turn of the century, was swirling in a human sea of turmoil stirred by centuries of czarist oppression. The festering boil of hatred for the royal tyranny that had kept its luxuriantly clad foot on the necks of its hopeless masses was brought to a head by a revolution. Over the succeeding decades, that revolution would grow and spread to infect everything it touched with purulence far more terrible than that inflicted on the people by any of the czarist regimes.

The 1917 Russian Revolution continues to impact almost every aspect of life in every part of our late twentieth-century world. That powerful influence is never more manifest than when it is observed upon consideration of the issues involved in wars and rumors of wars.

The Final Push Southward

This century began with the enraged Russian revolutionaries storming the czarist palace strongholds at St. Petersburg, a city shortly thereafter renamed in honor of the revolution's chief hero, Vladimir Ilich Lenin. The end of this century recently witnessed Leningrad's name changed back to St. Petersburg, symbolizing the fall from power of Soviet-style communism that had terrorized its victims for more than 70 years.

That so-called "second revolution" is still evolving in a dramatic transition that the expert observers of that part of the world tell us can end in one of two ways: with the establishment of an increasingly productive and peaceful market-style society or an armed confrontation that will plunge its people and the rest of the world into an abyss more dangerous than the war-making aggressions of Joseph Stalin and Adolf Hitler combined. How is this possible? Because a new absolute Russian tyrant would have at his disposal unfathomable nuclear power.

God, the great observer of all things, who knows the end from the beginning, has told through His prophet Ezekiel that just such an aggressor-force will one day storm southward into the land He promised Israel.

Twentieth-century Russia and its volatile neighbors concurrently occupy the land areas about which Ezekiel prophesied. Could this be the launching pad from which Gog's allies will thrust southward in the joint attack on Israel?

It is chilling to know that a Russian leader whom many believe could become a Hitler-like dictator over the new Russia has had published a book on his intentions for conquest. It is titled *The Last March South*. The author of that threat, despite his November 1994 political campaign-like visit to the United States, in which he described himself as not unlike a member of this country's Democratic Party, is Vladimir Zhirinovsky. He and a growing number of other would-be leaders of the re-formulated Russian empire have their sights set on the oil and mineral riches of the land.

The prophet Ezekiel wrote: "And thou shalt say, I will go up to the land of unwalled villages; I will go to them that are at rest, that dwell safely, all of them dwelling without walls, and having neither bars nor gates, To take a spoil, and to take a prey . . ." (Ezek. 38:11-12).

The Red Menace

Like that old dragon, the serpent Satan, Soviet communism promised heaven on earth, a utopia that would elevate every person to god-like status when its final results were achieved. Like Satan, too, the Soviet masters then set about to march throughout the world like roaring lions seeking whom they might devour.

The Red Menace spread like an unstoppable malignancy, absorbing its neighbors through armed aggression and bellicose threats, which none of them dared challenge. The Eastern bloc of European nations formed to emulate the ways and methods of the Kremlin in Moscow. The cancerous cells of Marxism-Leninism made their way eastward to begin their enslaving work in Africa and Asia.

The disease leaped continents and oceans and established footholds in the western hemisphere, at first manifesting itself as scholarly ideology in many of the western universities. The academicians acquiesced to or warmly embraced the philosophies of Marx, Engels, and Lenin. At the same time, they turned a blind eye and deaf ear to the genocide taking place in Middle Russia herself, where, over time, 30 million peasants would be murdered.

The way of tyrants is to stalk about seeking whom they may devour. Hitler, for a brief time, waged war on the Jews and "undesirables" during his reign of terror. Stalin and Mao Tse Tung slaughtered countless millions to secure for themselves their monstrous power and their places in historical infamy. Because the nature of man has not changed, the beastly ways of evil people who would gather absolute power unto themselves are still with us.

Indeed, when reviewing the proliferating provincial dictatorships around the world today and the bloody conflicts in which they are engaged, we can say with documentable certainty that the planet is no more civilized than during the time of the Spanish-American War, Russo-Japanese War, World War I, World War II, the Korean Conflict, or the Vietnam War. God's words tell that evil men and seducers shall grow worse and worse, and that the world will once again be filled with violence as in the days of Noah and Lot. Prophecy is coming to life before our eyes and in our ears through hourly updated news accounts gathered virtually instantaneously from the growing number of war-torn hot spots around the globe.

Jesus' words that there would be significant wars and news of wars and fears of wars in the days preceding His imminent return to earth have never been more worthy of consideration and analysis than in this present hour. Jesus said the generation alive at the very end of the age will be marked by bloodshed and violence on a planetary scale. Indeed, it is time for those who are called by His name to attune their spiritual senses to the prophesied reality of His sudden coming for them in the clouds!

Dashed Hopes for Peace

Hope for peace seemed to have a genuine foundation upon which to build following the Japanese signing of surrender concluding the most horrendous war to that date. Ticker tape parades welcomed home Dwight Eisenhower, Douglas MacArthur, and legions of American troops. Tested upon the crucible of war, and bone-weary from the mortal combat, these young soldiers had, through their courage and valor, at last brought World War II to an end. The ebullient and grateful masses of American citizens basked in the glorious light of victory. The beast-tyrants of the world were now vanquished. Peace lay just over the golden horizon; the black storm clouds were gone.

Joseph Stalin soon put an end to the tears of joy and the bright smiles. The Russian leader, given carte blanche in gathering to himself the broken pieces of Europe, partitioned the East from the West with what was quickly dubbed "the Iron Curtain." His gargantuan neighbor to the east, claiming a similar but even more dehumanizing brand of Communist ideology, erected its own intangible yet very real partition. China's "bamboo curtain" cloaked that little-understood land with a dark shadow that kept prying western eyes from witnessing the blood bath taking place under Mao Tse Tung's murderous direction.

Realization that the newly cemented Soviet Union had atomic, and abruptly thereafter, hydrogen bomb technology soon dampened the post-war euphoria. Nikita Kruschev, fresh from his victorious power struggle with Bulganin and Malenkov, sent tanks rumbling into Hungary and wherever else resistance to his megalomaniacal plans cropped up. These acts of aggression dashed all hope that world peace would be forthcoming. The Berlin Wall put the exclamation point to Kruschev's declaration to the West: "We will bury you!"

Soviet expansionism began in earnest during that era, and Communist Chinese hegemony followed suit. Both of these massive geopolitical and military powers established their control over peoples too tired and too hungry and militarily powerless to resist them. Where the East met the West, lines became sharply drawn and the pressures for war could not be suppressed for long. Each side — the great western bloc and that of the east — walked a diplomatic tightrope which, if broken, meant nuclear confrontation.

No longer could the planet afford to engage in world war. Now wars between small divided nations and regions exploded wherever the free world and the enslaved bumped against each other.

Decrying America and her allies as imperialist aggressors, the truly imperialistic Communist system fomented conflicts intended to extend its grip of enslavement. Each "revolution" was proclaimed to be a "people's revolution" to return power and control to the "oppressed masses." In reality, the power, if achieved, would ultimately reside in the hands of a dictator who was supported by a close group of like-minded thugs who commanded absolute support from the military.

Vietnam divided, as did Korea. Communist engendered schisms split vast areas of Africa into bloody tyrant-states. Wars raged and continue to rage today throughout that continent. Soviet Communist expansionism exploited centuries-old tribal conflicts in the region. Chinese communism gripped Asia and the Pacific Rim with its murderous tentacles. Russian-made armaments from small arms to anti-personnel instruments of death have long since replaced spears and primitive weaponry.

Peace is not to be found in the western hemisphere either. South America and Central America have long felt the influence of Russian-style revolution. The same types of free-world versus enslaved-world divisions can be found the world over. This emerging "New World Order," with the East and West coming together for the purpose of saving the planet, seems even more a world of disorder than was that dark age before the Berlin Wall collapsed and the Soviet Union dissolved.

The Sliding Scale of Diplomacy

This much-heralded dawning age that has grown from the evolving détente, upon close analysis, presents dangers far greater than those of the cold-war era. The danger, the terrifying prospects, can be discerned when considering the subtlety and incomprehensible aspects of the New Age sophistry that so influences current thinking in diplomatic circles. There are no absolutes anymore, according to this line of reasoning. Applied to the diplomatic process of working with the issues involved in matters of war and peace, such thinking destroys any potential foundation upon which lasting peace can rest.

Lines of demarcation have become blurred, even nonexistent, in this post-Soviet-Communist world of geopolitics. Boundaries of do's and don'ts, of can's and cannot's, no longer mean what they used to mean in documents that govern peace agreements. They are instead sliding scales of acceptable and unacceptable behavior, scales which no one seems to understand.

The process of diplomacy itself seems to be on this sliding track or slick surface that does not set firm limitations or erect immovable fences. Rather, it allows the parties involved to do whatever seems expedient to their cause or position. The last firm line of an unyielding nature seems to have been that one drawn by George Bush in the Arabian sands preceding Desert Storm.

Has this softer, more sensitive approach to facing down aggression made planet Earth a world less war-like? This New Age methodology of dealing with the beasts among us gives wide latitude by letting them, as God's word puts it, "do what is right in their own eyes." Could this approach actually be contributing to the fulfillment of Jesus' prophesied warning that just before He returns there will be an obvious increase both in the number and intensity of wars and that the rumors of even greater war will fill mankind with terror?

Tolstoy and Dostoyevsky

It is fascinating to note that the way in which societies deal with the governing of peoples has a direct effect upon the course civilization takes, for the better or for the worse. Two great writers, who wrote as much to warn as to record fictional history that entertains, left the world with massive volumes of thought we will do well to heed.

These two literary geniuses lived during the turbulent times of change leading up to the Bolshevik Revolution and were able to discern the causes and effects of the cultural decadence that surrounded them. Their observations led them to ponder and dissect the issues and events that constitute the profound biblical question: ". . .Why did the heathen rage, and the people imagine vain things?" (Acts 4:25).

Leo Tolstoy and Fyodor Dostoyevsky, both children of Mother Russia, gave us brilliant, incisive looks into what human lawlessness comes to when allowed to run its course. Separately, yet somehow seemingly together, Dostoyevky's deep thoughts and concern about *Crime and Punishment* validate and make sense of Tolstoy's masterful ruminations on *War and Peace*.

Whether one agrees with the postulates and conclusions reached by these writers, the preponderance of evidence provided by the history of humankind proves the subjects encompassed by the books' titles to be inalterably linked in consideration of how and why "the heathen rage" within human affairs. And how the heathen do rage!

On a Collision Course

A magazine article highlights the fact that Jerusalem, "the apple of God's eye," is the center of world attention. Those who analyze the issues and events pertaining to war and peace clearly have their journalistic senses trained upon the conflicts raging within that land mass near the top of the world the Bible terms "Magog."

The series of stories in that issue is prefaced by an interesting overview of violence between warring factions since the so-called "cold war" ended. It gives a discomforting prognosis for the future health of world stability. The forecast is one that portends a new world order requiring that national sovereignty give way to global policing authority.

"Violent Death of a Quiet American," reads the headline in the London-based weekly *European*, "Likable U.S. Spy Gunned Down in Georgia." According to the story on CIA agent Freddie Woodruff, most of his many friends in the Georgian capital of Tbilisi did not know he was a spy. But the normally tight-lipped CIA's willingness to acknowledge, even posthumously, that he was one, is certainly a sign that times have changed.

The fact that Woodruff was killed in Georgia is perhaps a sign, too, of the importance of the various republics of the former Soviet Union in the post-cold-war world. The feuding and outright warfare that riddle Moscow's old empire are the focus of this month's cover story. Georgia, after barely recovering from a civil war over national leadership, is locked in a bitter territorial struggle with the secessionist movement that Tbilisi says is supported by Russia. According to at least one report, Woodruff had been sent to train Georgia's security forces (the soldier responsible for his death may have come from their ranks) to fight the insurgents.

So the old Soviet empire may prove to be an arena for renewed competition between Washington and Moscow. As the *Economist* of London has forecasted darkly: "Russia and the West are on a collision course.... Over the next 10 years, the non-Russian bits of the former Soviet Union threaten to become a crescent of chaos stretching from the Baltic Sea to China." The Russians are concerned with what the U.S. is doing there, and vice versa.

As the conflicts in the former Soviet Union become bloodier, observers have called upon the United Nations to step in. A team of international monitors has entered Georgia under the UN flag. But as the feature story on the UN peace-keeping forces indicates, the blue helmets are already overextended.

While questions arise about their ability to relieve strife, a debate centers on just what the UN's proper role should be. Whatever happens in Somalia, Bosnia, Cambodia, and wherever else UN troops are called upon, one thing seems apparent: Today's conflicts place greater demands than ever before on the international organization and risk casting an Orwellian spin on the expression "peace-keeping."[1]

Finding a Unifying Purpose

The lifting of the inhumane Soviet totalitarian fist, while allowing the marvelous light of the gospel to be shined throughout the former USSR's enslaved territories, has given opportunity for dictatorships of a lesser magnitude to engage in power grabbing. This has kept the region at a constant boiling temperature.

If the former Soviet behemoth did nothing else, its iron grip held the lid of its own terrible kind of order on potential anarchic chaos. There seems no one capable of punishing crime; therefore, any chances of peace are totally consumed by war on many fronts.

Aleksandr Solzhenitsyn, the modern-day version of Dostoyevsky and Tolstoy, forewarned with great prescience of these things. Western journalists now must report what they denied as possible when Solzhenitzsyn's dire warnings emerged from the horrors of his gulag experience. That landscape is ablaze with numerous fires of wars and rumors of wars that prophecy indicates will only be brought under control by one inevitable union: the superamalgamation of nations whose burning common satanically-driven compulsion will be to obliterate Israel.

Dramatic changes taking place now in this prophetically crucial part of the world must be viewed by the true student of prophecy as among the most significant fulfillment of Jesus' words on the Mount of Olives. There He warned of wars and rumors of wars that will take place as His second coming approaches. More dynamic changes are in the offing.

The tremendous outbreak of conflicts in that region to the uttermost north of Jerusalem causes the wise student of prophecy to ask the question: Could the pressing need to put the lid back on the chaos and lawlessness be part of the "evil thought" that will come into the mind of "Gog" (the end-time leader of Magog)?

Certainly these many provincial wars, if not soon contained, will eventuate in a tremendously expanded arena of war. A Russian leader who could bring these many feuding factions together would need a unifying national purpose. One such common cause could be the turning of their collective attention to the south toward the oil and mineral-rich pockets and warm water ports of those lower regions. With that as his goal, such a leader could amass to himself a power bloc that the West could not or would not be willing to attempt to prevent invading Palestine.

Why the Russian Republic Dominates

The following armed conflicts and ethnic strifes have, since this overview assessment in 1993, divided in cancer-cell-like proliferation. These *World Press Review* stories mirror the extremely dangerous situations that have now more fully developed.

John Lloyd of the *Financial Times* chronicles the growing tension building in the states surrounding Russia. In his article, "New

World Wars: Conflicts Riddle the Old Soviet Empire," Lloyd writes:

> The former Soviet republics are again in ferment. North, south, and west, the now-independent states circling Russia are at least fragile and often convulsed by civil war.
>
> In the Caucasian states of Armenia, Azerbaijan, and Georgia, conflict between the political leadership and rebel movements has become increasingly bloody. In the Baltics, Estonia and Latvia are struggling to enforce a new definition of citizenship that would reverse the postwar flow of Russians into their tiny populations or, at least, assimilate them rapidly.

Lloyd then goes on to list the many struggles within the region and explains that these diverse crises have two common characteristics. First, "in each of the 15 former Soviet republics, a bitter conflict is taking place for control," writes Lloyd.

> Even the best politicians of these young republics (and many are opportunist and ruthless) grope in a fog of ignorance, which undertrained and inert bureaucracies do nothing to dispel. In the non-Russian states, "nationalist" wings seek to diminish involvement with other former Soviet republics while "pragmatic" parties seek to maintain minimal neighborly relations, especially with Russia.

The second factor is the relationship that all the former republics have with Russia. Russia dominates because it is the main provider of energy and "also because it retains hegemony over all former Soviet land space," Lloyd notes. Much of this power comes from the fact that Russia has troops loyal to it in every republic except Azerbaijan. In addition, "Russia retains the control systems for nuclear weapons based in three other republics."[2]

With its powerful military might and bureaucratic control, the Russian republic will do everything possible to maintain its dominance.

Kept on a Short Leash

An article titled, "The Federation's Shaky Center: Moscow's Own Unruly Republic," by Ryszard Malik for the Russian periodical, *Rzeczpospolita,* clearly defines the root cause of the volatility and the strife in the region. Concerning the October 1991 declaration of sovereignty by the autonomous republic of Tatarstan, Malik writes, in part:

> Having parted with the 14 other former Soviet republics and the satellite nations of Eastern Europe, Russia is finding itself at a starting point. Today, republics, districts, and counties long kept on a short leash — regions that were supposedly autonomous but actually remained dependent on the Kremlin in even the most trivial matters — want to have their own borders, governments, and foreign and economic policies.

It is painfully obvious from the many new reports in recent times about the bloody internal military conflict in Grozny, and other battle zones within that region, that there is no end in sight to the warmaking. Jesus' words echo again, "There shall be wars and rumors of wars."

> The battle for more rights, raging since the end of 1991, actually started somewhat earlier — immediately after the coup that toppled Mikhail Gorbachev in August of that year. On the basis of extraordinary powers granted him by the Congress of People's Deputies, Yeltsin selected the people to lead local executive bodies throughout Russia. Thus, he managed to keep his hand on the financial and economic policies of the republics, provinces, and districts of the federation. This strengthening of central power did not sit well with the local authorities.[3]

News from this volatile region, then, demonstrates beyond any doubt that the area called, in God's Word, "Magog" is in turbulent ferment that is not conducive to maintaining the status quo. Something is about to happen — something dramatic and violent and earth shattering.

The Rising Russian Star

The situation in some of the former Soviet Republics is eerily reminiscent of the situation immediately preceding Hitler's instigation of hostility that led to World War II. Hitler used the pretext of German citizens being persecuted by the Slavs to launch his aggression. Using the same tactics, Russian hard-line politicians, backed for the most part by the Russian military hierarchy, are decrying the harsh treatment of Russian citizens who live in the former Soviet republics. At the same time, they are demanding that action be taken, militarily as well as politically, to avenge what they self-servingly perceive to be persecutions.

There is yet another eerie and disturbingly similar parallel to be drawn between pre-World War II Germany and present-day Russia. There has emerged a leader in Russia who is being compared on all sides to Adolf Hitler, the former "Little Corporal/Paper-Hanger"-turned-bellicose-orator and defender of German pride. The Russian, hard-line parliamentarian is viewed as being everything from a hot-air-filled buffoon to a super patriot of the motherland whose brilliant visionary plans can make Russia once again an envied superpower.

The following report encapsulates the story of this rising Russian political star:

> The pompous proclamations of rabid Russian nationalist Vladimir Zhirinovsky have made headlines around the world. But perhaps his most amazing statement occurred recently in the presence of Rauf Gauffin, former Swedish ambassador to Moscow and reporter for the Italian geographical review, *Limes.*
>
> As reported in the February 10 (1994) *European,* Zhirinovsky swaggered his way to new heights of geopolitical ambition. During his meeting with Mr. Gauffin, the ebullient Zhirinovsky grabbed a felt-tip pen and spontaneously began to draw on a map of Europe that lay nearby.
>
> Scribbling vigorously on the map, he began to enunciate his vision of a new Europe. According to the account, it quickly became apparent that he believes in a "Greater Germany and a Greater Russia, both created by swallowing some of their neighbors." He told Gauffin that, "This Greater Germany and the new Russia will one day form an alliance which will neutralize Europe." His map shows Poland "dismembered and redistributed between Russia and Germany."
>
> He also believes that Slovakia should become Russian territory. Along the same lines, he envisions a "Greater Bulgaria," which eventually absorbs parts of Greece, Turkey, Romania, and the former Yugoslav republic of Macedonia.

Adding to his turbulent preview, Zhirinovsky modestly suggested that since Romania is "not a country but only a space where Italian gypsies live," Transylvania should be removed from its sphere of influence and redrawn as a part of Hungary. Then, he submitted that Serbia and Croatia should divide Bosnia between them.

The *European* reported that, "On the wall behind Zhirinovsky was his Liberal Democrat Party's emblem, a stylized map of the former Russian empire, which included Finland and Alaska. It was surmounted by an eagle and the words 'Liberty and Law.' 'Liberty and Law . . . and Russia,' declared Zhirinovsky, placing his pointer on Alaska." (He has often stated that Russia should take Alaska back from America.)

At present, Vladimir Zhirinovsky is being treated as something of an aberration . . . an odd duck who shoots off his mouth, but doesn't really represent the thinking of most Russians. In truth, he has demonstrated a remarkable ability to win votes from the Russian populace. Most Russians are deeply nationalistic. They long for a leader who will bring economic stability and a believable vision to the populace.[4]

It is worth noting again that Zhirinovsky's autobiography and official political statement is entitled, *The Last March South*. In it, he advocates a greater Russia that occupies territory from Moscow and southward to the Indian Ocean, engulfing much of the Middle East.

Zhirinovsky's Vision

Hal Lindsey, noted author and prophecy teacher, further enlightens us about present-day Russian realities by including within the "Strategic Perspectives" section of his *International Intelligence Briefing* some interesting observations about Zhirinovsky and his grandiose plans. Lindsey uses the words of Bill Sutton of the Sutton House to paint a graphic and troubling picture of what a future under the cloud of Vladimir Zhirinovsky, or someone like him, might portend:

Zhirinovsky's Vision: "I see Russian troops preparing for their last march to the South. The Middle East's riches and especially its oil, would save Russia." Further

. . . Zhirinovsky believes, "This conquest would be the last great re-division of the world and must be done as a form of shock therapy . . . suddenly, swiftly, and effectively." Further . . . "The Russian Army is capable of accomplishing this act, especially since this is the only way for Russia to survive. In fact, this would be a form of purification (cleansing) for Russia. What would the rest of the world do . . . precisely what they did when Hitler invaded other European countries . . . NOTHING! This is why Russia has developed a nuclear shield! Who in the Western World would risk total annihilation via nuclear attack . . . NO ONE!"

This is not a new idea, but rather an old one that has been put forth before by other nationalist Russian leaders. Russia has always looked South and seen . . . warm water ports and oil!

The Lindsey assessment goes on to point out two less-than-encouraging probabilities: Boris Yeltsin's health is getting worse, and one of the key figures who wants his job, Vladimir Zhirinovsky, is a KGB front man, financed both by the KGB and by Saddam Hussein of Iraq.

With the downsizing of America's military, administration leaders appear more inclined to depend upon diplomatic maneuverings. Such a strategy seems designed more to avoid confrontation with hard-line aggressors than to draw a line in the sand when such an action is clearly called for. As a result, America's current foreign policy makes Hal Lindsey's following assessment frighteningly plausible.

Zhirinovsky's VISION may foretell approaching events that will rock the world. Particularly worrisome is its timing of this VISION. In the past, Russia had far too much to lose . . . to risk a major conquest for the Middle East. But today, Russia may not have anything to lose and the Russian Military and KGB may now support this venture.[5]

Analyzing the Events

Is Russia the Magog of Ezekiel 38 and 39? Almost certainly. Is Russia, during our present generation, shaping up along the lines prophesied by the great prophet of God? Many scholars such as Mr. Lindsey think so. Is Vladimir Zhirinovsky the leader who is to be the Gog of the end-time Magog invasion into Palestine? Only God knows.

Hal Lindsey, however, presents some quite interesting forecasts based upon his always-biblically-centered search and analysis of events:

> 1. Russia's economic recovery efforts will . . . continue to fail. Russians will grow more impatient each day. Radical solutions will be tempting.
>
> 2. Personal health, a coup, and/or economic failures will . . . force Yeltsin out of office before or in 1996. (Note . . . his health is poor now.)
>
> 3. The next Russian leader and supporting cast will . . . support the Old Russian Dream . . . of acquiring warm water ports to the south.
>
> 4. Russian leaders will . . . be forced (by internal-external issues) to undertake a military conquest by or before the year 2000.
>
> 5. The reason for the conquest will . . . be economic failures, increasing ultra nationalist pressure, and treaties with other nations.
>
> 6. The Russian Conquest will . . . move south into the Mediterranean and Indian Oceans . . . not west into Western Europe as many believe.
>
> 7. Russia will . . . attack Israel, Lebanon, Saudi Arabia, Emirates, Bahrain, and Kuwait, plus other countries to the south of Russia.
>
> 8. Russia will . . . focus her conquests on the above nations, but Russia definitely has interest in . . . Iraq, Iran, Turkey, Baltics, Finland, and Alaska.
>
> 9. Russia will . . . attempt to utilize UN and world opinion to justify its conquest, i.e., sanctions against Israel supporting Arab complaints.[6]

Considering the rapid succession of earth-shaking events that have occurred in the recent past, e.g., the dissolution of the USSR; the fall of the Berlin Wall, and the re-unification of Germany; the swift thrust of Saddam Hussein into Kuwait; the reforming of the Old Roman Empire into the European Union; and the formation of a World Trade Organization that will undoubtedly at some time present a conflict in the matter of national sovereignty, who is to say that Mr. Lindsey's forecast will not become reality in the very near future?

Gearing Up for War

Although Russia is prophesied to be the nucleus of the aggressor-force that rides the red horse of Revelation 6, which will bring unprecedented war upon the earth, and present-day Russia is in violent disarray, all nations will ultimately share in the horrors of Armageddon.

Do other nations of our time seem to be gearing up for war? One day in the life of one newspaper, scanning only a few pages, provides the frightening answer.

Accounts of man waging war against his fellow man can be gleaned from any newspaper of significance any day of any year. Such reports bring home to our minds the fact that wars and rumors of wars are worldwide and occurring simultaneously, fitting the precise scenario given by Jesus.

On April 8, 1994, the following conflicts were occurring and reported on this one given day in one newspaper:

• U.S. Asks U.N. to Whisk Troops to Gorazde — Promises Air Cover

WASHINGTON — The Clinton administration is calling for the quick dispatch of hundreds of U.N. peacekeepers to Serb-encircled Gorazde in eastern Bosnia and vowing to have NATO air power defend them if they are attacked.

• With Leader Dead, Rwanda Runs Amok

NAIROBI, KENYA — Rampaging troops killed Rwanda's acting premier and as many as 11 U.N. soldiers Thursday during fierce fighting touched off by the deaths of the presidents of Rwanda and Burundi in a suspicious plane crash.

• 20 Million in East Africa Endangered

WASHINGTON — More than 20 million people in 10 East African countries are at risk because of civil strife and drought, government relief officials said Thursday. The country most affected, according to the officials, is Sudan, where the lives of about 5 million are threatened. The other countries with large numbers of people who could face severe malnutrition or perhaps starvation are Ethiopia, Somalia, Eritrea, Rwanda, Burundi, Uganda, Tanzania, Djibouti, and Kenya.

The ethnic strife in Rwanda and Burundi was underscored Wednesday when the presidents of both countries died when their plane went down in a mysterious crash as it arrived at the international airport in Rwanda.

• Next Move North Korea's, Arms Ace Says

WASHINGTON — North Korea has the next move in a dangerous game that, if played poorly, could lead to war with the United States, the Pentagon's top nuclear weapons expert said Thursday.

All eyes are on North Korea's small nuclear reactor in case it's shut down briefly to allow the fuel rods to be removed, an indication that the fuel then would be used for bomb-grade plutonium, said Ashton Carter, assistant secretary of defense for international security policy.

Another indication North Korea is going ahead with its bomb program would be if nuclear fuel is loaded into a new, 200-megawatt reactor, Carter said.

"What we don't want to see is a future spurt, and they are poised to spurt in two ways," he said. The Pentagon's objective now is "heading off those next steps, those leaps forward."

. . . The challenge now is to keep them from going further, he said, listing five reasons for blocking the North Koreans: preventing war on the peninsula; stopping them from coercing their neighbors; preventing a regional arms race; keeping a lid on nuclear proliferation around the world; and blocking them from exporting nuclear materials.

• Blood Flows in Natal Despite Army Pressure

DURBAN, SOUTH AFRICA — Twenty blacks were shot, burned, and hacked to death in scattered fighting throughout Natal Province despite the addition of 700 troops to the convulsed region, security forces said Thursday. . . . The security forces said 20 blacks were killed in 11 separate attacks that took place during the 24-hour period from Wednesday morning to this morning.

• 2 Killed, 21 Hurt in Bangladesh Protests

DHAKA, BANGLADESH — At least 2 people were killed and 21 injured Thursday after police fired tear gas and rubber bullets to prevent thousands of protesters from occupying the main government building.

The protest was the largest in months organized by the Awami League, the nation's biggest opposition party. The League is demanding the resignation of Prime Minister Khaleda Zia's three-year-old government.

• IRA Balking at Prolonging Cease-Fire

BELFAST, NORTHERN IRELAND — The Irish Republican Army is unlikely to extend its three-day cease-fire, the leader of its allied political party said Thursday. . . . Protestant-based "loyalist" gunmen fired several shots Wednesday at a taxi depot in west Belfast, a Catholic neighborhood where IRA support is strong.

• Letter Bomb Injures Radical Politician

LONDON — An explosion apparently caused by a small letter bomb injured a man Thursday at the headquarters of the British National Party, police said.

The device exploded shortly after noon, and a 57-year-old man was taken to a hospital for treatment of minor injuries to his hands and face, said police liaison officer Vishakhi Patel.

The party, which advocates an end to immigration and the expulsion of all blacks and Jews, won a seat on the local council in east London last year, its first election victory.

Scotland Yard said it had no indication who sent the device to the party headquarters in Welling, 10 miles southwest of London.

• Russia Backs Off From Plan for Latvian Base

MOSCOW — Facing an uproar in the Baltics, Russia hastily retreated Thursday from a plan to establish a permanent military base in Latvia. . . . "Latvia will never allow the building of a Russian military base on its territory," Latvian President Guntil Ulmanis said.

• Israeli Army Locks Out 1.8 Million Palestinians as

Deadly Attacks Go On

AFULA, ISRAEL — The army barred 1.8 million Palestinians from Israel for a week to combat a wave of attacks that claimed another Israeli life Thursday, while an angry crowd buried victims of a car bomb attack.

The order, one of the strictest ever imposed on the Palestinians, came a day after a Muslim fundamentalist, seeking revenge for a Jewish settler's Feb. 25 massacre in a mosque, set off a car bomb that killed eight in this northern town.

In new attacks Thursday, an Israeli was killed and four were wounded when a Palestinian opened fire at a bus stop in southern Israel. Two Israelis were also stabbed and slightly wounded by Arabs at entrances to the Gaza Strip.

Any newspaper on any given day contains numerous stories of war-caused death and dying and fears of even greater bloodshed such as in the excerpted report that follows.

• Elections Won't Wait, Mandela Insists

DURBAN, SOUTH AFRICA — Nelson Mandela rejected any delay in elections in volatile Natal Province, saying Wednesday that the army can end mounting bloodshed in the three weeks before South Africa's first all-race vote. . . . The South African army sent in 700 soldiers Wednesday in an attempt to quell the violence, bringing the deployment to 1,900. The 700 new troops gathered at Ladysmith in northern Natal; most were to be sent today to the area near Ulundi, the capital of KwaZulu.

Rumors based on facts, involving nuclear threat, portend the very real possibility of terrifying future wars:

• Pyong Yang Tries to Cut South Korea Out

SEOUL, SOUTH KOREA — South Korea has rejected a North Korean proposal that would effectively cut Seoul out of negotiations on the Korean nuclear dispute, a government source said Wednesday.

North Korea wrote to the United States in late March offering to allow new nuclear inspections if Washington drops its demand for an exchange of envoys between North and South Korea, the South's news agency reported Tuesday.

An envoy swap and full nuclear inspections have been a precondition for the United States holding high-level talks with North Korea on economic aid and diplomatic recognition. . . .

South Korean officials worry that with the envoy swap off the agenda, their country would be sidelined in the nuclear negotiations.

North Korea says its nuclear program is peaceful, but its refusal to allow inspections has deepened suspicion that it is developing atomic bombs. . . . The CIA believes the North has enough plutonium to make at least one atomic bomb.

Rumors persist, again based upon solid intelligence, that North Korea continues to establish relationships with nations that share her own hostility to the United States and to America's interests. Iran, it is generally conjectured, is likely providing both nuclear technology and delivery system technology that will make North Korea a nuclear threat to nations even several thousand miles distant. Korea's leadership has demonstrated it is volatile and irrational, perhaps more so than Saddam Hussein's regime.[7]

Wars and rumors of wars dominate the geopolitical landscape unlike any other time in recorded history. Christ's words echo across the centuries to sound the alarm of warning in the ears of everyone who will hear: "And ye shall hear of wars and rumors of wars. . . . For nation shall rise against nation, and kingdom against kingdom . . ." (Matt. 24:6-7).

The Wars Within

The wars between nations and provinces have, with few exceptions, been born of class envy. Most often that class struggle is steeped in ungovernable racial hatreds. Thus, those who would build a world of perfect harmony, a world for which they alone could provide a workable blueprint, always propose multi-culturalism/integrated racial arrangements.

If the world could be rid of bigotry, they say, envy would die and there would be no need for class struggle, which, they as did Marx, concede is essential to the process of ending the bigotry and envy.

Class struggle, they believe, must provide the impetus that ends racial hatreds and class envy, because only the masses have the kind of power necessary to force these changes of attitude of the bigots and materialistic hoarders of wealth. One-world utopianism, then, is really socialism in its purest form — which is nothing less than Marxist communism.

Jesus' prophesy, "nation shall rise against nation," is based upon the Greek word "ethnos." The Lord was prophesying that the generation alive at the time of His coming again will be characterized by tremendous violence based on racial hatreds. Again, Mother Russia, in her latter-day Soviet form, was the primary mover in the exportation of class-struggle. Post-cold-war Russia continues to be a tool in the hands of Satan, who has so enraged the masses by stirring racial hatreds and class envies that the world is a cauldron on the verge of boiling over to become man's last battleground.

America's inner cities, now the incubators of gestating class-struggle, threaten to bring to birth full-blown conflict between the races. Paradoxically, the utopian dreamers intensively promote multi-culturalism while desperately seeking to make the United States an harmonious part of the global order they are constructing. Similar to the wars that pit geopolitical factions against each other, society within America is aflame with wars, threatened wars, and fears of wars that are born of and fueled by racially-based class envies. Any major newspaper on any given day tells the story of where this generation of Americans stands with regard to the prophetic words of Christ: "nation shall rise against nation" — that is — "ethnic factions shall rise against ethnic factions."

We are all familiar with the Los Angeles rioting of 1993, involving the arrest of habitual lawbreaker Rodney King, whose resistance to arresting officers necessitated the use of force. That action, the latter part of which has since been shown hundreds of times on the television screens of American homes, sparked riots in the streets of Los Angeles the likes of which had not happened since the Watts riots decades earlier. Lawless elements of the black community burned and looted and destroyed randomly, damaging black as well as other ethnic minority homes and businesses. But the main focus of their wrath and "entertainment" was on whites, Latinos, Hispanics, and Asian-Americans living in and near the area.

Today, even reasons for celebration — such as the Chicago Bulls winning the NBA championship — are turned into opportunities for the criminals to vent their wrath. We watch as our news media reports neo-Nazi skinheads and other hate groups, both black and white, preaching hatred, some from behind pulpits in the name of one religion or another. From Norman Lincoln Rockwell, the assassinated leader of the American neo-Nazi movement, to Louis Farrakhan, high priest of a radical Muslim sect, we have emerged a generation unsurpassed in ethnic hatreds.

"Nation rising against nation" within America has taken its toll. It has engendered animosity toward law and order to the extent that murderous gang activity now threatens those who have fled near-city areas to the suburbs and countrysides to escape metropolitan violence. Children murder children while adults cringe in helplessness, exasperation, and fear. America's court system has become so soft-headed and convoluted that most of those who are charged with dispensing justice do not seem to know right from wrong, much less legal from illegal. Our inner cities have degenerated to become microcosms of the war zones that can be found on practically every continent.

These flash points of civil war, unless sanity prevails, will in spontaneous combustion-like fashion, ignite the firestorms that will engulf, then consume, this America we love. War is hatred come to fruition. Hatred springs from within. "From whence come wars and fightings among you? come they not hence, even of your lusts that war in your members?" (James 4:1).

Mankind, then, because of the sin-fueled rage within, seems destined for one great, final conflagration. Again, even the briefest perusal of any major newspaper's front page must cause the reader to come to that conclusion.

Potential World Hotspots

Analyzing the perils of our time, Hal Lindsey writes in his briefing paper:

> I believe that somehow oil fits into the Ezekiel 38-39 scenario. . . . The president of the World Bank recently stated that, ". . . the most dangerous situation facing the world today is the rate of decline in Russian oil production." The president of the World Bank went on to say, "If this problem is not corrected soon, all the money in the world won't be enough to keep Russia and its former republics afloat!"
>
> The decline of oil production in Russia is due to: (1)

the collapse of the USSR and (2) Russia's inefficient oil production and delivery systems. I also believe the timing of this event is extraordinary, and the consequences could and most likely will involve the whole world.

Oil is a critical world energy resource! I believe that oil will play a key role in some future end-time world drama. Ezekiel 38 predicts a great northern power (Russia) will invade the Mid-East, accompanied by some of the former Soviet Republics and most of the Muslim nations, including Iran, Libya, Syria, Iraq, and maybe Turkey. Russia's shrinking oil production could be a major factor in Russia's decision to invade and take over the Mid-East, including Israel, Saudi Arabia, and other Mid-East oil producing nations.

Note: The status of America's military will figure greatly in Russia's decision to invade the Mid-East. Clinton's plan to greatly downsize our military could make Russia's decision to invade the Mid-East very easy.[8]

That same briefing paper excerpted the following from the Prescott Group report on potential for conflicts around the world:

The . . . hot spots (for the immediate future) are projected to be:

African Hot Spots: Algeria, Sudan, Somalia, Eritrea, Nigeria, Egypt, Rwanda, Zaire.

Eastern Europe Hot Spots: Bosnia, Macedonia, Yugoslavia, some of the former Soviet Republics.

Far East Hot Spots: North Korea.

Mid-East Hot Spots: Iraq, India, Pakistan, Israel, Palestine.

Possible Hot Spots: Hong Kong, China.[9]

Persistent reports of nuclear-grade plutonium being stolen from former Soviet Republics and rumors of those republics selling nuclear weapons technology — and even nuclear weapons themselves — to unstable governments elicit nightmarish scenarios. Even the conventional war-making capability of the lesser powers portends an ominous future for world equilibrium. The following report encapsulates the threat:

Many Rumors of Wars: Third-world countries that

are potential enemies of the United States are amassing sophisticated hi-tech weapons, as the United States downsizes its military forces at a rapid pace. The list of hi-tech weapons being amassed includes: night vision goggles, satellite positioning systems (which use American satellites), anti-tank weapons, anti-aircraft missiles, cruise missiles, and submarines. In any future war with these countries, the risk of heavy U.S. casualties could impede the willingness of America to intervene, or, if the decision is made to become involved, the risk of massive U.S. casualties automatically increases drastically.[10]

The creation called man indeed appears destined for hate-generated self-annihilation. But take heart, such an end of the human race is impossible!

"Be Not Troubled"

"And ye shall hear of wars and rumors of wars: see that ye be not troubled: for all these things must come to pass, but the end is not yet" (Matt. 24:6).

Those words, by God himself, who came to this dying planet to redeem lost humanity from the soul-death that is the wages of sin, is like a sweet, soothing melody to the ears of those reconciled by His matchless grace. Jesus was saying — is saying today — that the child of God has no reason to be troubled by any madness of mankind, which will more and more, as the end of the age draws near, be raging all about him or her.

Jesus is telling us that war is inevitable, that it is the eruptive overflow of a sin-corrupt, volcanic world. "Be ye not troubled," Jesus is telling those who truly trust Him today. "For the end is not yet," He says to us in loving, consoling strains.

These are the words of blessed assurance from the Alpha and the Omega who knows in minute detail anything that has ever been, is now, or shall ever be.

3

Famines, Pestilence, Earthquakes, as Man Rebels

by Lester Sumrall

We're fat and happy in the United States today. Spreading the gospel isn't important to us. Terrible calamities are clutching our neighbors, and we sit and wonder if we can afford a second new car.

In America, the Church sings about Christ's coming and preaches about His return but lives as if Jesus is never coming back.

Famine stalks the earth. Pestilence, in many forms, desires our young and old. The earthquakes and other natural disasters Jesus spoke of 2,000 years ago are coming to pass.

We must wake up!

As Jesus was sitting on the Mount of Olives, the disciples came to Him privately. ". . . Tell us," they said, "when will these things be? and what will be the sign of thy coming, and of the end of the world?" (Matt. 24:3).

"Tell us about the end of the world," they requested.

First, He told them that false christs would come and try to deceive them. Then, he gave them several signs that would take place near the end:

> And ye shall hear of wars and rumours of wars: see
> that ye be not troubled: for all these things must come

to pass, but the end is not yet. For nation will rise against nation, and kingdom against kingdom: and there shall be famines, pestilences, and earthquakes, in divers places. . . . And then shall many be offended, and shall betray one another, and shall hate one another. And many false prophets shall rise, and shall deceive many. . . . For there shall arise false Christs, and false prophets, and shall shew great signs and wonders; insomuch that, if it were possible, they shall deceive the very elect (Matt. 24:6-7,10-11,24).

Ethnic Wars Around the World

The Holy Spirit said through Jesus that in the last days there would be wars and rumors of wars that will sweep the earth.

It is coming to pass. In this century, more kings — large and small — have been dethroned than during the rest of human history put together. Why? Because this is the end-time century.

In a few years, we will see the end of the decade of the nineties. It will also be the end of the twentieth century and the end of the sixth millennium.

The good and the bad are going to come close together in these last days. The unholy and the holy are going to live next door to each other. The putrid and the clean are going to rub shoulders together. As Christians, we are not of this world. We have been cleansed by the blood of Jesus, and we belong to another world.

The Lord told His disciples, ". . . nation shall rise against nation, and kingdom against kingdom . . ." (Matt. 24:7).

What does the word nation mean? It means ethnic.

Did you know that every war in the world now is an ethnic war? Did you know Yugoslavia has been smashed to pieces by a population that says, "I belong to this tribe; you belong to that tribe; he belongs to the other tribe; let's kill each other." As a result, they have gone through hell in the past few years, destroying that great nation and its rich heritage in the process.

What tore the Russian empire to pieces? Ethnic disputes. They said, "We don't belong to you. You don't belong to us. Your grandpa and my grandpa didn't get along; let's fight."

In Africa, there are dozens and dozens of civil wars going on right now, and though they are all tribal wars, the continent of Africa is killing itself from within. Millions have died from starvation because they had to run from the war. They couldn't plant or care for crops. In Rwanda, the people were on the verge of reaping bumper crops, but rival factions opened fire on each other and the food wasted.

Famine in Various Places

"There shall be famines . . . in divers places" (Matt. 24:7), Jesus explained. Jesus told me that millions and millions are going to die of hunger on this earth. It's beginning right now in Ethiopia and in Chad and in different countries.

Once, when I was in Africa, we drove several large trucks into a remote area to feed a group of refugees who had not had a bite of food in four days. They were eating pieces of bark off trees. When they saw our group coming through the jungle with trucks loaded high with food, they almost went berserk.

The Lord said that although there's great hunger in the world, "I don't want my children in the third world to die hungry. I want them to be fed! I love them as much as you in America."

Then, He said, "My children who cry out to Me in the morning and say, 'Give us this day, our daily bread,' and by evening, they haven't had a bite — they come back and ask, 'Are you there, God?' "

In Jerusalem, God commissioned me to feed His hungry people around the world. I told him I was very busy. And He paid no attention to it at all, just told me I had to do it . So I set out to do it.

The Lord told me the next revival that covers the whole earth will be a feeding revival — a feeding revival, and a teaching revival, and a demonstrating revival. Believers will call the people forward, and mighty miracles will take place, just as the Bible says.

When we go to a country, the boat is loaded with food that will be given to pastors from all over that country. We don't make a distinction between Baptist or Methodist or Presbyterian or Pentecostal; God loves everybody. We put it on a truck and take it to a church, and the pastor feeds His people with it. We tell them that the good people in America — by giving five dollars, ten dollars, and twenty dollars — provided this food for them. And these dear pastors and priests are so glad that we can feed their people.

A time will come when the churches are going to flow together, not separately with bickering and fighting. Food will become more important than doctrine.

When you are dying, you don't care which color the life raft is.

Dying people don't say, "I'll take a blue one." They take what they can get.

Everyone who names the name of Jesus is part of the family of

God. We must stop building walls around ourselves and start seeking to save the world. These are the last days. Millions and millions are going to be saved; and we must love everybody.

When China falls on its face, and communism is dead there, do you know what some in the Church will say? "Well isn't that something, I heard that the Chinese people were dying of hunger. Pass the mashed potatoes."

For the past few years, I've felt it was only a matter of time before the government in China collapsed like the former Soviet Union. The situation is perilous, but revival can come to the Chinese.

Now, in a copyrighted newspaper article, February 6, 1995, comes word from a U.S. Defense Department study that indeed, China's immediate future is in jeopardy. Longtime leader Deng Xiaoping is 90 years old and in failing health. His hold has been so strong that there is no clear-cut successor. The story says in part:

> The document presents the nightmare of all China experts: "There is no apparent internal balance of political forces, and Deng's death will create a political vacuum for both conservatives and reformers to move in."
>
> The study sees only a 30 percent chance of the country continuing on its present course. The document, which 13 China experts prepared in August for the Pentagon's Office of Net Assessment, shows little faith in the 'collective leadership' of head of state and party Jiang Zemin, Prime Minister Li Peng, and Deputy Prime Minister Zhu Rongji.[1]

There are believers and unbelievers alike who need help in that tragic but proud country. Jesus told us in Matthew 25 that there are two kinds of people in this world: those who help the needy, and those who shun them. There will be heaven for one, and hell for the other.

Will there be any heaven for you?

That rich man in the Bible — it lists just one thing he did wrong: He didn't feed the poor. The Bible gives six reasons for God's destruction of Sodom, and one of them was that the people had no compassion for the poor.

Pestilences in Various Places

". . . And there shall be . . . pestilences . . ." (Matt. 24:7).

What is pestilence? Cancer is a pestilence, cancer is a cannibal.

Cancers eat humans until they die. Our finite minds can't find a cure for cancer. Pestilence doesn't have to be something from the outside, it can come from within.

Potentially, the deadliest pestilence in the history of the world is AIDS. People talk of a cure, hoping this always-fatal killer can be wiped out. But AIDS is a last days' pestilence, and there won't be a cure for it. Billions of dollars are being spent on research worldwide, but no cure will be found.

Some countries still have their heads in the sand, hoping that AIDS isn't real and that when they wake up, it will have all been a bad dream. But many of them won't wake up because this terrible disease will kill them.

Japan just recently began to study the effects of AIDS on the population in this Asian country. As of last year, there were a little over 3,000 reported cases of HIV, and under 1,000 cases of full-blown AIDS. But as widespread testing comes about, those figures will grow at alarming rates.

This pestilence was caused by the sins of mankind.

India, in the last year, has been struck by pneumonic plague and bubonic plague. Medical professionals made slow headway against these killers. During one two-week stretch, people died every day. The panic caused hundreds of thousands to flee, thus spreading the plagues to other places.

Officials in Bombay worked desperately to catch and kill the rats that carry disease, but in India, some Hindus consider rodents to be gods! They won't kill them, and so the deaths of humans go on!

Age itself is a pestilence. It destroys the vital parts of a human until he has no resources left inside to even overcome a cold. The Bible says the last days will see an increase in this. The pestilence of various diseases has been happening since the great Flood.

Adam was created to live forever, but his sin derailed those plans. Under the climatic conditions at the time, Adam lived almost 1,000 years, and then he died. His early descendants had similar long life spans.

After the Flood, however, life spans immediately dropped to around 250 years, or less. Before the Book of Genesis ends, the span of a man's lifetime was around 75 years. And so it is today.

We have non-functioning glands in our bodies that apparently had purpose thousands of years ago.

Mankind brought pestilence on himself. An act of sin — basic to all our natures — destroyed our immune systems to the point that viruses that once took a long time to kill a perfectly-created human now kill babies when they are only minutes out of the womb.

Have you noticed that influenza outbreaks, even in North America, last longer and longer? Do you have scores of friends who used to be quite healthy, who now suffer through various viruses for months at a time? That is an example of the pestilence of the last days manifesting itself in the environment.

Our lakes, streams, and oceans are contaminated, creating breeding grounds for pestilence. That explains the cancers, viruses, and chronic sickness attacking people today.

A 1994 *U.S. News & World Report* article pointed to the terrible pollution problems of Chesapeake Bay in Virginia. Humans are dumping sewage, toxins, oil, and car exhaust into the water. Farming is also contributing to the problem, with animal manure and dirt finding their way into the bay. Fish, grasses, trees, and birds are dying there.

Early in Genesis, we see that God appointed someone to tend to the earth. Whom did He appoint? It wasn't a duck. It wasn't an elephant, or an otter. No, the Almighty chose Adam, a man, to take care of His creation.

And in only a few thousand years, we've managed to make quite a mess of it. Places like Chesapeake Bay are reaping the results of our mismanagement, and it will only get worse.

Earthquakes in Various Places

". . . There shall be . . . earthquakes, in divers places" (Matt. 24:7), Jesus told His disciples.

In this century, there have been more earthquakes than all the rest of history put together. Earthquakes have become commonplace, and yet they are increasing in intensity.

Every 10 years, earthquakes double in number, and so it has been for the last 10 decades. During the latter part of this decade, earthquakes will occur with increasing regularity, creating terror and panic throughout the world.

Jesus said that was one of the signs of His coming.

Indonesia, Japan, Turkey — these are scattered areas suffering from the effects of earthquakes. The earth is dying, and earthquakes represent the death rattle in its throat.

Earthquakes suggest that America's shores are not immune to destruction. Since 1987, the U.S. Geological Survey reports there have been 121,000 earthquakes recorded in southern California. That is over 100,000 shocks of death in one tiny area of this vast world.

The last days are seeing an enormous increase in terror in the daily lives of ordinary people.

What do you think those people on the California freeways were doing a couple of years ago when the killer earthquake hit? They were doing the same things you do — worrying about their children's education, racing to the store to pick up dinner, talking on their car phones. And then, before they could react at all, whole sections of freeway collapsed on them.

This didn't happen in some faraway country that most of us don't care two hoots about. The news pictures of this devastating earthquake were so severe, people still talk about them years later. The monumental job of cleaning up after such a disaster was impressively handled by rescue crews of all types. Rather than self-congratulations, the people involved in earthquake cleanup go about their business quietly — and still fearfully. So much for man's ability to control his environment.

Earthquakes scare us.

Mexico City residents understand earthquakes; they have almost destroyed them. Iran understands the devastation that earthquakes can cause; Russia has experienced the deadly results of the earth's fury. All over the face of this earth today, people understand well the reality of earthquakes.

The January 1995 earthquake in Kobe, Japan, which killed more than 5,000 people, dealt a devastating blow to this prosperous nation. In spite of all their earthquake drills and building codes, nothing could stop buildings from toppling and the infrastructure from being ripped apart.

The water-main breaks left firemen standing helpless to snuff out the flames that incinerated the people — some of whom were still alive — buried in the rubble of their homes. In spite of Japan's technological superiority, it took days for the government to send help to the desperate survivors of the quake. Thousands were left homeless and exposed to the harsh winter weather, resulting in a flu epidemic that brought further suffering.

The earth is shaking. Why? Our Lord is returning soon!

A few years ago, it was predicted that a devastating earthquake would split open at New Madrid, Missouri — right in the middle of the United States, where life is slow and pleasant!

Seismologists, amateur earthquake-watchers, psychics, and even church leaders put ears to the ground to hear the rumblings. Hardware stores made a fortune selling disaster-relief supplies. It was a sight to behold.

But the earthquake didn't happen. What does that tell us? Only God Almighty decides when and where nature will teach us a lesson.

During a New Madrid earthquake of 1811, it is alleged that the Mississippi River actually flowed backward for a few hours. There is geological evidence to back this up since it appears that a depression in the earth filled with water from the Mississippi.

A beautiful plantation in the state of Mississippi, built in 1790, bears a scar from this New Madrid earthquake that occurred hundreds of miles north. A column on the front of the house had to be improvised after damage occurred from this distant earthquake, and a huge crack runs the entire length of one side of the house.

At that time, folks in the middle of the country were convinced the end was near. The New Madrid earthquake of 1811 is a quiver compared to what's coming.

False Prophets Will Deceive Many

". . . Many . . . shall betray one another, and shall hate one another. And many false prophets shall rise, and shall deceive many" (Matt. 24:10-11).

This prophecy is repeated in 1 Timothy 4:1, ". . . In the latter times some shall depart from the faith, giving heed to seducing spirits, and doctrines of devils."

A year ago, CNN devoted a whole hour to a special program called "How to be a Muslim." A whole hour had to cost hundreds of thousands of dollars.

The Muslims can't save anybody. They don't believe in the blood of Jesus. They don't believe Jesus is the way, the truth, and the light. They don't believe Jesus is the Saviour of the world. They don't even believe Jesus died on Calvary. They say He sneaked away, and somebody else was killed.

Many Americans, however, are being deceived by the lies of Mohammed and the false teachings of the Koran. You don't have to listen to Louis Farrakhan or the messages of Malcom X to realize that theirs is a message of hate. They hate the Jews; they hate the Christians; they hate the whites; they hate anyone who does not agree with them.

Satanism, another religion based on hate, is growing in this country faster than you can imagine. Masked today in the philosophies of the New Age movement, its leaders speak of peace, tranquillity, and comfort.

Large corporations hire New Age consultants to lecture their employees on the latest mind-control techniques. "Now you breathe like this . . . and you put your hands out like this." That is exactly the way Hindus worship their idol gods and it is just another method of worshipping the devil.

If you question a New Age devotee about his doctrine, by asking: "Do you believe in the transmigration of souls?"

"Oh, yeah, my mother-in-law was a billy goat."

"Do you believe there is a hell?"

"Oh, no, no."

"Do you believe there is a heaven?"

"No, no."

"Do you believe Jesus is Saviour of the world?"

"No, no."

But they believe in bowing down to trees.

An enlightened nation like America has hundreds of thousands of people who are following Hinduism — a force of darkness that came from hell to India and from India to America.

You say "How did it happen?"

At one time these same people were Methodists and Baptists and Presbyterians, but they departed from the teaching of Scripture. And that falling away gave heed to false teachings like Hinduism.

Millionaires have given everything they own to convert this nation to the New Age. All the way from the White House to the outhouse, you've got people believing in the New Age. They're high in politics, and they can block you from doing what God wants you to do.

The Father said in the last days, "I will pour my spirit upon all flesh." And the Holy Ghost said some people will accept it. Others, though, would rather play with the devil than have a Holy Ghost revival.

They're in this country, saying, "No, no. Mary was not a virgin. No, no. Genesis is not like it is in the Bible. No, no, no." And they're on their way to hell, because they don't believe the Word of God.

You're not going to heaven if you don't believe the Word of God. It doesn't matter who you are.

There are powers that you and I haven't come into yet. Pride keeps us out. If God shows a little power to people, they start thinking they're big shots. The big shot's name is Jesus, not you or me.

A lot of evangelists were nothing when they started. Whatever they have to draw big crowds, Jesus gave it to them. And if they don't live right, they'll fall to the bottom.

Some of my finest pastor friends, whom I dearly love, in the last 10 years have committed adultery and lost their churches. They were not even middle-aged yet. But they gave way to the lusts of the flesh.

If you don't live right, you don't belong to God. The Bible says the pure in heart will see God; the rest are never going to see God.

False Christs and False Prophets

"For false Christs and false prophets will appear and perform great signs and miracles, to deceive even the elect — if that were possible" (Matt. 24:24;NIV).

This verse leads us to another thought: The Antichrist is ready to make his appearance. In fact, he has been trying to enter the world scene for the last 50 or 60 years, trying to get in.

The Antichrist cannot come, however, until about a hundred million or two hundred million of God's people go to the Marriage Supper of the Lamb.

Why has the Antichrist been held back? The prayers of God's people won't let him come.

When I first began preaching in 1929, I met the many remarkable people of prayer — most of them were older people. They were prayer warriors, and you could feel the presence of God in their prayers.

You may think that America's cities are wicked and violent places, but if God's people weren't living there, it would be a hundred times worse. Christians are the restraining power against sin. Our holiness pours itself out to God every day, and our witness and our testimony rises before God. I believe that is why God keeps slapping the Antichrist back in his place.

How to Live in These Last Days

If you really believe Jesus is coming soon, then you need to live like it. Let me give you some advice for living in these last days.

1. Read the Book of Revelation, not someone's interpretation of it. God worded this end-time prophetic word the way He wants it said. It's in the right order God put it.

2. Attend a Bible-believing church. If you stay with the Word and get settled in a good church, you can avoid being deceived. Christians who wander from church to church get in trouble. They're like grasshoppers; they don't know where to lie down next.

3. Live pure and simple lives. Get your mind off man-made ideas and the things of this life that will surely perish. Realize that we are living in the most dramatic moment this world will ever know. Keep your eyes focused up, for such an hour as you think not, the Son of Man is going to come.

4. Pray for revival. God told me the greatest revival in all of history would take place in China. That amazed me, too. He said there were going to be millions and millions of Chinese saved.

The president of the Bible Society told me recently that there are at least 45 million born-again Christians in China. They are secret believers who worship in the underground church, risking persecution and harassment for their faith. Many have been killed, some are in jail. But they refuse to give up; they won't quit.

5 Evangelize your world. Jesus told us to disciple all the world; that's the Great Commission. ". . . Go into all the world and preach the good news to all creation" (Mark 16:15;NIV).

Are we doing it? Do we have a burden for people everywhere? We should be reaching people for Jesus. This moment is the only time in history when we have had the facilities in our hands to reach a total world with the gospel of Jesus Christ.

6. Pass the sword to the last generation. Moses, being 120 years old, laid his hand on Joshua and, the Bible says, the spirit of wisdom came into him. No matter how old you are, God can use you to fulfill His purposes in these last days. Lay hands on your children and make sure they are firm in their faith in Christ.

In Acts 2:17, we read,

> And it shall come to pass in the last days, saith God,
> I will pour out of my Spirit upon all flesh: and your sons and
> your daughters shall prophesy, and your young men shall
> see visions, and your old men shall dream dreams.

Young men should see visions and old men will dream dreams. That means the old men will say, "This is the way it used to be, and this is the way the Word of God teaches it."

We need the young and the old — if we were all old, we'd dry up; if we were all young, we'd blow up. But if we work together we'll rise up for Jesus. Our children and our youth must be equipped to pass on the torch to their generation.

When God said He would pour out His Spirit on all flesh, He is talking about a worldwide revival! There have been revivals before, but nothing like this one will be.

Revivalist John Wesley only touched two countries: England and the United States. General William Booth with the Salvation Army only touched one: England. Evangeline, his daughter, went into France and had some great revivals over there.

I've never touched the world.

God has to raise up a kind of a new generation. You are that generation — the new generation of this final hour.

Now, I have studied all the great revivals of the twentieth century, because I have been involved in every one of them. But God is going to do something greater than anything He has ever done before.

Dead religionists will say it's fanaticism. But, God will say, that's My Spirit I'm pouring out. There's going to be one more mighty thrust from heaven. And I want to be in it!

Do you?

My Last Great Labor for the Lord

One night, while on a visit to Jerusalem, the Lord woke me up at ten minutes to midnight. He said, "I want to talk to you." He said, "It is also midnight in prophetic time." That shook me clear to my feet.

The Lord said, "I want you to listen to Me." Believe me, He had my attention.

Then He said the strangest thing. "One of My greatest concerns is My own people, part of My church. I don't want them to suffer death by starvation before I return. Will you feed My people?"

I wanted to say "No," so loud that He could hear it. I don't know anything about feeding anybody. I'm a preacher, not a fry cook. I had no intention of feeding anybody. But I listened carefully.

"To them it will be an angelic food supply. It will be a miracle to them."

I sat there writing it all down from midnight until five o'clock in the morning.

"Hunger is an agonizing death," He said. "I want you to give to those who are dying. If you will, I will see that you live happily and victoriously. I will prosper you."

He said, "I have spoken to you in Jerusalem. It is the city where I took bread, blessed it, and broke it, saying, 'Take and eat. This is My body that is broken for you.' I want you to take the bread of the Spirit and the bread of the soul, and the bread of the body to the multitudes who are hungry on this earth."

I asked, "Just what do You mean?"

"Never take just bread. Never! Never! Don't merely feed people's bodies. Take bread to My church and give it to those who are hungry. In the last days, there is going to be famine such as this world has never seen."

God spoke to me again and said, "Millions of My people who belong to Me get up in the morning and say, 'Our Father, which art in heaven, hallowed be thy name. Thy kingdom come, thy will be done, on earth as it is in heaven. Give us today our daily bread.' But when the evening comes, their bellies are empty."

I began to feel their pain.

The Lord asked, "Will you feed My little children?"

"Yes," I answered.

"You will greatly rejoice," He said.

I said, "Lord, I am willing to be an instrument. As old as I am, I need no honor from man. I need no prestige at all. As old as I am, I need no earthly goods of any kind. I can't take a thing of this earth with me. All I want to do is work for You until You come. I want to bless Your church and to bless those who are without."

In the years ahead of us there will be famine, and out of the plenty of American Christians there will flow blessings to the ends of the earth.

In the months after that vision, God began to speak to me about purchasing a large Hercules aircraft that could be used to transport food directly to those in need. After a series of miracles, we obtained a C-130 and began to prepare to feed the hungry.

One of our first trips came right after the Desert Storm War. We flew supplies to the starving Kurds in Iraq for two months, providing hundreds of thousands of pounds of food.

When we arrived, a thousand people a day were dying of dysentery. We took in water purifiers and a military field kitchen and began to feed them. Today, many, many Kurds are alive and praising God because of our C-130.

As the Bible says, there is famine in many places in our world.

Today people in Somalia are dying again. Americans have already grown cold to the cries coming from Somalia and Ethiopia and other places in Western Africa.

Albania is desperate, too — and things are very bad in Russia.

When we took food into Russia, I asked one company about meat and they said, "Yes. If you'll send me a check for $80,000, we'll give you meat." So I sent a check for $80,000 and they gave us $250,000 of the best Danish ham anybody has ever tasted. The Russians loved it.

On every flight, we've taken 10,000 pounds of meat along with flour and the other supplies.

I believe that the wealthy church in America and churches around the world have been called on to ensure that Christians worldwide do not go without food. I also believe that great evangelism and revival will occur if we will show compassion and feed the starving.

The Lord showed me in detail that all over the face of this earth there are the beginnings of famine.

Will you catch this vision? This may be my last great labor.

Join me to save millions from death by starvation.

Will you help feed God's people in the difficult days that are just around the corner?

Will you feed Christian children who are asking God to "give us this day, our daily bread?"

What does the Lord say to you? Will you obey?

4

Israel: Earth's Only Superpower

by Dave Breese

Consider the following scriptural references as we look into matters both ancient and modern involving the all-important prophetic subject called Israel — the nation often symbolized by the fig tree.

God says through the prophet Ezekiel:

> And I will make them one nation in the land upon the mountains of Israel; and one king shall be king to them all: and they shall be no more two nations, neither shall they be divided into two kingdoms any more at all: Neither shall they defile themselves any more with their idols, nor with their detestable things, nor with any of their transgressions: but I will save them out of all their dwelling places, wherein they have sinned, and will cleanse them: so shall they be my people, and I will be their God. And David my servant shall be king over them: and they all shall have one shepherd: they shall also walk in my judgments, and observe my statutes, and do them. And they shall dwell in the land that I have given unto Jacob my servant, wherein your fathers have dwelt; and they shall dwell therein, even

they, and their children, and their children's children for ever: and my servant David shall be their prince for ever. Moreover I will make a covenant of peace with them; it shall be an everlasting covenant with them: and I will place them, and multiply them, and will set my sanctuary in the midst of them for evermore. My tabernacle also shall be with them; yea, I will be their God, and they shall be my people. And the heathen shall know that I the Lord do sanctify Israel, when my sanctuary shall be in the midst of them for evermore (Ezek. 37:22-28).

About signs that will precede His return to earth as King of kings and Lord of lords, Jesus said:

Now learn a parable of the fig tree; When his branch is yet tender, and putteth forth leaves, ye know that summer is nigh: So likewise ye, when ye shall see all these things, know that it is near, even at the doors. Verily I say unto you, This generation shall not pass, till all these things be fulfilled. Heaven and earth shall pass away, but my words shall not pass away (Matt. 24:32-35).

The world is watching again!

The media spotlight moves around the world, at times circling a nation, a city, a battlefield, and brings us the emergent news from the latest hot spot. The world now watches that traveling spotlight with new and consummate interest.

While one or another nation is occasionally visited by that traveling lighted circle, there is one area of the world that appears again to be the focus of the world's present events as well as its past history. That area has generated more news and more crises with international implications than any other. It is, of course, the Middle East. Specifically, it is the land of Israel and the city of Jerusalem.

In September of 1993 world attention focused there once again as news cascaded out of the Middle East to capture the worried interest of all the world: The state of Israel and its mortal enemy, the Palestine Liberation Organization (PLO), signed — at least the beginning documents — of a peace accord.

The consummation of long negotiations came on September 13 when dignitaries from Israel and the PLO gathered at the White House in Washington, DC. Three thousand other "very important people" from Washington and the nation also attended to witness the signing of that peace accord. All who watched were struck by the almost surrealistic nature of the occasion as they observed a scene, at one time thought impossible — and yet there it was.

The high point came when Yitzak Rabin, Prime Minister of the state of Israel, and Yassar Arafat, chairman of the Palestine Liberation Organization, shook hands (we think reluctantly!) on that platform. That handshake and the related accords spelled for many "the dawn of a New Age."

Within moments, our telephones at Christian Destiny headquarters began to ring with people asking for radio interviews, television commentary, and a report of our interpretation of these incredible events. As a result, within an hour we found it necessary to produce a short commentary for distribution. We have included that essay as background against which a special analysis of the situation of Israel may be appropriate.

The Peace Accord Ceremony

"This is not just a piece of paper, it is the dawn of a new age," so spoke the President of the United States on the White House lawn on Monday, September 13. The occasion was what some have called "the watershed of history" and "the beginning of an era in which the whole world is invited to cooperate." The president said, "We are here to join together in a peace accord for the Middle East." He expressed the thought that after centuries of conflict, the wide differences represented there would now be resolved. He announced that "the conflicting claims of history" between Jews, Muslims, and Christians will now find a new resolvement. He said that the world was taking a "brave gamble for the future, betting that the future can be better than the past."

Not in recent history have Americans and citizens of the world heard speeches that express such a bright promise for the future, indeed a sense of destiny. Yitzak Rabin, prime minister of the state of Israel, said tearfully, "This is not easy, it is not easy for me and it is not easy for the others involved. I am a soldier and I say that we must now try to put an end to the long hostilities in the Middle East. I say enough! Enough of blood and tears!"

His words were given a standing ovation by more

than 3,000 dignitaries who attended the ceremony and we may be sure that there were additional millions across the world who were constrained to add to that ovation as they watched on global television. The response, by the way of approval from the crowd, showed that it sensed that soul-wrenching decisions had been made by the leaders of Israel and those of the PLO.

Then came what Tom Brokaw called "the moment." It was the occasion in which Yassar Arafat, chairman of the PLO, and Yitzak Rabin shook hands across a gulf of estrangement that had existed for the lifetimes of the two men. In that historic moment, the world remembered the years of death, destruction, hatred, the out-pouring of primordial passions in the violent, endless hostility between these two deadly protagonists.

The response, however, was not universal approval. There were riots in the city of Jerusalem as the Jewish Conservatives called this treaty a "recipe for disaster." One called this "a distortion of history" and "a moral distortion as well." One insisted that "Yassar Arafat should be arrested and put on trial for his crimes and his wickedness."

The passionate among the PLO and the Arab Fundamentalists denounced the treaty as a "shameful compromise" with the Israeli aggressors. They retained their conviction that the Jews should be pushed into the sea rather than become the object of some kind of spiritual merger.

Indeed, spiritual merger is what it seemed to be. In the speeches given in Washington there were quotes from the Torah, the Koran, and the Old Testament. These quotes were given under the assumed confidence that the passionate sense of destiny on the part of these three groups of people could be somehow resolved by negotiation.

There is no doubt that the earnest, impassioned call for peace carried the audience at the moment and certainly produced those wistful, earnest longings for what President Clinton called "the quiet miracle of peace." The presentation before an onlooking world was most impressive and will be the object of lengthy discussion in many nations.

The whole world was, in fact, looking on. Out of the activities of that morning, a call has already been extended for all of the Arab world to lay down the arms of hostility and get along with each other as well as find comity with the nations of earth. A call was also extended for the financial support of the world for the needed money that it will take to finance this dream of a new age in Gaza and in Jericho. Yassar Arafat is calling for world support in the amount of $6 billion to accomplish his desire in Gaza and the Jericho area.

It is interesting that the very day of the conference, September 13, 1993, the *Wall Street Journal* ran an article entitled "How Much Peace Can Western Money Buy?" The implication being that, after all the fair speeches, it is Western money and especially American dollars that will produce the big difference in the days to come.

The perceptive Christian will look upon these things and concern himself with the question, "What might this mean prophetically and what issues are involved?"

Many things can be said about this, but some especially should be noted. Obvious considerations include the following:

(1) We have now heard the largest call for peace which the world has ever lifted. The activities of that Monday were transmitted to the ends of the earth and were presented with a passion that was certain to touch the hearts of all who would hear. The call to peace is predicted in Scripture as one of the devices that the Antichrist will use at the end of the age in order to accomplish his will. The Scripture says about "the king of fierce countenance" (Dan. 8:23) that he "by peace shall destroy many" (Dan. 8:25).

(2) Peace cannot come by human machinations. The Scripture very clearly declares that "there is no peace, says my God to the wicked." God, who works all things after the counsel of His own will, has told us that, "There shall be wars and rumors of wars" until the end of the dispensation of the Tribulation. In fact, nation rising against nation is one of the signs of a period of time prelude to the Tribula-

tion, which is called "the beginning of the sorrows." When one thinks of this for just a moment, he remembers that God is a Holy God. Therefore, apart from conformity to His holiness, we will not, in fact, see man's bright desire of peace fulfilled in the world.

(3) Peace will only come upon the return of Jesus Christ in power and great glory. Until then, the world will be characterized by perpetual war on every hand. The time of the Tribulation, the seven-year period preceding the glorious return of Christ, will be characterized by such devastating wars that half of the population of the world will die. The Tribulation at its conclusion will gather all of the nations of the world in a great attempted military assault upon the Nation of Israel and upon the city of Jerusalem. God himself will ask, "Why do the nations rage?"

The peace of Jerusalem is a very sacred thing. The Bible scholar will remember that the peace of Jerusalem does not depend upon the peace of the world — it's the other way around. The peace of the world will depend on the peace of Jerusalem. Peace will only come when Jesus Christ reigns from the Holy City and imposes His righteous will upon the world.

(4) This time of great concern is now a time of spiritual opportunity. The world once again is talking about "the Holy City." It is quoting the Bible, it is talking about the God of Abraham, Isaac, and Jacob. Attention is being paid to the core of the Christian religion and, indeed, the religion of Islam, of the Koran, and of the Torah as never before. Because religious ignorance is so profound in the world, people will be asking the meaning of all these things. Happily, the Christian is in a position where he can explain from the prophetic Word the meaning of these things.

(5) A great call to peace will in fact be a prelude to war. The Apostle Paul tells us, "When they shall say peace and safety, then sudden destruction will come upon them as travail upon a woman with child, and they shall not escape" (1 Thess. 5:2). Therefore, we must remember that peace movements and especially gigantic peace initiatives

will not bring peace. Rather, predictably, they will bring war and they will make war more brutal when it actually comes to pass.

We must remember that the purpose of God is not necessarily to bring political peace, not in a world of sin. Rather, God has made life deliberately precarious, dangerous, filled with jeopardy so that we might seek a better world over which the Lord himself presides. More people have been won for Christ in times of trouble in this world than have been won in times of peace.

Therefore, we must labor, not primarily for peace, but rather for truth. Supposed peace which is built on moral falsity is not peace at all.

So the attention of the world once again is swirling in a larger circle around the Middle East — the place where it all began and where it's all going to end — making it wise for the believing Christian to look up for our redemption that draws nigh.

Remember again, this is a time of spiritual opportunity. We do not know what tomorrow will bring, but we know that today God is setting before us a gigantic open door to minister to a concerned world. The message, of course, is that peace for the soul comes by faith in Jesus Christ. Peace on earth awaits the brightness of His coming.

Peace: Just the Beginning

All who commented on that historic September occasion came to the same conclusion, in essence: "We have just been through an important beginning ceremony, but it will be worth nothing without the hard work of continued negotiations to bring peace in the Middle East."

A major part of the content of the speeches made that day included a set of characteristics that we should note:

(1) *The speeches were essentially utopian.* They promised everything would change now that we had seen the advent of "the New World Order." They pressed the idea of "the dawn of a new age." Implicit in this kind of talk is the idea that "the future can be better than the past," which were the very words of President Clinton. The suggestion is, therefore, on the table that a perfect or near-perfect world can be created out of these negotiations for peace.

(2) *They called for a composite religion.* Specific quotes given by one and another of the speakers were drawn from the Koran, the Torah, and the Bible, particularly the Old Testament. It was clearly implied that some kind of unified thinking could be developed out of a composite understanding of these three great religious books. Implicit within such a set of suggestions is the notion that a new, cooperative religion can be created that would be satisfying to all. By implication, the suggestion was not merely presented to the protagonists in the Middle East but was a call to all the world. Indeed, the basis for the religion of the last days could be found within those remarks.

(3) *The plans are dependent upon leadership known to be unstable.* Within the speeches made, and particularly within the commentary by the newsbrokers of the world, was that big question about the future: "Who will be in charge?" About Yassar Arafat many said, "Would you buy a used car from this man?" One of the comedians the following day even said, "Yassar Arafat has now hijacked a plane and returned home to Tunisia." Today's instability of leadership implies the possibility, perhaps the necessity, of a great call to a strong leader to "come and help us" in the future.

(4) *The peace accords assumed some kind of "mutual ownership" of the land of the Middle East.* In the totally secular discussions concerning the peace accords, there was no idea from whence final authority would come that could answer the question, "Who owns what in the Middle East?" Left completely out of the picture, and certainly unacceptable in the discussions, was the divine mandate of the Word of God: "In the same day the Lord made a covenant with Abram, saying, Unto thy seed have I given this land, from the river of Egypt unto the great river, the river Euphrates" (Gen. 15:18). So the question remains among the politicians of the world, "Who owns the land of Palestine?"

The student of the Word of God has no such unresolvable problem, for he knows the answer. "Israel does!" The only nation on earth whose borders are precisely named in Scripture is the nation of Israel.

Out of these discussions, confidence is running high in the world. The nations of earth have been invited to cooperate, especially with their money, with the new design for peace. The day after the signing, Yassar Arafat petitioned the United Nations for its financial help. His initial goal is $6 billion in order to reconstruct the infrastructure of the PLO. How would this $6 billion be used? To buy streets, sanitary systems, decent housing, food? Be sure that one of Arafat's first questions would be, "What is the price of 10,000 AK-47's on today's market?"

Beware the Three Princes

Against this background, we must lift a very earnest warning to the State of Israel. That warning is best expressed in the words, "Beware of the three princes."

Yes, there will be at least three notable princes of this world who will bear a tremendous impact upon the state of Israel. No leader of Israel could be called responsible who forgets that the destiny of the present and future state of Israel will be impacted by the activity of three princes. Who then are the three princes that will be of such great importance?

In the sixth century, before the coming of Christ, the prophet Ezekiel, in the very words given to him by God, lifted a voice of warning to the nation of Israel:

> And the word of the Lord came unto me, saying, Son of man, set thy face against Gog, of the land of Magog, the chief prince of Meshech and Tubal, and prophesy against him, And say, Thus saith the Lord God; Behold, I am against thee, O Gog, the chief prince of Meshech and Tubal: And I will turn thee back, and put hooks into thy jaws, and I will bring thee forth, and all thine army, horses and horsemen, all of them clothed with all sort of armour, even a great company with bucklers and shields, all of them handling swords (Ezek. 38:1-4).

Here we have the description of the beginning of a very serious military conflict. After telling us of the beginning of the war, Ezekiel instructs the nation of Israel in the name of the Lord, saying, "Be thou prepared, and prepare for thyself, thou, and all thy company that are assembled unto thee, and be thou a guard unto them" (Ezek. 38:7).

Israel, according to the Word of God, is instructed to institute a program of preparation to defend itself against the aggression of "the chief prince of Meshech and Tubal." When speaking about "the chief prince," the prophet Ezekiel actually uses the expression, which is literally, "the Prince of Rosh." Thoughtful evangelical Bible scholars all agree that this is a picture of that great power in the north, Russia.

We are even told by God the very words that will come into the mind of Gog, the leader of this massive army in the north:

> Thus saith the Lord God; It shall also come to pass,
> that at the same time shall things come into thy mind, and
> thou shalt think an evil thought: And thou shalt say, I will
> go up to the land of unwalled villages; I will go to them that
> are at rest, that dwell safely, all of them dwelling without
> walls, and having neither bars nor gates, To take a spoil,
> and to take a prey; to turn thine hand upon the desolate
> places that are not inhabited, and upon the people that are
> gathered out of the nations, who have gotten cattle and
> goods, who dwell in the midst of the land (Ezek. 38:10-12).

In this notable prophecy, we can gain knowledge from some special statements that help us establish a possible time frame for this great battle between Russia and the nation of Israel.

Why Was Israel Scattered?

Notice first of all that Israel has now been gathered out of the nations of the world. The scattering of Israel was surely the saddest chapter in that nation's history. So desolate is this picture that in Scripture is analogous to a valley filled with dry bones:

> The hand of the Lord was upon me, and carried me
> out in the spirit of the Lord, and set me down in the midst
> of the valley which was full of bones, And caused me to
> pass by them round about: and, behold, there were very
> many in the open valley; and, lo, they were very dry (Ezek.
> 37:1-2).

We cannot avoid asking, when we see this picture of spiritual desolation, why it was that Israel was scattered among the nations in such a manner. What was the reason for such judgment from God upon His people?

The Israelite people were the possessors of great spiritual advantage. They knew God. Their prophets were the channels by which the Word of God came to the world. They should have known better than to turn to the wickedness of the surrounding culture. But, of course, they did not. They played the harlot, committing literal and spiritual fornication with the pagan nations that were their neighbors.

The apostle Paul discusses this when he says, "What advantage then hath the Jew? or what profit is there of circumcision? Much every way: chiefly, because unto them were committed the oracles of God" (Rom. 3:1-2).

Advantage indeed! They possessed the sacred, living pages of the Old Testament and, as a result, every Jew on the earth should have been filled with the knowledge of God and been an expert at knowing His will. To Israel was given great light; it was even to be a light to the Gentiles.

What did Israel do with that light, that unique knowledge of the Word of God? In the pages of the Old Testament, we have the report again and again of deep spiritual lapse on the part of the nation of Israel. Despite its knowledge of God, its people turned again and again to worship idols in the high places and to follow after the pagan deities of the Gentiles.

Finally, Paul was constrained through his tears to write: "For the name of God is blasphemed among the Gentiles through you . . ." (Rom. 2:24).

Israel sinned in the midst of knowledge, illustrating that to sin against light is the worst kind of sin. Untold suffering has come upon Israel as a consequence of its backsliding and turning away from the will of the true and living God. There could be no other consequence than their scattering among the nations.

Spiritual Advice for the Nation of Israel

In spite of the fact that God's people have been scattered among the nations, Israel is still the demonstration to the world of the God of all grace. Despite its many eras of spiritual defection, God continued to promise that His covenant with Israel is eternal. He promised that He would bring errant, unbelieving Israel back to its own land. The divine covenant is particularly applicable to Israel in the land — the land which is theirs by divine mandate.

Looking at this from our present historical vantage point, we see that God has been progressively bringing this promise to pass. Israel, still largely in unbelief, is coming home.

One is left thoughtful about this: Is there any advice that we might presume to give to the nation of Israel, even at this time? Presumptuous as it may seem, the Church of our time would do well to advise Israel in several ways. Beyond the warning not to trust the Arabs, the PLO, or really anyone, we would presume to give spiritual advice that would include:

(1) *Turn to God in repentance of faith.* How else can your

miraculous return to the land be explained apart from letting God into the picture? It is inexcusable blindness not to see the hand of God in these things.

(2) *More specifically, turn to Jesus Christ.* Israel, you will, I promise, accept Jesus as your Messiah in a day to come. However, individual Jews who receive Christ as Saviour now become members of the Body of Christ. As a consequence, they become inheritors of the universe — joint heirs with Christ. Greater than David's kingdom on earth is Christ's kingdom of the heavens. Become a Christian now, and you are the heir of the greater promise.

(3) *Allow Christian evangelism in Israel.* Your great present mistake is to forbid the preaching of the gospel of Christ in your land. You, therefore, are living in continued rejection of Christ, thereby repeating the same mistake that you made 2,000 years ago.

(4) *Remember your best friends in the world are the Evangelical Christians;* especially is this true of the Christians of America! Don't simply promote affection with "the world religious community" (They don't really love you!); stay in contact with the Christians. They, I assure you, are the ones who really "pray for the peace of Jerusalem."

The First Prince Attacks

Despite talks of peace, Israel is at this very moment bordered by enemies who ravenously covet even the small bit of land that nation currently possesses. The threat presently confronting Israel, however, is nothing compared to what God's Word prophesies will come to pass just prior to Christ's return.

Although space limitations forbid an in-depth look at the Gog invasion of Ezekiel 38 and 39, it is good for our purposes to let the prophet's inspired words give a quick sketch of that attack. Keeping in mind that Rosh has been identified as the nation Russia, we notice that God speaks to the prince of Rosh, saying:

> After many days thou shalt be visited: in the latter years thou shalt come into the land that is brought back from the sword, and is gathered out of many people, against the mountains of Israel, which have been always waste: but it is brought forth out of the nations, and they shall dwell safely all of them (Ezek. 38:8).

Then, in most compelling fashion, God speaks further to the

prince of Rosh and says:

> And thou shalt come from thy place out of the north
> parts, thou, and many peoples with thee, all of them riding
> upon horses, a great company, and a mighty army: And
> thou shalt come up against my people of Israel, as a cloud
> to cover the land; it shall be in the latter days, and I will
> bring thee against my land, that the heathen may know me,
> when I shall be sanctified in thee, O Gog, before their eyes
> (Ezek. 38:15-16).

So we have the picture of Russia and its allies moving with
strength in the attempt to overwhelm and destroy the nation of Israel.

At this momentous time, God himself will fight for Israel as in
days of antiquity. Ezekiel says:

> And I will call for a sword against him (the invading
> prince of Rosh) throughout all my mountains, saith the
> Lord God: every man's sword shall be against his brother.
> And I will plead against him with pestilence and with
> blood; and I will rain upon him, and upon his bands, and
> upon the many peoples that are with him, an overflowing
> rain, and great hailstones, fire, and brimstone. Thus will I
> magnify myself, and sanctify myself; and I will be known
> in the eyes of many nations, and they shall know that I am
> the Lord (Ezek. 38:21-23).

As frightful as the attack from this northern confederation will
be, Israel, at some prophetic point in time, will face even more
terrifying prospects. The prince that shall come will hate Israel more
virulently than will the prince of Rosh.

Who is the Second Prince?

Europe is calling for a most unusual man. It needs a leader! He
must possess the personal intelligence, charisma, and communication
skills that will electrify the people of Europe. The call for such a man
grows stronger with each day that passes.

Will there be such a man who will rule Europe and then go
beyond that? Yes. Who is this person? He is "the prince that shall
come." He is "the Antichrist."

The day will come when the desperate cries of the people of the
world will bring this man to the place of the leadership of the revived

Roman Empire. That leadership will then develop into the base by which he is escalated to become emperor of the world and king of the earth. He will build his power on twin bases, political and religious. He will be the political leader of the world and will aspire to be its religious leader as well. To do this, he will labor to bring to pass a composite religion that can be acceptable to all the people of the earth.

It is a fascinating and moving experience to consider the teaching of Scripture concerning the Antichrist and the amazing power that he will possess as we move toward the consummation of history. (We suggest further reading on this, namely the books *The Religion of the Last Days* and *Before the King Returns,* published by the ministry of Christian Destiny.)

But the question remains: How will this person, "the prince that shall come," relate to the nation of Israel? The scenario suggested by the Word of God is fascinating indeed.

Europe Emerges While America Recedes

As a first step, he will make a covenant of peace with the people of Israel. The signing of the covenant and this mutual commitment will be another one of those memorable meetings to behold.

The Scripture says, "He shall confirm the covenant with many for one week . . ." (Dan. 9:27).

When we read this verse, we remember that Israel has been through five terrible wars with its Arab neighbors. In the midst of these wars, a faithful friend has stood by the nation of Israel, furnishing military equipment, intelligence, and help of many kinds. Who is this faithful friend? It is, of course, the United States of America.

What has protected Israel?

From a human point of view, Israel's protection has been America's military power and her willingness to use it. This has protected the nation of Israel (and the world) up until this point. One can even say that the United States has surely been Israel's only genuine friend in the world.

One can, therefore, speculate with interest on the question: What has happened to the United States at the time when Israel feels constrained to make a covenant with someone else, namely the leader of Europe? The answer to that question could be frightening for the people of America. Of this, more must be said.

Nevertheless, the indication is that Israel, no longer confident in the mentorship of America, seeks another alliance to vouchsafe its survival. By that time, the emergent power of the world is quite obviously Europe and the receding and distant power of America appears to be hardly as dependable as what Europe might be able to furnish.

So we see the leaders of Israel looking for an alliance with a closer, emergent power of the world. Europe emerges while America recedes. So a deal must be made!

What would be the advantage to Europe and to Israel of a mutual alliance? The advantage to Israel is obvious. Israel does not have the sustained military power to stand against a determined Arab invasion.

Remember, there are one billion followers of Islam in North Africa and the Middle East while only four million populate Israel. So the advantage of this new treaty to Israel is that Europe guarantees the borders of Israel. In order to do so, Europe may well move an army into the State of Israel on behalf of this guarantee. Israel, then, can reasonably be expected to be confident in the backing of a new and powerful ally.

The advantage to Europe is also obvious. Virtually 100 percent of the energy that runs the lamps and the limousines of Europe comes from the Middle East. Europe, with an army in the Middle East and with the cooperation of the state of Israel, would be in a much better position to protect those energy supplies than if Europe had to do it by mere diplomacy from a distance. The presence of a European military contingent in Israel guarantees the imperative flow of oil which the Middle East supplies. A covenant, a military alliance, then, is of obvious mutual advantage.

In the early days of that covenant relationship, one can surely suggest that there is great mutuality, even conviviality, between Europe and Israel. Israel has publicly stated on many recent occasions that it wants to be thought of as a Mediterranean power rather than as a Mid-East power. It therefore can be expected to develop many forms of commerce between itself and the individual nations of Europe by then coming together in the great unified Europe.

The Great Betrayal

God's prophet, Daniel, tells that when Israel signs an agreement guaranteeing the nation peace and security, it will actually be a covenant made with death and hell. The signing with Europe's evil genius leader, the Antichrist, triggers the seven-year Tribulation period termed by Jeremiah the prophet "Jacob's trouble," the most horrendous time of suffering in human history.

The dastardly heart of the Antichrist becomes obvious, and he betrays his covenant with Israel, disrupting the worship at the temple, which will, by this time, be rebuilt and the temple worship rituals reinstituted.

The apostle Paul gives us an expanded picture of this event, which is most telling. Speaking of the Antichrist, Paul says he is the one "Who opposeth and exalteth himself above all that is called God, or that is worshipped; so that he as God sitteth in the temple of God, shewing himself that he is God" (2 Thess. 2:4).

Here we have that astonishing picture of the Antichrist being overtaken by satanic megalomania. He travels from his base in Europe to the Middle East and actually sets himself up in the temple at Jerusalem to be worshipped, declaring himself to be God.

What can this be but the abomination of desolation?

For the Jews, this is the last straw. By this time, there is a strongly emergent consciousness in Israel of the true God and of one's obligation to Him. Consequently, Israel rebels against the leadership of the Antichrist, declaring itself a follower of God and a rejecter of the Devil's man who occupies now the twin thrones of religious and political leadership of the world.

An Army of Witnesses

There is initiated, as we may well understand, a terrible persecution once again against the nation of Israel. It has been suggested that this persecution is Israel's last cycle of discipline as, now brought to human extremity, it calls out to the Lord. On or about this time, we see the fulfillment of a remarkable promise made to Israel by the prophet Zechariah. God speaking through the prophet says:

> And I will pour upon the house of David, and upon the inhabitants of Jerusalem, the spirit of grace and of supplications: and they shall look upon me whom they have pierced, and they shall mourn for him, as one mourneth for his only son, and shall be in bitterness for him, as one that is in bitterness for his firstborn (Zech. 12:10).

Following the announcement of this pouring out of the spirit of grace upon the people of Israel are some of the most touching verses in the Bible. Describing a stunned and repentant Israel, Zechariah says:

> In that day shall there be a great mourning in Jerusa-

lem, as the mourning of Hadadrimmon in the Valley of Megiddon. And the land shall mourn, every family apart; the family of the house of David apart, and their wives apart; the family of the house of Nathan apart, and their wives apart; the family of the house of Levi apart, and their wives apart; the family of Shimei apart, and their wives apart; All the families that remain, every family apart, and their wives apart (Zech. 12:11-14).

Here we have a picture of the great sorrow and chagrin that will come upon the nation of Israel at this point in its history. Suddenly the nation recognizes that Jesus Christ is indeed the Messiah of Israel and the Saviour of the world. The mourning comes because they now look back at 2,000 years of fearful persecution and realize that all of this could have been avoided had they accepted Jesus Christ the Messiah when He announced himself to them. Many will remember when He spoke on the Mount of Olives and said:

> O Jerusalem, Jerusalem, thou that killest the prophets, and stonest them which are sent unto thee, how often would I have gathered thy children together, even as a hen gathereth her chickens under her wings, and ye would not! Behold, your house is left unto you desolate. For I say unto you, Ye shall not see me henceforth, till ye shall say, Blessed is he that cometh in the name of the Lord (Matt. 23:37-39).

But alas, God interrupts that mourning with another remarkable thing. Zechariah announces, "In that day there shall be a fountain opened to the house of David and to the inhabitants of Jerusalem for sin and for uncleanness" (Zech. 13:1).

A gracious God invites these people, His nation, the apple of His eye, to be forgiven and cleansed and washed in a special fountain opened to the house of David. Indeed:

> There is a fountain filled with blood; drawn from Emmanual's veins;
> And sinners, plunged beneath that flood, lose all their guilty stains.[1]

How then does the scenario of a redeemed Israel continue to unfold? We are certainly invited to be thoughtful in answer to this question when we read the Book of Revelation which says, "And I heard the number of them which were sealed: and there were sealed an hundred and forty and four thousand of all the tribes of the children of Israel" (Rev. 7:4).

As if emphasizing this most strongly, John announces every one of the tribes of Israel by name and the fact that 12,000 witnesses come from each one of the tribes. So it is that from one nation of the world will be produced an army of witnesses that are nearly three times the Protestant missionary force in the world today.

Israel will believe with a vengeance and accept its Messiah with overwhelming gratitude. Israel then will become the great witness preaching the gospel of the kingdom during the days of the Tribulation. It will fulfill the mission that God intended for it during all the time of its historical existence.

The consequences of this stunning new spiritual reality are many. Israel now becomes the world's most spiritual nation, the source of evangelism and spiritual provocation for all the earth. Zechariah announces the Lord as saying:

> Behold, I will make Jerusalem a cup of trembling unto all the people round about, when they shall be in the siege both against Judah and against Jerusalem.
>
> And in that day will I make Jerusalem a burdensome stone for all people: all that burden themselves with it shall be cut in pieces, though all the people of the earth be gathered together against it (Zech. 12:2-3).

So Israel becomes the focus of the world's spiritual resentment as well.

The Reigning Third Prince

Once again we have from the Word of God the awesome picture of warfare, this time by all of the nations of the world against the city of Jerusalem. In many places the Scripture announces that finally all of the nations will despise Israel and move with military power to destroy this great and now revived representation of God in the world — Jerusalem. The Psalmist describes this, saying:

> Why do the heathen rage, and the people imagine a vain thing? The kings of the earth set themselves, and the rulers take counsel together, against the Lord, and against his anointed, saying, Let us break their bands asunder, and

cast away their cords from us. He who sitteth in the heavens shall laugh: and the Lord shall have them in derision (Ps. 2:1-4).

Finally, Jerusalem will be surrounded by the hostile armies of all the world, bent on taking fatal vengeance against these people who now know and worship the Lord God. Israel, beware of the prince who shall come!

But, alas, this is not the end of the story. At the very moment Israel and the city of Jerusalem are about to be annihilated, and mankind, with its awesome war-making capability is about to commit collective suicide, the fabric of space scrolls apart, and the blindingly brilliant heavenly force begins its swift descent.

We are favored by the Lord to receive from John, the writer of the apocalypse, a stunning description of that great event. He says:

> And I saw heaven opened, and behold a white horse; and he that sat upon him was called Faithful and True, and in righteousness he doth judge and make war. His eyes were as a flame of fire, and on his head were many crowns; and he had a name written, that no man knew, but he himself. And he was clothed with a vesture dipped in blood; and his name is called The Word of God. And the armies that were in heaven followed him upon white horses, clothed in fine linen, white and clean (Rev. 19:11-14).

Here we have the picture of the glorious second coming of Jesus Christ. He will come at that time to judge the nations and then to rule them with a rod of iron, expressing the fierceness and wrath of Almighty God. He will be seen and recognized by all as the "King of kings and Lord of lords."

The result of that glorious return will be that the whole world will see, never again to forget, that God is God. But also, a parallel result will be that Christ in His second coming rescues the inhabitants of Jerusalem who by that time will be surrounded and probably despairing of their human lives. Christ will "smite the nations" and draw them back forever from their horrible intention of rebelling against God, which is represented by their angry siege of Jerusalem.

Looking upon that rebellion by the world against God, the Psalmist says, "He that sitteth in the heavens shall laugh: and the Lord shall have them in derision. Then shall he speak unto them in his wrath, and vex them in his sore displeasure. Yet have I set my king upon my holy hill of Zion" (Ps. 2:4-6).

What a day that will be!

The third Prince, therefore, must be seen as the deliverer of His people, the nation of Israel. He will come in that gigantic rescue, defeating the nations of the earth in their assault upon Israel and establishing in that hour His kingdom in this world.

Yes, Messiah the Prince will reign from Jerusalem and govern the nations of the earth for a thousand wonderful years.

> But in the last days it shall come to pass, that the mountain of the house of the Lord shall be established in the top of the mountains, and it shall be exalted above the hills; and people shall flow unto it. And many nations shall come, and say, Come, and let us go up to the mountain of the Lord, and to the house of the God of Jacob; and he will teach us of his ways, and we will walk in his paths: for the law shall go forth of Zion, and the word of the Lord from Jerusalem.
>
> And he shall judge among many people, and rebuke strong nations afar off; and they shall beat their swords into plowshares, and their spears into pruninghooks: nation shall not lift up a sword against nation, neither shall they learn war any more (Mic. 4:1-3).

So we see that one day Israel will be the leading nation of earth, and Jerusalem will be the capitol of this planet. From that place, Messiah the Prince shall rule the nations of earth.

Your Appointment With the Prince

Can anyone honestly deny that recent history has seen the tiny nation of Israel come again into existence, fight, and win what looked to be almost certainly unwinnable wars, and thrive and grow to be a truly Mediterranean power, not just a third-rate Middle East country? Is it not true that Israel is consistently reported by newscasts and newspapers around the world to be perhaps the most likely flashpoint that might ignite World War III? Indeed, Israel stands at center stage in the theater of global geopolitics precisely as God's word prophesies.

Just as God promised, last-days Israel has come from being the fig tree putting forth its leaves, in accordance with Jesus' words of Matthew 24:32, to Jerusalem becoming a burdensome stone to all the nations of the world as foretold in Zechariah 12. Amazingly, all this has happened in less than half a century! Be assured that every word within God's Holy Scriptures is absolute truth. All will come to pass exactly as God in His omniscience has said.

He tells us that Jesus Christ is the way, the truth, and the life; that no one comes to the Father but through Jesus. Jesus, the Messiah who makes Israel earth's only true superpower, is the same Jesus who gives to all who truly believe in Him everlasting life.

Today as the Saviour, Jesus Christ, He offers eternal life to all who believe in Him. When one accepts the finished work of the Lord Jesus on Calvary's cross and believes in Him as his personal Saviour, he becomes the possessor of eternal life. To know Christ and to have, therefore, His gift of life is the greatest experience possible in all of life.

However, if we avoid Jesus as our Saviour, we will meet Him one day as the awesome judge of the universe. The Scripture clearly indicates that every person who is not a Christian will one day stand before His judgment throne. John says:

> And I saw a great white throne, and him that sat on it, from whose face the earth and the heaven fled away; and there was found no place for them. And I saw the dead, small and great, stand before God; and the books were opened: and another book was opened, which is the book of life: and the dead were judged out of those things which were written in the books, according to their works (Rev. 20:11-12).

This passage of Scripture should shake the foundation of every soul when it says "And whosoever was not found written in the book of life was cast into the lake of fire" (Rev. 20:15).

Therefore, not for Israel alone, but for all of mankind, the proper warning is presented to "beware of the three princes." The ultimate Prince, the Lord of all things, is Jesus Christ. There is no avoiding that final appointment with Him when every nation and every individual will stand in the presence of that celestial throne. We prepare for that day by coming to know Him as personal Saviour today. Let no one miss Jesus' earnest invitation:

For God so loved the world, that he gave his only begotten Son, that whosoever believeth in him should not perish, but have everlasting life. For God sent not his Son into the world to condemn the world, but that the world through him might be saved.

He that believeth on him is not condemned: but he that believeth not is condemned already, because he hath not believed in the name of the only begotten Son of God (John 3:16-18).

Section II

Diary of a Mad Planet!

5

Perilous Times in a Wicked Generation

by Steve Butler

But as the days of Noah were, so also will the coming of the Son of Man be. For as in the days before the flood, they were eating and drinking, marrying and giving in marriage, until the day that Noah entered the ark, and did not know until the flood came, and took them all away; so also will the coming of the Son of Man be (Matt. 24:37-39;NKJV).

Likewise as it was also in the days of Lot: they ate, they drank, they bought, they sold, they planted, they built; But on the day that Lot went out from Sodom it rained fire and brimstone from heaven, and destroyed them all. Even so will it be in the day when the Son of Man is revealed (Luke 17:28-30;NKJV).

With these words, Jesus Christ answered His disciples' questions about the signs of the end of the age.

Christians today call this time the "second coming of Christ" and, like the first disciples, are very interested in the characteristics of earth's final generation. What will those times be like? How will they compare to the days of Noah and the days of Lot? Could our present generation be the one that Jesus was speaking about?

Jesus stated in verse 36 of the "Olivet Discourse," as this section of Matthew's Gospel is called, that ". . . of that day and hour knoweth no man, no, not the angels of heaven, but my Father only." The Lord was cautioning His followers not to speculate about the exact date and time of His return and the judgment of the world, but He did urge believers in every generation to ". . . be ready, because the Son of Man will come at an hour when you do not expect him" (Matt. 24:44;NIV).

In the Olivet passage, Jesus is describing some of the basic activities of human life — eating, drinking, marrying, and giving in marriage. Luke's inclusion of the activities of Lot's day also include buying, selling, planting, and building. What Jesus seems to be saying is that people will be going about their everyday business when He suddenly returns for His church and ultimately judges lost mankind.

Those Were the Days

What about the days of Noah and the great flood? Why did Jesus refer to Lot and the destruction of Sodom? Why were these two events linked together in Luke's record of Christ's discussion of the Second Coming? Because God's judgment came swiftly upon two civilizations that were perverse and wicked beyond turning back.

By examining the biblical record of the Genesis account of Noah's times and the days of Lot, some sobering light may be shed upon parallels between those days and the 1990s.

> And it came to pass, when men began to multiply on the face of the earth, and daughters were born unto them, That the sons of God saw the daughters of men that they were fair; and they took wives of all which they chose. And the Lord said, My spirit shall not always strive with man, for that he also is flesh: yet his days shall be an hundred and twenty years (Gen. 6:1-3).

The sixth chapter of the Book of Genesis describes the expansion of the human race both numerically and geographically upon the earth.

As mankind populated the earth, it seems that the sons of the descendants of Seth, the third son of Adam and Eve, desired the daughters of the descendants of Cain and intermarried with them. Apparently, the desire for Cainite wives, as well as for the daughters of the Sethite line, was based on sensual appetite rather than on love, common heritage, and especially, godly virtue.

This practice greatly displeased the Lord God because, by this time, the righteous Sethite line had departed from its former dependence on God and followed its debased yearnings that resembled the natures of ungodly and defiantly independent Cainites.

In Genesis 6:3, God said, ". . . My spirit shall not always strive with man, for that he also is flesh. . . ." The Holy Spirit of God would not abide as a moral, ruling force in the lives of straying rebellious people. There would be a limit to the patience of a righteous and generous God who was the only source of restraint upon a race that was willingly dominated by the "flesh."[1]

The term "flesh," in biblical terminology, refers to man's carnal nature, not to his creaturely kinship to the animal world through a material body. Mankind resisted the influence of the Holy Spirit and had become flesh.[2] As a result of sensuality and willfulness, the human race's days upon the earth were limited to 120 years.

God reveals His pending judgment even as He allows time for repentance through His grace.

Men of Violence

Along with marriages based on the unequal yoking of godly and ungodly partners, men of violence and lawlessness seemed to roam the earth, contributing to the general atmosphere of vanity and ungodliness that dominated the age before the flood.

> There were giants in the earth in those days; and also after that, when the sons of God came unto the daughters of men, and they bare children to them, same became the mighty men which were of old, men of renown (Gen. 6:4).

The term "giants" is better translated as those "who fall on others" or falling ones." Nephilim is a more accurate name from the Hebrew, Naphal, "to fall."[3]

The Nephilim were probably roving men of violence who preyed on the population as robbers and tyrants (according to Luther, Keil and other commentators).[4] They may have been warriors of large physical stature like the Rephaim (mighty ones) of Deuteronmy 2:11 and the Anakim (long-necked ones) of Numbers 13:22 and Joshua 15:13-14 in the Old Testament.

Whoever the Nephilim were, they were present before, during, and after the birth of the offspring of the Sethite men and the Cainite daughters. Many of these children grew up to be "mighty men," (Hebrew, Gibborim — the strong, impetuous heroes), and "men of renown," literally, "men of the name," known by many. They may have been, according to Calvin, "honorable robbers who boasted of their wickedness."[5]

> Then the Lord saw that the wickedness of man was great in the earth, and that every intent of the thoughts of his heart was only evil continually. And the Lord was sorry that He had made man on the earth, and He was grieved in His heart. So the Lord said, 'I will destroy man whom I have created from the face of the earth, both man and beast, creeping thing and birds of the air, for I am sorry that I have made them.' But Noah found grace in the eyes of the Lord (Gen. 6:5-8).

Through His patient oversight, God saw the wickedness of man was widespread on the earth and that every fashioned purpose of the thoughts of his heart (the seat of the emotions of the mind) was only set on evil literally every day.[6] Mankind had become depraved to the extent that evil was the race's sole identifying characteristic.

Such a state was the result of man's willful rejection of his Creator and moral guide and his enjoyment of brute force and self-gratifying indulgence as he oppressed those who were weaker. Obviously, the law of the jungle and the rule of the strongest prevailed over the moral restraint encouraged by God.

Verse 6 states that the Lord was sorry that He had made man on the earth and He was grieved in His heart. God was sorry that He had put men on His earth, and He grieved because He still cared for man. Man's depravity merited his destruction as the judgment of God would blot out man's reign of corruption. Even the lower animals would be recipients of the consequences of man's removal.

Fortunately for the race, during the 120 years of grace, Noah found approval before God, and he and his family would be saved when judgment would come through the great worldwide flood. This family would be God's remnant through which mankind would populate the earth after the Flood.

Divine Messengers

As the rains came for 40 days and nights upon the civilization of Noah's day, so fire and brimstone rained from heaven upon the wicked society of Sodom and Gomorrah.

> But on the day that Lot went out of Sodom it rained
> fire and brimstone from heaven and destroyed them all.
> Even so will it be in the day when the Son of Man is
> revealed (Luke 17:29-30).

In each of these biblical accounts, judgment came swiftly from God as the iniquity of people became full. Destruction was the final answer to continued sin and lack of repentance.

Jesus reveals to us that these same conditions will prevail upon the earth when He returns for His church and judges earth's last generation. How were the days of Lot like those of Noah?

The eighteenth chapter of Genesis describes a startling visitation of God and two of His angelic messengers to Abraham, the patriarch of the Hebrew people and uncle of Lot. This "theophany," or visible appearance of God in human form, was to announce the promised birth of a son to the aging Abraham and wife Sarah, and to conduct God's judicial investigation of Sodom and Gomorrah's sins.

Verses 20-21 record the Lord's statement that ". . . the outcry against Sodom and Gomorrah is great, and because their sin is very grievous, I will go down now and see whether they have done altogether according to the outcry against it that has come to me; and if not, I will know."

Of course, God already knew the sins of the "cities of the plain," but He apparently wished to demonstrate the justice of His judgment to His servant Abraham, who represented God's chosen, righteous people. Abraham and his family would be God's instruments for explaining His judgments to an unbelieving world.[7]

Being a man who had great compassion for others, Abraham seemingly did not understand the magnitude of God's grace and tolerance. The patriarch sought a reprieve for Sodom and Gomorrah by asking if the cities would be spared if 50 righteous men could be found in Sodom. God was patient with His servant, but after the number was reduced to 10, Abraham, too, realized that righteousness was not to be found within the city.

As soon as He was finished speaking to Abraham, the Lord disappeared. Grace was shown to Abraham's nephew, though, as the two angels continued on to Sodom where they encountered Lot.

Genesis 19 continues the narrative of the angels' interaction with Lot and the perverse men of Sodom. Lot was sitting in the gateway area of the city when he noticed the strangers. Hospitable like his uncle Abraham, Lot offered his own home as lodging for the angels to spend the night. There is no indication that he assumed they were anything but mortal men.

The divine messengers declined Lot's invitation at first but later gave in to his persistence. One can deduce that Lot's earnestness may have been a combination of the eastern custom of hospitality and his concern over the travelers' safety among the Sodomites at night.

God's Final Response

After eating supper at Lot's home before bedtime, the angelic guests and their host heard the presence of the men of Sodom who "... both old and young, all the people from every quarter, surrounded the house. And they called to Lot and said to him, 'where are the men who came to you tonight? Bring them out to us that we may know them carnally'" (Gen. 19:4-5).

Lot responded to the Sodomites' homosexual lust (hence, the term "sodomy" for such acts) by going out the door and imploring the men of Sodom not to violate the law of hospitality to strangers. Desperate to protect his guests, Lot offered his virgin daughters to the perverse mob (Gen. 19:8). By doing so, Lot revealed the effect that living in such a perverse city had on his own moral character.

The unruly multitude, which represented men of all ages from every part of the city, was so far gone in degradation of body and mind that it would not be satisfied with abusing the young women. Instead, it mocked Lot and threatened to do worse to him than to his guests.

As the men sought to break down Lot's door, he withstood them until the angels pulled him into the house and shut the door.

> And they struck the men who were at the doorway of the house with blindness, both small and great, so that they became weary trying to find the door (Gen. 19:11).

The angelic messengers struck the Sodomites with blindness, yet they still groped for Lot's door, until they all tired. This is another indication of the depths of sexual perversion and inordinate lust to which the people of that wicked city had fallen. Even blindness could not deter them from seeking to molest Lot and his guests. Only physical tiredness and the inability to enter the house caused them to depart.

Afterward the angels warned Lot to speak to his family and sons-in-law and prepare them to leave Sodom, "For we will destroy this place, because the outcry against them has grown great before the face of the Lord, and the Lord has sent us to destroy it" (Gen. 19:13). Lot's future sons-in-law thought he was joking with them and didn't heed his advice.

Sodom's attraction to Lot and his family seemed to continue as the angels sought to lead them out of the city the next morning. The messengers had to take Lot, his wife, and two daughters by the hand and lead them out of the city before punishment befell the area.

While being instructed to flee to the nearby mountains for safety, Lot begged to be allowed to go to the little town of Zoar (originally named "Bela") and that it might be spared as the other cities of the plain were destroyed. Lot gave the impression of being an obsessive urbanite.

After the angel allowed Lot to journey toward Zoar, the Lord rained down fire and brimstone out of heaven upon Sodom, Gomorrah, and the other cities of the plain, causing a geological upheaval that obliterated the once-fertile area. At the same time, Lot's wife disobeyed the angel's directive not to look back or stay anywhere in the plain, and she perished, becoming a pillar of salt (Gen. 19:15-26).

Fully Grown Sin

The wayward spirit of Sodom did not cease to influence Lot's family after the destruction of the cities of the plain and the death of his wife. Lot and his two daughters later left Zoar and took up residence in a mountain cave, "For he was afraid to dwell in Zoar" (Gen. 19:30).

Fearing that none of the local men would take them as wives, the older daughter persuaded the younger one to plot with her to get their father drunk and then to have sexual relations with him while he was in a stupor. The plan worked during two consecutive nights and eventually two offspring were born from their incestuous acts, and their father's lineage was preserved.

Lot's perverse daughters evidenced no shame for their abnormal sex acts because they named their respective sons in descriptive terms. The older daughter's son was called Moab, "from the father," and the younger daughter's child was called Ben-Ammi, "son of my people."[8] Each of these sons would be the forefather of nations that would be perpetual enemies of Israel after the conquest of the Promised Land. They were known as the Moabites and the Ammonites.

As the biblical record reveals, sin, if not repented of and

cleansed, will produce pride, lust, violence, and destruction. Though God is loving and patient, He is also just and righteous. That is, by His very nature, He will not tolerate the revolting activities of man's selfish desires forever.

The apostle James wrote that "Each one is tempted when he is drawn away by his own desires and enticed. Then, when desire has conceived, it gives birth to sin; and sin, when it is fully grown, brings forth death" (James 1:14-15).

The selfish desires of the citizens of Sodom and Gomorrah produced their own destructions. The twisted procreative desires of Lot's daughters resulted in the deaths of multitudes of Moabites, Ammonites, and Israelites in territorial wars that were waged among them over the centuries.

Sin, which is rebellion against the holy purposes of God and His authority to guide human lives, always leads to alienation and judgment. So it was in the days of Noah and so it was in the days of Lot.

New Days, Old Ways

What about our day, the 1990s? Is judgment coming upon our society in the United States and upon the world? Are there parallels in the lifestyles of our generation to those of these previously judged generations? Is man coming to that place in history when God says, "Enough!" and sends His Son Jesus Christ to retrieve His church and execute judgment on a wicked and defiant world system?

Jesus said, "Watch therefore, for ye know neither the day nor the hour in which the Son of Man is coming" (Matt. 25:13).

Our generation has suffered through 30 years of a gradual abandonment of what has been called "traditional values." These are the ethical mores and standards of right and wrong that guided the United States for more than 200 years. Actually, these values and standards of thinking, acting, and viewing life have been referred to as the Judeo-Christian ethic.

Since our nation and much of our western world has abandoned these traditional values, mankind has paid a heavy price for the illusionary and nonexistent happiness and "freedom" that moral relativism has promised but not delivered.

Writing in the August 8, 1994, issue of *U.S. News & World Report,* editor-in-chief, Mortimer Zuckerman asks "Where Have Our Values Gone?" He notes that three out of every four Americans think we are in moral and spiritual decline. Two out of three think the country is seriously off track. Social dysfunction haunts the land:

crime and drug abuse, the breakup of the family, the slump in academic performance, the disfigurement of public places by "druggies, thugs, and exhibitionists."

Zuckerman goes on to say:

> We certainly seem to have lost the balance between societal rights and individual freedoms. . . . Crime is sanctioned by the fact, real or imagined, that the criminal had an unhappy childhood. Gone are the habits America once admired: industriousness, thrift, self-discipline, commitment. . . . Instant gratification is the new order of the day. Personal impulses, especially sexual, are constantly stimulated by popular music and television, with other mass media not far behind. TV and music often seem to honor everything that the true American ethic abhors — violence, infidelity, drugs, drinking — and to despise everything that it embraces — religion, marriage, respect for authority. No wonder it is difficult to sustain parental values and parental continuity.

Zuckerman also laments that "altruism is not encouraged in a culture of acquisitive individualism."

Self-centeredness is definitely at the heart of man's problems, whether in America or the rest of the world. Generosity and self-sacrifice are necessary ingredients for marriages, families, and nations to prosper. The alternative is division, strife, and the splintering of a society.

According to Steven Roberts, in another article from *U.S. News & World Report*,[9] the family structure is continuing to change in America. The Census Bureau reports that the birth rate for unwed mothers has jumped 82 percent in the past 10 years, and the number of divorced Americans has increased almost four times since 1970. Roberts observes that more kids are being raised with less supervision and fewer resources, putting them at greater risk of delinquency.

An article by Phillip Elmer-Dewitt in *Time* magazine notes that single parents in America number more than 9 million.[10] Population watchers have pointed out that children raised by single parents are more likely to get in trouble.[11]

The most criminally active males are between 15 and 29 years old, and the number of teenagers is expected to increase in the general population by 23 percent over the next decade. From 1965 to 1990, juvenile murder arrests alone rose 332 percent. Citing these figures in *Newsweek*, Michel Marriott deduces that the trend is likely to continue in the years ahead due to deepening child poverty, destabilization of families, and more guns, drugs, and nihilism among young people.[12]

The Final Generation

If the grim state of American society is not enough to sober any thinking person, consider the international situation. Wars and rumors of wars blot the globe. Hundreds have been killed in Bosnia, as have possibly half a million or more Tutsis in Rwanda.[13] Haiti is still tumultuous, and Russia's democracy could easily fall. In the Middle East, peace is more prevalent but fragile. Instability seems to be the only consistent trend. The world needs a deliverer, but only One from heaven can do the job — Jesus Christ.

The days of Noah and Lot were much like our own: violent, proud, indulgent, and perverse. Noah's generation was noted for its defiance of God's rule and its tendency toward violence and sexual lusts. Lot's generation in Sodom was known for its obsession with sex to the point of homosexual rape and incest. This behavior was contrary to the laws of God and man. Our own society now condones sexual appetites of every persuasion, just as Sodom did.

Should we be spared?

Judgment may very well be upon us in reaping the bitter harvest of moral relativism that our modern world has so eagerly sampled. The fruit of this harvest is very bitter, and the solutions to our problems are beyond the resources of politics, economics, and academics.

The solutions are found only in the good news of a Saviour who has offered to enter the hearts and minds of every person who will accept His deity, sacrificial payment for their sins, and the forgiveness of a holy and gracious God. Obedience to God through a personal relationship with Jesus Christ will change the hearts of people. When a person's heart is changed, his life can change; and when people change for the better, societies and governments change for the better.

Jesus Christ told His followers nearly 20 centuries ago that ". . . This good news of the kingdom will be preached in all the world as a witness to all the nations, and then the end will come" (Matt. 24:14).

The good news is being preached on every continent on the globe today. Many people have heard the gospel, but others have not. When they hear, earth's final generation will see Jesus.

It may be very soon. Are you ready?

6

Sex for Fun and Profit

by Phil Arms

Sex. Sexologists have said that the average American male spends 60-70 percent of his waking hours musing, fantasizing, or studying the subject of sex, while he is actually only engaged in the activity less than 1 percent of his time.

Sex was one of God's greatest ideas; yet among all of man's activities, it has been subject to more perversion by Satan than any other of God's gifts to humanity. It is little wonder that this beautiful, tender, and compassionate expression between a man and a woman — with its ecstasy, its passion, and its power — would be the satanic tool of demeaning, humiliating, and embarrassing man, the ultimate of God's creation.

World history reveals that man, under the cloud of this demonic deception, has not only glorified but even deified sex. The Greek culture expressed deification of sex in its mythological goddess Aphrodite, the goddess of love, who was believed to have sprung from the foam of the sea. The wife of Hephaestus, the god of fire, Aphrodite supposedly had sexual liaisons with the gods, Ares and Dionysus, as well as with at least two lowly mortals, Anchises and Adonis.

This sexual license was not only permitted among the Greek gods, but it was preferred and encouraged in every pagan culture. The temples to sex goddesses were complete with their own stables of temple prostitutes. Temple rituals elevated sexual immorality to the status of holy sacrament.

The Greeks were said to have emulated the Orientals in their infatuation with the worship of sex. And each successive empire found a way to deify its own "goddess of love." There were, for example, the Roman goddess, Venus, and the Greek goddess, Aphrodite. The Apostle Paul described Diana of Ephesus as one ". . . whom all Asia and the world worshipeth" (Acts 19:27).

Even earlier perversions were expressed in the Old Testament in such places as Exodus 32, where Aaron allowed a golden calf to be the focal point of a rebellious children of Israel's sex orgy. So the worship of sex is definitely nothing new to the human race.

A Curse That Damns

The gift of sexuality, which God bestowed upon man, can only be satisfactory and completely fulfilling when expressed within the relationship of a man and a woman whose union has been sanctified by marriage. In that context God has said, ". . . the bed undefiled . . ." (Heb. 13:4). Outside that divine context and contract, sex becomes a curse that damns, pollutes, poisons, and debases the human spirit and soul. It becomes a selfish, self-centered enterprise that deteriorates into a downward spiral of acts, each more loathsome than the other in its attempt to satisfy a lust whose appetite becomes all-consuming and never appeased.

To understand the power of our sexuality, one must realize that sex has little to do with physiology and everything to do with spirituality. Since the Garden of Eden, it has been Satan's desire to lead humanity away from God. Satan has been so successful in the area of sexuality because the fall into sexual deviance and license rarely, if ever, occurs in one giant leap. Rather, the fall is a slow, downward descent, ever moving away from God's highly placed value of human sexuality.

No sin, especially sexual sin, is stationary in nature; it is digressive. God's Word states clearly that in the waning days of history, society's condition will become progressively worse. It is also clear, historically as well as scripturally and prophetically, that man will become more and more aggressive in his desire to satisfy the increasing sexual appetites that are stirred by his rebellion against God. Lust, however, can never be satisfied. It only grows, as a cancer, until it dominates and destroys its victims.

The decay of America's moral tone over the past 75 years is but a microcosm of a world gone mad for sex. And though every God-fearing person in this nation is appalled at the exponential rapidity of growing immorality, I fear we "ain't seen nothin' yet."

Prime-Time Perversions

Even in the '60s and '70s, America still exhibited some sexual restraint and moral scruples. For example, the early network television programs such as "Lassie," "Leave It To Beaver," "Father Knows Best," "I Love Lucy," and "The Andy Griffith Show" project an image of wholesomeness, basic values, and respect for traditional Judeo-Christian morality. Though none of the programs were overtly Christian, they never flew in the face of the moral fiber that existed in mainstream America. Television producers were reluctant to show a scene with a married couple in the same bed. Sexually laden terms — even the word "pregnant" — were anathema to producers, directors, and advertisers.

Today, the antithesis of sexual wholesomeness is pumped into our homes through the prime-time perversions of programming like "NYPD Blues," "Rosanne," and "Beverly Hills 90210," which come complete with profanity, overt sexual innuendo and diatribe, near nudity, and a mocking of the Judeo-Christian values still held dear by millions of Americans. The difference between the programming of yesterday and today has not only been brought about by the desire of the Hollywood and New York elite to be America's foremost change-agents, but also by the breakdown of resistance by a now very silent majority of program consumers.

This is not even to mention the unimaginable perversity discussed on talk shows such as "Donahue" and "Oprah," the ridicule of morality exercised on daily soap operas, or the pornographic and/or profane movies (we call them PG, PG-13, and R ratings) that cascade into millions of homes via cable television.

Furthermore, into our classrooms and living rooms across America, hell is vomiting out its greatest, vilest, most blasphemous and debasing of all sexual activity: homosexuality. Change agents in the media are successfully convincing our generation that such is normal, sane, and perhaps even preferred behavior.

Neither time nor space are available here to thoroughly deal with the fact that pornography (soft-core and hard-core) is now the third most profitable business in America. Today's pornography includes every grotesque assault upon human dignity imaginable, from homosexual and child porn to blatant bestiality — images of humans engaged in sexual acts with animals.

Flesh Worshippers

Humanity has always had its moral lapses, whether in ancient Greece and its preoccupation with the worship of sex, Rome with its destructive lust for flesh, or Sparta sporting its pride and infatuation with homosexuality. Every Spartan warrior traveled with his "boy" at his side. And yet, there have been pockets of resistance to the deviance, the abnormality, the "sexual revolution" of each succeeding empire and culture. A voice from some quarter has always registered repulsion to immorality and called for a return to moral purity.

The difference in our world, the entire world, is that the cry for repentance, the alarm against sexual license and deviance, the shock over immorality, are almost absent. Why? Because we are living in the waning days of human history as we know it. The Bible gives dire warnings and predictions concerning the collapse and decay of moral sanity in the last days. Paul clearly addresses this last days eruption of perversity and moral decadence:

> This know, also, that in the last days perilous times shall come. For men shall be lovers of their own selves, covetous, boasters, proud, blasphemers, disobedient to parents, unthankful, unholy, without natural affection, trucebreakers, false accusers, incontinent, fierce, despisers of those that are good, traitors, heady, high-minded, lovers of pleasures more than lovers of God, having a form of godliness, but denying the power of it; from such turn away (2 Tim. 3:1-5).

While Paul certainly deals with various areas of spiritual darkness and social depravity, there is no doubt he also deals with a last-days revival of moral darkness to be manifested in sexual deviance. His statement that "men shall be lovers of their own selves" not only establishes with clarity that humanity will increasingly become "flesh worshippers" but that all sexual appetites will be for the selfish fulfillment of his own lusts. Paul quickly reinforces the point as he says "men [in the generic sense men includes the female] will be without natural affection."

Among the natural affections Paul refers to are "sexual" affections demonstrated in normal sexual activity between a man and a woman. Here and in other New Testament passages, Paul clearly states that there will be an inordinate revival and evangelistic campaign among homosexuals in the last days.

Society's change agents have redefined the meaning of what is unacceptable, or "deviant," behavior. Indeed, we are witnessing the death of deviance. What was once considered blasphemous behavior, even by the irreligious, has become accepted, normal, cosmo, cool, and fashionable in many of our nation's most powerful circles.

We have a president who, for the first time in history, courted the homosexual political community for votes and quickly moved to reward its efforts to help elect him. He and his spouse have, according to leaders in the homosexual community, appointed more than 128 homosexuals to office and government positions, including some of the highest offices in Washington, DC.

Homosexuality, however, is only one small factor in the equation that has resulted in the demise of our nation's moral tone. Infidelity, adultery, and fornication are the hallmarks of a generation gone mad with the fleshly worship of its bodies.

Several years ago, a senior editor of *Life* magazine, when asked about America's infatuation with pornography, reportedly replied, "It is America's attempt to make love to itself."

And so it is.

Doing What Comes Naturally?

In "Infidelity: It May Be in Our Genes," a cover story for the August 1994 issue of *Time,* author Robert Wright suggested that America's continuing, illicit sexual feast is merely a result of our "evolutionary psyche."

Some believe that evolutionary psychology is giving us a new and fresh (actually, it's as old as the Garden of Eden) look at human sexuality. Wright has also written a book entitled, *The Moral Animal: Evolutionary Psychology and Everyday Life,* in which he asserts that, until now, evolutionary science has believed that the "evolutionary purpose" of human sexuality has been to sustain a healthy family unit. But now, according to Wright's article, evolutionary psychologists believe infidelity is "natural."

Wright suggests that, though people may indeed fall in love, they probably are not "evolutionarily" designed to stay in love. He then further suggests that males in the human species help advance the evolutionary process by sowing their seeds "far and wide." Of course, moral considerations and such are a non-issue to this animalistic behavior. Hence, the subliminal message is that all of us should chill out and relax our Victorian, moralistic views on traditional family values. After all, Wright suggests, man is just doing what comes naturally as he "hunts" around for another tryst.

Wright portrays the female of our species to be, by nature, a bit more discriminating in her mating choices, though still driven by her primitive desires. She, according to Wright, seeks out mates with the "best genes."

Here is a brief excerpt from Mr. Wright's Darwinian article:

> How can evolutionary psychologists be so sure? In part, their faith rests on the whole data of evolutionary biology. In all sorts of species, and in organs ranging from brains to bladder, nature's attention to the subtlest aspects of genitive transmission is evident. Consider the crafting of primate testicles — specifically, their custom tailoring to the monogamy, or lack thereof, of females. If you take a series of male apes and weigh their testicles (not recommended actually), you will find a pattern. Chimpanzees and other species with "relative testes weight" (testes weight in comparison to body weight) feature quite promiscuous females. Species of low relative testes weight are either fairly monogamous (gibbons, for example) or systematically polygamous (gorillas), with one male monopolizing a harem of females.

Mr. Wright, as we have seen, builds his thesis upon the animal kingdom and animal behavior. But then, without apology, he makes a quantum leap to apply those principles to human sexuality. Simply put, he re-phrases the question asked by the Tina Turner hit of several years ago entitled, "What's Love Got to Do With It?"

Man's attempt to dehumanize and emotionally neuter sex has been the single most blatant and harmful attack on the home and upon godly morality in our culture since the beginning of time. The effort to de-personalize sexual conduct and to relegate it to animalistic behavior is no more and no less than an effort to release man from his moral responsibilities and natural, God-given, moral restraints. It is, again, a revolution against our "natural affections."

New Age Sex — Cybersex

Decades ago, Winston Churchill prophetically wrote, "The empires of the future will be the empires of the mind."

Old sins re-packaged for the New Age seem to be the order of the day. Paul, in writing the book of Romans, gives us a bird's-eye view of man's moral regression over time. He says, "And even as they did not like to retain God in their knowledge, God gave them over to a reprobate mind, to do those things which are not convenient; Being filled with all unrighteousness, fornication, wickedness, covetousness, maliciousness . . . haters of God . . . inventors of evil things . . ." (Rom. 1:28-30).

The age of computers has allowed darkened hearts and depraved minds to invent more evil devices to give reality to their fantasized, inordinate affections. Computerized sex is here under the name of cybersex. This graphic, pornographic form of sexual expression is available on computer bulletin boards, on-line "chat lines," floppy disks, and interactive CD-ROMs. With computer simulation and photo-ready partners, one is able to verbally and visually participate in various sexual acts by interfacing and interacting with the computer program, any number of which are now being marketed through various respected secular book and computer stores.

This subject is so sordid and distasteful that I almost hesitate to discuss it here. However, it is vital that we do so to expose it, and especially to alert and educate ourselves and our children who may fall victims to such electronic seductions. Increasingly, our youth are being attracted to cybersex.

Interactive movies are the latest hot component of the cybersex publishing world. These videos offer extremely hard-core stories that give viewers the opportunity to choose their fantasy by making sensual decisions that guide the direction of the film's plot.

Virtual Reality or Non-Reality

Until now there has been only one kind of virtual sexual fantasy. It consisted of closing one's eyes and using the imagination. But now the purveyors of perversity are offering the ultimate cybersex experience through "virtual reality." This new technology promises, among other things, the experience of simulated sex. It is an unholy alliance between the most powerful of human drives and the most sophisticated and powerful new technology. Sex, via virtual reality, is an "invention of evil" that endeavors to re-define and more thoroughly vulgarize human sexual relationships.

In a book written by Philip Robinson and Nancy Tamosaitis called *The Joy of Cybersex: An Underground Guide To Electronic Erotica,* one regrettably can discover the menagerie of New Age sexual fantasies available on computers and through new Virtual

Reality technology. The ungodly book comes complete with a computer disk to open this whole new world of experiences for you.

In discussing the possibilities, the authors say:

> Just imagine yourself in the near future getting decked out in your cybersensual sex suit for a hot night out on the nets. You plug your jack into your cybernetic interface device, which then enables you to receive and transmit realistic tactile sensations. Suddenly you are in a strange new world where miraculously you can run your hands through virtual hair, touch virtual silk, unzip virtual clothing and caress virtual flesh. You would be having what might be called "neuromimetic sexual experience," where sensations experienced by your nerves are translated into electronic pulses. You don't have to feel the sensations, you only have to believe that you are feeling them. In a neuromimetic world, our tactile and other senses could be increased a thousand-fold in ways that boggle the mind.[1]

So, to reiterate Paul's description of man's love affair with himself, "And even as they did not like to retain God in their knowledge, God gave them over to a debased mind, to do those things which are not fitting" (Rom. 1:28;NKJV).

Prophecy clearly and repeatedly identifies a society in the last stages of depravity as this dispensation comes to an end. Man is pictured as fabricating, through his fallen and warped fantasies, additional descript ways of acting out his rebellion against the God of nature and the nature of God.

Tom Hawkins, founder of software makers Electronic Arts, speaking of the game machine company 3DO, says that soon "you'll be able to completely fool your brain into believing what you're seeing is real. You'll be able to suspend disbelief indefinitely."

R. U. Sirius, editor of a cyberpunk magazine called *Mondo 2000* writes, "People won't have complete isolation so much as identities that have less to do with physical body and appearance and more of how they choose to represent themselves."[2] And why? Because the relationships will be with those "perceived" by and through the technology and not by reality. Various sexual acts can be experienced by the mutual use of computers with an invisible partner sitting miles (or continents) away at their own PC, or one may use his own computer as his "consenting partner" to produce the sexual fantasy of his choice.

Amazingly, man is becoming increasingly adept at fooling himself by running from reality and calling it "virtual reality" which, in truth, is non-reality. Fantasy is the name of the game today. This computer age is facilitating man's downward spiral and accelerating the fulfillment of prophecy.

Sick as it is, you can currently find cybersex discs to download the following sexual fantasized activities from computer boards: Hot, Hot, Hot Girls; Sizzling Swimwear; Busty Babes; Hungry Amazons; Lingerie Ladies; For Adults Only; Gay Lifestyles; Hot Animations; Adult Games; and Women On Line.

Oh you can't afford a personal home computer system? Then let your fingers do the walking and just try. . . .

Phone Sex

Another sign of the times and of the continuing universal decay is the lackadaisical moral tone of not only the general population but also of our government's policing agencies (such as the Federal Communications Commission). Our government's attitude toward sex via the airways is abominable.

Police vice squads in every major city testify that for decades it has been possible to pick up a phone and order a prostitute by calling any number of escort agencies. You can utilize the services of your major credit card while doing so. However, you can now have what is called "phone sex" with a partner by calling a number and talking yourselves graphically through any sex act imaginable.

Telephone sex has become a multi-million dollar industry in America. 1-900 numbers are advertised in a multitude of major publications (and not only pornographic ones) as well as on television and radio. Of course, it, too, can be billed to your local phone number or to the major credit card of your choice.

Some of these phone sex clients and their call-in partners were featured as guests of the "Maury Povich Show" in August 1994. Their "defense" of this sordid activity was to repeatedly tout its virtues. Among the "positives" they cited were: "no one gets hurt," "it's innocent fun," and "it's safe sex."

A biblical perspective, of course, provides solid arguments to counter such excuses for acting out lewd fantasies. And yet the very existence, growing popularity, and economic rewards of such perverse behavior testifies to the fact that men are increasingly becoming lovers of themselves and that society is in a moral nose dive.

The countdown on the prophetic clock ticks on.

Truth or Consequences

When truth is rejected and spurned, the antithesis is the new reality. The only option open to those who refuse the truth of God is to accept the lie of Satan. The consequence of a global rejection of all that is holy, good, moral, and pure is darkness, deception, and, ultimately, destruction. Rejection of spiritual light opens a floodgate to spiritual darkness that leaves in its wake moral darkness and decay.

In 2 Thessalonians 2:10-11, the apostle Paul, looking through the portals of time by Holy Spirit revelation, received a preview of contemporary society: ". . . because they received not the love of the truth, that they might be saved. And for this cause God shall send them strong delusion, that they should believe a lie." Sin breeds ignorance and a profound stupidity. The deeper the sin, the greater and more profound the ignorance and stupidity.

In America we have a society inundated with venereal diseases, unwanted pregnancies, and a large, growing population of AIDS victims who still just "don't get it." Humanity is crazed with twisted sexual appetites, and people everywhere seemingly care very little about the consequences of throwing themselves into the flames of their own lust.

Once upon a time, even natural men without a relationship with Christ possessed a stout resistance to unbridled sexual gratification. Moral standards, social diseases, civil laws, and social stigmas helped restrain, temper, and direct men's sexual drives. When all else failed, the fear of social ostracism that came as a result of unwed parenthood, the embarrassment of moral failures, and even the thought of possibly contracting a "social disease" helped modify behavior.

But now that is all a thing of the past.

Man has "progressed." He's been unshackled from these "Victorian" concepts. Moreover, in most cases, venereal diseases now have cures or medicine to hold them in check. And after all, we are the most "sexually educated" generation in world history. Or so we have been told.

Why, then, are more than 50 million American teens and young adults infected with genital herpes, and why does one youth contract syphilis or gonorrhea every 30 seconds in America? Ten million victims of sexually-transmitted diseases last year were under 25. More than 25 percent of the people in the United States with syphilis or gonorrhea are between the ages of 10 and 19 years old. Thirty percent of sexually active teens in America are infected with chlamydia.[3]

And what of AIDS? In spite of the fact that this deadly disease is globally spreading faster than any other disease in history, the majority of America's youth say they are not worried about their chances of "getting it."

Experts now tell us that venereal diseases in America are no longer in an epidemic stage of societal infection but that they have been upgraded to the pandemic category, i.e., beyond control. Indeed, this nation is living under a great and strong delusion, believing "the lie" that living without moral considerations and spiritual constraints is a free ride.

In truth, America is "loving itself to death."

Sex — God's Way

God's first words to man and woman about sex were not to forbid it. On the contrary, God invented, sanctioned, ordered, and encouraged Adam and Eve (and every married couple since) to have sex — not only for the purpose of procreation but for pleasure. God is intensely interested in a man and a woman finding sexual fulfillment and enjoyment in their marriage.

One sees a beautiful, enthralling, and passionate expression of love between a married man and woman in the Song of Solomon, a poignant love story. The couple is neither discussing unpaid bills nor debating whose turn it is to take out the garbage or weed the garden. This couple is captured by each other's sanctified and seductive sex appeal.

In chapter 1:2 the woman says, "Let him kiss me with the kisses of his mouth: for thy love is better than wine." Then she says in verse 4, "Draw me closer to you." As this beautiful love feast continues, she says, "I am sick with love. . . ."

She describes the physical qualities and attributes of her lover, going on with rapturous praise of the delights she experiences while lost in his embrace. She exclaims, "His mouth is most sweet: yea, he is altogether lovely. This is my beloved . . ." (Song of Sol. 5:16).

The man, caught in a moment of splendor, later searches for his lady. He laments, "Return, return . . . that we may look upon thee . . ."(Song of Sol. 6:13). Soon he finds her, and continues to express his overwhelming and spellbinding enchantments with her beauty as he comments upon his sensual desires for her "beautiful feet . . . her lovely thighs," that, to him, are as "jewels; her navel that is as a vessel to hold that which he drinks of; her stomach as adorned with lilies," and her breasts, he compares to "beautiful, young, soft deer." Her neck he says is "as ivory"; her eyes as "crystal pools of water," her nose as a "well-placed ornament," and her head as a "majestic crown adorned by the beauty of her radiant hair worn as a halo."

He says, "How fair and how pleasant art thou, O love, for delights! . . . thy breasts shall be as clusters of the vine. . . . " He tells her "the roof of thy mouth like the best wine for my beloved, that goeth sweetly . . ." (Song of Sol. 7:6-9).

This is but a quick glance into sex, God's way.

Far and above a mere physiological experience entered solely for the purpose of self-gratification, this is a picture of two becoming one, losing themselves in a love fest directed at satisfying the wants, needs, and desires of the other. This sexual abandonment to the other "seeks not its own," and having not sought its own satisfaction, nevertheless discovers it in all its fury, its passion, and its ecstasy.

Indeed, a "bed undefiled" is such a bed where two people, exclusively covenanted to each other and sanctified by God, lose themselves in wondrous rapture that forbids either from holding back anything that would excite, satisfy, and bring sheer joy to the other.

God places no taboo on sex of any kind between a man and woman covered by the umbrella of His holy covenant called marriage. Their minds, bodies, and souls belong not only to Him, but exclusively to each other. Sexual expression and full satisfaction can only be experienced in abandonment of one to the other.

Ultimately, according to God's Word, that bed, that union, and that couple find consistent, thoroughly satisfactory, and repeated sexual joy that defies description and, with the passing of time, becomes more thrilling, more wondrous, and more satisfying. Sex, God's way, is so sensually fulfilling, sexually exciting, and emotionally titillating that no man or woman in that kind of relationship could be drawn outside of that relationship into infidelity. There is no sex like that sex, no joy like that joy, and no anticipation like that anticipation.

Yes, it involves discipline, sacrificial loving, and vigilance to maintain such a relationship, but the payoff is ultimate sexual joy without guilt, remorse, and sorrow.

Man's and woman's sex drive is a holy blessing. Sex only

becomes an unholy curse when humanity attempts to satisfy this God-given desire in a God-forbidden way. And as time winds down and humanity sinks further into the pit of depravity, he will continue to dig it deeper with his search for more ways to do what God said "don't do."

7

Government: Of, By, and for Whom?

by John Barela

Most of us sense a foul "wind of change" blowing our way, but we cannot put a finger on what makes this wind so different from past innovations.

Government seems to be getting out of control and invading our lives in ways unheard of a generation or two ago. We see a dramatic increase in crime that makes most Americans feel threatened — even in their own homes and in their own automobiles. Drive-by shootings strike horror in our hearts as they occur closer and closer to home.

The phenomenal increase in wickedness should not surprise the Christian who has studied his Father's Word. God himself long ago told of a diabolical plan that would be implemented as the time of Christ's return nears.

> And he causeth all, both small and great, rich and poor, free and bond, to receive a mark in their right hand, or in their foreheads, And that no man might buy or sell, save he that had the mark, or the name of the beast, or the number of his name (Rev. 13:16-17).

Such will be the outcome of the luciferian plot that is well underway. For example, did you know:

• Six million American workers are being monitored by new microchip computerized surveillance techniques that track their every move in the workplace. It tracks their productivity as well as when and how long they take for lunches, how much time they spend on breaks, even how long they spend going to the bathroom.

• Nineteen million California drivers are being issued new driver's licenses with microchip implants that contain their photo, fingerprints, and personal information, as well as their DMV records, criminal records, and any other information Big Brother deems relevant.

• One of the most suppressive surveillance techniques ever designed is now being implemented in Singapore. This "Smart Highway System" involves embedding microchips into the surface of the highways and equipping cars with electronically numbered license plates and small, black boxes mounted on their underside. Much like a homing device, this radio frequency transponder system tracks every movement of the automobile. Singapore will soon charge for the use of its highway system and bill its residents just as it does for electricity. At present, 2.7 million Singapore drivers are being monitored, and soon all Singapore cars are expected to be set up with the equipment.

Solutions for Supposed Crises

This, we can be assured by God's prophetic Word, is just the beginning. The agents of the plan, in order to implement it, will with hyperbole, manufacture supposed crises.

The "war on crime" is one of their greatest tools, and it will continue to be the topic of newscasts and a leading component in the political agenda. It is my opinion that the war on crime is specifically designed to act as a brainwashing, conditioning method of preparing us to receive "the mark."

FAMC (a Christian financial consulting group) says, "It is a planned phase of the "destabilization process" to move our country into the socialist New World Order."

The mind manipulators of the New World Order point out the problems:

- criminals rule our cities
- true political clout lies in the hands of drug lords and organized crime leaders
- tax revenues desperately needed by our economy are lost due to evasion by organized crime
- there has been a dramatic increase in drive-by shootings and homicide is at an all-time high
- the cost of crime is devastating to our economy
- prison overcrowding has reached unthinkable levels
- we cannot afford to build new prisons.

They will continue to cite momentous problems and present such remarkably persuasive solutions that implementing the mark will eventually seem like the right thing to do.

Here are some of their solutions:

• *Electronic tagging of released offenders.* To prevent prison overcrowding, a tamper-proof microchip transponder will be attached to the wrist of offenders. The device, which will respond to a receiver installed in the home, will beep to alert authorities the minute the person steps beyond prescribed boundaries.

• *Eliminate the "profit motive" of crime.* How? By eliminating cash. Cash is anonymous, and the drug trade would collapse if it could not be handled secretly. The underground economy, which operates independently of taxation, would not be able to succeed in a cashless society. The increased revenues gained from making transactions traceable could balance the budget in just a few years!

• *Eliminate kidnapping of children, government leaders, and top scientists.* How? With skin-implanted microchips containing homing devices that would emit radio signals, satellites could track kidnap victims anywhere in the world. The Israeli government is now working on a program like this to protect its government and army leaders.

The truth is . . . all this is so feasible that it is frightening. A massive amount of power in the wrong hands should be a serious concern to every citizen.

Programmed Propaganda

What most of us do not fully realize is that we are now poised on the verge of a quantum leap into a new and terrifying world which we have not anticipated and which we are not prepared to face. Our worst enemy is ignorance; therefore, it is vital that we learn the facts about conditions that will soon affect our lives and those of our families.

The alarming scenarios we present in this chapter will seem like tales from a macabre fiction novel — but they are not. At first, you may think I am one of those "conspiracy lunatics," but read on, anyway. What I say is very well documented; you cannot afford to disregard the evidence.

You will see how we have been subtly conditioned and programmed by a ruling elite, how our lives are being guided by an "unseen hand." Our government offices, institutions, and bureaucracies have been infiltrated, and are now occupied by their pawns. "Key people" have been cleverly placed to begin drawing in the net for the apocalyptic harvest.

Through a series of "manufactured crises," the planners-elite have set the stage for the takeover of our nation. As stated earlier, one of the key tools now being used to engineer our national enslavement is the pseudo-war on crime, which has been methodically designed to bring America to its knees.

The process of creating a "crime crisis" has been carefully incubated in the hotbed of liberal thought. Since traditional moral values constitute a major obstacle to The Plan, the plotters' first tactical strategy came in that arena.

New social pathologies have been instituted that have created the perfect conditions to develop an attitude of lawlessness. These ideologies have slowly been programmed into our thinking by cleverly disguised propaganda tactics. The media, including the motion picture industry, have played key roles.

The Communicators

It is a well-known fact that most esoteric organizations communicate their ideologies through the use of symbols. It is a clever way of identifying with those of like persuasions without verbiage.

It is interesting to note the symbols that identify our three major television networks: CBS is the most blatant; it is simply an "all-seeing eye." NBC, of course, has it's beautiful "all-seeing-eye" peacock, and ABC is more subtle in its use of the "sun disk," which still symbolizes the same ideology as the all-seeing eye.

By inviting these propaganda tools into our homes and lives, we have made ourselves willing participants in their programming process. Mesmerized by the media, it is no wonder that we are allowing these perverse social pathologies to have free reign. You will see documentation of the purposeful, gradual "decomposition" of our society.

Report Card on America

You will see the evidence that those who pull the strings behind our governmental offices have, I believe, intentionally designed the increase in crime and nurtured it to the current crisis point. Why? In order to create the perfect conditions for the demolition of our republic — and the institution of a new system of "total control" that will soon render us slaves of the New World Order.

Following are illustrations of how our government has been methodically maneuvered into a position of cultural decline that will sweep it up into the whirlwind of its own corruption. It will then be handed over to the "ruling elite" for the dictator of our new oligarchy to assume power — he is called the "Antichrist."

William J. Bennett, the conservative former director of the Office of National Drug Control Policy, Secretary of Education, and chairman of the National Endowment for the Humanities, saw the need for a report covering key "cultural" indicators. The information in this eye-opening report is a "key indicator" for the assessment of the general condition of the American culture.

Early in 1994, Bennett's shocking "report card" on America, titled, *The Index of Leading Cultural Indicators — Facts and Figures on the State of American Society* was published. In it, Bennett vividly documents that since 1960, while population, wealth, and welfare benefits have climbed, America's values have deteriorated. He draws information from the Census Bureau, the FBI, and other governmental sources that reveal one of the most comprehensive and frightening statistical portraits available of behavioral trends over the last 30 years.

Bennett shows powerful evidence that we are in a period of substantial social regression and decomposition. "When decomposition takes hold, it exacts an enormous human cost," he says. "Unless these exploding social pathologies are reversed, they will lead to the decline and perhaps even to the fall of the American republic."

According to Bennett's statistics, since 1960, the population has increased 41 percent, and during the same period:

(1) Violent crime has risen by more than 500 percent.

(2) There has been an increase in illegitimate births of more than 400 percent.

(3) The number of children living in single-parent homes has tripled.

(4) The divorce rate has doubled.

(5) SAT scores have fallen by almost 75 points.

(6) Teen suicide has tripled.

In the summer of 1990, a special commission of prominent political, medical, educational, and business leaders issued a report titled "Code Blue" on the health of America's teenagers.

They wrote that ". . . never before has one generation of American teenagers been less healthy, less cared for, or less prepared for life than their parents were at the same age." According to the commission, the explanation for teenagers' deteriorating condition lies with their behavior and not (as was the case in the past) with physical illness.

A disturbing and telling sign of the declining condition among the young is evident in an on-going teacher survey. Over the years teachers have been asked to identify the top problems in America's public schools.

In 1940, teachers identified talking out of turn, chewing gum, making noise, running in the halls, cutting in line, dress code infractions, and littering. When asked the same question in 1990, teachers identified drug abuse, alcohol abuse, pregnancy, suicide, rape, robbery, and assault.

What has caused the cultural decline in America? "A shift in the public's beliefs, attitudes, and priorities," writes social scientist James Q. Wilson. Why has this happened? Wilson notes that "the powers exercised by the institutions of social control have been constrained, and people, especially young people, have embraced an ethos that values self-expression over self-control."[1]

What does Wilson mean when he says that "the powers exercised by the institutions of social control have been constrained?" He means that the rights of parents, teachers, the law enforcement, and judicial systems have been taken away from those who formerly acted as instruments of "social control."

When Anarchy Reigns

When there is no control — anarchy results. That is precisely what the unseen hand intended to engineer by restraining all "outside" controls. They have now "manufactured a crisis" in order to step in and take "government" control. They have been successful in implanting the false illusion that government intervention is the only "logical solution."

Documentation will show that if logic is applied correctly, and if they are truly sincere about fighting crime, then our problems can be solved if they just reinstate the rights of the formerly successful control agents — parents, teachers, law enforcement, and judicial systems. But the plan is not a simple solution to the problem, it is to wrest any degree of control from the hands of "we, the people" and place it totally in the hands of government.

Let me give you some examples of how we have been deceived into believing government propaganda designed to convince us that a serious effort is being made to fight crime. If what they are telling us is true, let them answer the following questions:

(1) **Why** did we have "3.2 policemen in urban America for every violent felony committed" in the 1950s — but "now, the reverse is true, there are 3.2 crimes per police officer? In most big cities, the problem is even worse — 6.9 violent felonies per police office in Boston; 6.5 in New York and Chicago; and 10 in Los Angeles, Atlanta, and Newark."

(2) **Why** has our government not implemented even a minimum addition to our police force? "Estimates are that a 20 percent increase in the police forces of the 222 local police departments that in 1990 served populations of 100,000 or more would cost about $1 billion a year. The social benefits would almost certainly exceed the costs, as would be evident in reduced criminal victimization, revitalized local economies, and enhanced respect for government."

(3) **Why** is it that "from 1979 to 1990, total per capita spending by all levels of government on justice system activities rose 35 percent," but "spending for police, however, rose only 6 percent?" (The reason will be made clear later in this chapter. It is obvious that they do not want the U.S. police force to be sufficient for our needs — U.N., Hong Kong, and other foreign police have been, and continue to be brought into our country. Why? Read on.) Why did they give a whopping "31 percent increase for courts, 55 percent for prosecutors, and 99 percent for corrections?" (Read further about the reported detention centers [or concentration camps] that are alleged to have been set up all over our country. Think they are for hardened criminals? Think again. Could this have something to do with the enormous "corrections" increase?)

(4) **Why** has "the expected prison sentence for all serious crimes

decreased more than 60 percent since 1954?"

(5) **Why** are "three out of every four convicted criminals not incarcerated? In 1990, 62 percent of the estimated 4.3 million persons in correctional custody in the United States were on probation, and 12 percent were on parole."

(6) **Why** do "fewer than 1 in 10 serious crimes result in imprisonment"?

(7) **Why** was "the median prison sentence" in 1992 "for murder about 15 years, while the average time served was a little more than 5 years"?

(8) **Why** (in 1990) was "the expected punishment for someone committing a murder only 1.8 years in prison; for rape, the expected sentence was 60 days; for robbery, 23 days; and for aggravated assault, 6.4 days"?

(9) **Why**, when "fewer than one in three crimes is reported to police," do the police "arrest only 20 percent of the time? Nearly half of the people arrested have their charges thrown out by the prosecutor. When you take into account probation and other factors, one person goes to federal prison and one person goes to non-federal jail for every 100 crimes committed."

(10) **Why** do we so casually release criminals to roam our streets when "93 percent of prisoners are violent or repeat offenders? . . . Of all inmates released from state prison in 1983, 63 percent committed a felony or serious misdemeanor within three years of their release."

(11) **Why** are we so reticent to spend money on police when, "according to the Bureau of Justice Statistics, the direct economic cost to crime victims totaled $19.2 billion in 1990? A conservative lower-bound estimate of the social cost per crime is about $2,500. Thus, the typical prisoner when free can be said to cost society well over $25,000 per year — he commits approximately 10 crimes per year, each of them representing about $2,500 in social cost. For most prisoners, therefore, the social benefits of keeping them in prison are at least one and one-half times the social costs of incarceration" — we would actually save $12,000 per year per prisoner by keeping them off the streets where their crime cycles continue.[2]

Crime Without Punishment

Why is there so much crime without punishment in America today? "Because recent generations of social and political elites, both liberal and conservative, have liberated themselves from the belief that criminals are free moral agents and that publicly sanctioned punishments are what they justly deserve," writes John J. DiIulio, Jr. of Princeton University.[3]

Gordon Tullock of the University of Arizona explains how the "elites" reached this conclusion:

> It is clearly more appealing to think of solving the criminal problem by means that are themselves not particularly unpleasant than to think of solving it by methods that are unpleasant. But in this case, we do not have the choice between a pleasant and an unpleasant method of dealing with crime. We have an unpleasant method — deterrence — that works and a pleasant method — rehabilitation — that (at least so far) never has worked. Under the circumstances, we have to opt either for the deterrence method or for a higher crime rate.

Why does punishment work? Because it acts as "a kind of mirror image of praise," says Stanley Brubaker of Colgate University. "If praise expresses gratitude and approbation, punishment expresses resentment and reprobation. If praise expresses what the political community admires and what unites it, punishment expresses what the community condemns and what threatens it. Punishment, like praise, publicly expresses our determination of what people deserve."[4]

Instead of punishing criminals, the political elite seek to punish law-abiding citizens by taking away their constitutional "right to bear arms."

According to William Bennett in his book, *The Index of Leading Cultural Indicators — Facts and Figures on the State of American Society:*

> Armed citizens defend their lives or property with firearms against criminals approximately 1 million times a year. In 98 percent of these instances, the citizen merely brandishes the weapon and fires a warning shot. Only in 2 percent of the cases do citizens actually shoot their assailants. In defending themselves with their firearms, armed citizens kill 2,000 to 3,000 criminals each year — three times the number killed by police.

In light of this statistic, does it make sense:

(1) To abolish the Second Amendment rights of 100 percent of our citizens to own arms so 7 percent of the criminals will be deprived of buying their guns from legally recognized vendors? Ninety-three percent of guns obtained by violent criminals are not "purchased."

(2) To abolish the Second Amendment rights of 100 percent of our citizens who need firearms to protect their property and the lives of their families — because our government spends our tax money to keep the peace in Haiti, Kuwait, and other parts of the world — instead of on local police to keep the peace in America?

More and more, we are seeing blatant abuse of power by government entities. Our individual freedom and liberty are in serious jeopardy. The best protection against any opposing force is "knowledge." It is our duty to arm ourselves with knowledge of the enemy and pass this information along to those we care about.

If we allow these assaults on liberty to continue, unexposed and unopposed, it will soon be too late. America will become a nation of "slaves to the New World Order by default."

As one of our founding fathers, Samuel Adams, said, "It is natural for man to deal in the illusions of hope; but as for me, I want to know the worst, the truth, and prepare for it."

Gangs — Tools of the Government?

The March 1994 edition of *Monetary & Economic Review* reports:

They Have a Plan for You!

Our staff acquired a copy of a confidential memo of Handgun Control, Inc., outlining the "Notes and Minutes of Meeting of Friday, December 16, 1993" and "Rough Draft Proposal for Internal Memo and Five-Year Plan." The information is marked, "The following information is confidential!!! Do not distribute beyond the office of HCI unless hand-delivered to an approved state or federal legislator or law enforcement official."

This 20-page document would raise the hair on the back of your neck as you read about plans to disarm the American public and disarm the police force. Their plans would leave guns only in the hand of the military (whose army?)

If the true intent of this act is to protect American citizens from violence, then why is one of the goals outlined to "disarm the police force"?

If our government is so concerned about our safety, then why are reports surfacing that military weapons of all sorts are being stolen from our own military bases by high ranking military officers? Reports indicate that there is a continual stream of these contraband weapons that flows directly to street gangs.

Some time ago, we received a phone call from an employee of an institution in charge of rehabilitating young offenders and gang members. It sent cold chills up our spines, and we did not report it because it seemed so unthinkable. However, when the preceding report appeared in *Monetary and Economic Review,* we knew that it was time to tell the story and let you decide for yourself.

The caller (he identified himself to us, but he desires to remain anonymous as far as publicity is concerned, for job-related reasons) alleged that one West Coast gang leader he treated told him that he was actually in the employ of the government and had no reason to fear punishment by law enforcement officials. He told our source that he, as a gang member, was actually recruited by the government and specially trained to "eliminate undesirables," and carry out other various orders.

He went on to say that gangs (a veritable underground army) were valuable tools in the hands of government. The gangs could carry out unspeakable and illegal acts that no law enforcement agency could "get away with." These same agencies could, at the same time, appear to be the champions of law and order as they arrested the perpetrators of the crimes they had pre-designed.

Who would be so diligent as to keep track of the myriad acts of violence by street gangs? Who would be so diligent as to track the disposition of each case? The gang member said he is allowed to walk in the front door of the police department and out the back — and who is ever the wiser?

This all seems so horrendous that it is almost impossible to believe. So were the acts of Stalin and Hitler. Average Soviet or German citizens must have thought that the reports of torture, imprisonment, and mass murder were the wild machinations of unstable minds — until the pounding midnight knocks reached their own neighborhoods, then their own doors. The plans of these two monstrous personalities had been cleverly devised so that an uninformed and unarmed citizenry would have no ready defense against such tyranny.

Who's Afraid of the Big Bad Wolf?

The American public, for the most part, can be caricatured as Little Red Riding Hood merrily singing on her way to Grandma's house. She had no idea that the grandma whom she knew and trusted had been replaced by the "Big Bad Wolf." Many of us have heard bits of information about the new Crime Bill through various sources, but the "teeth" have been cleverly hidden until it is "time for dinner."

The Violent Crime Control and Law Enforcement Act has been presented as the end-all, cure-all for the rampant crime and violence that floods our cities. We are all seriously concerned about the dramatic rise in crime. We all, at times, fear for the safety of our homes and families. But is the cure worse than the illness?

The media has all but driven most citizens into hysteria by the colorful, vivid coverage of the macabre and unthinkable, the likes of which were once kept hidden from the public eye. Is there a reason that they have become obsessed with reporting every gruesome detail of the bizarre?

Why is Hollywood obsessed with producing the "blood-and-guts" horror films complete with life-like "special effects?" Some of these spine-chilling horror stories not only frighten us half to death, but they also serve as a platter of delectable suggestions offered before unstable minds. Like the beat of heavy metal rock, the obsession with blood, violence, and death is pounding ever nearer in an orgiastic crescendo of insanity. Why?

As reality and fiction blur into one ominous glob, a horrendous impression is made on the American mind — FEAR.

Fear is a very persuasive and compelling force. A manufactured crisis and manufactured fear have driven us through the forest to "Grandma's house," or should I say to "Uncle Sam's house?"

If the concerned caretaker under the ruffled bonnet is really Grandma, her lips will part and the corners of her mouth will turn up into her plump cheeks and the same sweet smile we remember with nostalgic warmth will greet us. However, if parting lips reveal huge, sharp teeth caging in a saliva-laden tongue, then it is not Grandma after all.

Let's lift the bonnet of the new Crime Bill to discover the true identity of our host.

Gun Control for Whom?

In a September 15, 1994, article titled, "Crime Bill Fraud," the *American Hunter* reports:

> On August 25 six "moderate" Republicans in the Senate followed their House counterparts and provided enough votes to pass a $30 billion "crime bill" that President Clinton touts as "the toughest, smartest crime bill in U.S. history."
>
> Not even the editorial writers in the liberal *Washington Post* believed the Clinton claim. The *Post* did comment that: "What the president calls the toughest, smartest crime bill in federal history is unlikely to have a traceable effect on the national crime rate, and some of the toughest-sounding provisions could perversely end up weakening rather than strengthening the ability of local and state officials to fight crime."

What most American citizens do not realize is that billions of these so-called crime-fighting dollars are actually allocated for non-crime-fighting social welfare programs. Worse than that, they have abandoned the principle that you attack crime by attacking criminals.

Instead, they have adopted the fractured logic that because of the acts of violent criminals, you must trample on the rights of law-abiding citizens by restricting their liberty. The passage of this bill is tantamount to tearing out one-tenth of our cherished Bill of Rights written by our founding fathers for our protection. Dare we recklessly "rip out the Second Amendment?"

According to Charles E. Bates and Derek W. Wilcox of FAMC, ". . . the authors of the Act do not understand the basic principles behind the Second Amendment. It was to be the last defense against a government that had become too big and too powerful. It is the authority of the people to take up arms, no matter what style they may be. You cannot defend your country or your rights with a hunting rifle. Perhaps we are not too far from the overwhelmingly large government that our forefathers feared most."

The *ILA Report,* September 1994, states that, "As long as criminals remain on the streets rather than in prison, the vast majority will continue to acquire guns as they always have: on the black market, through theft, or through second-party transactions."

The Index of Leading Cultural Indicators — Facts and Figures on the State of American Society, notes that "Of the guns obtained by violent criminals, 93 percent are not obtained through the lawful purchase and sale transactions that are the object of gun control legislation."

Tanya Metaksa, Executive Director, NRA Institute for Legislative Actions, says, "President Clinton condemned NRA for fighting his 'Crime Bill.' But we fought it because it's a lie. It's a lie that it would put 100,000 cops on the beat. It's a lie that adequate new prisons will be built. And it's a lie that banning firearms will stop violent criminals from preying on helpless victims."

On the surface, the Crime Bill sounds reasonable. Contained within its 960 pages are more severe penalties for rapists, burglars, kidnappers, and murderers. Stiffer, more extreme penalties will be placed on drug and gang-related activities. This sounds like we are on the right track, doesn't it?

Charles E. Bates and Derek W. Wilcox of FAMC have examined this bill and found that Grandma has "BIG teeth," and they are "all the better to strip away all your rights and leave you defenseless against an overpowered, tyrannical government."

At the same time the disarming of America is underway, the power to control is on the increase, as "Section 4501: Public Safety and Recreational Firearms Use Protection Act" makes clear. This section is a direct violation of the Second Amendment of the Constitution. It deals with the banning of so-called semi-automatic "assault weapons." This sounds like a good idea — what's wrong with banning assault weapons? Their "definition" of an assault weapon would ban almost every weapon — even our common hunting rifles.

Federal Police or the Gestapo?

Section 1121 of the Crime Bill covers "Police Corps and Law Enforcement Officers Training and Education," and provides for the extra 100,000-man federal police force. This section funds the recruitment of up to 20,000 additional members per graduating class of the prescribed training courses.

In the past, police have not been much more than a simple deterrent to crime, and at best, a recorder of events that have already taken place. It is proven that more criminal acts are prevented by the citizenry than by law enforcement officers. We need to examine the deeper motive behind flooding our streets with an army of law enforcement officers. In history such actions have taken in the form of the KGB, the Gestapo, and the Brown Shirts.

Clinton campaigned on adding 100,000 more officers to our police force. Isn't this provision in his Crime Act contradictory? Did you catch this deceptive statement that totally undermines our national police force? If more criminal acts are prevented by the citizenry than by law enforcement officers, how, then, can they propose to "keep the peace"?

If crime is so rampant as to require a radical Crime Act, then why does the Act itself say we don't need more police? Because they have a new kind of cop to introduce to you — the terminators!

Section 5108 of the Crime Bill is called the "Report on Success of Royal Hong Kong Police Recruitment." The section reads:

> Not later than 6 months after the date of enactment of this Act, the Attorney General, in concert with the director of the Federal Bureau of Investigation, the administrator of the Drug Enforcement Agency, the commissioners of the Immigration and Naturalization Service, and the commissioner of the Customs Service, shall report to Congress and the president on the efforts made, and the success of such efforts, to recruit and hire former Royal Hong Kong Police officers.

Why does the United States, who is about to hire an additional 100,000 federal officers, need more of the same from a foreign country?

Further research has indicated that the Royal Hong Kong Police forces are the most highly trained in the world. It also has been revealed that these officers are judge, jury, and executioner in their home country. Apparently, these men will not hesitate to fire upon their own, much less those with whom they have no affiliation.

According to our sources, this police force is composed of a group called "gherkas." The "gherkas" are apparently from Nepal and have been trained by foreign intelligence groups in urban and rural tactical warfare.

One must consider why we need professional soldiers roaming our streets with federal jurisdiction. Could these be the henchmen for the New World Order? This is a very important issue that the American people should know about. This was an all-important part to the proposed Crime Act that was expediently buried deep within the pages of that document.

The American public must wake up and take a serious look at what just might be the demise of our republic and the rise of the new power-hungry elite — then the new dictator of the New World Order.

It is obvious that citizens of Germany, the former Soviet Union, and China did not realize that the utopian promises made by the so-called liberators and champions of the working class were the lies of "Pied Pipers." Their melodious tune enchanted the masses and lured them willingly into the worst enslavement in modern history.

They heard some of the same promises we are hearing now: equality for all; protection from crime and violence; a paycheck for every citizen, whether he works or not; government assistance in the care of their children; educational programs paid for by the government; ad nauseam. They evidently had not learned that if you dance to the Piper's tune, you pay the Piper — someday.

In their case and ours, the payment is first extracted in sacrifice of personal freedom . . . little by little . . . inch by inch . . . until it is all gone.

These are only a few of a multiple number of provisions that fly in the face of the Constitution and just plain, common sense. It is evident that the Crime Act is not intended to stop the repeat felon, but to obtain greater control over our citizenry as a whole by stripping away our rights. These tactics are expected to continue as we get closer to the end days.

A Police State?

If you think these tactics will stop with just banning a few firearms, think again! Total control is the objective. In order to seize total control, they must do away with the rest of our constitutional rights, including our right to privacy in our own homes. Here, again, crime control is used as the excuse.

The *Prophecy Club Newsletter* quoted *The Los Angeles Times,* April 7, 1994, which reported:

Chicago Police Use Warrantless Sweeps to Seize Guns.

Chicago — Like soldiers in an army of occupation, [Wow! That sounds like "Occupation Army"] squads of police officers fan out each night through the Robert Taylor Homes, a tombstone row of high-rise tenement buildings that loom for 18 city blocks over the Dan Ryan Expressway in south Chicago. Ignoring taunts from gang members, they poke through bullet-pocked elevator shafts, boiler rooms, and laundry common, searching for automatic weapons.

I can hear the evil people planning. First create violence by removing prayer from the schools in 1964. Then by repeated movies and television, portray the glory of violence. When the violence goes to the street, we can take the guns. When we have the guns, we will be free to move into the New World Order. . . .

FAMC reported in their July 1994 *Monetary and Economic Review:*

> On a list of items presented to the Louisiana State Legislature by the Governor for consideration in the special session underway in Baton Rouge . . . is a measure that "would allow appropriate law enforcement officers to conduct a sweep search of any person for weapons, drugs and other contraband in a identifiable area with an inordinate amount of crime. . . ."
>
> The next giant step will be just such a measure as this, whereby, at the discretion of local law enforcement, any private housing area may be designated as having an "inordinate amount of crime," thereby relieving law enforcement of the necessity to obtain a search warrant. The question is, what is the standard for determining "an inordinate amount of crime"? Who is the appropriate law enforcement officer making the decision? And when? Five minutes before the search commences? Or, possibly after the search?
>
> "Crime control" efforts such as this may appear, on the surface, to be exactly what is needed in the war on crime. However, citizens need to be aware that when the checks and balances (such as the necessity on the part of law enforcement agencies to obtain a search warrant) in the exercise of power by law enforcement agencies are removed, the law enforcement agent potentially becomes judge, jury and executioner all in one! This measure, although touted as "justifiable in the light of high levels of crime," is extremely dangerous.
>
> If this kind of legislation is passed in the name of

crime control, we will soon be living in a police state. The right of American citizens to be 'secure in their person, houses, papers, and effects against unreasonable searches and seizures,' as guaranteed under the Fourth Amendment to the Constitution, will be a thing of the past.

Former President Nixon finished his book, *Beyond Peace,*[5] just before his death on April 22, 1994. In it, Nixon gives a memorable example of how legislation that began with "seemingly" right intentions can be perverted by government.

He said that he ". . . started the Environmental Protection Agency to find a balance between economic growth and protecting the environment. But, as so often happens with government programs, the pendulum has swung too far. . . Measures designed to protect endangered species such as bears, wolves, and the bald eagle are now being used to force Idaho farmers off their land for the sake of the thumbnail-size Bruneau Hot Springs snail."

He called "all 1,842 impenetrable pages" of the Clinton health care plan "a blueprint for the takeover by the federal government of one-seventh of the nation's economy."

The former president maintained that the criminal justice system "has abysmally failed to deliver what should be the first freedom; freedom from fear."[6] Ironically, the only ones who need fear our present criminal justice system are innocent citizens who are not "politically correct."

America's Cultural Elite

Stanley Rothman, S. Robert Lichter, and Linda Lichter, some of the country's leading authorities on the cultural elite, wrote in *Elites in Conflict: Social Change in America Today:* "Social and cultural changes in American society and culture have produced a new secular, liberal and cosmopolitan sensibility which partially rejects traditional bourgeois emphasis on work, frugality, sexual restraint, and self-control."[7]

William Bennett jumps into the middle of a war — the "politically correct" war — when he writes:

> The battle for the culture refers to the struggle over the principles, sentiments, ideas, and political attitudes that define the permissible and impermissible, the acceptable and unacceptable, the preferred and the disdained, in

speech, expression, attitude, conduct, and politics. This battle is about music, art, poetry, literature, television programming, and movies; the modes of expression and conversation, official and unofficial, that express who and what we are, what we believe, and how we act. . . .

Why is there a battle about our culture? Part of the answer lies in understanding that there is a fundamental difference between many of the most important beliefs of most Americans and the beliefs of a liberal elite that today dominates many of our institutions and who therefore exert influence on American life and culture.

The elite are most often found among academics and intellectuals, in the literary world, in journals of political opinion, in Hollywood, in the artistic community, in mainline religious institutions, and in some quarter of the media. . . . They exert a considerable amount of influence in official Washington — on the people who shape public discourse, who govern, who legislate, and who lead.[8]

Consider the disturbing though fascinating facts surrounding the elitists who have held the reins of government during our nation's most recent period of history. The picture that emerges from these statistics is that of government leaders whose primary interests are self-serving.

• They are less loyal to America and her domestic products.

• They manage to see that they are the highest paid citizens in America.

• They manipulate economic policy to benefit themselves first; the American public second.

• They manipulate lawmaking to perpetuate the "inner circle" benefits, and to make certain they remain in office to enjoy them.

In summary, these statistics reveal a corrupt, morally bankrupt circle of "elitists" who control our country and our lives. Maybe the word "elitist" needs to be re-defined. Bribery, fraud, tax evasion, crime, and sexual immorality were once the characteristics of those we imprisoned, not of people we trusted to run our country. Are a large number of our leaders "unfit to hold office"?

According to the report titled, "The Government Waste and Fraud Index," published by the National Taxpayer's Union:

Rank of Washington, DC, and suburbs in total number of citizens employed by the government: 1st

Rank of Washington, DC, and suburbs for total number of imported automobile sales in America: 1st

Rank of Washington, DC, and suburbs as measured by total number of high income families: 1st

Total losses of bank depositors in the Great Depression, measured in 1990 dollars: $25 billion

Cost to taxpayers for S & L collapse and congressionally-engineered bail-out: Over $350 billion

Number of 535 Congressmen who could become "Pension Millionaires" after 1993: 303

Number of states in which voters have been able to vote on congressional term limit laws: 15

Percentage of voters who support term limit laws for Congress: 75 percent

Number of times Speaker Tom Foley has permitted the U.S. House of Representatives to vote on term limit laws: 0

Percentage of popular vote won by Michael Dukakis in 1988: 46 percent

Percentage of popular vote won by Bill Clinton in 1992: 43 percent

Average total gifts by PACs to each Senate and House member for 1992 election: $208,052

Since 1970, more than 30 Senators and Congressmen have been convicted for bribery, mail fraud, tax evasion, sexual offenses, or other crimes.[9]

Unfit to Hold Office

The cultural war is much more serious than the debate over art, poetry, music, literature, films, and drama. It is a debate over the foundational values we wish our children to possess.

Most of us send our children to school to read good books and learn an appreciation for good music and art. We are convinced that these are building blocks that strengthen and improve the sensibilities of our youth. Conversely, we also need to realize that we may be unknowingly contributing to the moral decay of these same children by allowing them to listen to bad music, view bad art, and read bad books.

During the last two decades, we have seen a frightening annihilation of the traditional morals and values that have, in the past, made America strong. We have allowed the lines between right and wrong to be obliterated.

According to pollster Daniel Yankelovich, our society now places less value than before on what we owe others as a matter of moral obligation; less value on sacrifice as a moral good; less value on social conformity, respectability, and observing the rules; and less value on correctness and restraint in matters of physical pleasure and sexuality. Higher value is now placed on things like self-expression, individualism, self-realization, and personal choice.

Someone once said, "America is great because she is good. When America ceases to be good, she will cease to be great."

One of the best indicators of America's present condition is the leaders she has chosen. In the context of the declining morals and values of our young people, we need only look at the source of this abominable heritage.

It was not long ago that Gary Hart was forced to end his political campaign for presidential nominee because of a photograph depicting him as an unfaithful, adulterous husband. Well, we've come a long way in a very short time.

Who would have ever guessed that the high office of our nation could be occupied by a man who openly flaunted his promiscuity, and one who appointed the most despicably immoral crew ever to occupy critical government positions? President Bill Clinton, in a landmark move, appointed 22 open homosexuals to office. Until Clinton took office, it was still considered morally unacceptable — those in office kept it a deep, dark secret.

Has the "out of the closet homosexual agenda" made America a better nation — a better place to raise our children?

According to the headlines of the Saturday, March 19, 1994, issue of the *Washington Times,* the then-Surgeon General Joycelyn Elders "calls gay sex 'wonderful,' 'healthy.' " The article goes on:

> Gary Bauer, president of the Family Research Council, observed: "A large number of Clinton administration appointees have a rather unusual obsession with sex. Every time we turn around, they are talking about some

other aspect of it. Has anyone told these folks that the sixties are over?"

Paul Cameron, chairman of the Family Research Institute, said of Elders, "That woman would be a sorry joke if she didn't occupy such an important post. . . . Elders agonizes about secondhand tobacco smoke, yet gives the green light to sexual practices that are inherently dangerous, strongly associated with AIDS, hepatitis, and a host of other diseases."

Prior to the firing of Dr. Joycelyn Elders, Liberty Alliance had called for her resignation, saying, "Her own words show her unfit to hold any public office, much less the highly visible position of U.S. Surgeon General."

They quoted from the June 3-5 issue of *USA Weekend* magazine:

Q: Did you say you believe the Boy Scouts should admit homosexuals?

A: Yes. I also think girls who are lesbians should be allowed to join the Girl Scouts. None of us is good enough, or knows enough, to make decisions about other people's sexual preferences. . . .

Q: And are you in favor of homosexuals being permitted to adopt children?

A: Yes. The most important thing for children is nurturing parents. I don't think being gay has anything to do with the ability to nurture children.

Q: We haven't talked about teen pregnancy, your major concern. At what age should we dispense condoms in schools?

A: Whenever they need them. We have junior high school girls having babies, 12 year olds, 9 year olds. We had a girl in Arkansas who at 8 gave birth to twins. We must teach them responsibility and make sure they have the availability of a condom.

Q: How do you feel about decriminalizing drugs?

A: With all the money we're spending and so many young people involved with drugs in prison — yet the killing and robbing go on — we cannot afford NOT [emphasis ours] to study the issue.

Q: And if a study recommended legalization?

A: I'd be out on the street corner hollering every day. I'm not talking about putting them on the shelf like tobacco. When we say "legalize," I'm really talking about control. That we have doctors or clinics set up where addicts can get their drugs free, or pay $1.

We like to think of America as the number one country in the world. But sadly, because of the failures in our political leadership, we're claiming the number one spot in too many areas that don't make us proud. Here's what I mean:

We lead the world in rapes, muggings, and robberies.

America has more teen suicides than any other nation.

We lead the word in handing out diplomas to functional illiterates.

More American homes have burglar alarms than any other country.

Our government has a larger debt than any other. We owe $4.4 trillion now.

We now have more workers on government payrolls than on manufacturing payrolls.

We have more convicts in prison than any other nation.[10]

Just like you, I love America. There's no place in the world I'd rather live. But also like you, I wonder what's happening to our great country. I wonder how a country with so much potential and so many hard-working people has the kind of problems we do today.

Religious War in America?

Strategic Investment, June 27, 1994, carried a report titled, "The Holy War Hits Main Street:"

It's hard for most North Americans to imagine people fighting or dying for religion. But in the rest of the world, religious fanaticism has governments teetering on the edge.

Iranian religious radicals have purchased nuclear warheads from the former Soviet Central Asian republic of Kazakhstan. They've also put a price on the head of Egyptian President Hosni Mubarek. They plan to establish an Islamic fundamentalist state in Egypt (which would be a disaster for the Israeli stock market).

Meanwhile, Saddam Hussein has continued to rile Iraqi fundamentalist hatred toward "American imperialists." He's also replaced almost all the arms lost during the Gulf War. Further north, huge shipments of Islamic arms are being smuggled into Bosnia.

In India and Bangladesh, religious zealots continue to riot . . . all over Africa, fundamentalists are resorting to full-throttle guerrilla warfare to gain control of dying governments.

So far, it sounds like standard fare. Religious unrest is nothing new. But something's changed. Religious terrorism has crossed the border . . . the bombing of the World Trade Center . . . the holing up of a religious sect in Waco, Texas. With the rest of the world already under attack, religious fanaticism has come to the U.S.

What's so bad about this report?

(1) Its writers charge that religious zealots have governments teetering on the edge — that they are resorting to full-throttle guerrilla warfare in order to gain control of governments.

(2) It characterizes anyone with religious convictions as a dangerous fanatic who is ready to explode into horrendous violence at any moment.

(3) The word "fundamentalist" has been given a negative connotation and all "fundamentalists" are not painted with the same fanatical brush as Saddam Hussein, who hates American imperialists.

(4) It states that the world is under attack by religious fundamentalists.

(5) It points out that the same type of radical religious terrorist mentality has now become a challenge in America — referring to the religious sect in Waco, Texas, as an example.

It is dangerously naive to conclude that some governmental powers-that-be will not at some future date make a judgment based on the Waco precedent that your religious fundamentalism or mine should be dealt with for whatever reason it deems.

So many questions remain about the facts surrounding the fiery deaths of men, women, and children during the Janet Reno-ordered attack on the Waco compound because the government ordered the area bulldozed, thus destroying evidence of what really happened that terrible day. One allegation made by the government was that the children in the compound were being abused.

Texe Marrs, in his book, *Big Sister Is Watching You,* dramatically points out the ludicrous illogic of that assertion when he writes "Well, they can rest easy now; those kids will never be abused again."[11]

There can be no doubt that, regardless of David Koresh's guilt or innocence in the massacre, Janet Reno, acting on behalf of the government of the United States, in ordering her military-style force to assault the so-called compound, must be held, to some degree, responsible for the holocaust in which 86 men, women, and innocent children died horribly.

If you do not think that it is possible for such actions to one day be taken against Christians like you and me who adhere to the belief that God's Word is inerrant, think again. The entire nation stood by and watched this attack upon the Branch Davidians, a cult-like group with whom we would disagree on most points theological and philosophical, but who did not deserve to die just because they believed differently than others. Although some protested the government's action, there was no public outcry.

Fundamentalist Christians have already been branded religious fanatics and zealots. Wasn't this, in reality, why the Branch Davidians came to their fiery deaths?

Whether we recognize it or not, we are in the middle of a war.

> And when ye shall hear of wars and rumours of wars, be you not troubled: for such things must needs be.... there shall be earthquakes in divers places, and there shall be famines and troubles: these are the beginning of sorrows.
>
> But take heed to yourselves: for they shall deliver you up to councils; and in the synagogues ye shall be beaten: and ye shall be brought before rulers and kings for my sake, for a testimony against them (Mark 13:7-9).

Section III

Reaping the Whirlwind of Rebellion

8

The Global Church for a Godless Age

by David F. Webber

In just 10 generations from Adam, all mankind had turned away from God and was worshipping pagan deities — with the exception of the family of Noah.

By the time Noah was 500 years old and had three sons, Shem, Ham, and Japheth, the anti-diluvian world, with its population explosion and one-world society, was almost totally corrupted.

> And it came to pass, when men began to multiply on the face of the earth, and daughters were born unto them, That the sons of God saw the daughters of men that they were fair; and they took them wives of all which they chose. And the Lord said, My spirit shall not always strive with man, for that he also is flesh; yet his days shall be an hundred and twenty years. There were giants in the earth in those days; and also after that, when the sons of God came in unto the daughters of men, and they bare children to them, the same became mighty men which were of old, men of renown.
>
> And God saw that the wickedness of man was great in the earth, and that every imagination of the thoughts of his heart was only evil continually. And it repented the

Lord that he had made man on the earth, and it grieved him at his heart. And the Lord said, I will destroy man whom I have created from the face of the earth; both man, and beast, and the creeping thing, and the fowls of the air; for it repenteth me that I have made them. But Noah found grace in the eyes of the Lord (Gen. 6:1-8).

These eight verses tell the story of a violent world — a pagan world — a world without God.

The worship of the ancient world centered around the demigods and their shrines, referred to by Josephus as the basis for Greek mythology. The alien invasion by the fallen angels (originally sons of God by creation) and their depraved wickedness necessitated the judgment of the great Flood.

I suggest that the apostle Paul was writing of the Genesis scene when he spoke of God's wrath from heaven against a people who knew God but refused to worship Him and give Him the glory.

For the wrath of God is revealed from heaven against all ungodliness and unrighteousness of men, who hold the truth in unrighteousness; Because that which may be known of God is manifest in them; for God hath shewed it unto them. For the invisible things of him from the creation of the world are clearly seen, being understood by the things that are made, even his eternal power and Godhead; so that they are without excuse: Because that, when they knew God, they glorified him not as God, neither were thankful; but became vain in their imaginations, and their foolish heart was darkened. Professing themselves to be wise, they became fools, And changed the glory of the incorruptible God into an image made like to corruptible man, and to birds, and fourfooted beasts, and creeping things. Wherefore God also gave them up to uncleanness through the lusts of their own hearts, to dishonour their own bodies between themselves: Who changed the truth of God into a lie, and worshipped and served the creature more than the Creator, who is blessed for ever. Amen (Rom. 1:18-25).

After the cleansing waters of the universal Flood and Noah's building of an altar unto the one true God; even after the rainbow in the storm clouds, signifying that He would never again destroy all flesh by water — the rebellion of sinful man was again starkly evident at the time of the Tower of Babel.

The Modern Tower of Babel

The people's efforts to reach out again to the gods of other worlds lead us to believe they were erecting a pagan cathedral. "Tower of Babel," in the original languages, means "gateway to the gods."

In these early days after the deluge, God not only confused the languages of the people and scattered them abroad over the face of the earth, but He soon divided them into nations with distinct boundaries.

> Go to, let us go down, and there confound their language, that they may not understand one another's speech. So the Lord scattered them abroad from thence upon the face of all the earth: and they left off to build the city. Therefore is the name of it called Babel; because the Lord did there confound the language of all the earth: and from thence did the Lord scatter them abroad upon the face of all the earth (Gen. 11:7-9).

> And hath made of one blood all nations of men for to dwell on all the face of the earth, and hath determined the times before appointed, and the bounds of their habitation (Acts 17:26).

In spite of language barriers and national differences, mankind continues to seek unity through religion.

In 1893, a world parliament on religion was held. One hundred years later, from August 28 to September 5, 1993, another world parliament convened in Chicago. To give a brief report on this week-long ecumenical gathering, I refer to an article in the September 2, 1993, issue of the *Plain Dealer*.

The article, titled, "Religious Seek Common Language in the Modern Tower of Babel," by Joan Connell of Newhouse News Service of Chicago, states:

> At some moments, the Parliament of World's Religions is a chaotic Tower of Babel, crammed with 6,000 fervent believers, all convinced they have a corner on the truth. Other times, it is a temple of harmony, where historic enemies transcend their differences in a quest for common

good. This historic and high-decibel meeting of the world's faiths is a heated global discussion in which language itself is being invented. Speaking — and often shouting — the moral absolutes of their respective beliefs, participants are trying to shift to a new, more neutral tongue, from which they will fashion a declaration of common human values that all religions can support.

The parliament, which concludes Saturday, also seeks to shed light on one of religion's deepest paradoxes; why the pathway to God so often leads in the opposite direction.

"Ask Hindus and Buddhists, Christians, Muslims and Jews what is wrong with the world and how to overcome it and you get five very different responses," said theologian William Vendley, a consultant to the United Nations on inter-religious strife.

"Religion isn't simply sweet and comforting; it is tough. It grapples with tragedy, condemns human pathology and searches for salvation in cosmic terms of good and evil," Vendley said. "It is a great resource that can become a great danger when the battle between good and evil is allowed to collapse into a communal fight."

On the surface, the parliament is a celebration of differences and an experiment in unity, which has drawn major religious leaders and minor-league gurus seeking mainstream legitimacy. But in its undercurrents are lessons in how readily such collapses occur:

> • The Orthodox Christian delegation pulled out of the parliament citing concerns about "quasi-religious groups."
> • There has been Jesus-bashing by those who blame Christian missionaries for the killing and forced conversion of North American Indian tribes.
> • God the Father has come under fire from pagans who insist that the Deity wears a female face.
> • Chicago police had to quell a dispute among Muslims, Hindus, and Sikhs shouting litanies of grievances at a plenary session. The

combatants were finally drowned out when the assembly began singing "We Shall Overcome."

And the parliament itself seems haunted by the orgy of hatred, rape, and murder in the former Yugoslavia, where Orthodox Serbs, Croatian Catholics, and Bosnian Muslims are locked in a genocidal civil war.

"The malignant tribalism that sets members of one faith against another isn't simply a religious problem, it's a problem with the human species. We have to face up to our shadow side," said psychoanalyst Robert Moore of the Chicago-based Institute for World Spirituality.

At a week-long symposium on violence and religion, Moore contended that the impulse to turn against one's own is woven deep in the human psyche. "It is easy to preach about overcoming hatred and learning how to love, but it's enormously difficult to live," said Moore, a Jungian psychologist.

The Ecumenical Winds of Change

Movements and men for the New World Order are gaining momentum rapidly in the areas of politics and economics. However, as you will see in this chapter, religion is marching to the same drumbeat, involving the ecumenical winds of change.

To give examples, I refer to a report of the Southern Baptists' Annual Convention and a meeting of the Presbyterian Church USA in Wichita, Kansas. The excerpted article appeared in the June 19, 1994, issue of the *Oklahoman:*

> In a single week, Southern Baptists endorsed working with Roman Catholics on theological as well as political issues. It said that they will no longer accept money from some of their own brethren. Presbyterians united in a near unprecedented reaffirmation of their belief in God . . . as Father, Son, and Holy Spirit. In reaction to an ecumenical women's conference where some church leaders were involved in worship of Sofia . . . the Goddess of Wisdom.
>
> Hundreds of miles apart, actions of the 15-million-member Southern Baptist Convention and the 2.7-million-member Presbyterian Church USA embrace separate calls

to move past controversy . . . and on to the Christian business of helping people and spreading the gospel of Jesus Christ. Messengers to the Baptist Convention did yield in their long time animosity with the Catholics, calling for all Christian organizations to present united support for pressing social and moral concerns, and to recognize the right to evangelize among all people everywhere. They urge continued ecumenical efforts to oppose abortion and pornography, and promote their traditional values and religious freedom. And they also recognized areas of irreconcilable theological differences, such as the infallibility of the Pope . . . the way to salvation and the interpretation of baptism. Presbyterians meeting in Wichita also focused on the common ground rather than differences in resolving the controversy over the re-imagining conference that threatened to split the denomination . . . already resulting in the curtailment of funding from some congregations.

Although they number far fewer than Southern Baptists . . . or the nation's 57 million Roman Catholics, Presbyterians are a part of the mainline Protestant movement. It also includes United Methodists and the Christian or Disciples of Christ.

United Methodists and Disciples also are wrestling with church leaders' involvement in the conference that included personification of God with feminine attributes as well as spontaneous celebration of lesbianism. In its exhaustive process of listening to people torn by the controversy, the 57-member Presbyterian review committee concluded the issue was a theological crisis and that the answers would be found in the churches' theology.

A final quote: "Some Presbyterians center the ideas brought forth at the re-imagining conference that if it was in God's will, it would produce spiritual fruit and grow. The same concept has been voiced regarding the Cooperative Baptist Fellowship."

Running Out of Money — and Meaning

Another article that appeared in *Newsweek,* August 9, 1993, demonstrates drastic changes in religious organizations, and a trend toward more liberal guidelines and one-world embracing policies. Under the religion banner, this report asserts that the mightiest Protestants are running out of money, members, and meaning. It is headlined "Dead End for the Mainline?"

To join it, one would never know that the Community Church of Joy in Glendale, Arizona, is Lutheran — or that Pastor Walther Kallestad had been educated in a traditional Lutheran family, college, and seminary. From the Steven Spielberg-like Sunday school gimmicks to the generic Amy Grant music at worship services, everything is designed to "meet the needs" of his non-denominational baby boomers. "Be quick" is the first commandment. Moving faster than a Wendy's at lunch hour, the Church of Joy needs only five minutes to distribute communion to 1,000 worshippers. Still, pastor Kallestad insists, "It's a very meaningful moment for our people." Sermons take a bit longer because Terey Summers, Arizona's Actress of the Year, likes to stage skits in the sanctuary instead of having ministers preach from the pulpit. "People today aren't interested in traditional doctrines like justification, sanctification, and redemption," the pastor has concluded.

Whatever it is, it works. The Church of Joy has over 6,000 members and another 6,000 who participate in the more than 100 recovery and other special-interest programs that keep the church doors turning seven days a week. That's not what Martin Luther may have had in mind when he set out to reform Christianity — but that's the point. There's a new reformation in American religion, and this time it is not the Church of Rome, but Lutheran and other mainline Protestant denominations that are under siege. Like the officers of beleaguered IBM and other seemingly solid American institutions, the leaders of the nation's once robust Protestant establishment face the loss of brand-name loyalty.

Aging flocks: For 25 consecutive years, liberal Protestantism's seven sister denominations have watched their collective membership decline. Although the number of Protestants in general is growing — an evangelical church is opening somewhere almost daily — the mainline denominations are not. They now account for just 24 percent of the American population. Their flocks are aging, their budgets shrinking. Morale is low. Many local congregations rejecting control by denominational leaders and cutting back on funds to support their national programs. From every angle, mainline Protestantism is gripped by crisis: of identity and loyalty, membership and money, leadership and organization, culture and belief.

Presbyterian Membership:
>   1965:   4.2 million
>   1992:   2.8 million
>   Status: Church slashes budget by $7 million
>   and 175 staff positions

American Baptist Membership:
>   1965:   1.3 million
>   1992:   1.2 million
>   Status: Overshadowed by Southern Baptist,
>   now 12 times larger

Lutheran Membership:
>   1965:   5.7 million
>   1992:   5.2 million
>   Status: Made up for $14.8 million shortfall in
>   1988 by streamlining staff and spending.

Will the crisis among the main line denominations cause them to return to their historical evangelical roots? Or will it only make them more susceptible to false teaching and religious gimmicks to increase their membership?

The answer is found in the Book of Revelation, where the end-time church is pictured as a wealthy church; a church of spiritual compromise and fornication; a harlot church that blasphemes the name of God, commits abominations against the saints of Jesus, and martyrs many faithful Christians.

> . . . and I saw a woman sit upon a scarlet coloured beast, full of names of blasphemy, having seven heads and ten horns. And the woman was arrayed in purple and scarlet colour, and decked with gold and precious stones and pearls, having a golden cup in her hand full of abominations and filthiness of her fornication: And upon her

forehead was a name written, MYSTERY, BABYLON THE GREAT, THE MOTHER OF HARLOTS AND ABOMINATIONS OF THE EARTH. And I saw the woman drunken with the blood of the saints, and with the blood of the martyrs of Jesus . . . (Rev. 17:3-6).

How could this happen? What could possibly lead the established, organized church to turn her back on the teachings of Scripture and prostitute herself with the political forces of this world? The answer is simple: greed, power, and the satanic goal of religious unity.

Stamping Out Religious Conflict

In order to achieve religious unity, "religion" must first be identified by world leaders — and marketed through the media — as the source of the world's many conflicts.

In his book, *Moving Toward One World Religion*, Thomas K. Burke reveals that the process is already in progress:

> For many years, global thinkers have contended that the number one cause of war on earth is conflict among religions. Mikhail Gorbachev, in his now famous book *Perestroika*, stated that, in order to achieve peace and security on earth, we must stamp out religious conflict. His way of doing this would be to outlaw any religious exclusiveness, as to make speaking against another's religion a "hate crime."

> Those who have desired to abolish all religious conflict have dreamed of a common ethical framework upon which the different religions could agree. Just such a document was presented at the 1993 Chicago meeting of the World's Parliament of Religions. In this document are found the ideologies for a global ethic that could bond the varied religious beliefs into a one-world religious order.

> The Parliament's reason for being: The first global meeting of the Parliament of the World Religions was held in 1893. Its attendees were introduced to America, and consequently, introduced people of America to many eastern and mystical religions. From across the seas, these religious people came together in hopes of finding similarities in their religious and ethical beliefs. The meeting failed when certain Christian members refused to forfeit

their belief that Jesus, alone, was the Saviour of the world.

From August 28 to September 5, 1993, 6,000 religious leaders, representing 125 religious groups from around the world, gathered in Chicago. Like those who had come 100 years before, they also had visions of worshipping side by side in unity. With this dream intact, they penned the "Declaration of a Global Ethic."

Why a global ethic? Blais Pascal said, "Men never do evil so completely and cheerfully as when they do it from religious conviction." Many of the wars that are taking place today are due in part to religious differences. Whether it be a death sentence against Salman Rushdie or war in the Balkans, we can attest to the terrible atrocities that religious hatred can create.

It is believed that over two-thirds of the conflicts in the world are occurring because of some type of religious confrontation. Because of this, a document on global ethics was drafted by the Swiss-born Catholic theologian, Fr. Hans Kung. With this document Baha'i, Buddhist, Christian, Confucian, Hindu, Jain, Jewish, Muslim, Native American, Neo-Pagan, Shitos, Sikhs, Taoists, Theosophists, Rastafarians, Unitarians, and Zoroastrians leaders are moving their followers towards a new world order for religious practices.[1]

We should not be surprised by these recent developments and growing unity among religionists. Jesus warned us, nearly 2,000 years ago, that deception and persecution would be rampant at the end of the age:

> And Jesus answered and said unto them, Take heed that no man deceive you. For many shall come in my name, saying, I am Christ; and shall deceive many. And ye shall hear of wars and rumours of wars: see that ye be not troubled: for all these things must come to pass, but the end is not yet. For nation shall rise against nation, and kingdom against kingdom: and there shall be famines, and pestilences, and earthquakes, in divers places. All these are the beginning of sorrows. Then shall they deliver you up to be afflicted, and shall kill you: and ye shall be hated of all nations for my name's sake. And then shall many be

offended, and shall betray one another, and shall hate one another. And many false prophets shall rise, and shall deceive many (Matt. 24:4-11).

Why would Christian believers be the objects of hate by all the nations? Because they will refuse to become part of the "religious unity" movement and will be seen as a threat to world peace and harmony.

A Church for All Nations

To establish this world religion, all other religions must agree to come under the same banner, including Judaism and Christianity. How can that happen?

Judaism, a monotheistic religious movement, will have a role in forming a universal church, especially since they are back in the land of their fathers. The Church of Rome, which is also venerable and thought by some to be the ecclesiastical representative for God, must also play a major role in forming a one-world church.

The diplomatic relationship recently confirmed by Israel and Rome will doubtless hasten the formation of a church for all nations, as described in this article from *Parade* magazine, April 3, 1993:

> The attitude of the Church toward the people of God's Old Testament — the Jews — can only be that they are our elder brothers in the faith. I have been convinced of it from my youngest years in my native town of Wadowice.
>
> Pope John Paul II, the Polish-born pontiff of the Roman Catholic Church, continued: "It must be understood that Jews, who for 2,000 years were dispersed among the nations of the world, had decided to return to the land of their ancestors. This is their right."
>
> "And this right," he said, "is recognized even by those who look upon the nation of Israel with an unsympathetic eye. This right was also recognized from the outset by the Holy See, and the act of establishing diplomatic relations with Israel is simply an international affirmation of this relationship."
>
> He was referring to the agreement on diplomatic relations between the Vatican and Israel, signed in Jerusalem last December 30 — a breakthrough 45 years after the birth of the Israeli state, culminating a process of quiet

diplomatic relations personally set in motion by the Pope two years earlier and directed by him on a day-to-day basis. The Vatican and Israeli diplomats at the ceremony then toasted each other with champagne.

Remarkably, the agreement comes after an often-difficult relationship between the Vatican and Israel, in which a major obstacle to diplomatic ties between the two was the unresolved political situation involving Israel and its Arab neighbors, as well as Palestinians in occupied territories. The Vatican moved toward diplomatic relations after Israel and the Arab states and the Palestinians launched their peace negotiations in Madrid in October 1991. (And, last month, the Vatican announced the establishment of diplomatic relations with Jordan, Israel's Moslem neighbor to the east.) The question of the status of Jerusalem, whose internationalization had earlier been demanded by the Vatican and others but resisted by Israel, ceased to be an issue in recent years. However, the Vatican continues to seek stronger guarantees for free access to Jerusalem as a holy place for all religions.

Having emphasized the right of the Jews to their own nation in Israel and given the reasons for its recognition by the Vatican, the Pope's thoughts turned to the holy city of Jerusalem, identified in his mind — as he made clear in recalling the 147th Psalm — with the biblical history of the Jews. His "greatest dream," he is telling friends and visitors these days, is to go there on a religious pilgrimage as soon as possible. John Paul II had visited the Holy Land as a bishop more than 20 years ago, but a return to Jerusalem as Pope has a crucial spiritual and peacemaking meaning for him. (Pope Paul VI went to Jerusalem in 1964). Israel already has invited John Paul II for a state visit.

"We trust," the Pope said, "that with the approach of the year 2000, Jerusalem will become the city of peace for the entire world and that all the people will be able to meet there, in particular the believers in the religions that find their birthright in the faith of Abraham."

This was an allusion to the fact that Jews, Christians, and Moslems — followers of the three great monotheistic religions spawned in the Middle East — trace their roots to Abraham, the first of the great biblical patriarchs.

The Church of Rome has long had a particular interest in Jerusalem because it owns property there and believes it will have a role in governing the nations of the world when Christ returns. The prophet Isaiah wrote about the period of "peace" that will result from this worldwide religious unity:

> And it shall come to pass in the last days, that the mountain of the Lord's house shall be established in the top of the mountains, and shall be exalted above the hills; and all nations shall flow unto it. And many people shall go and say, Come ye, and let us go up to the mountain of the Lord, to the house of the God of Jacob; and he will teach us of his ways, and we will walk in his paths: for out of Zion shall go forth the law, and the word of the Lord from Jerusalem. And he shall judge among the nations, and shall rebuke many people: and they shall beat their swords into plowshares, and their spears into pruninghooks: nation shall not lift up sword against nation, neither shall they learn war any more (Isa. 2:2-4).

A World Religion?

Even the Freemasons, who do not claim to be a religion, have a special interest in a central religion.

Quoting from the book, *Born in Blood,* by John R. Robinson, which is hailed by Freemasons as their current battle cry:

> The other problem in Israel brings us right back to Freemasonry, because it is squarely centered on the original site of the Temple of Solomon on Mount Moriah, the Temple Mount in Jerusalem, the birthplace of the Knights Templar. Perhaps no spot on earth cries out for the brotherhood of men of different religions more than the site of the original Temple of Solomon, in a situation so tense that some writers have speculated that it could well trigger World War III.
>
> It is of vital importance to three great religions — Judaism, Islam, and Christianity. Although Israel got possession of Jerusalem in 1967, it has been reluctant to

take possession of the Temple Mount. It is still policed by Moslems, because instead of a Jewish Temple to God, the Mount is crowned with two Moslem mosques built during the days of Islamic rule.

Yet to the Jews this Temple Mount is the most sacred place on earth. The Temple predates Christianity by a thousand years and Islam by many more. To the Christian it is sacred ground, for it is where Christ tossed out the moneychangers and debated and taught.

The Catholic church has suggested that Jerusalem become an international city, a concept which may have merit, but which does not solve the problem. It is not the city itself but the few sacred acres of Mount Moriah that sits at the center of controversy.

Listen carefully to this question posed by Robinson, and his solution:

Can the followers of three great religions, three great ways to worship God, find a way to come together in peace and brotherhood in this tiny place? This is the place where, more than anywhere else, the central religious attitude of Freemasonry could be applied with the most beneficial effect to the rest of the world, where men who avow their beliefs in a Supreme Being could meet in brotherhood and bear full respect for the other man's mode of worship.

Is it practical to leave the Dome of the Rock as it is, but build a Jewish Temple and a Christian shrine on the mount, all connected with a common courtyard? A sensible plan needs to be made and sold to the Jews, the Christians, and the Moslems. Just mounting a move in that direction might help thwart the plans of those willing to risk war in a maniacal game of king-of-the-hill, to set their God above all gods, whichever of the three He may be. It is time that men stop dying over how merciful and caring is their God.

What I am suggesting is that about 5 million Freemasons in the world, who do accept brotherhood with men of all faith, in that spirit might take the lead in solving the problem of the Temple Mount by combining their religious attitudes with their veneration of the Temple of

Solomon, to the benefit of the whole world. It would give new meaning to each man shaping himself into the perfect ashlar ready to take its place in the Temple of God. It would be a wonderful way to complete a full-circle circumambulation back to the very first purpose of their predecessor Knights of the Temple, the safe passage of all pilgrims to that holy place.

The plan of freemasonry has always been to meld all men into a universal brotherhood. This, to them, is the highest truth. If there is to be a New World Order, there must of necessity be a World Religion. Evidently the Pope is suggesting the same thing.

In the month of April the Pope will address the United Nations. The U.N. is calling it one of the most significant speeches of modern times. Has the Pope taken the cue from the Masons? Has he compromised the narrow path for the broad path?[2]

Man is forever trying to solve the problem apart from God.

The World Council of Churches

It was no coincidence that the World Council of Churches was founded in 1948, the same year that Israel became a nation. The intentions of the World Council of Churches was to socialize the church, featuring a watered-down social gospel, and to ultimately amalgamate all religions and denominations into a one-world ecclesiastical organization.

This body is working hand in hand with the proponents of world government and internationalism. They operate as far as possible within the framework of the United Nations. The ultimate world government, under this plan, will have a political arm and a religious arm. The WCC plans to be in control of the ecclesiastical or religious arm.

The apostle John visualized just such a one-world church married to a revived Roman Empire of political hue. The apostle John described the end-time super church:

. . . Come hither; I will shew unto thee the judgment of the great whore that sitteth upon many waters: With whom the kings of the earth have committed fornication, and the inhabitants of the earth have been made drunk with the wine of her fornication (Rev. 17:1-2).

In August 1948 the Federal Council leaders went to Amsterdam, the Netherlands, to form the World Council of Churches. In Amsterdam, clergymen of varying political beliefs met, including mouthpieces for the Soviet Union from behind the Iron Curtain.

Time magazine of September 13, 1948, captured the scene: "This greatest church meeting since the Reformation could not even agree on a definition of the word 'church.' The talk at Amsterdam was mostly on the comparatively low level of diplomacy. Czech theologian Joseph Hromadha (a Soviet mouthpiece) said: 'It won't embarrass me at all in returning to Prague. Of course, it's pretty negative and doesn't offer much in the way of action.' "

Substituting Revolution for Religion

Harvey T. Hoekstra, elected moderator of the Reformed Church and former missionary among the forest people of Ethiopia, has added another voice to the rising concern over evangelism in the WCC. As a minister whose church has been a member of the WCC from its inception, Hoekstra has studied the constitutional commitment of the WCC to support the churches in their worldwide missionary and evangelistic task.

Hoekstra questions whether the present WCC understanding of the mission of the church provides the churches with the support they need for this task. We quote from a review of his book, *The World Council of Churches and the Demise of Evangelism,* in *Christianity Today,* April 4, 1980:

> First, there are deep and historical changes in the definition of evangelism in the WCC. The International Missionary Council abandoned historical evangelism at the conference in Jerusalem, 1928, and revived a neo-orthodox evangelism at Madres . . . in 1938. The WCC changed a basically evangelical understanding of evangelism expressed in the First Assembly at Amsterdam in 1948, to a humanistic salvation quietly recognized by the central committee in 1959. . . . The problem does not seem to lie in the structure . . . within the WCC, with the basic theology of sin, Christology, redemption, the world, eschatology, and universalism. WCC evangelism was totally redefined. . . . Second, the leadership of the WCC is

now preoccupied with Roman Catholic relationships in anticipation of a councilor church. . . . Third, the doctrine of universalism is so extensively accepted by the WCC churches . . . that it seems very unlikely that there can be a sincere and unequivocal evangelistic movement addressed to non-Christian religions and non-Christian ideologies. Dialogue with them has replaced proclamation, and the humanization of society has utterly obliterated the historical evangelical understanding of personal evangelism.

The January 1983 *Reader's Digest* article, "Do You Know Where Your Church Offerings Go?" asks some pertinent questions:

What is the attraction of leading churchmen to Third World, Marxist-Leninish societies that have severely restricted and in some cases all but eliminated religion? . . . A major obstacle to reform is the unwillingness of the average churchgoer to acknowledge what has happened to his church. "People just can't believe that their church, the church they've loved all their lives, can be financing all these Marxist-Leninist projects," says David Jessup. "The very idea seems preposterous, an affront to common sense." If there is to be a change, it will have to be made by the men dependent on the church bureaucracy to take the lead. Several Methodist ministers who urge their congregations not to pay their (Church) World Service apportionment have been punished, some actually forced out of the church. Methodist evangelist Edmund Robb, who heads the Institute on Religion and Democracy, a new Washington-based organization of distinguished ministers and laymen, recognizes that there are churchgoers reluctant to take action for fear that it will divide the church. But he feels that, on the contrary, action is essential to renew and restore the church to its fundamental task. . . . "At the root of the problem," says Robb, "is the secularization of the church. The NCC (and WCC) has substituted revolution for religion."

Apostasy is predictable. The denial of Jesus Christ as the only begotten Son, His atoning death, and His literal resurrection, by ecclesiastics opens the way to political insurrection.

Second Peter 2:1-3 describes the methods of the end-time false teachers:

> But there were false prophets also among the people, even as there shall be false teachers among you, who privily shall bring in damnable heresies, even denying the Lord that bought them, and bring upon themselves swift destruction. And many shall follow their pernicious ways; by reason of whom the way of the truth shall be evil spoken of. And through covetousness shall they with feigned words make merchandise of you: whose judgment now of a long time lingereth not, and their damnation slumbereth not.

The apostle Peter indicated that many would come in the name of Christ, yet deny Him as both Lord and Saviour. The Apostle also said that these same apostates would make merchandise of the members of the churches. In other words, like the Nicolaitans, they would use the money and the name of the memberships as merchandise to gain advantage (Rev. 2).

If you are a member of a church that belongs to the WCC, then the WCC leadership speaks for you. They use your name, and in the eyes of the non-Christian world, the WCC represents you.

The Worship of Angels

When we read in Revelation 13:4 that people will worship the dragon (devil) and the beast (Antichrist), we can conclude that there will be religious activity during the final seven years of man's day. And there will be a global church and a central religious authority over all the earth.

Metaphysical activities and the revival of ancient religions indicate the world is already being prepared for such a massive delusion.

> For the mystery of iniquity doth already work: only he who now letteth will let, until he be taken out of the way. And then shall that Wicked be revealed, whom the Lord shall consume with the spirit of his mouth, and shall destroy with the brightness of his coming: Even him, whose coming is after the working of Satan with all power and signs and lying wonders, And with all deceivableness of unrighteousness in them that perish; because they re-

ceived not the love of the truth, that they might be saved. And for this cause God shall send them strong delusion, that they should believe a lie (2 Thess. 2:7-11).

The resurgence of activity in the spirit world brings to mind a departure from the historic Christian faith as emphasized by the apostle Paul in 1 Timothy 4:1: "Now the spirit speaketh expressly, that in the latter times some shall depart from the faith, giving heed to seducing spirits, and doctrines of devils," and 2 Timothy 3:5: "Having a form of godliness, but denying the power thereof: from such turn away."

This turning away is evident in the renewed interest in angels, the goddess religion, nature worship, and Eastern religions, as this report of the First Angel Conference confirm:

> NIRR — The convinced and the curious hoped to commune with the celestial at the first Angels and Nature Spirits Conference, held August 15-22 in Angel Fire, New Mexico. "If you watch the news or pay too close attention to world affairs, it gives you a sense of 'Who is in control here?' " said Terry Lynn Taylor, conference coordinator and author of how-to guides for contacting and working with angels.
>
> "Technology is not filling our souls with happiness. People are re-evaluating what this is really about. The angels are helping people have hope, letting us know there is another force," Taylor told NIRR. Among the other rarely seen nature spirits are gnomes, leprechauns, and genies.
>
> The 55 attendees who paid $1,200 each included "traditional Catholics to very way-out thinkers," Taylor said. Presenters included Spiritual Church ministers, clairvoyants, psychics, aromatherapists, oracles, astrologers, tarot card readers, and healers who cure with tuning forks and crystals. One woman "channeled" an age-old Himalayan spiritual entity. New Age musician Iasos coordinated "an evening of inter-dimensional games with local fairies, angels, and elementals as a fun way for humans to become acquainted with them in a mutually loving manner."
>
> But you don't have to be religious to believe in

angels, Taylor said. "A few people were atheists or agnostics who could never let go of their belief in angels," she said. "No one here is putting down religion. People are learning from one another's experiences with angels," Taylor said. "At this point in evolution, people are more able to accept the unseen, to have faith," she told NIRR, citing a Gallup poll that showed belief in angels is growing. "Angels are spiritual helpers who work in direct alignment with God for our spiritual well-being and understanding. They are not the forces we pray to, but intermediaries. God's in charge."[3]

The Revival of Goddess Worship

Another growing deception centers around goddess worship, which is even infiltrating our public schools, as this news report shows:

> "The Great Goddess is in the Divine Feminine that has been gradually disempowered, then suppressed by patriarchs to the detriment of men and especially women." So said the introduction to an in-service scheduled for Edmonton Public School Board teachers this August. The two-and-one-half hour seminar, called "Remembering the Goddess," was canceled, however, after the superintendent received complaints from "three or four people" about its content.
>
> "When I see this opposition, this misunderstanding, I get very hurt," says Dr. Nadia Torrens, who teaches Arabic and English half-time at Glengarry Elementary School, and two courses about the goddess in the University of Alberta women's program.
>
> Fed by a feminist desire for a non-male divinity, goddess worship has blossomed in the United States and is taking root in Canada as well. "The goddess movement is a rich, unstructured, multi-disciplinary wave of artistic, intellectual and spiritual activity," say the authors of *Megatrends for Women,* who estimate that between 100,000 and 500,000 U.S. women are active in it.
>
> The term "goddess worship" encompasses a smorgasbord of spiritual offerings. The Egyptian goddess Isis is

popular, as are the Greek Artemis and Athena. Hopi Spider Woman is one of the many goddesses from native Indian spirituality, and the European Wiccan tradition, purged of its masculine elements, offers a tantalizing prescription of rituals, spiels, and chants for women to practice while circling darkened rooms at Women's Spirituality conferences. Some Hindu forms, Jungian therapy, and a revamped Virgin Mary also figure prominently, as does a generous helping of Gaia (Mother Earth), an environmental mysticism whose adherents have been known to condemn cutting grass or tilling soil.[4]

Other false gods are also raising their heads. Native worship is being revived under many guises as demonstrated in an article titled, "Spirit in the Hills:"

> Like a tree sloth, Paul DuBose dangles from a Hill Country oak, arms and legs gripping a low branch.
> He's a guest at Dancing Waters, a Wimberly bed and breakfast inn dedicated to providing healing and spiritual renewal.
> DuBose does admit to being bonded with the Earth. Intimately. Experientially. Vocationally. Religiously. He and his wife, Patricia, have created DuBose Natural Farm, a 1,700-acre place dedicated to healing and restoring the land of a former cattle ranch. So his bond with nature runs deeper than just a tryst with a tree.
> The DuBoses' commitment to nature has led them beyond organic farming and sustainable development for an environmentally sound future to the creation of a religion for themselves and others who feel the same sacred bond.
> Somehow the Hill Country attracts people like the DuBoses.
> Some even say the hills flow with a special kind of energy that comes from the earth itself.
> Whatever the reason, the cedar-dotted Texas hills are home and refuge to spiritual explorers practicing everything from ancient earth religions to life in an East Indian Ashram. Practicers of witchcraft, known as Wiccans, danced naked by the light of the moon, "sky-clad," as they

call it. And admirers of American Indian spirituality purify body and soul in sweat lodges tucked away throughout the hills.[5]

The pores of their skin may be cleaner, but there is only One who can purify the soul.

Living in the Age of Enlightenment

Since Maharishi Mahesh Yogi founded his university in Fairfield, Iowa, Transcendental Meditation (his invention) has been used in business, school, and churches. Now the appearance of America is changing as an entire village near Austin, Texas, practices TM:

> The sign outside an idyllic subdivision thirty miles southwest of Austin reads, "Welcome to Radiance, an Ideal Village Practicing the Transcendental Meditation Programs."
>
> Aside from the sign and a gold-domed meditation center, a visitor would find it hard to tell the difference between Radiance and any other upper-middle-class, hill country subdivision with a pool. At least, on the surface.
>
> But the 125 people living in the thirty or so homes all practice TM, or transcendental meditation, as taught by the Maharishi Mahesh Yogi.
>
> A number of the Radiance children attend school at a small frame house in a hollow down the hill from the cluster of homes. The Maharishi School of the Age of Enlightenment looks like Little Schoolhouse on the Prairie. But the accredited school for pre-schoolers through grade six has its differences.
>
> Like all elementary classrooms, that of Carol Tavares has visuals on the wall. But instead of the usual posters of Mr. Sunshine or springtime flower, there is a hand-lettered poster of the TM precepts for learning.
>
> Inside nearly every home in Radiance, at least one portrait of the Maharishi hangs on the wall. He is revered as a saint for bringing the practice of TM to the world. His concepts, such as the TM Sidhi program, are accepted by those at Radiance.
>
> The TM Sidhi program is an attempt to assemble a core group of mediators in geographical areas with the

belief that this will stabilize the city or even the nation, if the group is large enough.[6]

AT&T and Their Homosexual Friends

The religious appearance of America is drastically changing, and it is becoming a pagan wilderness. Perversions are open and advocated in every walk of life. The media and religious liberals are working feverishly to obtain total acceptance for sexual perversions the Bible designates as abominations to God.

As graphic examples, I refer to a shocking article that appeared in the *Christian World Report*, February 1994, headlined, "Business, Celebrities, Religious Left Support Homosexual Causes":

> AT&T recently sponsored the production of the musical Falsettos in Atlanta. Billed as the "story of a typical family with a not so typical dilemma," Falsettos includes a gay father, his wife, a psychiatrist, and two lesbians from next door.
>
> In the story the father, Marvin, struggles to explain to his son that he is moving in with his male lover, Whizzer. Meanwhile, the mom moves in with the family therapist. The whole family comforts Whizzer when he dies of AIDS.
>
> Also in June, AT&T celebrated Gay and Lesbian Awareness week in the company. The week culminated with a workshop on homophobia in the workplace.
>
> Tennis legend and open lesbian Martina Navratilova recently wrote a fund raising appeal for the National Gay and Lesbian Task Force. The letter, on her personal stationery, says: "We've all grown to appreciate that for too long, the rules have been made by and for white, Christian, heterosexual males. All the rest of us were left out." She calls for readers to "put your voices and pocketbooks where, for many of us, our hearts have been for years."
>
> Navratilova is also the subject of the October cover story of the *Advocate,* a leading gay and lesbian news magazine. (In the 1970s, *Advocate* ran regular ads for homosexual boy prostitutes who were advertised as "chicken." A forthcoming book by Dr. Judith Reisman exposes the magazine's history of promoting pederasty and gay prostitution.)

Actress/comedienne Lily Tomlin wrote a letter in September asking for money to make a film of Vito Russo's book, *The Celluloid Closet*. Russo, who died of AIDS in 1990, was co-founder of ACT-UP and GLAAD, two radical homosexual political action groups.

Russo's book, first published in 1981, tells how Hollywood has depicted homosexuals in movies.

Liberal diva Barbara Streisand will produce and Glenn Close will star in an upcoming, yet-to-be titled NBC movie about Co. Margarethe Cammermeyer, the Army officer dismissed from service after revealing her lesbianism.

At the National Lesbian and Gay Journalists Association Convention in September the following companies were listed as "progressive" because of their support for homosexual causes: Apple Computers, AT&T, Ben and Jerry's Homemade Ice Cream, the Boston Globe, Digital Equipment Corp., Gannett Co., Harley Davidson, Lotus Development Corp., Microsoft Corp., RJR Nabisco, Warner Brothers, and HBO, all of which offer full benefits to same-sex partners.

Focus on the Family's *Citizen* magazine reports that David Geffen, the Hollywood billionaire who made his fortune in the record business, donated $20,000 to defeat Colorado's Amendment 2. Amendment 2, which passed in Colorado last fall, declared that sexual behavior is not proper grounds for protected legal status. Geffen announced last November that he is a homosexual.

Miller Lite and a Washington nightclub, Tracks, purchased a full-page ad in the *Washington Blade,* a homosexual newspaper. The ad promoted a fundraising event for the Fourth Annual Gay Games.

Secular humanism and blatant homosexuality has always brought about the decline of nations and empires. Sodom and Gomorrah received the judgments of God because of their abominations. The ultimate abomination will be the global church that accepts what God categorically condemns.

For this cause God gave them up unto vile affections: for even their women did change the natural use into that which is against nature: And likewise also the men, leaving the natural use of the woman, burned in their lust one toward another; men with men working that which is unseemly, and receiving in themselves that recompense of their error which was meet. And even as they did not like to retain God in their knowledge, God gave them over to a reprobate mind, to do those things which are not convenient (Rom. 1:26-28).

The willful king of Daniel 11:36-37 will doubtless lead the gay parades and Olympic games; for he will not regard the God of his fathers, nor the desire of women.

Worshipping at the U.N. Altar

Every universal movement must have a political arm, an economic arm, and a religious arm to form the triangle for the global empire. Although the United Nations does not endorse any religion, it will most assuredly promote the world church in the last days.

The global church that directs worship toward the beast and his image will blaspheme heaven and the Lord Jesus Christ, and all His saints.

> And they worshipped the dragon which gave power unto the beast: and they worshipped the beast, saying, Who is like unto the beast? who is able to make war with him? And there was given unto him a mouth speaking great things and blasphemies; and power was given unto him to continue forty and two months. And he opened his mouth in blasphemy against God, to blaspheme his name, and his tabernacle, and them that dwell in heaven. And it was given unto him to make war with the saints, and to overcome them: and power was given him over all kindreds, and tongues, and nations. And all that dwell upon the earth shall worship him, whose names are not written in the book of life of the Lamb slain from the foundation of the world (Rev. 13:4-8).

The great unseen church of Jesus Christ has innumerable followers, who will only become visible to the world when the Lord returns. The foundation of the true Church is set forth in Matthew 16:13-18:

When Jesus came into the coasts of Caesarea Philippi, he asked his disciples, saying, Whom do men say that I the Son of man am? And they said, Some say that thou art John the Baptist: some, Elias; and others, Jeremias, or one of the prophets. He saith unto them, But whom say ye that I am? And Simon Peter answered and said, Thou art the Christ, the Son of the living God. And Jesus answered and said unto him, Blessed art thou, Simon Barjona: for flesh and blood hath not revealed it unto thee, but my Father which is in heaven. And I say also unto thee, Thou art Peter, and upon this rock I will build my church; and the gates of hell shall not prevail against it.

Today the watchword of the organized church is unity. Bible prophecy indicates in the last days there will be a global church that will ultimately embrace all faiths, creeds, and cults. We have observed many signs and much evidence of formative movements in the building of such a worldwide mega-church.

One sign we have but briefly mentioned in a single paragraph is the United Nations.

The one-world forces that are already riding like the four horsemen of the apocalypse are rapidly promoting the power and the proliferation of the United Nations. The U.N., already in stage two, is also beginning to show a religious aura in its august sessions.

Although the world took little notice of the reconvening of the United Nations January 31, 1992, for the first time in its historic assembly the security council included a king, five presidents, six prime ministers, a chancellor, a premier, and two foreign ministers.

William F. Jasper, writing in *Global Tyranny . . . Step by Step,* describes the religious verbiage of the U.N. Charter and the religious overtones of their "summits":

The assemblage took on a religious aura as, one by one, the national leaders worshiped at the U.N. altar, referred to the U.N. Charter with a reverence usually reserved for Holy Writ, and recited the by-now familiar doxology always heard at these increasingly frequent "summits": a new world order; peace, equity, and justice, interdependence; global harmony; democracy; human rights; the rule of law; collective engagement; an enhanced and strengthened United Nations, etc.

President Bush enthusiastically extolled "the sacred principles enshrined in the United Nations Charter" and, recalling its messianic mission, proclaimed. "For perhaps the first time since that hopeful moment in San Francisco, we can look at our charter as a living, breathing document."

The U.N.'s newly-installed Secretary-General, Egypt's Boutros Boutros-Ghali, was no less caught up with the spiritual purpose of the world organization. He called for additional summit-level meetings of the Security Council, since this "would also help to assure that transfiguration of this house which the world hopes to be completed before its fiftieth anniversary, in 1995." How he divined what the world's "hopes" for the organization on its fiftieth birthday might be, he did not say. And he did not have to explain the motive behind his use of biblical metaphor. That was transparent enough. Webster defines "transfigure" this way: "to give a new and typically exalted or spiritual appearance to." To the Christian mind, of course, "transfiguration" recalls the Gospel account of Christ's manifestation of His divine glory.

Boutros-Ghali undoubtedly knows the power of the symbolism he chose and, like his fellow true believers in the one-world gospel, he realized that much more of his evangelization is necessary if the masses are to be sold on the idea of the U.N. as the world's savior.[7]

Obviously, when the U.N. turns 50 in 1995, it wants to be ready for stage three — total domination of all nations by this august body. It will function with a world court, a single mega-bank, a new currency, and a global U.N. army. A global taxation will soon follow.

Stage Three — Total Domination

In order to bind the people of the nations together in a cohesive fashion, the United Nations will do more to promote a syncretic religion as part of the New Order than the World Council of Churches, the Roman Catholic hierarchy, and religious parliaments around the world.

In *Global Tyranny* the author says this about "The New World Religion:"

We have meditations at the United Nations a couple of times a week. The meditation leader is Sri Chinmoy, and this is what he said about this situation: "The United Nations is the chosen instrument of God; to be a chosen instrument means to be a divine messenger carrying the banner of God's inner vision and outer manifestation. One day, the world will . . . treasure and cherish the soul of the United Nations as its very own with enormous pride, for this soul is all-loving, all-nourishing, and all-fulfilling."

In times past, when critics of the United Nations described the organization as a modern Tower of Babel, most were making reference to man's act of spiritual arrogance that the Book of Genesis tells us earned God's displeasure. To back up such an unflattering characterization today, they could point to the confusing and combustible melange of tongues, cultures, ideologies, and politics for which the "house of peace" has become justly famous. The U.N., along with its programs and policies, is becoming ever more worthy of comparison to the Tower of Babel, as rampant idolatry and militant paganism thoroughly permeate the organization.

The United Nations is steadily becoming the center of a syncretic new world religion, a weird and diabolical convergence of New Age mysticism, pantheism, aboriginal animism, atheism, communism, socialism, Luciferian occultism, apostate Christianity, Islam, Taoism, Buddhism, and Hinduism. The devotees and apostles of this new faith include the kind of strange admixture of crystal worshippers, astrologers, radical feminists, environmentalists, cabalists, human potentialism, Eastern mystics, pop psychologists, and "liberal" clergymen one would normally tend to associate with the off-beat, sandals-and-beads counterculture of the 1960s. But today's worshippers in this rapidly expanding movement are as likely to be scientists, diplomats, corporate presidents, heads of state, international bankers, and leaders of mainstream Christian churches.[8]

The purposes and actions of those who join and participate in this new world religion will be known by these ungodly characteristics:

As it is written, There is none righteous, no, not one: There is none that understandeth, there is none that seeketh after God. They are all gone out of the way, they are together become unprofitable; there is none that doeth good, no, not one. Their throat is an open sepulchre; with their tongues they have used deceit; the poison of asps is under their lips: Whose mouth is full of cursing and bitterness: Their feet are swift to shed blood: Destruction and misery are in their ways: And the way of peace have they not known: There is no fear of God before their eyes. Now we know that what things soever the law saith, it saith to them who are under the law: that every mouth may be stopped, and all the world may become guilty before God (Rom. 3:10-19).

"The world will be guilty before God." Why? Because the religion of the United Nations promotes man's law instead of God's law; secular humanism instead of acknowledging God's authority; and chains of bondage instead of the liberty of the Lord.

When the King Comes

Only those believers who refuse to be part of this new world religion will be welcome as children of God by the Father. It is mandated that we must separate ourselves from all unrighteousness:

Be ye not unequally yoked together with unbelievers: for what fellowship hath righteousness with unrighteousness? and what communion hath light with darkness? And what concord hath Christ with Belial? or what part hath he that believeth with an infidel? And what agreement hath the temple of God with idols? for ye are the temple of the living God; as God hath said, I will dwell in them, and walk in them; and I will be their God, and they shall be my people. Wherefore come out from among them, and be ye separate, saith the Lord, and touch not the unclean thing; and I will receive you, And will be a Father unto you, and ye shall be my sons and daughters, saith the Lord Almighty (2 Cor. 6:14-18).

Peace will not come to planet Earth until the prince of peace returns, the Lord Jesus Christ who is literally our peace, and the glorious fulfillment of Isaiah's prophecy.

For unto us a child is born, unto us a son is given: and the government shall be upon his shoulder: and his name shall be called Wonderful, Counsellor, The mighty God, The everlasting Father, the Prince of Peace. Of the increase of his government and peace there shall be no end, upon the throne of David, and upon his kingdom, to order it, and to establish it with judgment and with justice from henceforth even for ever. The zeal of the Lord of hosts will perform this (Isa. 9:6-7).

The Church triumphant will fill the whole earth, and ultimately God's universe, when the King comes back. And every knee shall bow and every tongue confess that Jesus Christ is Lord to the glory of God the Father; of things in heaven, and things in earth and things under the earth.

Even so, come Lord Jesus.

9

America and the New World Order

by Don S. McAlvany

America in the mid-1990s is declining as rapidly as did Germany in the mid-1930s, or Rome as it was approaching its terminal stages. Morally, culturally, spiritually, politically, and financially, America is now plunging down the slippery slope to collapse. And, as with most countries in decline, the majority of Americans do not recognize the descent and would argue vehemently that America is as great as ever.

Alexander Solzhenitsyn wrote:

> The strength or weakness of a society depends more on the level of its spiritual life than on its level of industrialization. Neither a market economy nor even general abundance constitutes the crowning achievement of human life. If a nation's spiritual energies have been exhausted, it will not be saved from collapse by the most perfect government structure or by any industrial development. A tree with a rotten core cannot stand.

Edward Gibbon, the great British historian, wrote (between 1776 and 1788) in his classic, six-volume, *History of the Decline and Fall of the Roman Empire,* about the five primary causes for the collapse and destruction of Roman society:

>   1) The rapid increase in divorce and the undermining of the sanctity of the home;
>   2) The spiraling rise of taxes and extravagant spending;
>   3) The mounting craze of pleasure and the brutalization of sports;
>   4) The building of gigantic armaments, and the failure to realize that the real enemy lay within the gates of the empire, in the moral decay of the people; and
>   5) The decay of religion and the fading of faith into a mere humanistic form, leaving the people without a guide.

All of these and much more of Gibbon's great work, as well as much of William Shirer's epic history of *The Rise and Fall of the Third Reich,* describe America today. In my opinion, we are in a state of moral collapse, with homosexuals and sexual degenerates now running our government, our entertainment industry, and much of our public education system. Free, uninhibited sex outside of marriage is now being promoted, and the largest pornography industry in the world produces, promotes, and distributes its filth on a global basis.

That the family has disintegrated in America is a gross understatement. More than half of all marriages in America (including Christian marriages) end in divorce. More than half of American children are either being raised by a single parent, in a home with a stepparent, or by the state. More than 25 percent of American children are born out of wedlock into a single-mother family. Statistics about teenage crime, rebellion, gang warfare, pregnancy, and suicide are the highest in the world in America, as are those statistics describing domestic violence and physical and sexual abuse against children and wives.

More than 25 years of poisonous women's liberation philosophy directed at two generations of American women is now bearing its ugly fruit. Record numbers of American wives are leaving their husbands, children, and families to "find themselves" or "do their own thing," and record numbers of American women are turning to lesbianism for fulfillment.

As the Romans Do

Like Rome, America is the most highly-taxed major country in the world, with 50 to 60 percent of the income of her most productive class now going to income re-distribution and welfare. Half a century of explosive economic growth, extravagant materialism, overindulgence, and prosperity (since the end of World War II) has given way to gross over-indebtedness, record personal and business bankruptcies, and a declining "real" standard of living for most Americans.

As in Rome, Americans now worship the "god" of entertainment, pleasure, and distraction, whether that "god" is sports (participatory or spectator), travel, television, movies, videos, recreational drugs, or sex. These diversions preoccupy almost all of Americans' leisure time, leaving little time for reading, thinking, reflecting, or observing what is happening to our people, our country, our culture, our families . . . ourselves.

"Anger," "brutality," and "distraction" characterized the Roman circuses of ancient times, as well as the other diversions designed by wicked leaders to keep the masses' minds off of the realities of a declining decadent empire. These same words aptly describe our spectator sports and television in America today.

As in ancient Rome or in Germany in the mid-1930s, the socialists have captured the U.S. government and are systematically destroying virtually all of the freedoms, traditions, and morality of the American people. Having forgotten America's history, heritage, and greatness, her people, many times, can no longer tell the difference between right and wrong or good and evil. Like the people in ancient Rome and Nazi Germany, the American people, I fear, risk becoming slaves robbed of their freedom. The frightening part is that many don't seem to realize it.

The great patriot of America's War for Independence, Patrick Henry, said:

> Bad men cannot make good citizens. It is impossible that a nation of infidels or idolaters should be a nation of free men. It is when a people forget God that tyrants forge their chains. A vitiated state of morals, a corrupt public conscience, are incompatible with freedom.

Thirty million babies can be mutilated and killed in their mothers' wombs, yet most Americans no longer seem able to discern that abortion is wrong — that it is murder.

A man of highly questionable character, accused of womanizing, adultery, drug use, draft dodging, and wartime collaboration with America's most deadly enemy can run for president and be elected by a constituency that doesn't really object to his background. Why? Because they don't believe his moral comportment will affect his ability to govern and improve the economic condition.

And, as did Rome and the Germany of the 1930s, America has gone into a spiritual and moral free fall, leaving her people without an anchor or a compass. In my opinion, a number of America's mainline religious denominations are as immoral, socialist, and devoid of spiritual content and truth as their counterpart state-sanctioned churches in Nazi Germany and the old Soviet Empire. From a social gospel and liberal theology devoid of almost any redeeming spiritual content; to the morality of the day; to homosexuals in the clergy; to most of the tenets of socialism, collectivism, and big government control of the people; certain mainline religions have gone along with, or even been in the forefront of the decline.

America has gone into spiritual decline and substituted the secular humanist gods of man, materialism, pleasure, high technology, etc., for the God of the Bible, His Son Jesus Christ, and His biblical blueprint for successful living.

As Antonio Gramsci, founder of the Italian Communist Party, said, "If you want to take down a capitalist country and convert it to communism, first undermine its morality, its culture, and its spirituality — and the subsequent transition to communism (and slavery) will be a short and easy one."

This chapter will examine the global plunge toward world government, targeted for the end of the decade, and the efforts of a socialist government (i.e., Big Brother) to control the American people. Such control will come via electronic surveillance, a national ID card, a national police force, a financial dictatorship, growing police state tactics, the confiscation of private property and wealth, gun control, socialized medicine, and much more.

We will analyze how Big Brother is programming Americans for socialism and the New World Order; how the persecution of Christians, conservatives, and traditionalists by the socialist "change agents" now in control of America is approaching. We will also study how the judgment of a righteous God — who, according to the Bible, takes a very dim view of baby killing, homosexuality, promiscuity, pornography, rampant divorce, immorality, and rebellion to His laws

— could be descending upon America in the 1990s.

A World Government by the Year 2000?

Both the New World Order and the New Age movement proclaim that their world government will be in place by the year 2000 — the dawning of the Age of Aquarius!

Elitist groups (such as the Trilateral Commission, the Council on Foreign Relations, the Bildebergers, the Club of Rome, the Socialist Internationals) which have staffed most of the key positions in the Clinton administration (and, previously, the Bush administration), and most of the major European governments, have written very openly for years about their plans for world government by the elite.

The Council on Foreign Relations, the CFR, founded by globalists in 1921, was, in my opinion, established to surreptitiously gain control of the U.S. government. The majority of U.S. presidents, vice presidents, and secretaries of state, treasury, commerce, and defense for more than 50 years have come from the CFR or its sister organization, the Trilateral Commission, which was founded in 1973 by David Rockefeller. At least 15 of 20 secretaries of state since the founding of the CFR have been members.

The late Rear Admiral Chester Ward, himself a former 16-year member of the CFR, warned of the evil intentions of these globalists:

> The most powerful clique in these elitist groups have an objective in common — they want to bring about the surrender of the sovereignty and the national independence of the United States. A second clique of international members in the CFR . . . comprises the Wall Street international bankers and their key agents. Primarily, they want the world banking monopoly from whatever power ends up in control of global government.

People who deny the power and influence of the CFR and other elitist groups in the world's major governments have simply not read their writings or studied their membership rosters. Most alarming is the fact that many of the key positions in the U.S. and top governments of the world are staffed from these groups.

Thomas Jefferson was aware of the danger that such elitist group pose when he wrote:

> When all government, domestic and foreign, in little as in great things, shall be drawn to Washington as the

center of all power, it will render powerless the checks provided of one government on another, and will become as venal and oppressive as the government from which we separated.

For almost 50 years (since the end of World War II), the globalists have systematically and secretly been building the edifice or superstructure for this world government. Take a look at some of the major developments over the past five decades:

- The Korean and Vietnam wars.
- Desert Storm (described by George Bush as "a major stepping stone to the New World Order").
- The establishment of European Economic Community (now giving way to the United States of Europe).
- The NAFTA agreement (described by Henry Kissinger as "a major stepping stone to the New World Order"), which is designed to economically, and then politically merge the U.S., Mexico, and Canada.
- The massive western financial/industrial/high-tech aid to the former Soviet Union (now Russia).
- The western betrayal of South Africa.
- America's present gun control and environmental movements.

These events, and many more have all been part of an elaborate, long-term strategy to move the world toward one giant world government — which will be an Orwellian socialist dictatorship (a giant global Tower of Babel).

The Bloomfield Memorandum

The organization that gave birth to the United Nations was the Advisory Committee on Post War Foreign Policy, set up by Secretary of State Cordell Hull in 1941. Ten of its 14 members were members of the CFR.

To sell the American people on the U.N., the organization was located on an $8.5 million piece of land (donated by John D. Rockefeller) situated on the East River in New York. The chief salesman for the U.N. and the first Secretary General for the U.N. Formation Committee was Under Secretary of State Alger Hiss (CFR), who, while selling the U.N. to the American people and Senate, was also functioning as a Soviet agent.

More than 30 years ago, in a study known as Memorandum No. 7, titled, "A World Effectively Controlled by the United Nations," by Lincoln P. Bloomfield of the Council on Foreign Relations (delivered to the State Department on 3/10/62), the elitists wrote:

> A world effectively controlled by the United Nations is one in which "world government" would come about through the establishment of supranational institutions, characterized by mandatory universal membership and some ability to employ physical force. Effective control would thus entail a preponderance of political power in the hands of a supranational organization.... The present U.N. Charter could theoretically be revised in order to erect such an organization equal to the task envisioned, thereby codifying a radical rearrangement of power in the world.

The Bloomfield Memorandum was commissioned by the State Department, then headed by Secretary of State Dean Rusk (CFR), to study how disarmament could be used to usher in "world government." The document stated:

> The principal features of a model system would include the following: 1) power, sufficient to monitor and enforce disarmament, settle disputes, and keep the peace — including taxing powers; 2) an international police force [which is now openly called the New World Army], balanced appropriately among ground, sea, air, and space elements, consisting of 500,000 men recruited individually, wearing a U.N. uniform, and controlling a nuclear force composed of 50-100 mixed land-based mobile missiles and undersea-based missiles, averaging one megaton per weapon; 3) a government divided among three branches; and 4) compulsory jurisdiction of the International Court.

Deceiving the American Public

Socialism has dominated many of Europe's most powerful nations such as England, France, and Sweden (with periodic regressions — such as in England under Churchill and Margaret Thatcher) for more than 80 years. Socialism is by definition the government ownership or control of the means of production and distribution. The democratic socialism practiced in Europe for decades is essentially a dictatorship over the economy and over people's lives by leaders whom the people get to elect.

Some would argue that Americans think differently (more independently and individually) than Europeans, so socialism and globalism has had to be sold to Americans in a more subtle, disguised, and gradual manner — the ideologies have had to be "re-packaged" for the American public.

H.G. Wells, the British Fabian Socialist and internationalist, makes this point clear in his 1908 book, *New Worlds for Old:*

> Socialism would cease to be an open revolution, and would instead become a subtle plot. Functions were to be shifted from the elected representative, to the appointed official . . . a scientific bureaucracy appointed by representative bodies which would have diminishing activity and importance. . . . The replacement of individual action by a public organization could achieve socialism without public support (without the public even knowing it or being in favor of it).

And that is how it has happened in America — so subtly, disguised, and gradually that the nation has become socialized without its people knowing or even supporting it.

Such deception is in total opposition to the wishes of our founding fathers, as Thomas Jefferson wrote:

> A wise and frugal government which shall restrain men from injuring one another, shall leave them otherwise free to regulate their own pursuits of industry and improvement, and shall not take from the mouth of labor the bread it has earned. This is the sum of good government.

The New World Constitution

A World Constitution has now been drafted by the World Constitution and Parliament Association in Lakewood, Colorado. The preamble to the World Constitution says, in part:

> Realizing that Humanity today has come to the turning point in history and that we are on the threshold of a new world order, which promises to usher in an era of peace, prosperity, justice, and harmony; . . . Aware of the interdependence of people, nations and all of life; . . .

Aware that man's abuse of science and technology has brought Humanity to the brink of disaster, through the production of horrendous weaponry of mass destruction and to the brink of ecological and social catastrophe; . . . Aware that the misery and conflicts caused by the ever increasing disparity between rich and poor; Conscious of our obligation to posterity to save Humanity from imminent and total annihilation;

Conscious that Humanity is One, despite the existence of diverse nations, races, creeds, ideologies, and cultures and that the principle of unity in diversity is the basis for a new age when war shall be outlawed and peace prevail; when the earth's total resources shall be equitably used for human welfare; and when basic human rights and responsibilities shall be shared by all without discrimination; Conscious of the inescapable reality that the greatest hope for survival of life on earth is the establishment of a democratic world government;

We, the citizens of the world, hereby resolve to establish a world federation to be governed in accordance with this Constitution, for the Federation of Earth.

The World Constitution goes on (in Article III, titled "Grant of Specific Powers to the World Government") to propose to: "Supervise disarmament and prevent re-armament; prohibit and eliminate the design, testing, manufacture, sale, purchase, use, and possession of weapons of mass destruction and all such weapons as the World Parliament may decide." Total gun control and disarmament of the American public is an essential part of this program.

Other sections call for regulating transportation, communications, and migration of people; regulation of supranational trade, industry, corporations, businesses, cartels, professional services, labor supply, finances, investments, and insurance (NAFTA is a big step in that direction). These programs will be funded by "raising the revenues and funds, by direct and/or indirect means" (i.e., heavy taxation) which are necessary for world government.

In addition, they plan to establish a world financial, banking, credit, and insurance institution designed to serve "human needs" — an establishment that would establish, issue, and regulate world currency, credit, and exchange.

Section 21 calls for the development of a means to control

population growth and to solve problems of population distribution. Sections 22 through 24 casually outline taking control of the world's land, oceans, and atmosphere.

Section 30 says: "Peace under world government will control essential natural resources which may be limited or unevenly distributed about the Earth. Find and implement ways to reduce wastes and to achieve distributive justice when development or production is insufficient to supply everybody with all that may be needed."

Section 35 would "develop a world university system. Obtain the correction of prejudicial communicative materials which cause misunderstandings or conflicts. . . ." (That means that conservative, traditionalist, constitutionalist publications will be shut down in order to stifle dissent and gain a 100 percent information monopoly for the New World Order.)

The World Constitution also calls for a World Police Force (now openly called the New World Army) "to handle intra-state violence or problems, should they occur." This world police force (which is already being formed at this writing) would cooperate with the National Police Force (also being assembled in the U.S. at this writing) to control or apprehend (i.e., neutralize) opponents of the new world government (i.e., the New World Order).

Global Population Control

The globalists believe that the world is dramatically overpopulated. The New Agers believe that the world's population should be reduced by at least 2 billion people. This is why we have Planned Parenthood and the U.S. (and world) abortion movement (which was started in the '60s by the globalist establishment), and this is why we have a growing movement toward euthanasia in America and around the globe. It could even be why we have an AIDS plague.

The World Constitution calls for global population control and so does the Clinton administration, which has been an enthusiastic supporter of abortion since it came into power. On January 11, 1994, the Clinton administration announced that the centerpiece of its "global affairs" agenda will be an effort to make family planning (i.e., abortion) available to every woman on earth. The Clinton administration proposed contributing $500 million in 1994 to world population control programs such as the United Nations Population Fund.

The Clinton State Department's top official on world population control, Tim Wirth, says the world's population will grow from 5.5 billion at present to 11 billion within 35 to 40 years — posing significant danger to the entire globe. Hence, Wirth said recently: "Our goal by the year 2000 in population is to provide comprehensive family planning to every woman in the world who wants it" (i.e., global abortion on demand, funded by the U.N., the U.S., and the new world government).

Controlling the American People

"When the righteous are in authority, the people rejoice: but when the wicked beareth rule, the people mourn" (Prov. 29:2).

The strategy of the Liberal Eastern Establishment regarding the American people is to control the people and to confiscate their wealth. This people-control agenda kicked into high gear during the second year of the Clinton administration.

The government is moving to control private property; nationalize the family; monitor and keep the public under surveillance from the cradle to the grave; replace old standards of merits with affirmative action and quotas; force banks to loan based on race instead of merit; tax and regulate business (especially America's 5.3 million small businesses) out of existence; license all U.S. gun owners as a prelude to total gun confiscation; control all aspects of the American medical system; put a condom in every child's pocket; and on and on, ad nauseam.

More than 2,500 laws were passed in 1993, to be implemented by 86,000 pages (in fine print) of new regulations in the Federal Register in 1993, at a cost to the American economy of more than $800 billion. Most of these laws and regulations carry criminal (as well as civil) penalties, including property seizure and forfeiture provisions.

The FDA is now talking about a total ban on smoking in America. This writer hates cigarette smoke and is allergic to same, but if the federal government can arbitrarily ban cigarette smoking today, then why not gun ownership tomorrow, political dissent the next day, etc.?

Ron Paul, in his *Survival Report,* describes the following situation as an example of federal controls on the people:

> Up to 30,000 home seamstresses operate illegally in the Dallas-Fort Worth area. Hundreds of thousands of similar workers do sewing in their homes nationwide. Since World War II, this wonderful form of work for mothers, the elderly, the disabled, etc., has been illegal thanks to labor union-induced laws. Recently the U.S.

Department of 'Justice' issued 35 injunctions against companies who use these home seamstresses. Criminals roam the streets, in BATF uniforms and otherwise, and the government is worried about women sewing at home.

Carroll Quigley, who is Bill Clinton's mentor, wrote these frightening words in *Tragedy and Hope:*

Our aim is nothing less than to create a world system of financial control in private hands, able to dominate the political system of each country and the world economy as a whole. Freedom and choice will be controlled within very narrow alternatives by the fact that every man will be numbered from birth, and followed as a number, through his educational training, his required military or other public service, his tax contributions, his health and medical requirements, and his final retirement and death benefits.[1]

Totalitarian societies are surveillance societies. To control people, a government must be able to watch people and know their every move. In a democratic society, the only way for Quigley's plans to be implemented is to create a sense of crisis so that citizens demand more surveillance. As a result, "crises," real or contrived, such as the "drug crisis," the "crime crisis," the "Social Security crisis," the "budget crisis," the "child abuse crisis," etc., become excuses for greater government interference in our lives.

The National ID Card

Congress is presently passing laws imposing mandatory surveillance over our financial transactions, monitoring firearms purchases, requiring registration of children at birth, increasing the power of the IRS, the EPA, the FDA, the ATF, of OSHA, etc.

The newest "crisis" is health care; so, in response, the Clinton administration introduced legislation (S 1757 and HR 3600) mandating that every American be issued a tamper-proof "Health Security Card" (HSC) through which medical data on each citizen can be collected, catalogued, and transmitted to a federal computer center. Failure to register for the card would be a criminal offense, punishable by jail, heavy fines, or both.

As Mark Nestmann wrote in a recent issue of *Low Profile:*

Clinton's plan doesn't call for HSC to be a "smart card" (capable of recording health care 'transactions' on its own), only a "dumb" card that only verifies the patient's identity when treatment occurs. But the HSC could still be involved in a federal plan to impose nearly continuous electronic surveillance over the population.

The centerpiece of Vice President Gore's "Report on Reinventing Government" is to establish a state-of-the-art nationwide electronic transmission network. Thus the "Information Highway" for which Gore has been seeking funding for more than a decade, his "Reinventing Government" idea, and the Health Security Card are part of the same plan. Their common denominator: linking government computers capable of collecting, transmitting, and analyzing massive amounts of personal and financial data.

In other words, the government will soon have access to total financial data (all computerized) on every American.

Bill and Hillary Clinton have consistently pushed for a National ID card. In the Clinton-Gore campaign book, they pushed for a national identification card (an internal passport) to be forced on every American. They pushed for a "smart card" that could encode and computerize not only our entire medical histories, but virtually all government records on individuals. Because of flack about this aspect of the ID card, its proponents have agreed to settle for a "dumb card," as a phase 1, before progressing to a "smart card" after the public becomes accustomed to the concept.

Government Technology, a publication for state and local government in the information age, published an article, titled "Health Card: A Technological Tattoo," in December 1993. The article described the card as "an ingenious device for keeping track of the personal lives of Americans" and "designed to keep permanent, accessible records of all aspects of your health care, including the details of every doctor visit, every drug store prescription, and every hospital treatment."

Other potential uses for the card outlined by the article included cracking down on welfare fraud, tracking down deadbeat dads, supplanting Social Security cards and passports, and controlling voter fraud. Since the card "will become so ubiquitous, so necessary in order to comply with government regulation . . . we will be obliged to carry it with us at all times."

The article goes on to suggest that since carrying the card with one at all times might be inconvenient, a "tiny microchip the size of a grain of rice" and containing identification data might be implanted in the skin. The data could be accessed and digitally displayed when the microchip passed over a scanner.

"True, an implanted transponder can't yet hold anywhere near as much material as a smart card. But if the desire is there, larger size implants and tiny microchips could soon increase its data storage capacity." (Full details of these devices are outlined in the March 1994 issue of the *McAlvany Intelligence Advisor*.)

The purpose of the Clinton National ID card is not convenience (although it will be sold under that pretense). The purpose is enforcement of the government's will over the people.

When the "smart card" is finally employed, its computer chip will hold at least 60 pages of data per person, to be updated at will. These pages will be full of highlights of each citizen's entire federal dossier, including tax, employment, medical, marital, child, passport, and other records.

Ira Magaziner, head of Hillary Clinton's health and ID task force, suggests imposing one of these cards on every American at birth.

Keeping Track of You, Your Money, and Your Children

The methods by which the government is watching us are multiplying rapidly. Virtually all forms of electronic communications are now, or will soon be, monitored (i.e., telephone calls, cellular phone calls, faxes, computer communications, voice mail, e-mail) and can be recorded by government eavesdroppers for use against an individual. One should never assume that such communications are private and should not use such means for communicating "sensitive" information.

Trucks are now being monitored under a new high-tech system recently installed in British Columbia, Washington, Oregon, California, Arizona, New Mexico, and Texas. With the help of a white box called a transponder mounted on a truck's bumper and a square plate buried in the road, a computer instantly calculates the speed, weight, and length of a truck cruising at highway speeds. Taxes for highway use can be electronically assessed, speeding tickets electronically levied, and the whereabouts of any truck determined at any time.

A centralized computer could instantly determine the truck's cargo, the driver's identity, and whether the truck has the proper permits to operate in the state. In addition to automated tax collections, the system will be used to determine the hours a truck has been driving each day, the hours a truck has been in service, and its location.

This technology will soon be installed all over America and applied to passenger cars, giving local, state, and federal authorities the ability to monitor the movement and location of any automobile in the country. The system will be in place around the country for cars, trucks, buses, etc. by the end of the decade.

In Dal-Worth, Texas (a high drug-usage neighborhood in the Grand Prairie/Dallas/Fort Worth metroplex), the police have begun to monitor all cars driving through the town via hidden cameras, and to notify businesses and individuals with vehicles that drove through by letter that their vehicle was seen driving in Dal-Worth.

Lawrence, Massachusetts (a city of 70,000 about 28 miles north of Boston), has been combating drug crimes by photographing motorists and sending letters to them telling them that they are being watched, as well as by setting up barricades and check points for auto searches. Citizens in these and other communities say that these techniques are reducing drug trafficking, but at what price in privacy, civil liberties, and in freedom from unwarranted searches and seizure?

The government has begun to monitor all wire transfers of funds domestically and internationally as of January 1, 1994. Banks must now keep detailed information on all senders and receivers of bank-wired funds, and that information must be transmitted with the wire. Withdrawals from automatic tellers and fund transfers requested by telephone, telex, fax, or payable by credit card are also covered. Nearly $1 trillion is wired daily in the U.S. or across its borders. Tracking it will require massive investments by both financial institutions and the government.

In Washington's Sea-tax Airport, DEA agents have begun to walk up randomly to travelers and question them about who they are, their travel plans, where they have been, whether they are carrying cash and how much, etc. The technique is called "dragnetting." A Seattle federal prosecutor defended the practice, saying: "If you're in a public place, you don't have any expectation of privacy . . . there is nothing wrong with a police officer following someone. . . . You don't need probable cause to follow someone."

Any American who has traveled internationally in recent years has probably been subjected to government sniffer dogs as the traveler comes through U.S. customs to claim his bags. The dogs, trained to sniff out drugs (and probably cash if it has any drug residue on it — and most cash now does) sniff hand luggage and checked bags. God help us if the dog wags his tail or barks — we're in deep trouble. Many U.S. travelers now hold their breath in fear that the dog (or its government handler) may be having a bad day.

Forced government inoculations of all children is another back-door method of computerized surveillance and people-tracking. The "Comprehensive Child Immunization Act" was introduced (but not passed) in 1993 by Senators Ted Kennedy (D-MA) and Don Reigle (D-MI) and in the House by Congressman Henry Waxman (D-CA). This Act called for the government computerization of all children from a day-old baby up through the teens and the government tracking of these children (and their parents) to "make sure their parents comply."

Refusal to have one's child computerized or inoculated would result in jail sentences for parents (as in criminal child abuse), heavy fines, or loss of custody of children to government social services. Pushed hard by Hillary Clinton, this horrific legislation did not pass in 1993, but is likely to be reintroduced in the very near future.

Toward a National Police Force

Much evidence suggests that a national police force is being contemplated by the current administration. It is thought that the super-police agency will consist of the Drug Enforcement Agency; the Federal Bureau of Investigation; the Bureau of Alcohol, Tobacco, and Firearms; the Customs Service; and the criminal divisions of the Post Office and the Internal Revenue Service; and will be called the Directorate of Central Law Enforcement.

The new head of the national police (which many fear would be the American equivalent of the KGB or the Nazi Gestapo) would be the U.S. Attorney General. Apparently, the DCLE would also have a White House supervisory council appointed by the president, which would insure a politicized institution that would go after the government's political enemies first.

Reportedly, also being recruited into the National Police Force (the DCLE) are ex-Navy Seals, Force Recon, Rangers, Green Berets, and (incredibly) Royal Hong Kong police officers. Are these person-nel for fighting street crime, gang warfare, and drug dealers? Or are they to be used for attacking dissidents, constitutionalists, gun own-ers, and patriots who oppose the sovietization of America, and to be utilized for house-to-house searches for unregistered firearms?

Why are Royal Hong Kong police officers being recruited for the new National Police Force? Are any of them agents from Red China?

The February 1994 issue of *Modern Gun* included a report that the commanders of the U.S. Navy Seal Team Six handed out a questionnaire to his Navy Seals in September 1993 that asked, "Would you fire on U.S. citizens while in the process of confiscating their guns?"

My newsletter, the *McAlvany Intelligence Advisory* (MIA), keeps receiving unconfirmed but very disturbing reports that the National Guard, National Police, and military are being aggressively trained for house-to-house searches and area sweeps for firearms.

The new National Police Force is being brought directly into local law enforcement. In Washington, DC it was announced last July by Janet Reno that a "mega force slated to fight crime in DC" had been formed, made up of the Washington local police, the FBI, the DEA, the BATF, and the U.S. Marshals Service. This experiment with an anti-crime, local/federal police force is expected to become a model for other cities, and represents a quantum leap forward in the federal government's takeover of local law enforcement. The Clintonistas National Police Force is planning to coop and take over our local police.

In early July, claiming it was tackling America's number one problem, crime, the Clinton administration proposed a 24 percent increase in the Justice Department's fiscal 1995 budget — to more than $13 billion. The increase would be for hiring more local and national police, restricting handgun sales, and tightening U.S. borders — $1.7 billion would be for grants to state and local governments for 50,000 new police and for expanding federal control over local police departments; $6 billion would be provided for '96-'99 for Bill Clinton's 100,000-man National Police Force; $100 million to help states implement the Brady Law; $450 million to expand prison facilities for an additional 10,000 prisoners; etc.

The White House Office of National Drug Control Policy is also to receive $13.2 billion (a 9 percent increase) for the drug war — much of it to be used for "fighting crime."

Although I am very much for legitimate crime control efforts against real criminals, it is clear that much of this $26.2 billion for the "war on crime" will be used in harassment and seizures against honest, law-abiding citizens, in gun control efforts, in money laundering [i.e., anti-cash/anti-privacy] cases, etc. Is the $26.2 billion really to fight crime, or is it to advance the police state?

The CIA and the Black Helicopters

Every CIA director since its inception during World War II has been a Council on Foreign Relations member. Since the so-called end of the Cold War, however, the "spy agency without a mission" has been getting deeply involved in domestic affairs, politics, and business in the U.S. — serving as a police arm of corporate America.

Worth magazine reports that the CIA played a decisive role in lobbying Congress for passage of NAFTA.

Before Congress adjourned in November 1993, it voted an estimated $28 billion in secret funding for one year (the real number may be higher) for the CIA. No one in the Congress has any idea how those funds are spent, but it is a great deal of money with which to do a huge amount of good or evil.

It appears that in the post-Cold War era the CIA will do more and more domestic industrial spying, industrial espionage, and surveillance of the American people. This writer is not alone in believing that the CIA is the private army (though publicly funded) and enforcement arm of the Liberal Eastern Establishment and New World Order crowd.

Unmarked black helicopters (painted with flat black paint) continue to fly over cities, towns, and rural areas all over America. Ex-military personnel who have seen these choppers are puzzled by the lack of markings or identification numbers on these planes.

Low-level flights over neighborhoods, homes, and businesses (often hovering for minutes at a time over one location) are common. Some are seen to be photographing buildings or people below; some are seen to be armed. Most inquiries are met with official denial of their existence.

It is believed that these helicopters are part of the Multi-Jurisdictional Task Force, but the air force has said that they are part of the Special Operations Command conducting routine night navigation, aerial, and urban training. But that does not explain the thousands of daytime occurrences around the country, the low-level photographing and surveillance, or the lack of legally required markings.

It is rumored that some of these flights are U.N. training missions and that they could be part of some future state of emergency, martial law, or house-to-house roundup of firearms. These are unconfirmed reports, but the fact is that the ominous flights of the black helicopters still continue. Why???

House Raids by Militant Police

American freedoms are being devoured rapidly by bureaucracies and by militant police authority.

Paul Craig Roberts, in the following excerpted editorial, titled "A Police State or A Nation of Laws," which appeared in the *Washington Times,* August 31, 1993, points out why all Americans should be concerned:

> What will become of "law and order conservatism" now that we know our law enforcement agencies from the Justice Department to local police forces can be as criminal as the miscreants they are supposed to pursue? Unspeakable acts of cold-blooded murder and fabricated evidence now routinely characterize everyday acts of law enforcement.

Roberts described the 1992 murder of Donald Scott, a Malibu, California, millionaire by a 30-man raiding party composed of Los Angeles County sheriff's deputies, federal drug agents, and the California National Guard. Federal agents, who had targeted Scott's $5 million, 200-acre ranch for seizure under federal drug forfeiture laws, had with them a property appraisal of Scott's ranch along with notes on the sale price of nearby property.

Roberts wrote:

> In pre-democratic times, this behavior was known as "tax farming." Government officials simply seized whatever they could, and raked off a commission. Today the commission is in the form of the bureaucracy's budget. Ever since President Reagan's budget director David Stockman invented "budget savings" from tougher IRS and drug enforcement, the pressure has been on these marauders to farm more revenues. The result is mounting abuse of citizens (now subjects) and occasional deaths.
>
> . . . shades of Waco, Texas, where the FBI and Alcohol, Tobacco and Firearms folks killed nearly 100 men, women, and children, while the attorney general, looking on, took all the credit to show how tough she is. Her message did get out: "Don't mess with us, or we'll kill you, too."

According to the Associated Press, on 7/22/93, noted defense attorney Gerry Spence told the Montana Trial Lawyers Association that he had never been involved in a case with the federal government in which it had not told lies and manufactured evidence in order to get a conviction. "These are not the good guys," he said of federal agents and prosecutors. "These are people who do whatever is necessary to do to bring about a conviction. The law gets hung with the victim."

Nothing makes it clearer that we are no longer "a nation of laws" than federal wetlands regulations. These "laws" have no statutory basis and have been created entirely by bureaucrats and courts. All over the United States people are finding their use of their property circumvented and themselves in jail because the regulatory police decided to apply a law that they themselves invented.

Consider the following violations of our quickly disappearing individual liberties.

More than 60 homes in Tulare County, California were raided without search warrants in 1993, looking for suspected illegal immigrants. Police said if they had obtained warrants, the suspected illegal immigrants would have escaped. One woman died during the raids when Border Patrol agents burst into her house without a warrant.

Fifty California residents have filed suit against the Immigration and Naturalization Service, charging unlawful and unconstitutional raids on private homes.

Is America a Police State?

Billy Kelly, a Chicago conservative activist, attended Bill Clinton's "Town Hall Meeting" on July 26, 1993. He asked Clinton from the floor, during the question and answer session, why the president insisted upon blaming Republicans for "gridlock" on his proposed tax hikes when he clearly had a Democratic majority in both houses of Congress.

Clinton didn't like the "unfriendly question" and had the Secret Service agents arrest Kelly at his home later that evening and charge Kelly with "willfully and knowingly entering and remaining in a cordoned off and restricted area of a building where the president of the U.S. was temporarily visiting." Kelly, who had no previous police record, was kept for two days in a holding pen secured with leg shackles and handcuffs. A federal indictment is asking for a six-month prison term.

On October 9, 1993, 15 armed agents from the Department of Agriculture and four Highway Patrol troopers, wearing bullet-proof vests and with guns drawn, entered the Circle Land and Cattle Company, held the three employees present at gunpoint, and seized most of the company's business and accounting records. A week after the raid, the government agents still refused to say what they were looking for or why they conducted the raid.

The puzzled owner of the business, which of course could not function without its records, said, "It was federal agents. Gestapo agents with their bullet-proof vests and their guns. . . . I have no idea who or what they're looking for. . . . It's Germany, 1939, with its SS troops."

A resolution has been passed by the council of Kansas City, Missouri, expressing its "strong desire that the chief of police and city attorney explore the feasibility of conducting weapons checkpoints in order to curb the violence associated with access to illegal weapons." This resolution was unanimously passed by the council with the mayor casting the only vote against it. A companion resolution calling for "an aggressive anti-violence and illegal gun sales and confiscation plan" was also passed.

In fiscal 1993, the IRS paid out $5.3 million (up from $1.7 million the year before) to 829 people who turned in fellow Americans for alleged underpayment of taxes. Since the late '60s, according to the *Wall Street Journal*, January 12, 1994, the IRS has had 177,298 snitches turn in fellow taxpayers and has paid out rewards 8.4 percent of the time.

The various agencies of the government are paying out far more in finders fees for people who turn in others for alleged violation of some rule or regulation that results in a property seizure. Between 10 and 25 percent is paid out to informants for successful seizure/forfeitures. There are many definitions of tyranny, but one is a government that pays its citizens to turn in friends and neighbors for money.

A police state could be described as a nation in which the police wear federal uniforms and confiscate the people's guns; where the government levies confiscatory taxes; where the government keeps its citizens under surveillance and prosecutes the politically incorrect; where the government usurps parental authority and steals the children and/or their minds; where the government raids church schools for being unregulated or unlicensed and jails their leaders; where the government jails landowners for improving their property and seizes that property; where the government destroys businesses for violations of pathetic ridiculous bureaucratic regulations; where the government burns and kills whole communities for simply trying to live in peace and worship God as they see fit; and where the government shoots the wives and children of political dissenters.

Does this describe Russia in the 1920s, Nazi Germany in the 1930s, Red China in the 1950s, Cuba in the 1960s, or America in the 1990s? All of the above were and still are (except for Nazi Germany) socialist police states and treat their subjects essentially the same.

Think about it!

No More Trackless Cash

Whoever controls the financial system of a city, state, country, or the world is likely to control that entire sphere of influence. There is a reason why banks and insurance companies usually have the largest buildings in town. To control the world, as the globalists believe they will over the next five to 10 years, they believe they must control wealth, the movement of funds, and ultimately consolidate the world into one large monolithic financial system which they control.

This financial control is done through central banks (including the Federal Reserve) which they control, through the IMF, the World Bank, the Bank for International Settlements, and their ability to manipulate markets, currencies, and economies via interest rates.

A key element of the globalists' plans for a world financial dictatorship is a one-world central bank, a one-world currency, all leading, they believe, to a cashless society where all financial transactions down to parking meters, pay phones, newspaper purchases, grocery, and other staple purchases will go through the computerized banking and credit card system.

If you have ever been turned down for a transaction using a credit card, especially if you had no cash on you, you know what a helpless feeling that is. If the elitists are able to install their credit, debit, or smart card system for most (or all) financial transactions over the next three to seven years, we will all be at their mercy for buying and selling. The "politically incorrect" may well have their financial plug pulled at some point.

Formed in 1990, the Financial Crimes Enforcement Network (FinCEN) is a huge, highly sophisticated computer system housed in the Treasury that compiles financial profiles on all American citizens, using data from all available sources (i.e., tax returns, gun registration forms, credit card records, banking records, credit bureaus, school records, military records, speeding records, criminal records, marriage license records, passport records, etc.).

With a staff of 200, FinCEN is among the most secretive agencies in Washington and is the most ambitious data collection operation ever assembled by a western government. Only federal law enforcement officials are allowed entry. It is guarded by one of the nation's most sophisticated security systems.

FinCEN provides detailed citizen profiles to the ATF, FBI, DEA, FDA, EPA, U.S. Marshals, CIA, IRS, and the various federal agencies, which will make up the National Police Force. It represents the world's most sophisticated spying arm and surveillance of a populace.

From FinCEN data, a sophisticated psychological profile of every adult American and every family in America can be generated for various federal agencies. In fiscal 1993, FinCEN received 4,100 requests from 154 federal, state, local and foreign agencies for data in identifying, investigating, and prosecuting alleged money launderers. Most of its information requests are related to cash reporting.

Many laws, domestically and internationally, have been passed over the past decade greatly restricting the use of cash, the movement of cash, and the ownership of cash. Cash is trackless and therefore anathema to the globalist planners. You cannot control what you cannot see. Hence, we have seen a plethora of cash/privacy-controlling money laundering/structuring laws instituted all over the world over the past 10 years (mostly at the instigation of the U.S. government and the establishment/globalists) in an effort to dry up the free flow of cash.

The Catch in the Clinton's Crime Package

Americans (especially conservatives) are fed up with violent crimes and lenient sentences by liberal judges. As a result, they are demanding a major crackdown on crime and criminals in America. What they don't understand is that millions of honest, law-abiding citizens are now being reclassified by tens of thousands of new laws, rules, and regulations as criminals by our socialist masters.

They do not understand that, in my opinion, the new Clinton crime control package is not really about fighting crime or real criminals at all. I believe it is about controlling the people. It is about the Feds taking over local and state law enforcement. It is about disarming honest, law-abiding citizens via Draconian gun control measures. It is about establishing a socialist police state in America. And it is about stifling dissent and resistance to the socialist police state that is presently being installed.

When the leftist bureaucrats and regulators get through interpreting and writing regulations to implement the package, I'm sure that it will be three times worse than what was passed by Congress. It will centralize all U.S. law enforcement in the hands of the federal government and especially in the hands of the new National Police Force.

In the end, the new crime package will be used to lock the chains on the American people in the emerging new United Soviet States of America. Every tyrannical regime in world history has marshaled a centralized police force to control the citizenry and prevent any political dissent. That, I believe, is the real design of the Clintonistas.

The War on Private Property

One denominator common among communists and socialists all over the world is that they hate private property and believe the state should own (or control) all private property "for the good of the people." The actions of the U.S. government against private property and its owners over the past decade or so have been just as confiscatory, just as Draconian, just as totalitarian as in any Communist country.

Legal rights and protections that Americans have cherished for hundreds of years have been increasingly violated during the past two decades. Most of what we learned in school about our legal rights and protections is no longer true. A combination of rising crime, the growing power of government, and increasing concern about drugs has done tremendous damage to the Bill of Rights and our heritage of liberty.

Few Americans realize how grave and how ominous that damage has been. Today the government has the power legally to seize our bank accounts, our houses, or our businesses — without trial, hearing, or indictment. Everything we have worked for and accumulated over a lifetime can now be taken away from us at the whim of authorities.

Black or white, rich or poor, we are all potential victims. And unless the laws are changed, there is very little we can legally do to protect our property.

Tom Geary, president of the Idaho Farm Bureau Federation,

wrote in the *Idaho Farm Bureau News*, January 1994:

> All across the United States, good people have gone to jail or been fined enormous amounts of money because they worked their own land, and some bureaucrat found a way to make a case against these individuals under the auspices of the Clean Water Act or the Endangered Species Act.
>
> Under the burden of these laws, some homeowners have had the lives of their families threatened by fire because they were not allowed to disturb the soil to cut a firebreak around their property.
>
> Under the burden of these laws, even the agencies in charge cannot agree as to the best way to proceed. For example, if both the bald eagle and the salmon are considered endangered or threatened, how do you protect both at the same time? You cannot prevent the eagle from eating the salmon without threatening the eagle's existence. And you cannot permit the eagle to eat the salmon without endangering the lives of salmon.
>
> Meanwhile, as the government agencies are trying to figure out the best way to be the Grand Protector of Every Living Thing, people have been left out of the equation. In the government's zeal to protect all life, entire cities are threatened with having their water supply substantially shut down, as is happening right now in San Antonio, Texas, where a federal judge ruled that the water supply to 1.4 million people could be slashed as much as 65 percent in periods of drought. This is to protect the wild rice plant, fountain darter, San Marcos salamander and the San Marcos gambusia, four species that rely on the same aquifer as the city of San Antonio.
>
> Using similar logic, the government shuts down logging operations to protect a supposedly 'endangered' owl, only to find out a few years later that the owl isn't endangered at all. Then they go after protection of snails, using flawed scientific research to justify shutting down the water supply to farmers and ranchers in Idaho.
>
> And it's the same story all across the nation. It isn't really a War on the West, so much as it is a War on Private Property Rights, using Wetlands and the Endangered

Species Act as weapons. It's a war on the rights of people to exist and to work and to progress.

Don't Mess With the DEA or the FDA!

Jarret Wolstein recently described in the *Freeman* the following examples of Big Brother's socialist police state attitude against Americans and their property rights.

Thirty-year-old Ken Brown owned and operated Chemco, a small pool and gardening chemical supply company in Albuquerque, New Mexico. A few months after he opened his doors in 1986, agents of the Drug Enforcement Administration (DEA) stopped by and told him to "get out of the chemical business." A year later Ken found out why. His chief competitor in Albuquerque had an arrangement with the DEA, and neither the DEA nor the competitor wanted any competition.

When Ken refused to close his doors in 1987, harassment from the DEA began and got steadily worse. First his UPS packages were opened and inspected. Then his deliveries were seized, his drivers were searched, and his suppliers were threatened. Next his house was searched by armed DEA agents. They found nothing.

On November 19, 1991, the DEA arrested his manager and padlocked the doors to Chemco. The IRS was also brought in to investigate the company. The DEA charged Chemco with selling chemicals that could be used to manufacture drugs. On May 8, 1992, the DEA seized Ken Brown's house and cars, and told him to sign an agreement to pay rent to the U.S. Marshals or "hit the street with my wife and eight-year-old son." In May 1992 the DEA made Ken Brown an offer : "Give us Chemco and we will give you all your personal belongings back." Ken Brown refused and is still fighting.

Dr. Jonathan Wright operated the Takoma Medical Clinic in Kent, Washington. On May 6, 1992, nearly two dozen armed police and Food and Drug Administration (FDA) agents broke down his clinic's door and pointed their weapons at him and his 15-person staff. For the next 14 hours, the staff was held at gunpoint while the FDA ransacked the clinic. Neither Dr. Wright nor any of his employees was ever charged with a crime. That didn't stop the police and FDA from seizing Dr. Wright's books, laboratory equipment, supplies, patient records, reference books, and computers. The raid was part of a national FDA crackdown on nutritional therapists.

Such blatant acts by these agencies contradict every right we have as American citizens, as Supreme Court Justice Sutherland wrote:

> Life, liberty, prosperity. These three rights are so bound together as to be essentially one right. To give a man his life, but to deny him his liberty is to take from him all that makes life worth living. To give him his liberty, but to take from him the prosperity, which is the fruit and badge of his liberty, is still to leave him a slave. The next step in the logical chain (after life, liberty, prosperity) is privacy — the right to be unmolested, left alone. Without this right, each of the other three is compromised and vulnerable to destruction by an omnipotent state.

All of these rights — life, liberty, prosperity, and privacy — are now threatened in the United States — by our own government.

Environmental Landgrabbers

Jack Ward Thomas, the new head of the U.S. Forest Service, said it is his intention to make protection of the environment a priority; but he will succeed only if that includes public and private land. He said in the *Wall Street Journal* (12/17/93): "I don't mean to imply that we seek any regulatory authority over private land, but there are mechanisms."

In 1993, Bill Clinton and his Interior Secretary Bruce Babbitt teamed up with Merchant Marine Committee Chairman Gerry Studds (D-MA) and House Natural Resources Chairman George Miller (D-CA) to push one of the greatest attacks ever on private property — the National Biological Survey (NBS).

The Clinton-backed HR 1845, if passed by both houses of Congress, would direct federal bureaucrats to "inventory" all privately owned property in America for the purpose of cataloging the nation's "biological resources" and to determine if properties are in keeping with a correctly managed "eco-system." In other words, passage of this bill would entitle federal bureaucrats to enter private property, inspect it for environmental "compliance," and arbitrarily restrict its use, or even seize it.

Draconian controls on land use and development will follow.

I believe the National Biological Survey legislation is in reality a socialist scheme to destroy private property rights forever. Proponents said that it would simply authorize a survey of all plant and animal species in the U.S. — much like the 10-year government census of people.

Right? No, wrong!

The bill will create an agency dedicated to property confiscation. The Clintonistas want a legislative mandate to move forward with the national land inventory and already have 1994 appropriations giving them $163 million to get started.

Proponents of NBS want the Interior Department to recruit volunteers from the environmental movement to conduct the survey. This would enable radical environmentalists, acting under the federal authority of the Interior Department, to march onto private property to interrogate citizens and find potential environmental crimes.

As Rep. Studds, the openly avowed homosexual from Massachusetts, says, "NBS catalogs everything that walks, crawls, or flies around the U.S."

A major goal of the Clinton administration has apparently been to create a federal data base to monitor the use of private property in the U.S., and to set up a "hit list" of privately-owned land to be seized by the government. A national map will be created that details animal and plant life down to every last bug and weed.

Every U.S. landowner would become a potential environmental criminal, subject to having his property seized for some manufactured environmental infraction. With the map in hand, the government will have a ready-made excuse to veto any economic development it opposes.

If a farmer wants to plant a few more acres, he may find bureaucrats opposing him based on NBS. The same will be true for house builders or developers. Property values are likely to plunge where NBS is being implemented.

The true intent of Studds, Babbitt, and the Clintonistas was made clear when they fought tooth and nail against two amendments. One amendment would have required survey workers to get written permission from landowners before entering their private property.

The second amendment would have given property owners the right to review the results of government property surveys and to contest their accuracy.

The people anointed to carry out the leftist agenda and hundreds like them are not just environmentalist, hug-a-tree freaks. They are dedicated socialists — they want to control the American people and their use of both public and private lands, and they want to ultimately abolish all private property in America.

Many of them, such as Gore, Babbitt, Rivlin, Browner, etc., are (or were) also members of the globalist Council on Foreign Relations and/or Trilateral Commission, which are implementing a strategy to push America into a socialist police state and into the New World Order. Radical socialism, in the guise of environmentalism, is to be one of their primary vehicles for accomplishing these goals.

Disarming Honest Americans

The socialists and the New World Order crowd must disarm the American people before they can subject them to total control, as in the former Soviet bloc countries, Red China, Nazi Germany, etc.

The socialists may have bitten off more than they can chew in moving to register American gun owners and their weapons, and confiscate those firearms. An estimated 75 million American households own an estimated 200 million firearms. The great majority of those Americans have those firearms not just for hunting, but for self-defense for themselves and their families — at a time when the domestic crime rate is the highest in the world and the highest in U.S. history, and family protection is essential.

Most of those gun owners (this writer would guesstimate 75 percent or more) will not license themselves, will not register those firearms, nor will they turn them in. The American people may be apathetic and complacent; they may be fat, dumb, and happy after almost 50 years of uninterrupted prosperity since the end of the great war. They may be ignorant of the devices and strategies of the socialists and New World Order types, but they are not total pussycats, either (they have the reputation of being the most violent people in the world). When the sleeping giant, which is the American people, is aroused, it is an awesome thing to behold — as the Japanese found when they bombed us at Pearl Harbor.

If the Clintonistas go too far, too quickly, with their gun grab, they could provoke the biggest government/public confrontation since the Civil War. Perhaps that is why they are rapidly recruiting a

National Police Force; are training U.N. troops on U.S. soil; are training National Guardsmen for house-to-house searches for firearms; are flying black unmarked surveillance helicopters everywhere; and are building huge federal detention centers by the dozens.

Perhaps they expect major political/social upheaval when they go for the guns and are preparing for same.

The Brady Bill

The American public will not simply roll over and play dead for the Clintonista socialists and their "comrades," or bark and wag their tails on command like Pavlov's dogs. How do we know? Because in the 90 days after the Brady bill passed, there was the greatest stampede to buy firearms, magazines, and ammunition in U.S. history. Amazing!

Millions of people did not stampede to register their firearms or turn them in — they stampeded to buy more before the February 28 launch date for Brady. That says a lot about the mindset of the American people, versus what we are told in the polls and the press (i.e., how the majority are against firearms ownership). It is not a mindset of surrender, at least not for a certain large segment of the public.

On February 28, the day that the Brady Bill became effective, Jim Brady announced the unveiling of Brady II, which is essentially the mandated federal licensing of all gun owners. This has long been a goal of the political left; of Handgun Control, Inc., and of the Clintonistas.

Licensing would computerize every gun owner in America; and it would make mass confiscation an easy matter. It would also make it easy to revoke licenses, deny them, etc. Part of the licensing process will probably involve the listing of all the firearms, magazines, and ammunition that we can own.

The argument for licensing gun owners is "If you license car owners, then why not gun owners?" The answer is that the government doesn't plan to confiscate cars (at least not yet), but it does plan to confiscate firearms as soon as they are registered or their owners are pinpointed via licensing.

Part of Brady II will also be the licensing of "arsenals" — defined as 10 to 20 weapons owned in one household, the higher or lower number depending on which version of the legislation might pass, and/or 1,000 rounds of ammunition.

The establishment media has started massive propaganda, calling for the licensing of all gun owners.

USA Today editorialized on January 3, 1994 that "licensing motorists makes us safer. This is indisputable. Licensing firearms users also will make us safer. . . . Indeed, aside from the usual off-planet carps about government intrusion and mythical gun rights, responsible lawmakers should find no fault in this idea. Licensing is easy, effective, and inexpensive. . . . As for motorists, so for shooters. States could easily create Departments of Firearms to administer gun safety and operational exams. This would surely help staunch the number of accidental gun deaths pegged at 1,441 in 1991." However, there are 50,000 auto deaths per year, in spite of licensing.

The Five-Year Gun Control Plan

A "secret internal document" from Handgun Control, Inc. has recently surfaced, which appears to be genuine. It details a five-year plan to disarm the American people and which is probably parallel to, if not identical to, the government/ATF plan to do the same.

Included are the following items:

1) The banning of all semi-autos and magazines which can hold more than six rounds. (That includes virtually all semi-automatic pistols and rifles.)

2) The banning of all parts for firearms.

3) Banning of all pump shotguns that could potentially hold five or more rounds (that includes almost all pump shotguns).

4) Banning all machine guns, destructive devices, short shotguns, rifles, assault weapons (i.e., semi-automatics), Saturday night specials, and non-sporting ammunition.

5) Licensing of all arsenals (described above) with an annual fee paid to the government of $300 to $1,000 for possessing same, and reduction of the number of guns to qualify as an arsenal to just a few.

6) Banning all arsenal licensing in counties with more than 200,000 people.

7) Abolition of the Department of Civil Marksmanship, which has trained American shooters since before World War I.

8) Banning ownership of all firearms within 1,000 feet of a school.

9) Banning all toy guns.

10) Providing for gunshot victims to sue gun manufacturers and dealers.

11) Placing Draconian fees and taxes on guns, ammo, and dealers' licenses (up to 1,000 times such present fees).

12) Licensing all rifles and shotguns.

13) Requiring state and federal licensing for any firearms.

14) Requiring federally approved storage safes for the mandatory storage of all firearms, and the federal registration of all such safes and firearms contained therein and periodic government inspections of the safes.

15) Banning all types of hunting ammunition, any type of expanding bullet, possession of gun powder and reloading components.

(16) Requiring national registration of all ammunition and ammo buyers.

(17) Eliminating most gun ranges, licensing those which remain, restricting their access in communities of a certain size, imposing heavy range taxes, and establishing waiting periods for pistol and rifle rental at firing ranges.

(18) Eliminating all hunting on public lands.

(19) Banning more than four armed individuals being in a group at one time (except for military and police).

(20) Making gun owner records and photos part of the public record.

(21) Setting up random police checks of homes and cars for weapons.

Obviously, all the elements of this five-year plan to disarm the American public cannot be implemented at one time, but HCI/government gun grabbers plan to implement most of these elements on a piecemeal basis during the next five years.

Why They Want Our Guns

The biggest obstacle to the socialists and New World Order crowd imposing a socialist police state on America is the possession of more than 200 million firearms in the hands of 75 million Americans. The American people must be disarmed. It has nothing to do with crime or accidental shootings. Disarming honest, law-abiding citizens (but of course not the criminals) will increase crime, not reduce it — and the government knows that.

Washington, Jefferson, Madison, Adams, Patrick Henry, and our other founding fathers knew that the government will have a very difficult time subjecting the American people to slavery or tyranny as long as citizens are well armed.

It should be apparent to any thinking American that our country and our Constitution are in deep trouble. The socialists and the New World Order crowd, though they represent only a small minority of our population (i.e., far less than 1 percent, and with support from liberals of probably another 5 percent) control the levers of power in America: the government, the judiciary, the media, the educational system, and the police and military.

This is another parallel to Nazi Germany in the 1930s, where the Nazis only had solid support from about 5 percent of the populace but manipulated and coerced the rest into following them.

The socialists in America (like a runaway horse) have the bit in their mouth and are trying to stampede America toward a socialist police state. Their ultimate goal, over the next five to seven years, is to push for a world government.

They have become very bold, brazen, and arrogant about their plans to subjugate Americans to their will; to control every aspect of our lives; to keep us under 24-hour lifetime surveillance via high-tech, a National ID card, etc. They want to regulate and control us via a National Police Force and cashless, computerized financial dictatorship; to seize and forfeit our property in flagrant disregard of the U.S. Constitution and all of our traditional values. They plan to disarm the American people prior to taking down the Constitution and subjugating us to the New World Order.

Get Mad and Get Mobilized

The British politician Edmund Burke said, "All that is necessary for evil to triumph is that good men do nothing." In America, the great majority of good men and women (including Christians) have been doing nothing for 30 or 40 years, as the socialists and destroyers of our Constitution and traditional way of life have marched into power almost unopposed.

Opposition to the socialists will not come from the top down — it will come from the bottom up — from the grassroots. With the power of that great silent majority, who outnumber the socialists about 50 to 1, Americans could flex their collective political muscle and send the socialists packing.

Fortunately, a potentially potent remnant of several million people is beginning to stir and wake up — and just in time!

The socialists are pushing an incredibly awful education bill, HR-6, which represents a near total government takeover of all public education (and an attempt to take over private education as well). The government will impose a national educational curriculum that will eliminate virtually all local and state curriculum, traditional values, and traditional history teaching materials, etc. This new curriculum is designed to program all children by the year 2000 for a socialist America, a New World Order, and world class intellectual mediocrity.

Recently, the socialists quietly sneaked language into HR-6 that would have effectively eliminated all home schooling and most private Christian schools within three to four years.

All home school teachers and private school teachers would have had to become fully certified by the state in all subjects taught (a virtual impossibility) or cease and desist from teaching. They would have also been brought under government control and forced to teach government-approved curriculum. Had this passed, almost 1 million home-schooled children and in excess of a million private-schooled children would have been forced back into the government schools.

Mike Farris and the people at the Virginia-based Home School Legal Defense Association picked up on the socialist subterfuge in mid-February 1994, and put out an urgent red alert to home schoolers, private schools, conservative and Christian radio talk shows, and other conservative and Christian political action groups around America.

Almost instantly, congressional switchboards in Washington and home district offices began to light up. Hundreds of thousands of calls, faxes, mailgrams, and letters began to pour into congressional offices in the greatest outpouring of protest and wrath in a three-or-four-day period that the Congress has ever seen.

James Dobson, aided by Gary Bauer of the Family Research Council, Marlin Maddoux, Rush Limbaugh, and hundreds of other radio talk show hosts grabbed their microphones and stirred up the greatest firestorm of protest in modern congressional history — and in an election year, hundreds of congressmen froze in their tracks.

Republican Congressman Dick Armey of Texas, a great patriot and statesman, had submitted an amendment to exclude home schooling and private schools, but Congress voted this down on party lines (the Democrats against and the Republicans for) — before the "great protest" broke out.

But on February 24, votes were again taken on two amendments that excluded home and private schooling form HR-6, an amendment by William D. Ford (D-MI) and one by Dick Armey. These exclusionary amendments passed 421 to 1, and 374 to 53, respectively, — a spectacular come-from-behind, upset victory for home and private schooling. This is an incredible example of what an aroused and angry public can do to reverse the course of events.

Did all those Democratic congressmen who reversed their votes the second time around suddenly have a philosophical change of heart and become "born-again pro-home/private schoolers?" Not on your life! They were simply made to fear for their political lives in the November 1994 congressional elections if they voted to kill home and private schooling.

As the late GOP Sen. Everett Dirksen used to say with a twinkle in his eye: "When we feel the heat, we see the light!"

Conservatives, traditionalists, patriots, and Christians should use this home/private schooling victory as an example of what we can do on many issues from A to Z if we will simply get mad, get mobilized, and go into action. Admittedly, there was a quasi-organized constituency in the home/private schooling camp, but the same can be said of gun owners, traditional medicine advocates, hard money advocates, hunting advocates, etc.

We need to quickly organize and network various interest groups around the nation and begin to fight back — as the home/private schoolers just successfully did.

These are not Republican versus Democratic issues, conservative versus liberal issues, or even in many instances exclusively Christian versus non-Christian issues. They are issues of freedom versus slavery, our Constitution versus the New World Constitution, traditional values versus perverted values, etc., that affect all Americans.

Get Prepared

First, we must realize and prepare ourselves for the fact that it's going to get a lot worse before it gets better.

Next, we must understand that we are in a spiritual battle as well as a political battle, which was the case as the Communists came to power in Russia, China, Cuba, etc. and the Nazis in Germany, and indeed in almost every period of political cataclysm, or upheaval in world history.

As Ephesians 6:12 says: "For our struggle is not against flesh and blood, but against the rulers, against the authorities, against the powers of this dark world and against the spiritual forces of evil in the heavenly realms" (NIV).

We need to gear up in God's spiritual armor as never before; we need to seek God for direction as never before; we need to walk more closely to Him than ever before; and we need to study our Bibles and seek God in prayer as never before.

"Therefore put on the full armour of God, so that when the day of evil comes, you may be able to stand your ground, and after you have done everything, to stand" (Eph. 6:13;NIV).

"The prudent see danger and take refuge, but the simple keep going and suffer for it" (Prov. 27:12;NIV).

Personal Bible study and Scripture memory should become a daily habit, and home fellowship or Bible study groups should be considered. If present trends continue, if persecution of Christians in America becomes commonplace, if "politically incorrect" churches in America come under increasing government pressure, then the true believers may be forced underground — into low profile home churches such as still meet secretly in Communist countries all over the world.

Advanced contingency planning for such a development should be made now. This writer strongly believes that persecution of the Christian church in America is on its way and that Christian pastors (many of whom are in a comfort zone themselves and do not wish to rock their boat) should be preparing their congregations for the same. Most are not doing so!

It is indeed wise to prepare for emergencies, no matter what their nature, be they man-made or natural. For practical guidance in preparing for such eventualities, the *McAlvany Intelligence Advisor* offers specific suggestions. (For example, see the *MIA* March 1994 issue, pages 26-27.)

Time to Take a Stand

It's time for Americans (including Christians) to wake up and get angry over what wicked, evil men and women are doing to destroy our beloved country, our traditional values, our heritage, and our Constitution.

Too many Christians in America only think of passively "turning the other cheek," and forget the Jesus who, in righteous anger and indignation, drove the moneychangers from the temple with a whip. Too many Christians are waiting passively for the return of Christ and feel they have no real responsibility to actively stand for God, country, and our biblical values, and against the evil of our day until He returns.

Many of our founding fathers were godly Christians who were strong followers of the Lord Jesus Christ, but they were also fighters and activists for liberty, freedom, and against tyranny. They recognized evil in their day, and were not afraid to take a stand against it.

The Bible teaches us to stand against evil:

> Let those who love the Lord hate evil . . . (Ps. 97:10;NIV).
>
> To fear the Lord is to hate evil . . . (Prov. 8:13;NIV).

They fought against the evil of their day, but they did so in the power and strength of the Lord. And, as the prayer in the chapel near George Patton's grave at a military cemetery near Luxembourg says: "Grant us grace fearlessly to contend against evil and to make no peace with oppression."

In the conflict between good and evil, which is now exploding on the scene all over the world, we can only stand and be victorious if we do so in the strength of the Lord. The forces of darkness and evil in this world are formidable, but the Bible describes our God as an awesome God (Ps. 47:2; 66:5; 68:35) who will easily triumph over the forces of darkness.

The present thrust for world government (i.e., the New World Order) will not succeed because it is anti-God and anti-Christ. It will help to de-stabilize the planet, however, and create times of tremendous political and social upheaval, and persecution of Christians and traditionalists.

If a person understands the true nature of what is happening in America (and globally) today — the plunge toward socialism and the New World Order and the crumbling of our culture and society — and doesn't have a close relationship with the God of the Bible and know the final chapter, he or she could easily be quite depressed or discouraged.

On the other hand, if a person knows the God of the Bible and His Son, Jesus Christ, in a personal and intimate relationship, and understands His provisions of strength, peace, wisdom, guidance, and deliverance for His people, then there is nothing to despair about. In fact, these are the most exciting of times.

As the apostle Paul wrote:

> We are hard pressed on every side, but not crushed; perplexed, but not in despair . . . struck down, but not destroyed. . . . Therefore we do not lose heart. Though outwardly we are wasting away, yet inwardly we are being renewed day by day. For our light and momentary troubles are achieving for us an eternal glory that far outweighs them all. So we fix our eyes not on what is seen, but on what is unseen. For what is seen is temporary, but what is unseen is eternal (2 Cor. 4:8-9,16-18;NIV).

And, finally:

> "For I know the plans I have for you," declares the Lord, "plans to prosper you and not to harm you, plans to give you hope and a future" (Jer. 29:11;NIV).

Editor's note: Questions regarding specific source references should be directed to Don McAlvany, P.O. Box 84904, Phoenix, AZ 85071.

10

Aids: Plague of Deception

by D.A. Miller

Laughing children hold hands as they gaily dance around singing, "Ring around the rosie, pocket full of posies, ashes, ashes, all fall down."

These children of the twentieth century reciting a familiar old rhyme know nothing of the tragic history behind their song. Silenced by time are the voices of fourteenth-century children who sang of rose petals that doctors carried in their pockets believing that the fragrance would ward off deadly infection from the black plague. Originally, the song ended with, "Ashes, ashes, all fall dead," in reference to victims whose bodies were stacked and burned after dying of the highly infectious bubonic plague, which destroyed one-fourth of Europe's population.

Today, we look back at the fourteenth century and say, "What ignorance! Imagine using rose petals to stop the black plague!"

In mankind's future, however, will people also look back at the twentieth century and say, "What ignorance! Would you believe people tried to stop the AIDS plague with the slogan, 'Safe Sex'?"

Certainly the historians of tomorrow will reflect in wonder at the ignorance of twentieth-century society. Those historians will no doubt record incredulous dismay over the ineptness of leaders and their failure to mandate the proven methods of stopping epidemics.

Living today in an "enlightened scientific and medical era," we look back in sadness at the countless lives lost unnecessarily to the bubonic plague as we see how ignorance allowed innocent men, women, and children to die. Employing the correct methods of containment, which were known as early as 1490 B.C., came too late for them.

How to Stop an Epidemic

God had recorded through His servant Moses the standards for long life, guidelines of hygiene to avoid sickness, and rules for the separation and isolation of people infected with contagious diseases (Lev. 11-15). Historically, killer plagues and infectious diseases have only been controlled by those God-given guidelines.

For example, leprosy claimed even more lives than the black plague, yet whenever God's instructions were applied, the plagues of leprosy were assuaged. And during the late nineteenth century, the killer plague of syphilis was first curtailed as a result of aggressive testing, contact tracing, and the voluntary celibacy of those infected with the highly contagious disease. Only in the next century were penicillin and other antibiotics discovered.

Ironically, our society's permissive attitude toward sex has produced an alarming resurgence of syphilis, even though penicillin still affects a cure.

Added proof demonstrating the correct method for stopping contagious epidemics is the handling of tuberculosis. During the epidemic of the late nineteenth and early twentieth centuries, those infected were instantly isolated. No one cherished the idea of pulling family members apart, but society conformed to this proven method of containment.

Those involved knew that love for others demanded self-sacrifice in order to halt the spread of the disease. Fortunately, in the late 1940s, drugs were discovered that cured most TB patients, who then returned to their family members who had been spared from the disease by the separation.

Since 1985, TB infections have risen sharply. The U.S. Health Department still treats the carriers of this contagious disease quite strictly. In fact, any TB patient who refuses medical treatment faces criminal charges.

The procedure of isolation continues to be prescribed today for such common contagious ailments as measles and chicken pox. Notice that the aforementioned ailments now have either preventive vaccines or medicines to bring about a cure. In spite of the fact that contracting them is no longer considered a stamp of death, infected individuals are still isolated from well persons until the disease is gone.

Why have the proven methods for epidemic control not been applied to AIDS? Can we, in the "enlightened" twentieth century, avoid devastation from the worst plague in the history of mankind?

As with all the major questions of life, the ultimate answers cannot be found without considering the spiritual factors. Remember, Proverbs 1:7 says, "The fear of the Lord is the beginning of knowledge: but fools despise wisdom and instruction."

In examining the AIDS epidemic, I will include information drawn from history, medicine, education, politics, and the social arena, and we will view this information through the microscope of biblical truth. From the verifiable information available, I will address the following questions:

1. What is AIDS, and is it really an epidemic?
2. Who prepared the fertile ground in which AIDS could grow?
3. Who planted the seeds of AIDS?
4. Who protected the seedlings of AIDS?
5. Who keeps this plague alive?
6. What can we do to stop this plague — or is it too late?
7. Is AIDS a judgment from God or a sign of the end times?

What is AIDS?

What is AIDS?

Viruses are among the smallest living things in existence, yet they can kill. They cannot reproduce themselves, but they can redirect the reproductive machinery of cells to produce their progeny in such numbers that a cell can literally burst apart in exhaustion.[1] Most scientists believe that AIDS is a virus called HIV, which stands for human immuno-deficiency virus. The AIDS virus attacks the immune system, which, in basic terms, is the inner army God designed to protect people from disease.

When an HIV virus enters the body via some kind of bodily fluid, it is camouflaged with human sugar. Fluids in which the HIV virus have been found include, blood, urine, saliva, breast milk, semen, and vaginal secretions. Masquerading as a human virus in these fluids, HIV finds its way to the lymph nodes, then seeks to bind itself to a CD-4 carrying cell.

These CD-4 receptors are found mostly in the mucous membranes, but Langerhans cells found in the skin also have these CD-4 receptors! Once attached, the HIV virus invades the cell and replicates itself inside the human cell.

AIDS is a retrovirus, which means that it has the ability to change the structure of the cells it enters. Slowly, these new counterfeit cells destroy the immune system made up of T and B cells, leaving the body open for attack. Currently, 28 opportunistic diseases are known to take advantage of an AIDS-compromised system, bringing sure death to its victims.

Because it is a retrovirus, AIDS develops with a long delay between infection and the expression of the disease; consequently, it does not immediately show in the infected person. The delay can be anywhere from four months to 14 years.

Figures from 1994 show that 80 percent of those infected with AIDS were involved in either homosexual sex or IV drug use with shared, contaminated equipment. These two high-risk activities also produce unusually elevated rates of other sexually transmitted diseases and diseases that compromise the immune system.

The more compromised a person's immune system is at the time of infection, the sooner full-blown AIDS surfaces. Early in the epidemic, the average time from infection to the onset of AIDS symptoms was one year; but as the epidemic slowly spreads to the healthier members of society, the average delay time seems to be increasing.

A Fragile Virus?

Most governmental sources would have us believe that "AIDS is a fragile virus," and that "no one ever should be afraid of casual contact." But let's look at the facts.

On September 28, 1985, the British medical journal *Lancet* published results of tests carried out by top scientists at the Pasteur Institute in France. Pasteur scientists are now credited with being the first to isolate the HIV virus as the cause of AIDS.

Take note of their results: "The agent causing AIDS has been isolated from body fluids [blood, semen, saliva, tears]. Its isolation in saliva prompted us to investigate the possibility of transmission by saliva."

Scientists found that the AIDS virus lives outside the body, wet or dry, up to 20 days, and is highly infectious for four days.[2] The following information demonstrates the alarming viability of AIDS.

As early as 1985, the medical textbook, *AIDS: Etiology, Diagnosis, Treatment and Prevention,* documented AIDS infections from casual contact. It recorded that a healthy woman contracted AIDS although her "only exposure appeared to be kissing her AIDS-patient husband."

Again, on November 15, 1985, the Associated Press reported that a nurse contracted AIDS from a baby who had gotten it from a transfusion. In December 1985, *Discover* ran a story featuring a nurse who had contracted AIDS from a man diagnosed posthumously as having had the disease.

The *Dallas Morning News* published an Associated Press story on April 12, 1985, which stated that "People who live with AIDS victims run a higher risk of becoming infected, according to federal study." And as early as December 1984, a New York State Department of Health bulletin stated that a number of cases had been reported in which health care workers not belonging to any AIDS high-risk group had come down with the disease. These people had no known contact with AIDS patients' blood.[3]

In late 1993, I attended a teleconference, "HIV and the Health Care Worker," at our local hospital. The video-seminar was presented by Walter Stamm, M.D., a professor of medicine at the University of Washington School of Medicine and head of the Division of Infectious Diseases at Harborview Medical Center in Seattle.

The health care workers in attendance gasped in disbelief when Dr. Stamm relayed his statistics that through 1993, 1,400 health-care workers had contracted AIDS in the workplace!

Is AIDS Really an Epidemic?

The root meaning of the word, epidemic, is "among the people." Its usage pertains to "something spreading rapidly among many people . . . said especially of a human contagious disease."

On every count, AIDS qualifies as an epidemic!

AIDS first surfaced in Africa during the late 1970s, and in 1980 began to afflict homosexuals in the United States. At first, the Center for Disease Control in Atlanta (CDC) saw the incidences of AIDS double every 10 months. Because of this doubling factor and the belief that one in every 10 men were homosexual, a huge epidemic was expected to race through the world immediately. However, the number of cases didn't explode as expected, so the CDC lowered its projections.

Then the discovery of an up-to-14-year-latency-period drove the projections back up. As the danger to groups other than homosexuals became obvious, the numbers rose even more. The CDC continues to increase projections by including additional opportunistic illnesses (diseases that end up killing by taking advantage of a patient's depleted immune system) to be registered under the AIDS umbrella.

In Kinshasa, Zaire, an area hard-hit by AIDS, 70 percent of the population tests HIV positive. In Africa, equal numbers of women and men have died from AIDS. The percentage of new cases in the United States among gays and IV-drug users has dropped recently, but only because a high proportion of homosexuals and IV-drug users already have AIDS. Estimates during the early nineties indicated that between 76 and 90 percent of the gays in San Francisco had AIDS.

Giving an accurate account of how many AIDS cases we have worldwide is extremely complex. Since technically, death comes from one of the 28 opportunistic diseases, a doctor can count a death as either being from AIDS or from TB, cancer, or one of the other diseases. Most doctors record death as being from AIDS for anyone who dies HIV positive, regardless of which opportunistic illness or combination of illnesses actually caused the person to expire.

Critics of this counting method say that in Africa many people already were dying of many of the listed "opportunistic" diseases, but now the deaths are moved over into the AIDS category simply to raise the statistics on AIDS deaths. They speculate that this is done in order to obtain funding, supposedly to stop AIDS.

It is this author's opinion that although these critics may be somewhat correct, the affected AIDS-belt area in Africa has had such an alarming rise in deaths that the HIV-positive dead must be considered as AIDS-related.

Also, in our search to determine the scope of the AIDS epidemic, should the count include persons who are HIV positive, but who do not yet show any symptoms of AIDS?

Because of all these complexities, I'll give estimates of the epidemic ranging from the most conservative to the most alarming projections. A few medical researchers (who hold the opinion that the condition of being HIV-positive does not even relate to AIDS) set the count as low as 250,000 worldwide. For further investigation of this view, readers may want to examine the work of Dr. Peter Duesberg.[4]

The Ticking Time Bomb

In 1994, at the Tokyo AIDS conference, the World Health Organization (WHO) set the number of people worldwide who either currently have AIDS or who have already died of AIDS at over 4 million. Amazingly, a scant five months later, the WHO statistics jumped from 4 million to 4.5 million. This startling announcement came during the February 1995 Conference on Women and AIDS. In 1994 WHO estimated the number of people infected with HIV to be more than 17 million.

Considering the delay characteristic of the AIDS retrovirus, WHO's estimate seems to be somewhat low. It is, of course, just an estimate, but increasing occurrences of "casual contact" cases may force the estimates to go much higher. It's difficult to calculate HIVs because most people in the world are in what they've been told is a "non-risk for AIDS" category, so they have never even been tested!

More alarming in the elusive search for the number of people affected are the statistics for the United States. The CDC, an arm of the National Institute of Health (NIH), has projected the count of AIDS cases in the USA, through 1994, to be nearly 500,000. This number does not include HIV-positives who haven't yet developed full-blown AIDS.

By early 1995 federal researchers announced that AIDS had become the *leading cause of death among all Americans aged 25 through 44.*[5]

According to AIDS expert Dr. Robert Strecker, "In the field of retroviriology, there is a rule of thumb for the spread of retroviruses. For every case you have of AIDS, by the time the first person who gets infected knows he has the disease, he has probably infected over 100 others. In other words, in every case of AIDS you see, there are probably 100 others in the population infected."[6]

After 1984, the CDC realized that the doubling time of every 10 months had stretched into two years. Observing the rise of AIDS since the first 50 cases of 1980, to the nearly 500,000 cases of 1994, we see an exponential rise. This upward curve shows not just added cases every year, but an ever-increasing rate of increase!

For example, look at the new (not the total) AIDS cases each year since 1983. To the nearest hundred we see: 1984 — 4,400 nc (new cases); 1985 — 8600 nc; 1986 — 12,300 nc; 1987 — 22,100 nc; 1988 — 32,400 nc; 1989 — 33,500 nc; 1990 — 45,000 nc; 1991 — 46,200 nc; 1992 — 46,800 nc; 1993 — 106,000 nc; and 1994 — 85,000 nc. (In 1993, the CDC added three more clinical conditions to the list of AIDS diseases as well, including HIV positives who had a T-cell count of 199 or less. These additions caused a transient increase in the count of new cases.)

Using the rate of progression for these years (which is a doubling time slightly longer than two years), we could conservatively project that by the year 2002, the USA alone would be facing more than 4 million cases of full-blown AIDS. Besides the unspeakable tragedy in human suffering and loss of lives, the financial burden will present the USA with a financial crisis. Each case of AIDS costs taxpayers about $100,000. By these projections, our health-care bill in the year 2002, for AIDS patients alone, would be $400 billion dollars!

If AIDS continues to double every two years, then the world faces even worse news. Take the known 4 million worldwide cases and apply the doubling time of two years. Doing this, we see that without some change in the current spread of AIDS, by the year 2002, 128 million people will have full-blown AIDS.

When we recall that each case of full-blown AIDS has already produced 100 HIV-positives, we see nearly 13 billion people HIV-positive and sentenced to death from AIDS. That would be more than the total population of planet earth! Plainly, AIDS, gone unchecked, could wipe mankind off the earth.

Fortunately, extinction of humankind will not occur. This we know because the Bible describes an eventual time of man living at peace on earth, ruled by Jesus, and living tremendously long lives. So before mankind can be killed off by AIDS, something cataclysmic must, and will, happen soon.

Whether the epidemic will slow down, a cure will be found, care for patients will stop, our nation will dissolve, or — more likely — the prophetic episodes scheduled on God's time clock will transpire, the time-bomb of AIDS ticks away for society as we know it today.

Who Prepared the Fertile Ground in Which AIDS Could Grow?

As stated earlier, AIDS first surfaced in Africa during the late 1970s and appeared in the USA in 1980. As we now know, this virus is carried mostly in the blood and spread through transfer of body fluids. The majority of transfers occur in sexual contact, so I will explain how, particularly in the USA, the ground was prepared early for the spread of this disease.

Many leaders gave us the fertilizer that allowed the AIDS pandemic. I have selected a few of the people most responsible. Space won't permit detailing how ideas of past leaders prepared the way for AIDS; however, an examination of history reveals principles that brought debilitating doubt into the moral fabric of American thinking:

(1) The dismissal of man's eternal soul and spirit, introduced by Charles Darwin, in his *Evolution of the Species*;

(2) Higher criticism, led by John Welhausen out of Europe, which led people to doubt the reliability of the Bible; and

(3) The encouragement of nouveaux-sociologists, taught by Sigmund Freud, the father of modern psychology, to believe that sex controls every aspect of people's lives.

In the first half of the twentieth century, three leaders in particular dumped lots of "fertilizer" that prepared the ground for AIDS:

1. John Dewey is known as the father of "Progressive Education." Although it sounds good to be progressive, let's examine the direction of his progression.

His stated ideals were:

(A) It is useless to teach children any moral absolutes. He felt that fixed moral laws and eternal truths were outdated and restrictive. (B) Truth was relative, and (C) believing in God was not admissible.

Dewey was chief designer of the 1933 Humanist Manifesto, which declares that the universe is self-existent — not created — and man is a part of nature that has emerged as a result of a continuous process. John Dewey brought chaos to the American educational system. His pagan system of education stripped morality and restraint from four generations of school children.

2. Dr. Benjamin Spock wrote *Common Sense Book of Baby and Child Care,* which was published in 1946, just in time to influence the parents of the "baby boomers." He introduced the idea of never spanking children but, rather, reasoning with them and letting them develop and unfold as one would let a rose blossom.

Countless numbers of families and government agencies followed these principles, thereby spoiling three generations who were raised without discipline. Reportedly, Dr. Spock belatedly said he ruined a generation of children.

No, Dr. Spock. It was *three* generations, and we're still counting. The government has your precepts set in stone. No matter that they don't work. If any reader doubts the government's position on corporal punishment, try spanking your children in public if they misbehave!

3. The most putrid fertilizer of all came from Dr. Alfred Kinsey, whose research reached the public in 1948 under the title of *Sexual Behavior of the Human Male*.

According to the *Wall Street Journal,* March 31, 1993, "The Kinsey 'findings' are based on criminal experiments conducted by pedophiles who sexually stimulated infants [as young as two months] and children against their will." Kinsey viewed bisexuality as normal, indeed superior, in uninhibited people and considered cross-generational sex (adult sex with children) necessary for full development of sexuality.[7]

Unbelievably, 25 percent of the 1,500 men interviewed for Kinsey's studies were prison inmates, most convicted for sexual offenses. He obtained more cohorts for his studies from names given to him by the prisoners he interviewed. His advertisements invited people who wanted to take part in a sex study to "please apply." Considering the fact that sexual modesty still existed in the 1940s, Kinsey was hardly interviewing a group from "middle America"!

Researchers of Kinsey's day scoffed at his biased work, yet a gullible public bought his book and, even worse, "bought" into the premise that homosexuality is just another natural expression of sexuality. Out of his slanted, scurrilous studies came the familiar statistic that "one in ten males are natural homosexuals."

Even after more than a decade of efforts to legitimize homosexuality, reputable studies (done in recent years) reveal far lower incidents of homosexuality than Kinsey promoted. The April 15,1993, headline in *USA Today* states, "Only 1% of Men Say They Are Gay," while the *Wall Street Journal,* March 31, 1993, lists studies from USA and Europe that show less than 1 percent of the male population is homosexual.

Another not-so-obvious but equally fatal flaw in Kinsey's studies was the assumption that discovering a norm among people somehow validates their behavior. Using that logic, one could use a survey done among SS troops in Nazi Germany during the holocaust to validate the correctness of gassing six million Jews. After all, exterminating Jews was the norm.

The truth is that even if 100 percent of the people polled on a certain moral issue agreed, they might all be wrong. Morality is not obtained from a consensus, it comes from God.

Who Planted the Seeds of AIDS?

How AIDS began or perhaps even who started it is yet to be

proven. Let me list just a few of the theories.

1. One popular theory (without much evidence) proposes that humans were either bitten or involved sexually with Green monkeys in Central Africa. These monkeys test with a virus similar to HIV but do not come down with AIDS.

The CDC traces its earliest cases of the virus to Central Africa — now known as the AIDS Belt. They call a French-Canadian airline host, Gaeten Dugas, "patient zero," tabbing him as the person who brought AIDS to the USA from Africa. The CDC did contact tracing on Degas and found that he infected more than 200 men with AIDS.

2. For a while, the cry was, "Haitians brought AIDS into the USA." A high percentage of Haitian refugees did carry the virus, which fueled this view. Some adherents of the idea accused the CIA of infecting Cuban pigs with AIDS virus and then spreading the pigs throughout the Dominican Republic, Haiti, and Cuba. This was a favorite story of the Russian KGB.

3. Another idea for the origin of AIDS is that the Club of Rome, an elitist group of geopolitical one-world thinkers, produced and spread the virus. Dr. David Webber presents this possibility, and again the motive projected is one of depopulation and world control.[8]

4. Dr. Peter Duesburg says, "It's not a virus. It's an immune system breakdown caused from drug abuse." He points to a few cases of people who have died of AIDS but who never did test positive with HIV.

It's true that intravenous drug users and many in the highly promiscuous section of homosexuals use lots of drugs that break down the immune system. However, many victims of AIDS in Africa and some in the USA who contract AIDS neither take drugs nor have compromised immune systems before infection, as Dr. Duesburg would assert.

A Method of Population Control?

The fifth theory, which sounds as unbelievable as the rest, cannot entirely be discarded when one looks at some of the rhetoric coming from the movers and shakers of our world.

Dr. Robert Strecker proposes that the World Health Organization organized a scientific study to discover an animal virus that could be transmitted to humans. Dr. Strecker and a number of other doctors assert that the experiments actually took place in the laboratories of the National Cancer Institute at Fort Detrick, Maryland. There, it is claimed, researchers combined the BLV (bovine leukemia virus) with sheep visna virus (which causes brain rot in sheep). Presumably, this virus was unleashed in Central Africa, Brazil, Haiti, and Japan by the WHO through smallpox vaccine and then released in the USA.

In this view, the Public Health Service orchestrated the USA contamination through an "experiment" on homosexuals by administering a "special" Hepatitis B vaccine at clinics in New York, Los Angeles, and San Francisco. This alarming, somewhat unbelievable, scenario is based partially on the following information:

1. Countless previous unauthorized experiments have been done on unsuspecting humans, as documented, among other sources, by the book, *A Higher Form of Killing*.[9]

2. Some of the doctors and groups overseeing the administration of these vaccines were already on record discussing the value of developing a retrovirus that would blow out the immune system of humans. The intended purpose of these experiments was to find a way to accelerate population depletion.

If this assertion is correct, the perpetrators must be congratulated for their morbid success. Actually, the *London Times* ran a front page article on October 5, 1987, that alleged this same conspiracy.

Along with this theory (and some of the other conspiracy views listed) is the speculation that an AIDS cure now exists — such as pulse-electro-magnetic-energy. The information is being stifled, the theory suggests, until enough of the right people have died and enough others are infected. Then, the conjecture follows that a new controlling power will offer the "cure" to those who pledge allegiance to a new government.

Others write about an oxygen cure they claim works, but they say its proponents are arrested before they can prove their results. Dr. Strecker and Ed McCabe write separately about some of these ideas.

Certainly I do not know which, if any, of the theories listed qualify as the true origin of AIDS. Noticeably, though, most of the suggestions about the origin of AIDS (as well as the "non-attack" against the epidemic) fall into a "conspiratorial" category. Even the mention of conspiracy causes most of us to be weary (or at least wary). But before we dismiss the thought that any human being or group of humans would ever devise such wicked thoughts, we must review some recent history.

Too Many People on Earth?

Twentieth century leaders have seen fit (for either political or ideological reasons) to execute 70 million persons in Russia, exterminate 13 million "undesirables" under Nazi control, instantly immolate 132,000 civilians in Nagasaki and Hiroshima, and use chemicals to wipe out whole villages in Iraq. Some humans have purposely starved whole people-groups in Africa and Yugoslavia, while others orchestrated the mass butchering of a half-million rival tribespersons in Rwanda.

This horrendous list only includes some of the massacres of this century. Don't ever think that humans are not capable of setting a deadly virus loose on an unsuspecting population. History tells us differently.

Why should we be surprised? God's Word tells us over and over again that apart from regeneration through faith in Jesus Christ, men's "tongues practice deceit. . . . Their feet are swift to shed blood; ruin and misery mark their ways" (Rom. 3:13-15;NIV). God even says "the heart is deceitful above all things and beyond cure . . ." (Jer. 17:9;NIV).

Even the apparent "noble" cause of population control can only be understood from a spiritual perspective. The Bible says "in the image of God made he man" (Gen. 9:6). God also said to ". . . replinish the earth" (Gen. 9:1).

Today the lies (yes, I said lies) of overpopulation and of a world food shortage are designed to cause panic. This alarm is intended to bring people to such feelings of desperation that they will embrace the distortion that only through a one-world government can mankind survive. Readers who really want to understand this agenda and recognize the lies about the inability of God to provide for man as He promised, must read the landmark book *Environmental Overkill* by Dixy Lee Ray.[10]

Daily, the media bombards us with alarming new environmental catastrophes that threaten to destroy us. Most are situations amplified totally out of proportion or completely baseless. Why would anyone concoct those dire predictions? Again, only through spiritual understanding can we know why. The Bible says that Satan desires to control man. To accomplish this, Satan will bring into existence a global government headed up by his own appointed messiah.

To illustrate the mindset of those who show complete disregard for human life and who seek not just to stabilize earth's population but to massively lower it, I submit the following quotes. As you read these, ask yourself if this kind of thinking could lead people to justify using the AIDS virus to obtain their desired goals.

1. In response to banning DDT, Dr. Charles Wurster, who was then chief scientist for the Environmental Defense Fund, stated that in his opinion there are too many people, and "this is as good a way to get rid of them as any." Again Dr. Wurster stated in congressional testimony, "It doesn't really make a lot of difference because the organophosphate (pesticide) acts locally and only kills farm workers, and most of them are Mexicans and Negroes."

2. Dr. LaMont Cole, a respected environmentalist at Yale University, asserted that "To feed a starving child is to exacerbate the world population problem."

3. Dr. Van den Bosch of the University of California chided others about their concern for "all those little brown children in poor countries."

4. Dixy Lee Ray gives us the outline of celebrated environmentalist Paul Ehrlich of Stanford University. He and his wife propose (among other programs, to prevent or ameliorate the population explosion) to institute the Chinese Communist system of compulsory abortion and various forms of infanticide. . . . The rich and intelligent must not propagate. They are "dangerous because they promote overproduction [and have] the heaviest impact on the planet."

5. Ted Turner, owner of CNN, said, "Right now there are just way too many people on the planet." His plan is to cut back from the current 5 billion human beings to no more than "250 million to 350 million people."

6. David M. Graber, research biologist with the National Park Service: "Until such time as Homo sapiens should decide to rejoin nature, some of us can only hope for the right virus to come along."

7. David Brower, founder of Friends of the Earth and former director of the Sierra Club, asserts that "Loggers losing their jobs because of spotted owl legislation is, in my eyes, no different than people being out of work after the furnaces of Dachau shut down."[11]

Who Nourished the Seedlings of AIDS?

Regardless of where or how the AIDS virus originated, it came. And when it began to surface as a deadly, communicable disease, nothing sensible was done to thwart its spread, which would have saved millions of lives. It's horrifying to realize that apathy, ignorance, denial, greed, fear, manipulation, perversion, and irresponsibility combined to cause wholesale slaughter.

A few voices have spoken up with truth. *Science* magazine states, "Throughout history, true humanitarianism has traditionally involved the compassionate but firm segregation of the afflicted with communicable diseases from the well." Dr. James Curran, a Harvard health official, states, "This is a plague. I see nothing wrong with quarantine."[12]

Since the epidemic in the USA began in the homosexual community, I'll begin by showing the homosexuals' part in nourishing the epidemic.

In the U.S. in 1980, scattered AIDS cases surfaced among men, who all happened to be homosexuals. But it wasn't until January 1982 that doctors named this new killer Gay Related Immune Deficiency, or GRID. Some heterosexuals reacted to the disease with apathy, suggesting, "If gays die of a weird homosexual disease, it really doesn't matter much."

Since these early cases in the USA were confined to homosexuals, the fear was great among most gays that this stalking killer wouldn't be stopped. They didn't want AIDS perceived as a "gay disease" because they feared that if it was, scant funds and attention would be given to locate the cause and cure. They insisted that the word "gay" be taken out of the disease's name, so the disease became known as Acquired Immune Deficiency Syndrome, or AIDS.

From the beginning, groups formed and pressure was exerted to save the reputation of the homosexual community, which demanded that there never, no, never, be any mandatory reporting, victim isolation, contact tracing, or any other handling of AIDS as a communicable disease. As a result of these and other restrictions, AIDS became the first disease with "civil rights"!

AIDS brought the gay community to a fork in the road. Inroads toward societal acceptance had begun in the benchmark riot in 1969 against the New York Police Department's raid of the gay bar, the Stonewall Inn. They could have questioned the deadly results of the great freedom they had recently gained in "coming out," or they could have insisted on their "civil rights." They chose to treat the fight against AIDS as a civil matter rather than a health issue concerning a deadly communicable disease.

This decision marked the beginning of a self-inflicted death march. The march became one of open defiance against any doctor or agency that would suggest personal responsibility or sexual restraint. An editorial in *U.S.A. Today* ranted about public reaction to AIDS "threatening human and civil rights," while the *Guardian* informed everyone that "the real plague is panic."

No leaders in the health or political arms of our government insisted on curbing the spread of this highly deadly disease by mandating that the Health Department handle AIDS the same as it handled all other contagious diseases. Members of the homosexual community lobbied and screamed for their "rights." So they got their rights and lost their lives.

A Lifestyle or a Death Style?

Listen to the reasoning of homosexuals and that of their supporters.

Joel Wachs is the Los Angeles city councilman who sponsored the first law to prosecute anyone who bars AIDS patients from schools, refuses to hire them, will not rent to them, or restricts them from restaurants. He states, "A society which should be showing compassion to people who are ill is often shunning them like lepers." (Presumably, Mr. Wachs would invite a typhoid carrier home for dinner.)

Mark S. Senakof, legal services director of Gay Men's Health Crisis in New York, fights AIDS testing on the basis that "a positive test becomes as insidious and loathsome an instrument of discrimination as a yellow star was in Germany."

"As late as October 1984, *Frontiers,* a Los Angeles homosexual publication stated, 'There is at this time no documented proof that AIDS is a sexually-transmitted syndrome.' "[13]

Larry Kramer, founder of the homosexual activist group, ACT UP, writes, "Intentional genocide is going on.... A society that hates gays has allowed them to become this decade's Jews.... Morality and moral norms are not operating ... same world is sitting by as millions of gays and others are murdered."[14]

The problem in understanding AIDS is that many untruths caused this epidemic. Frankly, the 99 percent of heterosexuals and 1 percent of homosexuals have been lied to in many ways.

People have been told to call the homosexual lifestyle "gay." We have been told that being gay is just an alternative lifestyle. We are told that same-sex partners are just as loving and committed as heterosexual marriage partners. We have been told never to say, "Being homosexual is a choice," but rather to recognize that some people are born gay.

With sadness I say, "Homosexual conduct is not gay, it is tragic." This behavior leads to endless searching for love, to disease, and to early death. Compare the facts with what we have been told to believe.

First, we must ask whether homosexual relationships are really as loving and committed as we're told. The statistics would not say so.

From columnist Mike McManus, we read, "A 1978 study found 43 percent of white male homosexuals had sex with more than 500 different partners during their lifetime and 28 percent estimated they had sex with more than 1,000."

McManus adds, "An American Psychological Association study in 1984 showed that the average homosexual promiscuity did drop after the onset of AIDS. Instead of 70 partners a year, they had 50."[15] These statistics are backed up by other studies, such as that of Masters and Johnson. This kind of partner-swapping leads to many violent deaths from jealousy and most of all disease.

Here are some examples of the "loving" and "committed" attitudes of some of those who have practiced homosexuality. Movie star Rock Hudson callously continued kissing and having sex with people after he knew he had AIDS. He lied about having AIDS to his live-in lover for more than a year after his diagnosis so that he could have sex with his lover until he (Hudson) died. His lover, Marc Christian, says, "I was the last to know."

Dr. John Dwyer, former chief of immunology at Yale-New Haven Hospital in Connecticut, has treated more than 400 AIDS patients. He states, "There are people who say, 'I know I'm going to die, and I'm going to take as many people with me as I can.' "[16]

Caryl Matrisciana, producer of documentaries on AIDS, says:

> While filming "Aids: What You Haven't Been Told," we interviewed 97 homosexual men dying of AIDS. We asked each one, "How long after being diagnosed with AIDS did you stop having sex?"
>
> Ninety-six answered, "We kept having sex until our AIDS was so obvious that no one would have us." The one man who stopped having sex had just become a Christian. He said, "Remaining celibate until I die is the hardest thing I ever set out to do, but now I'm even thankful that I have

AIDS, because that's what brought me to Jesus."

Randy Shilts, an outspoken homosexual who died of AIDS in 1993, was a highly acclaimed author and expert journalist on the AIDS epidemic. Writing about the early 1980s, he said, "Gay men made up about 80 percent of the 70,000 annual patient visits to the city's (San Francisco) VD clinic . . . the clinic was considered an easy place to pick up both a shot and a date."[17]

"Gays are three times more likely to have alcohol or drug abuse problems than heterosexual men. . . . More than half of all reported cases of syphilis in the United States occur in homosexual men."[18]

When we consider the 1 percent figure on gays in the population, it looks more like being gay is a "death" style. Consider life spans. Among those gays dying of AIDS, the average age of death is 39. From all other causes, the average age is 41. That's rather a short life compared to a heterosexual male's life span of 70!

Born That Way?

Incidentally, no evidence exists proving that men are born homosexual.

God says homosexual behavior is a choice, and try as they will, homosexual researchers cannot come up with any proof to justify their perversion. The next time you we see an article headlined "Gays Born That Way," read it for the propaganda that it is. The article will be full of "may be," "could," and "might show," because "Born That Way" cannot be validated by medical science.

I have even heard Christians fall prey to the propaganda and suggest, "Well, maybe some people are born gay."

To them I say, "Would the God who loved you so much that He gave His Son to die for you, be so unfeeling as to condemn a person for living the way he was born? We know the Bible condemns homosexual acts, so it must be a choice."

Even secular sociologists Masters and Johnson report a 79.1 percent immediate success rate for their patients who attempt to discontinue homosexual activity. Some eventually go back, but the 136 ex-gay groups attest to the truth that being gay is a choice, not an in-born trait.

Times have changed, and so have the morals and restraints of our populace. So to fully understand the AIDS epidemic, we must consider the depravity of man and his acts of perversion.

How does the changing of morals relate to the tragic early deaths of homosexuals? What is it about the homosexual life that cuts men off in their prime? It's what they do.

When men leave the natural function of their sexual design and begin to use every body orifice to pursue stimulation, the body can't stay healthy. Long before AIDS hit, those who committed homosexual acts were contracting and spreading sexually-transmitted diseases and hepatitis in record numbers.

God's Word states that our bodies are "fearfully and wonderfully made," which would include the body parts designed for sex and procreation. If, however, we leave the godly mandated design for our bodies (which prescribes one woman and one man to be committed solely to each other in marriage, for life), we take the risk of destroying those bodies.

That people seek sexual stimulation from multiple strangers and from unspeakable acts involving urine and feces is no surprise to God. He warned about this kind of perversion in the Bible in Romans 1:24-32:

> Wherefore God also gave them up to uncleanness through the lusts of their own hearts, to dishonour their own bodies between themselves . . . unto vile affections . . . the men, leaving the natural use of the woman, burned in their lust one toward another; men with men working that which is unseemly . . . as they did not like to retain God in their knowledge, God gave them over to a reprobate mind, to do those things which are not convenient . . . Who knowing the judgment of God, that they which commit such things are worthy of death, not only do the same, but have pleasure in them that do them.

Initially, because of the AIDS epidemic, there was a call to close the gay bathhouses so popular in New York and San Francisco.

In the early 1980s, when I first read of the attempts to close "gay bathhouses," I assumed that these were some kind of special men's club frequented by homosexuals. I thought perhaps this close camaraderie might escalate gays' contacting each other, thereby in some way raising the possibility of spreading AIDS. My naiveté showed.

These bathhouses are male whorehouses designed for homosexuals to meet and have multiple sex encounters with total strangers. Some, which specialize in quick, anonymous sex, sport walls full of "glory holes" which allow participants to only connect sexually through the wall. It's a kind of assembly-line sex and certainly as noncommittal as could be imagined.

According to Lorraine Day, the orthopedic surgeon who blew the whistle on the AIDS blood-scandals in San Francisco, the use of amyl nitrate "poppers," speed, heroin, and cocaine, enable men to engage in as many as 50 encounters a night.

Randy Shilts, commenting on the bathhouse situation as it was just before AIDS hit, said, "Promiscuity, however was central to the raucous gay movement of the 1970s . . . (it) spawned a business of bathhouses and sex clubs. The hundreds of such institutions were a $100 million industry across America and Canada."[19]

The ACLU quickly volunteered its wisdom by labeling as "repressive" any movement to curtail the spread of AIDS by the closing of bathhouses. We would assume that now, since homosexuals know the dangers involved in participating in the abhorrent promiscuous practices performed in the bathhouses, the bathhouses have been closed. However, that's a wrong assumption.

According to the *New York Times,* February 16, 1993, "There are more sex clubs in New York City in 1993 than there were in the early 1980s." By April of 1994, bathhouses existed in 43 cities nationwide.

The Red Badge of Courage?

The studies of Pavlov demonstrated that the shorter the time between behavior and the result, the quicker the subject learned. One reason for the continued deadly behavior of homosexuals may be found in God's statement, "Because sentence against an evil work is not executed speedily, therefore the heart of the sons of men is fully set in them to do evil" (Eccles. 8:11).

Actually, AIDS infections are on the rise again, and experts fear a new wave of AIDS that began in 1994.

Ron Stall, a behavioral scientist at the Center for AIDS Prevention Studies at the University of California at San Francisco, says, "Many gay men say they are numb with loss, fatalistic about their own survival, unwilling to face a measure of sexual deprivation, and eager for the attention showered on the sick and the dying, so they are again practicing unprotected sex."

Reasoning that boggles the mind surfaces in the words of a 32-year-old airline mechanic who recently became infected. "I thought if I was HIV positive I'd be so much gayer." He added, "People are looking for the red badge of courage, and you get that when you convert from being HIV negative to carrying the virus."

Dick Sargent, star of TV program "Bewitched," and an outspoken homosexual, recently died of cancer. Before his death, Sargent summed up this bizarre mentality. "I don't have AIDS . . . but if I did, I would wear that badge as proudly as everybody else who has it."[20]

Michael Callen, who has AIDS, realized the error of his homosexuality, and admitted it. He founded "People with AIDS New York," and started a crusade to close the bathhouses. His efforts brought the wrath of the homosexual world, and he was forced to resign from the AIDS Medical Foundation. "It was my use of that word 'promiscuity' which blocked my effectiveness."

What does all this have to do with AIDS? Plenty. The very practices that define men as homosexual are the very practices that are killing them. The more perverted and the more frequent the encounters, the higher the risk of contracting AIDS or giving it to someone else. Yet the bizarre behavior continues.

Lest we think these risky behaviors are limited to a few big cities known for high concentrations of homosexuals, we should note the problem in the men's bathrooms of East Tennessee State University and the University of California at Los Angeles. The custodians have given up trying to repair "glory holes" between the stalls in the bathrooms. They couldn't keep up with the young men who used the school bathrooms for anonymous sex between classes.

City parks throughout my area of southern California, specifically in San Diego, Riverside, and the small town of Hemet, are besieged with complaints from area residents who say they cannot use the public parks because of the blatant daytime trysts of homosexuals. Roving men cruise the parks looking for willing partners.

The police say they simply cannot — or have chosen not to — control the problem. One officer stated to the *Hemet News,* "There's no point in chasing them out of the parks 'cause they'll just go somewhere else and do it."

Ironically, Fairmont Park in Riverside, recognized as a mecca for multiple-anonymous homosexual trysts, is referred to in a newspaper article reporting about an AIDS Day celebration: "1,800 take steps to fight AIDS. The balloon-carrying walkers grieved for friends and relatives as their 5-kilometer walk wound through the city and past Fairmont Park."

Good grief! If the walkers really cared, why didn't they forget their balloons and go into that park and encourage, cajole, or otherwise persuade men to stop committing the acts that cause them to get AIDS?

Recruiting Young Boys

The loving, committed relationships that homosexuals portray to the "straight" world are actually rare to non-existent. The homosexual community seeks always to expand itself. It can't propagate; it only kills, so it must recruit. For an accurate look at the recruiting practices of homosexuals, read some of their own words.

The *San Francisco Sentinel,* San Francisco's premier homosexual publication, printed an editorial, "No Place for Homophobia," on March 26, 1992, that asserted, "The love between men and boys is at the foundation of homosexuality".

The North American Man Boy Love Association (NAMBLA), a regular group participant in gay-pride parades, promotes "intergenerational" sex. The age of consent has already been lowered to 14 in San Francisco, but NAMBLA would like to see all age restrictions abolished!

Some media-wise homosexuals would like the International Gay and Lesbian Association to disavow its connection with NAMBLA, but it hasn't and can't. Members acknowledging that one kind of sex is improper (i.e., sex with children), would set a precedent that certain kinds of sexual activity should be restrained. And gays cannot take that stand because that position involves morality, and morality in sexual matters is what homosexuality is not about.

Tell me. What is the difference between pedophiles and men in the Rene Guyon Society who express their philosophy as "sex before eight or it's too late?"[21]

Gene Antonio, AIDS author, writes concerning the Club Dallas Bathhouse in Texas: "This establishment, with a reported patronage of over 30,000, has recently been advertising special cheap locker rates for teenagers."[22]

There is an agenda among homosexuals.

The Jeremiah Films video, "Gay Rights, Special Rights," reveals the agenda, as stated by gays in their own words. Michael, writer for *Gay Community News,* brags, "We shall sodomize your sons, emblems of your feeble masculinity. We shall seduce them in your schools, your dormitories, in your gymnasiums, in your locker rooms, in your sports arenas, in your seminaries, in your youth groups."

"Ten percent is not enough! Recruit! Recruit! Recruit!" was the chant by lesbian activists (recorded in the Jeremiah video) at the 1993

Washington March For Gay Equal Rights and Liberation.[23]

God has seen this agenda before. Then He showed not only righteous judgment, but also demonstrated His grace when He spared the world's population from extinction. He destroyed Sodom and Gomorrah before the agenda of those cities' homosexuals spread their sure death via sexually transmitted diseases.

Are we approaching the time that God will have to bring judgment on the world, once again to preserve mankind?

Homosexuals are killing themselves and asking the rest of us to condone, sample, and share in the AIDS risk produced by their deadly behavior. To anyone still not sure of the accuracy of the preceding information, I strongly recommend obtaining some of the illuminating books and videos listed at the end of this section.

Who Keeps This Plague Alive?

Many groups of people have been involved in the spread of this fatal epidemic.

In the following sections, I will illustrate how blood banks, hospitals, the CDC, literature to "stop" AIDS, governments and politicians, the liberal media, proponents of sex education, and misguided religionists all hold responsibility for the pandemic of AIDS.

Blood banking is a business. In fact, it is a billion-dollar-a-year business. We donate blood, and the banks sell it at a profit to hospitals.

Randy Shilts commented that in 1980, 5 to 7 percent of the blood donated in San Francisco was given by gays. As early as December 1982, Dr. Bruce Evatt of CDC warned blood-bank owners about the blood-related AIDS cases. Yet, up until the spring of 1985, the general public was allowed to believe the assurances of Dr. James Curran, chief of the AIDS Task Force for CDC. He had reassured the public as late as February 1984 that the risk of getting AIDS from a blood transfusion was "one in a million."

Sadly, estimates show that 29,000 people became infected by bad blood before 1985.

An exposé reported in the *Press Enterprise,* May 15, 1994, substantiated that all the banks knew blood carried the AIDS virus, but they conspired to decide not to tell the American public about the risk until they could develop a cheap test for AIDS contamination in blood. A test was available at that time, but since the cost-effective analysis showed it to be too expensive, they opted to lie.

Of the estimated 20,000 hemophiliacs in the U.S., close to 75 percent are now infected with the AIDS virus. It is clear that 2 percent of the AIDS cases in adults and almost 10 percent of the cases in children were results of blood transfusions.

Now that there's an economical test for HIV, the blood supply is safe, right? That's what we are told; but in reality, the test is for HIV antibodies, and they sometimes don't show up in the blood for three and one-half years after a person has contracted the disease! That indicates a dangerous window of time when a person's blood could infect others although it doesn't show positive in a test!

Let us for a moment disregard the danger from AIDS activists (who have repeatedly threatened to purposely contaminate the blood supply to draw attention to the plight of AIDS sufferers) and look at yet another risk. Tainted blood could be given unknowingly by people who are HIV positive. Remember, the latency period of up to 14 years could allow a person to be infected without knowing it because he or she may have never even been tested for HIV.

Is the Blood Supply Safe?

Most experts claim that the blood supply has been safe since 1985 because of the HIV-detection test and blood-donor screening. Notable sex-sociologists Masters, Johnson, and Kolodny disagree with this contention.[24] Other experts, writing in the *New England Journal of Medicine,* disagree also. "The AIDS virus may lurk undetected for as long as three years in the blood cells of some infected men."[25]

Lorraine Day, head of orthopedic surgery at San Francisco General, believes that the negative window factor, the weakness of self-deferral, and mistakes in blood labs (which have repeatedly occurred) leave our blood supply still unsafe.

Self-deferral means that those who think they might be in a high-risk category will not give blood. This thinking smacks of "Pollyanna" when we realize that most carriers continue to knowingly subject their "lovers" to risk. Why would these same AIDS carriers be concerned about protecting total strangers? Also weakening the self-deferral safeguard is the denial that goes along with high-risk behavior. To some, donating blood is an act of bravado that states to the world: "I'm different. AIDS can't get me!"

A 1994 documentary shown on PBS gives chilling proof that even though there is a test that screens out most of the tainted blood, some banks dangerously cut corners while testing. Others cheat on their records to hide the fact that they don't test for AIDS at all.

In late 1993, blood banks in Germany, France, and Romania all hit the headlines with their blood-bank scandals. In Germany alone, more than "1,500 people have been infected with AIDS from tainted blood since 1984."

Even knowing the dangers connected with taking blood from members of high-risk groups, the third quarterly blood drive in San Francisco on July 30, 1988, was scheduled in the Castro district. This was blatant disregard for human life because "Castro had the highest per capita rate of AIDS-infected people in the nation."[26]

In California, Paul Gann, a 75-year-old politician who contracted AIDS from a blood transfusion, saw the defeat of Proposal 102, which asked for mandatory HIV reporting from physicians and contact tracing (as is required for 58 other communicable diseases). Currently in California, a $10,000 fine is levied on doctors who do report the names of persons testing positive for HIV.

An article in the *San Jose Mercury,* October 1988, states, "1 of 4 current blood donors would stop giving blood if Proposition 102 passed . . . if 102 became law, the current blood shortage would become far worse and precipitate a crisis that could cripple the health-care industry."[27] This might be a Freudian slip. Obviously, opponents of Proposition 102 knew that a high percentage of blood was being taken from donors in high-risk categories. Currently, less than half the states allow physicians to report AIDS infections, even to spouses or sexual partners of the carriers.

The *Los Angeles Times,* April 25, 1990, printed information about 671 IV-drug users in Baltimore who said they had sold or donated blood during 1988. One hundred and forty-two of these donors tested positive for AIDS. In light of this information, which represented only one segment of high-risk people in only one city in the USA, how confident can we feel about the following assurance of blood safety?

" 'The current products out there are considered to be 100 percent safe,' said James Reilly, spokesman for the American Blood Resources Association."[28]

Hospitals and Tainted Blood

When hospital administrators realized they had transfused millions of pints of tainted blood, they too were at a crossroads. Should they contact patients who had received blood over the past five years? Most decided not to. They said, "It would be too hard, too expensive, and it might scare those who would register a false positive."

Incidentally, the panic-from-false-positives-excuse is given over and over as a reason to avoid a mandatory reporting of names of HIV-positive persons in order to do contact tracing and testing of possible victims. False positives occur once in 130,000 on the ELISA test. Anyone who tests positive can make sure by taking a slightly more expensive test called the Western Blot, which is very accurate.

Meanwhile, those who unknowingly contracted AIDS from tainted blood were allowed to infect their spouses, newborns, and other innocents. No one yet knows how many thousands were infected by tainted blood and continue to unknowingly infect others.

Elizabeth Glaser, wife of actor Paul Michael Glaser, contracted AIDS from tainted blood she received when their daughter was born. She was never tested. Only after giving birth to their son four years later did she become sick with AIDS. The worst part of the tragedy is that because she wasn't tested, she gave AIDS to both of her children. They are all dead now.

Anyone facing surgery that could require blood should give some of his or her own ahead of time and speak with the doctor about recycling his or her own blood during the operation. This method proves quite successful.

The CDC and Safe Sex Myth

The CDC sponsors and promulgates the "Safe Sex" and condom lies. A typical newspaper headlines reads, "CDC says condoms, if used properly, work." This article complains that condom critics are spreading myths and assures us that condoms aren't 100 percent effective, but they can be very, very close if used consistently.

The hype admonishes, "If you must participate in risky sex, be safe, use a condom." That makes no sense. The intrinsic voids (holes) in a condom are five microns in size. Compare the size of those holes to the HIV virus which is one-tenth of a micron in size (four-millionths of an inch.)

Stopping the AIDS virus with a condom is a little like a basketball player shooting baskets with marbles and expecting them to get caught in the net! Is this scare tactics, as the media suggests? No, it is scary truth!

Try this next information for another fright. The HIV virus is 450 times smaller than sperm. Condoms have proven to allow a 14 to 36 percent pregnancy rate — and remember, conception can only occur a few days out of each month.[29]

AIDS can kill any time. Comparing the size of sperm and the

amount that slips through condoms to the size of the HIV virus shows us that "safe sex" is just another nice name to alter the truth. Wouldn't "slightly less deadly sex" be more appropriate?

Using condoms to stop AIDS is akin to playing Russian roulette and leaving five bullets in the chamber. Oh yes, if you want to play safely, put a condom over the barrel first!

The point here is not that if condoms were safe it would be morally right to have promiscuous or deviant sex. The point is that, from the beginning, the public has been lied to by the private and government groups who are supposed to be working for our welfare.

Remember, the Pasteur Institute proved conclusively that the HIV virus lives up to 20 days outside the body in saliva specimens, yet these special interest groups continue to propagate the lie that AIDS is a "fragile virus."

The CDC tells health care workers not to worry about needle pricks. They assure workers by telling them, "You have only a 1 in 200 chance of getting AIDS infection from an accidental prick with an AIDS-tainted needle." Don't you health care workers feel relieved now? Those comfortable odds are the same as the odds of contracting AIDS from the most deadly form of homosexual deviancy, anal sex! As stated, through 1993, 1,400 health care workers in non-risk groups have already gotten AIDS from job-related exposure.

The Unknown 9 percent

In a brochure entitled, "How You Won't Get AIDS" distributed by the U.S. Public Health Services Center of Disease Control, we read a long list of ways and places where we can't get AIDS, including parties, stores, swimming pools, telephones, toilet seats, eating utensils, and contact with body fluids such as tears, sweat, or saliva.

The brochure urges readers not to "worry about getting AIDS from everyday contact with a person with AIDS." Then it states that we should "take precautions such as wearing rubber gloves only when blood is present."

Now remember, the law prevents us from knowing who might be AIDS infected, yet in every one of the "safe" casual contacts listed, blood could be involved. People get cut, and people bleed. Blood carries AIDS. AIDS is not a fragile virus. This Sunday, would you like to go to a shopping mall and let your daughter have her ears pierced?

Even Arthur Ashe, who contracted AIDS from a transfusion, fell for this hype, stating that Magic Johnson should never have quit basketball. Ashe added, "The chances are so small that anyone would get HIV from him you can't measure it." How strange that Ashe, who lost his life by trusting in the assurances of the AIDS experts, should trust and promote the assurances of the medical "experts" concerning casual contact.

One of the most vital pieces of information in understanding the seriousness of the AIDS epidemic is this: At first the disease in the U.S. was confined to the homosexual community. But when that changed, AIDS educators tried to make the public believe that only a few high-risk groups of people could contract AIDS.

That party line continued, even though a close look at CDC literature from June 1986 shows the agency admitted it could not account for 6 percent of the AIDS cases. And the alarming news does not stop there. The percentage of AIDS cases contracted from unknown sources is rising. As of June 1994, CDC literature states regarding the 146,145 new AIDS cases (January 1993-June 1994) that "9 percent occurred among persons whose risk has not been identified."

This government health organization assures us AIDS can only be contracted four ways: through risky sex (i.e., no condom, with an infected partner); using a dirty needle from an AIDS-infected, IV-drug user; pre-natal infection from mother to child; or being transfused with AIDS-tainted blood. At the same time, the CDC tells us that it can't account for 9 percent of the AIDS cases. The obvious conclusion is that there are ways AIDS is transmitted that the CDC either doesn't know about or will not discuss.

Very few studies have been done about the percentage of AIDS spread in other ways: by "aerosol transmission," which involves breathing in viruses as when one catches a cold; or the possibility of "vector infection," which involves mosquitoes, bed bugs, biting flies, etc.

One study, a staff paper done for Congress by the Office of Technology, tries to dismiss the possibility of vector transfer but concludes by saying, "Experiments with mechanical transmission of viral diseases have shown that under the right conditions, transmissions through insect vectors can occur. Experiments designed to answer the question of whether HIV can survive in bloodsucking insects long enough to be transmitted if interrupted feeding occurs have shown that it is theoretically possible."[30]

While aerosol or vector transmission do not seem to be much of a factor in the AIDS cases reported in the USA, conditions in other countries may be more conducive to these methods of transfer.

On August 5, 1986, the *Wall Street Journal* quoted a study from Zaire which showed that those who lived under the same roof with an AIDS sufferer have a "300 percent greater risk of becoming infected than the general population."[31] The AIDS belt in Africa covers the tropical zone, where numerous infectious diseases are spread by vectors.

How Not to "Stop" AIDS

Examine AIDS literature. Does it curtail or expand the epidemic?

The San Francisco AIDS Foundation's brochure, "AIDS in the Workplace," asks, "Should people with AIDS be allowed to work?" My answer would be certainly. But jobs that could put other people at risk should not be included.

Then the publication confidently states, "The companies having experience in dealing with employees with AIDS have determined that AIDS can be treated like any other life-threatening illness, such as cancer or heart disease." It's odd that they should compare AIDS with cancer and heart disease, rather than with other communicable diseases such as TB or smallpox.

An AIDS Education Project, Inc., brochure announces, "Being gay didn't give him AIDS . . . lifestyles don't cause disease, germs do." But wait a minute. We know viruses give us colds, and yet we say, "You gave me your cold!"

Let's face the truth: Certain behaviors put us in contact with people who carry viruses, so certain lifestyles can expose us to viruses. If we allow ourselves to be sneezed on by a person with a cold, we may get sick. If we allow ourselves to contact the body fluids of an AIDS-infected person, we may die.

Another piece of literature is meant to dispel panic although it, too, contains a paradox. "Your Child and AIDS," published by the San Francisco AIDS Foundation, reads, "Can MY Child Get AIDS from Another Child? NO," in big bold letters.

It then gives another long list of safe activities including breathing, coughing, biting, sneezing, wrestling, hugging, touching, kissing, and playing. However, if these activities are so "safe," then why does the publication go on to say, "A child with AIDS should stay at home or go to school with specially trained teachers if this child has (1.) open sores; (2.) is too sick to go to public school; (3.) has uncontrollable diarrhea; or (4.) bites other children."

How are we supposed to know when a young child might bite another, or even simply bump into another child, breaking the skin on his or her knee or elbow, and accidentally exchange blood? If it is safe to wrestle, why isn't it safe if a child bites? For that matter, why were the playground monitors in our local school district instructed in an AIDS-prevention seminar to wear rubber gloves while on playground duty?

If AIDS is such a fragile virus, why must school janitors wear rubber gloves to protect themselves from AIDS when they handle trash?

Presumably, AIDS literature is provided to the public in order to calm our fears and protect us from infection. However, each piece of literature we've surveyed contains contradictions that dreadfully undermine our confidence in these groups' objectiveness and truthfulness.

A Cure in 100 Years?

Although the Secretary of Health and Human Services announced on April 24, 1984, that "a cure for AIDS will be found within the next two years," the end of 1994 passed with no cure in sight.

A budget of $1.3 billion yearly for research has put us no closer to a cure than we were in the beginning. The dreadful multiple-design of AIDS (being 9,000 to the fourth power) makes its destruction virtually impossible. Added to that is the virus' ability to mutate 1 million times faster than most other organisms.

Stunned attendees at the 1994 International Conference on AIDS in Japan heard chilling words when they learned the sobering information that it would be 100 years before a cure will be found for AIDS. This announcement makes sense.

Throughout history, any scientist who could have discovered a cure for the common cold virus would have become an instant billionaire. But it hasn't happened. Even the much more simply designed cold virus has eluded destruction. Prevention through behavior change, contact tracing, and isolation (practices which demand personal sacrifices from us all) is still being dismissed; yet these are the best and only ways we know of to stop the epidemic.

Additional bad news surfaced at the conference in the statistic that the number of strains of HIV, which early on was believed to be three, has now stretched to 30 — most of which are not detectable by the present tests for HIV. (The potential danger of blood-supply contamination increases greatly from this information.)

A small ray of hope in the struggle to bring sanity to the effort of stopping AIDS appeared on March 20, 1994, in an article by Keith Stone in the *Los Angeles Daily News:* "Lawrence Gostin, a Georgetown University law professor, says today's people are saying AIDS is no longer a politically protected disease, and we are no longer going to hold back. They are proposing mandatory testing . . . mandatory partner reporting, and criminalization." The article mentions scores of city and state governmental leaders in favor of this new direction.[32]

The Politics of AIDS

Why wouldn't the leaders of all nations support God's moral guidelines that are vital in stopping the spread of AIDS?

The Lord gives insight on this question. "The kings of the earth set themselves, and the rulers take counsel together against the Lord and against his anointed, saying, Let us break their bands asunder, and cast away their cords from us" (Ps. 2:2-3).

Proverbs 1:22-31 tells us that "Fools hate knowledge . . . because I have called and you refused . . . you have set at naught my counsel . . . when your destruction cometh . . . I will not answer . . . they hated knowledge and did not choose the fear of the Lord . . . therefore shall they eat of the fruit of their own way."

How has the U.S. government reacted to the epidemic?

President Clinton favored lifting the ban on immigration (and even visiting the U.S.) for those with communicable diseases including AIDS, syphilis, gonorrhea, leprosy, and non-active TB. During the Gay Games in New York in 1994, President Clinton had his way as AIDS carriers from around the world converged on an already sick city.[33]

Attorney General Janet Reno, in an effort to stop discrimination "based on unfounded fear and factual understanding," named dental offices in Houston and New Orleans in a lawsuit. The Justice Department said the dentists were violating the Americans with Disabilities Act by withholding treatment from patients with the AIDS virus.[34]

While our valiant and dedicated Justice Department goes after those "evil" dentists, Frank Bridges, a man who knew he had AIDS when he raped and infected his bride's seven-year-old daughter during the wedding celebration, gets a possible three-year slap on the wrist. The law does not support an attempted murder charge because it cannot be proven that he intended to kill the girl.

It seems that if those responsible for policing such things were really doing their jobs conscientiously, they would, rather than attacking dentists who are trying to survive the epidemic, go after people who knowingly infect others with death. It seems the best our government can do, besides pouring billions of dollars into a black hole of virus research, is to make commemorative stamps, cheer obscene marchers, display memorial quilts, and encourage the wearing of red ribbons. Nice touches, but not very effective in stopping an epidemic.

Other countries aren't doing much better. Asia now shows the largest increase in AIDS cases. In some countries, military recruits are testing positive at the rate of 20 per 100.

U.S. News & World Report, January 18, 1993, revealed, "France is now hit worse by AIDS than any other European country, with an estimated 200,000 people testing HIV positive and 22,000 struck down with the disease." The worst blood scandal to "become public" occurred in France when politicians "ordered continued use of contaminated stocks until they ran out." This decision apparently was both financial and for reasons of prestige since France wanted to develop its own system of blood safeguarding.

During the 1980s, Haiti's Minister of Health admitted his cover up of AIDS. He stated he would not divulge AIDS information that was threatening their tourist industry: "Scientifically I have no reluctance to provide the information to the CDC. But if those data will destroy my country, I will not do it because my main duty is to my country."[35]

Halfdam Mahlar, Director General of the World Health Organization, warned against the use of a "racist and fascist approach to stop the spread of AIDS" and against "discrimination and fear." The WHO opposes routine testing in America.

In America, the *People's Daily World,* a Communist newspaper, objected to routine testing because of the dangers to constitutional rights. At the same time, by 1990, the Soviet Union had performed over 50 million blood tests, screening its population and that of other Soviet bloc nations, including three-fourths of Cuba. As of December 1988, less than 100 people had HIV, and only three or four had died.[36]

According to the *New York Times,* February 16, 1993, "Cuba has the same population as New York City. New York has 42,737 cases of full-blown AIDS. Cuba has 159."

The Liberal Media's Subversive Mission

The information industry is brazenly dominated by liberals. This wouldn't matter if news was presented in a bi-partisan manner. But according to statements of industry icons, the media is no longer content with just reporting the news, now they must "shape" the public's thinking.

Bernard Goldberg of CBS' "48 Hours" reveals, "We in the press like to say we're honest brokers of information, and it's just not true."

Dianne Dumanoski of the *Boston Globe* brags, "The press does have an agenda. There is no such thing as objective reporting. . . . I've become even more crafty about finding the voices that say things that I think are true. That's my subversive mission."[37]

Unfortunately, the liberal slant concerning AIDS elevates the civil rights of infected people over the rights of the yet disease-free population.

Note the "60 Minutes" program in October 1993. Reporter Steve Kroft highlighted the success of the isolation program in Cuba, yet the objection prevailed on the program that the Cuban's "civil rights" were being violated! Unbelievably, the expert on "60 Minutes" who kept pressing this civil rights issue is none other than Jonathan M. Mann, the first director of the WHO's AIDS program.

Mann carries the mantle of "the leading public health specialist in the global fight against AIDS." Speaking at the 1994 International AIDS Conference, he had the audacity to inform attendees that "even if governments did everything called for in the current global strategy, AIDS would not be brought under control."[38]

Mann may be correct, but if so, it seems reasonable to charge that those who have used media propaganda to treat AIDS as a civil rights matter rather than as an infectious disease have been chief among the contributors to its spread. Additionally, any reporters brave enough to buck the credo of the liberal press and criticize the government or special-interest groups concerning their mishandling of the AIDS epidemic simply lose their contacts, if not their jobs. A reporter without contacts cannot survive.

Sadly, even the seemingly innocuous columnist, Ann Landers, adds her liberal bias to expansion of the AIDS epidemic. In one column she advises a distraught mother whose 15-year-old son is having sex with his 13-year-old girlfriend. After two paragraphs of sage advice, Ann Landers says, "Meanwhile, stay cool, non-judgmental, and pray a lot." Pray to whom, Ann? If there are no judgments, then there must be no judge.

After printing a doctor's letter listing factual evidence on the failure of even well-educated people to use condoms, the failure rate of those condoms, and the obvious need to avoid AIDS by abstinence and monogamy, Ann Landers commits another media crime by writing, "Dear Readers, powerful piece, isn't it? Now I am going to stick my neck out by suggesting a far more realistic solution than abstinence. The sex drive is the strongest human drive after hunger . . . there must be an outlet. I am recommending . . . mutual masturbation."

Thanks, Ann, for your confidence in one's ability to stay chaste until marriage. Too bad you weren't around to help God sort these things out before He wrote His book! Shame, shame on you, Ann, for helping to break down the morals of our youth, resulting in further spread of AIDS in their ranks!

That same perverse wisdom came from the mouth of Joycelyn Elders while she was serving as U.S. Surgeon General. This final straw in her long line of recommendations for school children to learn uninhibited sexual practices cost Elders her job.

Even doctors writing information columns fall into the uninformed, dis-information category. Dr. Donohue, syndicated columnist, assures people that AIDS can only be contracted through one of the four "party-line" methods. A reader asked about information he had seen stating that the AIDS virus could be viable for many days outside the body. The doctor assured him there was no problem of contamination, then mentioned that although he was not familiar with the medical reference, he was going to research the matter. But then he decided not to.

Promoting Sex Education — or Sex?

We have been told that if we give our children comprehensive sex-education programs, teenagers would have less pregnancies, abortions, and sexually transmitted diseases. We're constantly admonished with "Education is the best way to stop AIDS." Let us look at some of the helpful information, under this umbrella of education, that schools offer to our children.

The sex-ed program by Gary Kelly describes how to have anal sex and "non-harmful" sex with animals. Virginia Uribe, Los Angeles High School teacher and lesbian founder of Project 10, states, "Its goal is to persuade school children, beginning in kindergarten, to accept homosexual behavior as normal and desirable." (For her efforts in creating and bringing this program to schools throughout America, Uribe received the award of creative leadership in human rights from the National Education Association.)

Gus G. Sermos, former public health advisor and AIDS researcher at the CDC, reveals ominous information in his book, *Doctors of Deceit*. He details how the chief sex educator for Florida's Dade County AIDS Division (who was supposed to be teaching students how to protect themselves from AIDS), continued to participate in anal sex in public places until he eventually died of AIDS.

Parents, we must look at the information presented to us and our children that supposedly "teaches" us how to avoid getting AIDS. Most of the literature is monitored and/or produced by homosexuals and lesbians. The bias, which encourages sexual experimentation, promiscuity, and same-sex encounters, dominates the content of these propaganda pieces.

Barbara Nevins, reporter for CNBC, writes, "Adults who insist on a rigid standard of morality are as reckless as kids who have unprotected sex."[39]

Well, let us look at statistics on the success rate of liberal, comprehensive, sex-education programs.

"From 1971-1981, government funding at all levels for contraceptive education increased by 4,000 percent. In that time, teen pregnancies increased by 20 percent and teenage abortions nearly doubled."[40] As for comprehensive sex-education, a Harris Poll reveals, "Those who receive it have a 50-percent higher rate of sexual activity than those who have not had 'comprehensive' sex-education courses."

Excellent sex-ed programs such as "Sex Respect" teach abstinence as the only way to avoid STD's, AIDS, and pregnancy. This, and other programs like it, teaches the transcending values of self-control and commitment.

Statistical studies from independent research groups such as the Institute for Research and Evaluation in Utah prove that abstinence-based programs do lower sexual activity. Consequently, they lower the pregnancy rate, the abortion rate, and the spread of sexually transmitted diseases among teenagers. The sexually explicit, permissive, non-values curriculum taught in most sex-ed courses have proven to have devastating impacts on the youth of America.

Former Surgeon General Joycelyn Elders, during her tenure as director of the Arkansas Health Department, established 24 of the country's 200 school-based health clinics. The clinics' goals were to combat the "deadly disease" of teen pregnancy. During the run of her controversial programs, "pregnancies rose, syphilis rose 130 percent, and HIV infections went up 150 percent. . . . Elders attributed the failure of the clinic program to poverty, ignorance, and the Bible-belt mentality."

One goal Elders had said that she hoped to achieve was to see all K-12th-graders receiving comprehensive sex education. Her advice to high school girls to "put a condom in your purse" when going out on dates prompted the homosexual community to dub her the "Condom Queen."[41]

Speaking in New York to the Lesbian and Gay Health Conference, Elders castigated the religious right for its opposition to sex and AIDS education. "We've got to be strong," Elders challenged, "to take on these people who are selling our children out in the name of religion." Elders said she feels that if the religious community would stop moralizing the issue and educate "our" children, we could eradicate many of these problems.

True Christian home life promotes biblical morality, thus our children are encouraged to abstain from harmful activities. Obedient children within such homes need not fear falling into drug abuse nor acquiring venereal diseases. Do the methodologies Dr. Elders espoused guarantee these same desired results?

Kristine Gebbie, President Clinton's ex-AIDS czar, endorsed a New York City Youth Conference in February 1994, at which she was the keynote speaker. The literature handed out there is so depraved I choose not to exhibit its contents. Children as young as 12 received the graphic information. The pamphlets, produced by the Gay Men's Health Crisis, a New York AIDS group, were nothing more than initiation and instructions to perverted sex under the guise of AIDS education.

Recently, U.S. Congressmen displayed these pamphlets (and other homosexual and lesbian literature designed for children) before Congress. Viewers watched on CSPAN, but the pamphlets were so raw that they could not, by law, show them on television.

A ray of hope on the horizon may have occurred after this presentation: the inclusion of an amendment in the 1994 education bill, which stops funding to any school districts that allow the teaching of homosexual or lesbian behavior as a normal, alternate lifestyle, was voted in!

Freedom to Die and Kill Others

Too long pulpits have been silent about the major vehicle for the spreading of AIDS — promiscuous sex.

Somehow Christians have been deluded into thinking that the loving thing to do is to never criticize the lifestyle of another person. Many religionists seem more concerned with picking up broken bodies at the bottom of the cliff than climbing to the top and persuading people not to jump.

God warns us in 2 Timothy 3:1-5 that "in the last days perilous times shall come" and that people will love themselves and perverse pleasure more than God, and, worst of all, that people will have, ". . . a form of godliness, but denying the power" of God.

Let's look at a city in America named "Freedom." Around the turn of the century, the local citizens of this city bought their first automobiles. How wonderful to speed across town at the unbelievable speed of 20 miles per hour. It wasn't long, however, before the cars began crashing into one another as they crossed busy intersections. The town council wisely voted to set out stop signs to prevent the wrecks.

Later, as the speed of cars increased and technology advanced, the city fathers erected signal lights to control the flow of traffic. Even later, the addition of freeways necessitated the building of median dividers to separate the cars as they whizzed past each other in opposite directions.

Sometimes citizens didn't like to halt completely at the stop signs, especially when they could see no cars coming. Likewise, they sometimes found waiting at a signal when they were in a hurry to be an aggravation, and occasionally, when drivers missed a freeway turnoff, they wished they could simply execute a "U" turn in order to go the opposite direction. But these people truly realized that these forms of traffic control were necessary for the protection of everyone's safety.

One day there came into this idyllic town a traveler who hated the traffic control system. This newcomer attended the town council meeting and voiced his objections. "You call this town Freedom. What a joke," he chided. "You can't even make your own decisions when you drive. Who gave anyone the right to tell you to stop, especially when you can see there are no cars coming?"

The traveler hammered on the podium. "Folks," he warned, "this is about your civil rights. Nobody has a right to tell you how to live. You ought to be able to drive your cars the way it seems right to you!"

At first, the citizens were aghast at the traveler's suggestions, but as they discussed it among themselves, they began to realize he had made a great case. After all, their town was named Freedom. Its citizens ought to start living that way. So they voted to pull out the stop signs, disconnect the signals, and remove the median dividers from the freeways.

Now, at last — just as the traveler had recommended — the townspeople had true freedom. And so on the roads they killed themselves and they killed others. But they had freedom.

God gave mankind a free will. The Lord also gives us guidelines for every area of our lives. These guidelines are designed for our protection — to make our lives flow smoothly and to keep us from experiencing head-on collisions.

The guidelines of heterosexual sex and lifelong commitment in marriage have been given to us in order to safely channel the gift of sexual appetite. Ignoring God's guidelines and demanding no restraints in the name of civil and personal rights leads to disappointment, pain, and sometimes death.

Anyone having experienced the grief of a home shattered by sexual unfaithfulness can attest to this. As if the tragedies of broken lives, STDs, unwanted pregnancies, and abortions were not enough, we now have — through our insistence of "no mandates" from God or man — allowed a deadly epidemic to envelope the earth.

Is it too late to go back to God's control? Not for you.

God always wants you to humble yourself before Him so that He can offer you forgiveness and hope, but great damage has already been done to the world's population.

God gives us a vital principle in Galatians 6:7-8, concerning the consequences of our actions. "Be not deceived; God is not mocked: for whatsoever a man soweth, that shall he also reap. For he that soweth to his flesh shall of the flesh reap corruption; but he that soweth to the Spirit shall of the Spirit reap life everlasting."

In the AIDS epidemic, our world is reaping what our rebellious hearts have sown.

What Can We Do To Stop This Plague?

We must learn the truth about AIDS and not be afraid to tell others what we know. Beginning in our own homes, then branching out into our communities, and finally into our state and federal government, we must model, teach, and support the principles of chastity, abstinence, and commitment within heterosexual marriage.

The truth we need to disseminate is described by statistician Dr.

Stan Weed, who states, "Numerous abstinence-based curricula evaluations show that teens are not only able to discipline and postpone their sexual desires . . . they have a greater sense of self-respect and accomplishment when they do."[42]

A national chastity program, "True Love Waits," spearheaded by Youth For Christ, encourages teenagers to sign a pledge stating they will wait for sex until they are married. In the first year of the program, 500,000 pledged to remain chaste.

Leaders in one of the countries hardest hit by AIDS have discovered the value of teaching abstinence to young people and of respecting the ability to exercise self-control.

Dr. S. I. Okware, Director of Ugandan AIDS Control Program, said, "We don't pass out condoms. . . . Our president says that if we pass out condoms, we give our young people the wrong message. Condoms tell our youth that promiscuity is all right. Our program in Uganda is to encourage morality, and our program is working. It used to be that our sexually transmitted disease clinics would have 10 or 15 cases of STDs a day. Now we have perhaps one case a week, if that. We are cutting back on the transmission of HIV disease and venereal disease in our country."[43]

The recommended literature and videos at the end of this chapter will help spread these truths to our family and friends. We should make sure that our school districts use abstinence-based sex education programs, and most of all, we must not believe the lies that have led our world into this plague.

If mankind doesn't adopt policies of compulsory testing, mandatory reporting, contact tracing, and some type of isolation, all the world's inhabitants are at risk. Remember, this plague could have been avoided had mankind paid attention to the guidelines God set down in the Bible regarding life-long commitment in heterosexual marriages and separation of people with contagious diseases.

AIDS — a Judgment From God or a Sign of the End Times?

The same God who tells us how to live healthy and moral lives also says that He will give people over to a reprobate mind if they continue to blatantly disregard His guidelines of sexual behavior.

He also tells us of a future time when people who believe in Jesus Christ as Saviour will be taken out of this world to heaven. At this time, among those left on earth, the last vestiges of moral restraints will be thrown off. Under the tutelage of a satanically inspired leader, people will totally disregard God's rules.

The plagues that will come on mankind at this point will make even our AIDS epidemic look like child's play. Because the world has not taken responsibility for the moral decay that has brought us to the AIDS crisis, the AIDS epidemic may destroy billions as part of a self-inflicted plague during the future Tribulation.

In Revelation 6, we see listed the familiar four horsemen of the Apocalypse. The fourth and most devastating horseman brings death. "And I looked, and behold a pale horse: and his name that sat on him was Death, and Hell followed with him. And power was given unto them over the fourth part of the earth, to kill with sword, and with hunger, and with death, and with the beasts of the earth."

Notice verse 8 describes a time that one-fourth of the earth will be subject to death from war, famine, and beasts of the earth. Will these "beasts" be predators such as lions and tigers — or will, perhaps, a microscopic virus such as AIDS be the fulcrum of this worldwide carnage? So often throughout history, God has allowed the sins of men to double back on them and become the instrument of their undoing.

God's Word says that evil men would become ". . . worse and worse, deceiving, and being deceived" (2 Tim. 3:13). In a little more than a decade, the AIDS virus has spread from a community killer to a worldwide pandemic disease. The way world leaders (and the populace as a whole) continue to ignore, even disguise, the growing threat of AIDS, provides a graphic of that verse. Perhaps the whole deception we've seen connected with AIDS is a precursor of the powerful delusion that will accompany the rise of the final satanic world-ruler (2 Thess. 2:11).

God has a plan for the world, and the end of that plan is unfolding in our world today. Darwin, in his theory, tried to explain our existence apart from God so that he wouldn't have to honor God. But Darwin made a deadly mistake.

Psalm 14:1 says, ". . . The fool hath said in his heart, There is no God . . ." but nonetheless Darwin had to answer to the Lord. We know he did because God warns us, "And as it is appointed unto man once to die, but after this the judgment" (Heb. 9:27). God also states, ". . . Every knee shall bow to me, and every tongue shall confess to God" (Rom. 14:11).

The most vital truth to embrace today is that regardless of our previous lifestyle or how many of God's laws we've broken, Jesus paid for our disobedience when He died on the cross. Our debts are paid, and we are forgiven if we humble ourselves by asking for forgiveness from God through Jesus.

Jesus said in Matthew 11:28, "Come unto me, all ye that labour and are heavy laden, and I will give you rest." Today you have that choice.

As Joshua said in the Bible, ". . . Choose you this day whom ye will serve . . ." (Josh. 24:15).

Resources

Antonio, James, *The AIDS Cover-Up* (Ignatius Press, San Francisco, CA, 1987). History of AIDS epidemic with responsible ideas on how to stop it.

Adams, Moody, *AIDS: You Just Think You're Safe,* (Baker, LA: Dalton Moody Publishers, 1986). (918-234-0462) One of the best overviews of the AIDS plague that richly intersperses biblical quotes and applications

Cameron, Paul Ph.D., *Exposing the AIDS Scandal* (Lafayette, LA: Huntington House Inc., 1988). Excellent treatment of the motives and agenda behind the AIDS crisis.

Day, Lorraine M.D., *Aids: What the Government Isn't Telling You* (Palm Desert, CA: Rockford Press, 1991). (1-800-537-2437) Account of apathy, greed, fear, and irresponsibility in protecting people from AIDS by the past head of orthopedic surgery at San Francisco General Hospital.

Dixon, Patrick Dr., *The Truth about AIDS* (Eastbourne, UK: Kingsway Publication, 1987). Extremely practical treatment on AIDS. Both the truth and care giving are presented by this British cleric.

Exodus International (414-454-1017) A fine example of the more than 130 ex-gay organizations.

Gage, Rodney, *AIDS and SEX* (Nashville, TN: Broadman Press, 1992). Good material for mature teens looking for the Christian perspective on AIDS.

Jeremiah Films, *AIDS: What You Haven't Been Told; No Second Chance; Gay Rights Special Rights.* (1-800-828-2290, 1-800-633-0869) Hard hitting documentaries on AIDS, abstinence, and agenda.

Masters, William H. M.D.; Johnson, Virginia E.; Kolodny, Robert C., *Crisis: Heterosexual Behavior in the Age Of AIDS* (New York, NY: Grove Press, 1988). Alarming clinical research statistics of the AIDS crisis. Exposes blood supply risk, danger, and misinformation.

Miller D. A., *AIDS — Lies We've Been Told.* (909-658-1619) Audio capsulizing the AIDS information in Apocalypse III.

Monteith, Stanley M.D., *AIDS The Unnecessary Epidemic* (Sevierville, TN: Covenant House Books, 1991). A superb and riveting account of AIDS and the success of gay lobbies in preventing physicians from monitoring or controlling the AIDS epidemic.

Ray, Ronald D. Colonel USMCR, *Military Necessity & Homosexuality* (First Principles Inc., 1993). (1-800-837-3544) Powerful presentation on the problems of lifting the ban on homosexuals in the Military. Christian ethics applied to dilemma.

"The Report," (Lambda Report Publishers). (1-800-462-4700) Monitors homosexual agenda in American politics and culture. It offers many resources.

11

Decline and Fall of the American Family

By Chuck Missler

America is engaged in a civil war. The battle lines are drawn, the strategies are in place, the casualties are mounting. And the winner takes all.

From the shattering of families to a staggering rate of crime and lawlessness, the secular assault on the moral fabric of this country is unraveling every facet of life as we have known it. Even our most basic liberties, including our freedom to worship God without government interference and censorship, are now threatened.

It almost seems redundant to consider once again the statistics that, by now, have become familiar to most of us. On every side, in almost every place, we are beset with child abuse, rape, abortion that occurs at the rate of one per minute, drug abuse, senseless violence, sexual perversion, pornography, divorce, gang warfare, and finally, teenagers who are committing suicide at the rate of one every 90 minutes. No wonder.

It is not so much a situation in which Americans are merely breaking the law; it is more grave than that. It is a situation where people have actually overturned the law. God issued a severe warning to Israel in Isaiah 5:20: "Woe unto them that call evil good, and good evil; that put darkness for light, and light for darkness; that put bitter for sweet, and sweet for bitter!"

Boards of education across America sanction the teaching of homosexuality as an acceptable lifestyle, but the Supreme Court has banned them from using any reference to the word "God" in their official writings. We seem to have lost the standard, and there is no longer any consensus of what is true and what is honorable.

Ten years ago, we were shocked at revelations of declining moral values in America. Today, the shocking thing is that nothing shocks us anymore. We have seen it and heard it so many times that we have almost become desensitized. But as Christians accountable to God, we must wrestle with serious questions: How did this happen to our once great nation? What do we do and where do we go from here?

Facing Reality

For those of us engaged in the study of end-time prophecies, there is a subtle danger in all of this. We read 2 Timothy 3:1-5, and we know that, in the latter days, men are destined to become selfish, proud, disobedient to parents, without natural affection, despisers of those that are good, and lovers of pleasure more than lovers of God.

We debate the conspicuous absence of the United States in the final biblical scenario, and we somehow conclude that maybe America's decay is just a predestined prelude to the return of our Saviour. And so we become passive.

But if our Lord did return today, what would we have left to give Him from the wreckage of our rich spiritual heritage and the incredible blessings that He has bestowed on this country? We know from the parable of the talents that God expects a return on the truth that He has invested in us. How many talents would we have to offer?

When Jesus pronounced sentence against Judas, He made an interesting point. Personal responsibility for sin is never excused on the basis of the inevitability of events. "For the Son of Man is going as it has been determined, but woe to that one by whom he is betrayed!" (Luke 22:22;NRSV).

Whatever God chooses to do with the United States, we as Christians are still responsible for our stewardship of the liberties and the freedoms that He has given us. Jesus will not return in order to rescue us from a corrupt situation. He will return when His work on earth, through His church, is completed. The hope of His imminent return should compel us all the more to strive toward restoring the character of our country and the honor of His name.

That is where the going gets tough. Christian leaders everywhere are sounding the call to arms. We're challenged to fill the voting booths, call our congressmen, boycott the offenders, change the school systems, impeach our leaders. Frustrated Americans are proposing everything from a military takeover in Washington to secession from the union.

We are told to pray for revival and to stand up for God's Word. But it is on this last point that we come face to face with a very tough reality. We are trying to hold a nation of people accountable to God's Word when, in fact, a significant number of them no longer believe that God even exists.

Saving the Next Generation

It's plausible that the cause of our moral and spiritual dilemma, and the solution to it, may be something more simple and more profound than we have considered. Throughout Scripture, there seems to be a plan, ordered by God, that is designed to keep us corporately in God's blessing. It isn't just the type of government we set up or the people we elect or even the laws we institute. It is the simple commandment that we teach our children to keep the way of the Lord.

The concept goes back as far as Genesis 18:19 when God said of Abraham, "For I know him, that he will command his children and his household after him, and they shall keep the way of the Lord, to do justice and judgment. . . ." In Deuteronomy 4:10, He states again ". . . and I will make them hear my words, that they may learn to fear me all the days that they shall live upon the earth, and that they may teach their children."

The powerful impact of teaching children should not surprise us. Our enemies have understood it well. Communist countries made it policy to remove children from their homes at an early age in order to educate and indoctrinate them. Adolf Hitler pronounced that "who controls the youth, controls the future."

Liberal engineers of social change have made the claim that, given just one generation, they can radically alter a society. And they have proven their point.

Psalm 78:5-7 states:

> For he established a testimony in Jacob, and appointed a law in Israel, which he commanded our fathers, that they should make them known to their children: That

the generation to come might know them, even the children which should be born; who should arise and declare them to their children: That they might set their hope in God, and not forget the works of God, but keep his commandments.

Perhaps we need to consider that God doesn't hold us as accountable for governments and policies and social orders as much as He does for the spiritual inheritance that we give to our own children. Perhaps, in His providential plan, it would be enough if only we would master the task of safeguarding God's truth from father to child, one generation at a time.

For many Christians, teaching our children God's truth may seem routine. But therein lies the danger. It doesn't mean that we passively sit back and tell our children what we believe. It doesn't mean that if they see us going to church and to Bible studies that they will somehow get the message.

Teaching is not just exhibiting faith but laboring to implant everything that we know and understand about our God into the hearts and minds of the next generation. It is teaching God's Word and using every possible opportunity to demonstrate its validity. It is a labor of love.

Of His Word, God says: "And ye shall teach them to your children, speaking of them when thou sittest in thine house, and when thou walkest by the way, when thou liest down, and when thou risest up. . . . That your days may be multiplied, and the days of your children, in the land which the Lord sware unto your fathers to give them . . ." (Deut. 11:19-21).

However close our relationship with God, no matter how strong our own convictions, we need to understand this principle of teaching the next generation. Otherwise our faith dies with us, and our children are left to fashion a world of their own choosing.

Where Did America Get Off Track?

The fallout from the takeover of secular humanism in America has been staggering, and nowhere is it more evident than in the lives of our youth. When we examine the course of the last couple of decades in this country, we see a chronicle of what happens to a nation that turns its back on God.

The first chapter of Romans details a progression of sin and rebellion against God that is stunningly like the progression of life in

America. It begins: "Because that, when they knew God, they glorified him not as God, neither were thankful; but became vain in their imaginations, and their foolish heart was darkened" (Rom. 1:21).

There is no lack of historical evidence that this country was founded on Christian principles. Document after document confirms an original commitment to God and to His laws.

Patrick Henry stated, "It cannot be emphasized too strongly or too often that this great nation was founded not by religionists but by Christians, not on religions but on the gospel of Jesus Christ."

If we assume that 200 years ago the majority of people in America were followers of God, then what happened in the intervening years to bring us to where we are today? The answer may be that we lost something crucial. We lost the foundation, the reference point, of our Christian faith. And without the foundation of God's authoritative Word, we no longer had anything substantial to pass on to the next generation. So we substituted relativity for truth, and "values clarification" for God's moral absolutes.

After the Great Depression and the powerful impact of World War II, a generation of Americans suddenly found itself in a time of peace and prosperity. Life was easier, families were stable, and there was a general sense of order and rule. People trusted each other. Furthermore, they trusted the government and those in authority, and that proved to be a fatal mistake.

Instead of obeying God's command to teach our children diligently, we delegated that responsibility to Sunday school teachers and public schools — to authorities outside the home. At that time, there was no reason to assume that anything would be lost in the process. But we didn't see that the foundation was beginning to crumble.

Altering the World View of Life

Ken Ham, a scientist with the Institute for Creation Research, wrote that "the meaning of anything is related to its origin." Many who agree with that premise believe that the domination of evolutionary thought in America probably delivered the first and most extensive blow to the foundation of Christianity.

Of Genesis, Ham states that "all biblical doctrines are, in one way or another, founded in this first book of the Bible."[1] Thus, the evolutionary thought that undermined the creation of man, effectively undermined the whole authority of biblical teaching.

Many Christians still do not realize the enormous impact of the teachings of one man, Charles Darwin, and how he has forever altered the world view of life.

Public educators took the theory of evolution, which from the beginning was riddled with unanswered questions and inconsistencies, and presented it to an entire generation as the factual account of man's origin. With one broad stroke, they took out the Creator, which eliminated man's personal accountability, stripped away the value of a human life as having been created in the image of God, and erased the natural division between man and animal.

In his book, *The Long War Against God,* Dr. Henry Morris states that: "Evolutionism and its corollary teachings in the schools have so undermined the Bible by discrediting its record of creation and divine purpose that the whole 'Christian experience' has likewise been completely discredited in the minds of young people. . . ."[2]

It would be impossible to fully assess the amount of damage that the teaching of evolution has left in its wake. Since man is just a random accident in the universe, then life itself is of no real value beyond the existential seeking of momentary pleasure. No life is any more significant than any other, so there is really nothing and no one worth sacrificing for, and man has no more right to the earth's resources than the lowest animals.

In the words of Dr. David Jeremiah, "Abortion, infanticide, and euthanasia are logical behaviors for those who have so easily disposed of the image of God in the eternal soul of man."[3] Evolution effectively takes God out of the picture and allows man to justify anything and everything that he deems is a means to his own.

We could hardly have sent a more devastating message to our children. Instead of teaching them that they were uniquely designed by a loving and compassionate Creator, in His image, with value and purpose, we set them adrift into a world of futility and meaninglessness.

One of the intriguing things about the theory of evolution is that we embraced it so fully in the academic world when it was still suspect in the scientific world. In the book, *Origin of Species Revisited,* the author quotes a noted biochemist, that 100 years ago, ". . . even Darwin himself had increasing doubts as to the validity of his views. . . . His general theory, that all life on earth had originated and evolved by a gradual successive accumulation of fortuitous mutations, is still, as it was in Darwin's time, a highly speculative hypothesis entirely without direct factual support. . . ."[4]

Yet the theory of evolution was brought full-scale into the classrooms of America, even to the exclusion of the theory of creation. Evolution was introduced not so much as a scientific doctrine, but as a social doctrine that would completely redesign our view of life.

Dr. Morris goes so far as to state that "evolutionary thought is basically responsible for the lethally ominous political developments and the chaotic moral and social disintegration that has been accelerating everywhere in recent decades."[5]

Again, we find in Romans a reference to these engineers of social change: "Who changed the truth of God into a lie, and worshipped and served the creature more than the Creator, who is blessed for ever. Amen" (Rom. 1:25).

Abandoning the Places of the Heart

The progression of rebellion against God as outlined in Romans 1 denotes three areas where God "gave them up," or gave men over, to suffer the logical consequences of their own sin. First, He gave over their hearts to uncleanness (verse 24), then He gave over their bodies to "vile affections" (verse 26), and finally He gave them over to a reprobate mind (verse 28). We see around us today the same consequences in the lives of those who reject God, and in the life of our nation as a whole.

When we began to reject God, we first felt the damage in the "places of the heart." After the foundation was sufficiently weakened, the first major casualty of the war against God was the family. Every weapon that could be used to break down family structure was employed.

Once Americans achieved a high standard of living and the money supply was tightened, the pressure was on to reconcile the two. Many researchers report that financial pressure within a marriage is the number one cause of divorce. Many women were forced to enter the workplace in order to provide a second income, and at the same time, the new left began to denigrate the role of full-time mothers and homemakers.

Neil Postman, a professor at New York University and a secular author, discusses this shift in his book, *The Disappearance of Childhood.* Although he basically commends the women's liberation movement as one that "deserves the full support of enlightened people," he nevertheless sees it as "devastating to the power of the family."

Postman concludes: ". . . it cannot be denied that as women find their place in business, in the arts, in industry, and in the professions, there must be a serious decline in the strength and meaning of traditional patterns of child care. . . . Thus, as parents of both sexes make their way in the world, children become something of a burden, and, increasingly, it is deemed best that their childhood end as early as possible."[6]

Marie Winn, who writes for the *New York Times* magazine, continues this same line of thought, also from a secular perspective, in her book, *Children Without Childhood*. Her indictment states: "Instead of being willing as a society to sacrifice for children, to consider their care a primary duty, adults have transformed the very image of childhood from one that deserves protection and nurture to one that justifies their own sometimes monstrous abandonment of children."[7]

The sexual revolution also left its scars on the family in terms of infidelity. Therapists, however, reassured us that, no matter what we did, it was most likely someone else's fault. The concepts of sin and personal accountability became more or less obsolete. Increased self-esteem became the new goal, and it didn't matter what it took to achieve it.

The ideas of sacrifice and commitment, to anyone or anything, were quickly set aside if they interfered with the ultimate fulfillment of individual potential. As we mastered the art of putting "self" first, the divorce rate skyrocketed. And millions of pregnancies ended in abortion because we were unwilling to make a place in our world for the children we conceived.

And all the time, our children were watching us.

Since 1960, the teenage suicide rate has tripled. A recent interview on CNN "Headline News" featured a counselor who works with children affected by divorce. He described the impact on the child as being something similar to a drive-by shooting. "He is sitting there, minding his own business, when suddenly, out of nowhere, he takes a direct hit."

Josiah Gilbert Holland once wrote, "No nation can be destroyed while it possesses a good home life."[8]

With the disintegration of the family, we do not yet know where America's youth will end up in the final analysis. But we know a lot.

Give Kids a Benchmark

While the hearts of the children were at risk on the home front, their minds were being attacked on a different front. "And even as they did not like to retain God in their knowledge, God gave them over to a reprobate mind . . ." (Rom. 1:28).

Behavioral psychologists and secular forces began to infiltrate the public education system. Their influence gradually extended beyond academics and into the moral and philosophical realm.

Along with evolution, secularists brought with them the philosophy of humanism as set forth in two humanist manifestos, signed in 1933 and 1973. They introduced naturalism and supported it through the teaching of evolution. They replaced moral absolutes with relative values and situational ethics. And in 1962 they succeeded in persuading the Supreme Court to outlaw prayer and later, Bible reading, in the classroom. Quite an agenda for change.

Since that pivotal Supreme Court decision, teenage pregnancies have risen 556 percent, venereal disease is up 226 percent, divorce, which had declined for 15 years, has tripled every year since, and S.A.T. scores, which had previously been stable, began their remarkable decline, which continues today.

It stands to reason, however, that the real problem came not because of what children were being taught in school. The real problem may have been what they weren't being taught at home.

As a result of entrusting our children to outsiders, Postman notes that: "Psychologists, social workers, guidance counselors, teachers, and others representing an institutional point of view invade large areas of parental authority, mostly by invitation. What this means is that there is a loss in the intimacy, dependence, and loyalty that traditionally characterize the parent-child relationship."[9]

Secular teaching succeeded, in large part, because it went unchecked at home. Over and over, God charges the parents, specifically the father, to teach children His truth. ". . . the father to the children shall make known thy truth" (Isa. 38:19). "And, ye fathers, provoke not your children to wrath: but bring them up in the nurture and admonition of the Lord" (Eph. 6:4).

God makes no provision for the delegation of that responsibility, even to Sunday school teachers. It may be part of God's plan that, for children, truth is intrinsically validated when it comes through the life of the parents.

A poll conducted by *U. S. News and World Report* in the summer of 1994 found that 60 percent of respondents "say they hold their current religious beliefs because of their parents' example." Children who are taught foundational biblical truth will have a benchmark against which to measure every other doctrine and philosophy, and their minds will not be such easy prey for the enemies of God.

"Train up a child in the way he should go: and when he is old, he will not depart from it" (Prov. 22:6).

Rebellion and the Sexual Revolution

God gives men authority over in a third area — the physical realm. Nothing so graphically illustrates rebellion against God as the so-called sexual revolution.

The vast majority of teenagers today are presumed to be sexually active and are encouraged through school-sponsored programs to practice "safe sex." This assumption is so predominate that a curriculum teaching abstinence was ruled to be unconstitutional because the concept of abstinence was deemed to be "religious" in nature.

As a result of secular sex education, however, teenage pregnancies have skyrocketed, and 35,000 new cases of venereal disease are reported every day. Many of the pregnancies end in abortion, and there is continuing debate over the right of a minor to obtain an abortion without parental knowledge or consent.

In addition to sexual promiscuity, the market for pornography, including child pornography, is widespread.

Before his execution, confessed murderer Ted Bundy stated, in an interview with Dr. James Dobson, that one of the most powerful influences in his life of perversion was that of pornography. There is an end result of this progression in Romans — unclean hearts, vile affections, and reprobate minds — and it is a portrait of a people who have rebelled against God.

> Being filled with all unrighteousness, fornication, wickedness, covetousness, maliciousness; full of envy, murder, debate, deceit, malignity; whisperers, Backbiters, haters of God, despiteful, proud, boasters, inventors of evil things, disobedient to parents, Without understanding, covenantbreakers, without natural affection, implacable, unmerciful (Rom. 1:29-31).

Verses 26 and 27 deal with homosexuality, and the consequence of men ". . . receiving in themselves that recompense of their error which was meet."

The homosexual lobby is one of the strongest forces in American politics today and is openly advanced by the current President and his administration, despite the fact that homosexuals reportedly represent only one percent of the entire population. At the same time, AIDS continues to defy any vaccines or cures, all the while claiming thousands and thousands of lives every year. In the last year alone, the number of estimated AIDS cases has risen 60 percent, to almost 4 million people worldwide.

On August 6, 1994, Dr. George Lundberg, editor of the *Journal of the American Medical Association,* addressed the 10th International Conference on AIDS with a particularly somber prediction: that by the end of the next century "no successful method of treatment or prevention will have been fully implemented . . . and AIDS will still be a serious endemic disease throughout the world."

What happens when a group of people rejects the God of the universe and finds itself in this category? And what happens to the children of the generation that turns away?

The Journey from Light into Darkness

Frank Peretti, a well-known Christian author, once made a presentation in which he related the transition of life in America to a somewhat obscure verse in the Bible: "For rebellion is as the sin of witchcraft . . ." (1 Sam. 15:23). His premise is that there is a progression of sin beginning with rebellion against God that, when it runs its course, ends up in the realm of the occult.

There may be some interesting parallels to what we see around us today. One of the intriguing recurrent themes in Scripture is the contrast between light and darkness. Writing of Jesus, the Gospel of John proclaims, "In him was life; and the life was the light of men. And the light shineth in the darkness; and the darkness comprehended it not" (John 1:4-5).

Jesus marks His own identity with references to the light: ". . . I am the light of the world: he that followeth me shall not walk in darkness, but shall have the light of life" (John 8:12). "Then Jesus said unto them, Yet a little while is the light with you. Walk while ye have the light, lest darkness come upon you: for he that walketh in darkness knoweth not whither he goeth" (John 12:35).

According to Scripture, light represents the kingdom of God and His revealed truth, and darkness represents the realm of Satan. It is logical, then, that when we traverse outside the boundaries of God's truth, we run the risk of crossing over a type of spiritual boundary into the domain of darkness, or the occult.

Jesus said He came: "To open their eyes, and to turn them from darkness to light, and from the power of Satan unto God, that they may receive forgiveness of sins, and inheritance among them which are sanctified by faith that is in me" (Acts 26:18).

Man was created with an inherently spiritual nature. When twentieth-century scientists and behavioral psychologists tried to strip away the basic foundation of Judeo-Christian thought, what they left in its place was a spiritual vacuum. And into that vacuum, we are seeing the rush of New Age religions, the occult, eastern philosophies, and a wide range of teaching that seeks to replace the light with the dark.

When we took away from future generations the underpinnings of Judeo-Christian faith, they turned to find a faith of their own, and there was no shortage of leadership to help guide them in their search for spiritual fulfillment.

Old Enticements for a New Age

While it is true that Christianity is no longer allowed in the public school system, we would be very wrong to assume that religion has been removed from our schools. Secular humanism, once defined by the courts as a religion, is now giving way to more aggressive New Age precepts and doctrines. In almost every school subject, children are taught holistic education, values clarification, and transpersonal psychology. No longer is the major emphasis on academics as much as it is on behavioral and social strategies that will prepare the coming generation to be good global citizens.

But the New Age isn't really new at all. A blending of religions and doctrines that are rooted in Hinduism, including hedonism, pantheism, and humanism, it is as ancient as time itself.

In the garden, Satan tempted Eve with two enticements. First, he said that it was possible to be like God. Then he reassured her that "ye shall not surely die." These two concepts are the basic tenets of New Age thought, and the reason why it is so attractive to a nation without God. The idea that man can achieve "godhood" is to be found everywhere in New Age thought.

Stephanie Herzog wrote a book titled, *Joy in the Classroom,* claiming that every student can achieve personal inner fulfillment and strength through consciousness-raising exercise that put him in touch with "his true God-Self."[10]

In a December 1987 article in *Time* magazine, Robert J. L. Burrows stated: "You can see the rise of the New Age as a barometer of the disintegration of American culture. Dostoyevsky said that anything is permissible if there is no God. But anything is also permissible if everything (or everyone) is God."

Synonymous with the idea of godhood is the availability of power. The media is saturated with this idea of supernatural power, from "the Force" of *Star Wars* to *Field of Dreams* to *Dungeons and Dragons,* and beyond.

The latest example of this quest is the card game, "Magic: The Gathering," that has sold more than 10 million cards and continues to sell out before the game even hits the shelves. The game, created by Wizards of the Coast, deals with building up property, which is your "mana," and accumulating cards in order to acquire "the power" that each card carries.

The other facet of New Age comes from Satan's promise that "ye shall not surely die." The biblical understanding of death is that it is an integral part of man's redemption. God prevented Adam and Eve from eating of the tree of life so that they should not "eat, and live forever," which would have left them in their sinful, separated state of existence.

Jesus Christ triumphed over death when He rose from the grave, and in so doing, He robbed Satan of his most powerful weapon. It is no wonder then that Satan should try to negate the power of Christ's victory by convincing man that there is no death. Reincarnation allows New Age followers to live forever, and it takes out the uncomfortable specter of "accountability to a righteous God."

The Beautiful Face of Evil

Why is New Age teaching so easily pervading the American mainstream? And what does it have to do with the fall of the American culture? Isaiah 2:6 states, "Thou hast forsaken thy people the house of Jacob, because they be replenished from the East, and are soothsayers like the Philistines . . ." (NASB).

We know from 1 Samuel 6:2 that the Philistines practiced the art of divination. That practice, which is forbidden by God's Word, seeks to achieve power, control, and a knowledge of the future through the intercession of spirit beings or demons. What God denounced in Israel more than 2,500 years ago is no different from the trends that are sweeping through American culture today.

The eastern mystical religions have always been antithetical to God and to His revealed plan for mankind. Their influence has been called the beautiful face of evil. "And no marvel; for Satan himself is transformed into an angel of light" (2 Cor. 11:14).

Many scholars believe that, as we draw near to the return of Jesus Christ, it is only natural that those within the dominion of Satan will become more and more aggressive as they approach the final battlefield. New Age thinking is in perfect harmony with the end-time prophecies of a one-world global society under the leadership of one man, and the concurrent one-world religion that accompanies his rise to power.

That is why, when we decided we would no longer impose our system of spiritual values on our children, Satan was more than happy to impose his.

How to Change the World

It appears that as a nation we have traveled the full spectrum from the loss of our Christian foundation to open rebellion against God's moral truth, which had led many into the realm of occultic beliefs and practices.

How do we begin to turn an entire nation around and to reclaim the godly heritage that once was ours? We begin one person at a time.

One of the enigmas of Christianity is that ever since Jesus chose a handful of men to change the course of history, God has carried on His master plan for the ages through the transformation of one life at a time. We are not asked to perform supernatural feats or to overthrow principalities. We change America the same way we change our families. Lives are turned around, when one on one, we are willing to be used by God to make known the gospel of Jesus Christ.

The real challenge to us as Christians is to run the hard race. We need to measure our lives against the standard of God's Word and be willing to make changes where there are discrepancies. We need to alter our priorities, take a stand, teach our children, make the tough choices, and seek God's face.

We need to give our children a sure foundation, a certain knowledge of absolute truth that will transcend governments and philosophies and powers of darkness.

The greatest thing that we can do for America is to fight the good fight, finish the course, and keep the faith. Then possibly God will be able to use us in the way that He used John the Baptist 2,000 years ago: "... to turn the hearts of the fathers to the children, and the disobedient to the wisdom of the just; to make ready a people prepared for the Lord" (Luke 1:17).

12

How Near Is the Mark of the Beast?

by J. R. Church

The idea for a New World Order is not new. Over the centuries it has been a subject discussed only in the secrecy of smoke-filled conference rooms in the upper echelons of secret societies and under the cover of top secret government agencies.

Only in the past few years have politicians started talking about the concept openly and publicly. Why now? Because these well-planned programs for world government are almost ready for implementation. As we approach the turn of the century, the time has finally come, they think, to prepare mankind for the transition.

A slick multi-faceted advertising campaign has been launched to convince the human race that we should no longer think of ourselves as citizens of our respective countries, but instead, as members of some sort of global village. We are children of the universe!

Briefly, let's review the history of this conspiracy for world government and see just what our favorite politicians have in store for us.

Men have always fallen prey to would-be dictators, who, under the guise of noble causes, have strewn the battlefields of history with the carcasses of their victims. There were the ancient

Babylonians, Persians, Greeks, and Romans.

In almost every generation there has been at least one powerful monarch or politician who has sought to enslave as much of the human race as he could.

In the fifth century a Frankish monarch by the name of Merovee established a dynasty which, over the centuries, has attempted to revive the prestige of the Roman empire. Offspring of this family of European monarchs have scarred the face of the earth with their programs for world conquest.

In the Middle Ages, they attempted to revive the throne, the crown, and the title "King of Jerusalem." Five European armies, under the command of Godfrei de Buillon, drove the Moslems out of Jerusalem and attempted to establish mankind's long-awaited utopia. The year was 1099. Godfrei de Buillon died the following year, and his brother Baldwin eventually ascended the Crusader throne. This revival of the throne of David was supposed to last a thousand years. But alas, the so-called "kingdom of heaven" was defeated by the Moslems in just under 200 years.

The European Crusaders were told that they were in the service of a man who had descended directly from Jesus Christ and Mary Magdalene, and, therefore, had a divine right to rule the world. King Baldwin II converted the El Aksa Mosque, which stands today on the south side of the Temple compound, into his palace and changed the Mosque of Omar into a Christian shrine.

The Knights Templar

In 1118 a new order of knights was established. They were called the "poor Knights of the Temple." The French term is "Knights Templar." These so-called Knights of the Temple spent the next nine years excavating the temple site — not for the purpose of rebuilding the house of God, but to find the fabulous treasure, which had been hidden from the Romans a thousand years before. According to a copper scroll found in 1952 in a cave near the Dead Sea, some 138 tons of gold and silver had been buried in 64 locations.

In 1127 these "poor Knights of the Temple" returned to Europe wealthy beyond belief! In the years following, they established an international banking cartel capable of loaning gold to various governments and implementing a system of taxation for repayment.

The citizens of each country were called upon to support their "national debt." Today, the London financial district, which houses the Bank of England and all of its partners in the International Banking

Cartel, is located on 22 acres in downtown London — in the middle of which stands the Church of the Knights Templar. The Knights Templar own the International Banking Cartel to this very day.

The sordid story of these money manipulators is well documented in my book, *Guardians of the Grail and the Men Who Plan to Rule the World.* On page 11, I wrote, "The members of this secret sect are neither Christian nor Catholic, they are neither Jew nor Moslem. Their doctrine sidesteps the basic tenets of those beliefs and replaces them with the teachings of their greatest prophet — whom they believe to be Buddha."[1]

Their plan for world conquest has been a simple one. Over the centuries they have succeeded in setting up a central bank in every country of the world. They create money (reserve notes) out of nothing and loan it to the various governments in the form of paper currency.

This currency is not an asset but a debt. It is called a note — similar to the note of a loan at the bank. The currencies of all nations have become debtor's notes — upon which interest is levied and paid to the Class A Stockholders of the central bank. Pretty slick idea, isn't it!

The Knights Templar have bought the world. In his book, *Morals and Dogma of the Ancient and Accepted Scottish Rite of Freemasonry,* Albert Pike wrote of the Knights Templar, "Their watchword was, to become wealthy in order to buy the world."[2] And indeed, that is exactly what they have done!

I am indebted to Gary Kah and his tireless research published in his book, *Enroute to Global Occupation,* for insight into the history of Albert Pike and his involvement in the world's most secret society. He wrote that Albert Pike was a brigadier-general in the Confederate army, who, upon the defeat of the South, was tried and found guilty of treason. However, on April 22, 1866, President Andrew Johnson pardoned him.

Both men were members of the Masonic Lodge, and President Johnson was Albert Pike's subordinate. A statue honoring Albert Pike stands today in Washington, DC, even though he fought against the Union on the side of the Confederacy. It is the only such monument to a confederate soldier in our nation's capital. Albert Pike's book virtually became the text book of the Masonic Lodge.

Kah reports that on July 14, 1889, Albert Pike delivered "Instructions" to 23 Supreme Councils of the world, in which he said,

"The true and pure philosophic religion is the belief in Lucifer, the equal of Adonay; but Lucifer, God of Light and God of Good, is struggling for humanity against Adonay, the God of Darkness and Evil."[3]

This teaching, I might add, is revealed only to members of this secret society who reach the upper echelons of its power structure. The average member knows nothing of their real secret doctrine. This secret society, one of many which evolved from the Knights Templar, virtually controls the political power structure of every country in the world. Even President Affez Assad of Syria and King Hussein of Jordan are members of the Masonic Lodge.[4]

Currency Control and the Federal Reserve

Some historians say that the Revolutionary War, the War of 1812, and the Civil War were fought over an attempt to control the issuance of America's currency. The Bank of England was determined to establish and control a central bank in the United States.

Finally, in 1913, the Federal Reserve Act was passed by our well-intentioned politicians, creating a central bank for the United States — under the control of the Bank of England and its European-based International Banking Cartel.

When the Federal Reserve System was established in 1913, the United States had no national debt. Today, however, our government owes this International Banking Cartel more than $4 trillion. By the end of this century, all of the taxes collected in America will not cover even the interest due on our national debt.

Kah reminds us of what Thomas Jefferson said when he first learned that Alexander Hamilton had been given a permit to establish a central bank. He said, "If the American people ever allow private banks to control the issue of their currency, first by inflation and then by deflation, the banks and the corporations that will grow up around them, will deprive the people of all property until their children wake up homeless on the continent their fathers conquered."[5] That is exactly what is happening.

After the Civil War, Abraham Lincoln voiced his concern about the prospects of private control over America's currency. He said, "As a result of the war, corporations have been enthroned. And an era of corruption in high places will follow and the money power of the country will endeavor to prolong its reign by working on the prejudices of the people until wealth is aggregated in the hands of a few and the Republic is destroyed."

In 1913, Colonel Edward Mandell House, a secret representative of the International Banking Cartel, persuaded President Woodrow Wilson to support and sign the Federal Reserve Act into law. Some years later, President Wilson admitted, "I have unwittingly ruined my country."[6]

And who was Colonel Edward Mandell House? He was a proponent of world government. Kah reports that during the Civil War, his father, Thomas House, had been an agent of the Bank of England and had made a fortune by supplying the South with equipment and ammunition from France and England.

Colonel House called himself the "unseen guardian angel" of the Federal Reserve Act. He was not only an advisor to President Woodrow Wilson, he was the unseen administrator of the Wilson White House.

In 1912, Colonel House published a novel called, *Philip Dru, Administrator,* wherein he laid out a plan to bring America into a New World Order. He wrote, "America is the most undemocratic of democratic countries. . . . Our Constitution and our laws served us well for the first hundred years of our existence, but under the conditions of today they are not only obsolete, but even grotesque."[7]

His book tells of a bloody revolution in the United States wherein the "Socialism of Karl Marx" would be established. Colonel House wished the same for Russia. And that revolution came in 1917 — only five years after the publication of his book.

Over the years, there have been several attempts in our Congress to dissolve England's hold on America's currency. But all attempts have failed. Our government is filled with politicians on the payroll of the International Banking Cartel.

Gary Kah reports that by the middle of the 1980s, some 20 states had passed legislation calling for an audit of the Federal Reserve System — or for a repeal of the Federal Reserve Act. But did you hear about this in the news media? No. The big networks are effectively controlled by this powerful and fabulously wealthy secret society.

By the late 1980s the battle was once again taken to the floor of the United States Congress. House Resolution 1469 called for the abolition of the Open Market Committee of the Federal Reserve System, and House Resolution 1470 called for repeal of the Federal Reserve Act of 1913.[8] Another House Resolution called for an annual audit of the Federal Reserve. But again, they all failed.

How can this be? Who are these people who have a stranglehold on American politics? And what is this secret society which plans to bring all nations under their control?

The Council on Foreign Relations

On May 1, 1776, the infamous Illuminati was organized in Germany by Adam Weishaupt, a prominent member of one of the secret societies evolving from the Knights Templar. His sinister organization conspired for the overthrow of all governments and the establishment of a New World Order.

Weishaupt wrote, "We must do our utmost to procure the advancement of Illuminati into all important civil offices. By this plan we shall direct all mankind. The occupations must be so allotted and contrived, that we may, in secret, influence all political transactions."

According to some historians, this ultra-secret organization was short-lived. But not so! They have continued to flourish under the cover of several sister organizations until this very day. In the late eighteenth century they carried out the French Revolution. In the nineteenth century they conspired with Karl Marx to produce a plan for world conquest. In America, this secret society, funded by the International Banking Cartel, established a group called the Council on Foreign Relations.

Gary Kah quotes from the handbook of the Council on Foreign Relations concerning it's origin: "On May 30, 1919, several leading members of the delegations to the Paris Peace Conference met at the Hotel Majestic in Paris to discuss setting up an international group which would advise their respective governments on international affairs." The United States branch was officially formed on July 29, 1921, and called the Council on Foreign Relations.[9]

Over the years, this group has accomplished some astonishing feats. It established the United Nations, the Trilateral Commission, and the Club of Rome. Its tentacles reach into every facet of American life. It influences our educational system from the earliest grades to the university level. It provides politicians for local, state, and federal legislatures. It educates our lawyers and controls our judicial system. And it effectively controls both political parties in our nation.

It provides the candidates for our federal government in both the Democratic and Republican parties. We are told that the candidates differ in their approach to government; but in reality, it doesn't matter who is elected. Both will work for the establishment of world government. This is true not only in America, but in almost every nation in the world.

They are moving quickly to establish a New World Order by the year 2000.

Ten Horns, Seven Heads, and the Little Horn

Some 2,500 years ago, the prophet Daniel wrote about a coming world government headed up by an Antichrist. He used several metaphors to describe Lucifer's plan to enslave mankind. Daniel called this world government "a dreadful beast with ten horns" rising out of the sea of humanity. Then he described another "little horn" which would arise and conquer three of the first horns.

In Revelation 13:1, this beast is said to have seven heads along with its ten horns. The biblical view of the prophecy tells of seven heads, ten horns, and a little horn who will pluck up three horns by the roots. These numbers are fascinating in the light of modern developments toward a New World Order.

The Council on Foreign Relations established the United Nations to be the catalyst upon which world government will eventually emerge. More than 160 nations now belong to the United Nations — corresponding quite nicely to a prophetic "sea" of humanity.

The Club of Rome was organized in 1968 to oversee the unification of the entire world. On Sept. 17, 1973, the Club of Rome released a report wherein it proposed to divide the world into 10 political and economic regions. Its original document calls these 10 divisions of our world 10 "kingdoms." It seems to correspond quite nicely to the 10 horns on the beast in the Books of Daniel and Revelation.

Also in 1973, the Trilateral Commission was established, bringing the leaders of the three richest nations in the world together to foster a new era of "global economic interdependence."[10] Japan and the United States, along with Great Britain, represent the most powerful industrial base in the history of mankind. Each of these three nations funds their gigantic corporate structure and industrial base with a colossal stock market — the London Stock Exchange, the New York Stock Exchange, and the Tokyo Stock Exchange.

Since 1973, the Trilateral Commission has evolved into the G-7 (or Group of Seven). The Far East is dominated by Japan. The Western hemisphere is spearheaded by the United States and Canada. Europe is represented by Britain, Germany, France, and Italy.

The seven heads of these fabulously wealthy nations have met each year since 1973. They are preparing to establish a New World Order. These seven nations seem to correspond quite nicely to the prophetic "seven heads" on the creature described in the prophecies of Daniel and Revelation.

Most students of Bible prophecy have been watching the rise of a unified Europe as a possible fulfillment of the prophetic beast. As long as there were 10 nations in the Common Market, we were convinced that they constituted the revival of the Roman Empire. We were frustrated, however, by the inclusion of two other nations. There are now 12 nations in the EEC and plans have been laid to include several more.

Perhaps the unification of Europe will fulfill the prophetic scenario by providing a platform for Daniel's "little horn" to rise to power. According to the prophet, the Antichrist will destroy three nations. He will pluck up three horns by the roots.

If the Antichrist comes from a family of European monarchs — and personally, I am inclined to believe he will — he could rise from the ranks of the European-based International Banking Cartel. He could be guiding the trilateral nations and their partners to establish a New World Order, based upon those 10 divisions of the world suggested by the Club of Rome, and then step forward to foreclose on these three richest nations by collapsing their colossal stock markets.

Breaking the World to Pieces

Why will the Antichrist foreclose on England, Japan, and the United States? Because the world's three richest nations will soon owe more money to the International Banking Cartel than they can collect in taxes to cover their payments. It's just a matter of time. How could he do it? By instituting his prophetic "mark of the beast."

In Daniel 7:23 we are given details of the prophetic scenario: ". . . The fourth beast shall be the fourth kingdom upon earth, which shall be diverse from all kingdoms, and shall devour the whole earth, and shall tread it down, and break it in pieces."

First of all, this kingdom will be different from all kingdoms. This could be referring to a New World Order using the United Nations as a power base to divide the entire world into 10 economic and political divisions. Nothing like that has ever existed before in history.

Secondly, this kingdom will devour the whole earth — not just Europe. It appears to be larger in scope than just the development of a United Europe. According to the prophecy the kingdom will last only three and one-half years — the last half of the predicted seven years of Tribulation.

Then third, this kingdom will break the world in pieces. This so-called New World Order will utterly fail to unite the world. Once these super rich megabankers have control of all nations, they won't know what to do with them. Society will begin to fragment and revolt. Their elaborate scheme will crumble. They will break the world in pieces.

Yes, mankind is about to become enslaved to the most diabolical and ruthless dictatorship ever unleashed upon civilization. This dictatorship will be worldwide and headed up by none other than Lucifer!

Over the course of its rise and fall, half of the population of our planet will be slaughtered. A series of devastating wars will ultimately lead to the awesome battle of Armageddon.

Christ once said, "And except those days should be shortened, there should no flesh be saved . . ." (Matt. 24:22). But I've got good news for you. Mankind's long-awaited dream of utopia will soon come.

Out of Lucifer's final attempt to steal the dream, Christ will return. His planned appearance will come at the darkest moment for the human race. In the midst of Armageddon, Christ will judge the wicked and establish the kingdom of heaven on earth.

The New World Order

Past president of the United States, George Bush, along with Mikhail Gorbachev, popularized the terms, "New World Order," "New International Order," and "new partnership of nations."

The entire theme and focus of George Bush's address to a joint session of Congress on September 11, 1990, was "The New World Order." Speaking of the Persian Gulf crisis, Bush warned, "This is the first assault on the new world we seek, the first test of our mettle." He then summed up, "a new world order" may emerge from the crisis in which the world is "freer from the threat of terror, stronger in the pursuit of justice and more secure in the quest for peace. . . ." Bush had just returned from the summit meeting in Helsinki with Mikhail Gorbachev. He said the meeting laid the groundwork for "a new partnership" between Moscow and Washington, which would play a key role in a "new world order."[11]

I'm convinced that communism was just another pawn in their game plan. To prepare mankind for global control, they chose to provoke revolution, riots, race wars, and anarchy.

Seventy years before Karl Marx came on the scene, Weishaupt told his disciples that to achieve One World Government, his conspirators would have to infiltrate every agency of government. They first used Masonic lodges to institute their plan. By sitting in the top seats of all governments, Illuminati agents eventually guided nations toward their "Novus Ordo Seclorum," a New World Order.

This has been the goal of the International Banking Cartel. Gary Allan's statement in his book, *None Dare Call it Conspiracy,* could not make it any plainer. He wrote:

> "Communism" is not a movement of the down-trodden masses but is a movement created, manipulated and used by power-seeking billionaires to gain control over the world . . . first by establishing socialist governments in the various nations and then consolidating them all through a "Great Merger," into an all-powerful world socialist super-state, probably under the auspices of the United Nations.[12]

Were the International Bankers pulling the strings that controlled the affairs of communism? Yes. The leaders of Russia, China, Cuba, and other Socialist nations worked hand-in-hand with super-rich International Bankers.

The Council on Foreign Relations (CFR) was organized on July 29, 1921. Its headquarters building is located on the west side of fashionable Park Avenue at 68th Street in New York City. Facing it on the opposite corner is the Soviet Embassy to the United Nations.

The CFR's Study No. 7, published November 25, 1959, openly declared its true purpose: ". . . building a New International Order [which] must be responsive to world aspirations for peace [and] for social and economic change . . . an international order [code word for world government] . . . including states labeling themselves as 'Socialist.' "[13]

The first attempt in the twentieth century to unite the world followed the close of World War I. President Woodrow Wilson on January 8, 1918, laid out a 14-point plan to Congress for lasting peace. Within this package of world peace was a neatly hidden plan to get all nations to give up their sovereignty. It was labeled the "League of Nations."

World War I became a tool to frighten war-weary people into believing that all governments could unite into a New World Order and put a stop to all wars. The League of Nations could work to achieve world peace and security. But the Congress and Senate would not agree to it. By the end of World War II, however, their proposed world parliament finally became a reality: the United Nations.

The Call for Globalism

A current buzzword, or catch-phrase for One World Government, is "globalism." One of the most compelling arguments for globalism, today, is the danger of global annihilation. We are warned by a multitude of voices that this danger alone warrants the final sacrifice required to bring about global peace.

What is that sacrifice? For nations to surrender their sovereignties and armaments in a manner consistent with United Nations planning. If that were to happen, they say, this could end the threat of global war and begin an era of unprecedented peace and safety. But this requires the supreme sacrifice of nationalism.

The United Nations itself was founded upon a policy of globalism. It requires us to submit to the decrees of the United Nations General Assembly (or a similar body) as law — for the benefit of all world citizens.

Globalism has been a growing trend since 1973, when many famous and influential people signed the Humanist Manifesto II. They declared: "We deplore the division of humankind on nationalistic grounds. We have reached a turning point in human history where the best option is to transcend the limits of national sovereignty to move toward the building of a world community . . . a system of world law and world order based upon transnational federal government."[14]

Tal Brooke, in his excellent book, *When the World Will Be As One,* wrote:

> The pieces of the New World Order seem to be fitting into place very quickly. Economic Babylon is unfolding. The political powers of unity are marching ahead. And a social corrupting process combined with a spiritual apostasy is moving at an unprecedented rate. But no one looking on can really set the timetable. . . . Most likely the New World Order must be set in place before the final world ruler can ascend the throne.[15]

Ralph Epperson has written what I consider to be the comprehensive work on the conspiratorial view of history. His 490-page book, *The Unseen Hand,* is a classic work on the movers and shakers in world politics. Epperson actually shows us the proposed time frame for the New World Order.

He quotes Roy M. Ash, an official with the Office of Management and Budget during the Nixon administration, who, on May 18, 1972, predicted the time frame for world government: "Within two decades [sometime before 1992] the institutional framework for a World Economic Community will be in place . . . [when] aspects of individual sovereignty will be given over to supernational authority."[16]

His predicted time frame was apparently achieved! On November 19, 1990, the leaders of 34 nations gathered in Paris to sign the largest peace treaty in history. In the euphoria of the moment, world leaders could scarcely conceal their optimistic delight over the birth of international government.

The November 20, 1990, issue of the *New York Times* reported on the front page, "Mr. Bush said the treaty, signed beneath the glittering chandeliers of the Elysee Palace, 'signals the new world order that is emerging.' "

France's President Mitterrand noted, "It is the first time in history that we witness a change in depth of the European landscape that is not the outcome of a war or a bloody revolution. We do not have here either victors or vanquished but free countries equal in dignity." He proclaimed to those present that they were "putting an end to the previous age." In making this statement, he was announcing the advent of a new age.

Chancellor Helmut Kohl of Germany praised the treaty, saying it could build "a Europe of eternal peace." He added that the new Europe should found its conception upon the ideas expressed in the French Revolution, the Magna Carta, and the Declaration of Independence, as well as the philosophies of Emmanuel Kant, whom he cited as an eighteenth-century advocate of European unity.

Consent or Be Conquered!

Epperson quotes from the writings of James P. Warburg,[17] whose father, Paul Warburg, personally promoted the passage of the Federal Reserve Act. In his book, *The West in Crisis,* James P. Warburg, following in his father's footsteps, stated his support for a world government:

> A world order without world law is an anachronism; and that, since war now means the extinction of civilization, a world which fails to establish the rule of law over the

nation-states cannot long continue to exist. We are living in a perilous period of transition from the era of the fully sovereign nation-state to the era of world government.[18]

On February 17, 1950, James Warburg also told a Senate Committee how the peoples of the world would receive this world-government: "We shall have world government whether you like it or not, if not by consent by conquest."[19]

His proposed world government also includes plans for a world police force. Epperson quotes historian Arnold Toynbee, who once said: "We are approaching the point at which the only effective scale for operations of any importance will be the global scale. The local states ought to be deprived of their sovereignty and subordinated to the sovereignty of a global world government. I think the world state will still need an armed police [and the] world government will have to command sufficient force to be able to impose peace."

In Epperson's opinion, it would be a monumental task to convince people to give up their national sovereignty. However, U.N. spokespersons don't see the problem as insurmountable.

The former director of the World Health Organization, Dr. Brock Chisolm, stated, "To achieve world government, it is necessary to remove from the minds of men their individualism, loyalty to family tradition, national patriotism, and religious dogmas. . . . We have swallowed all manner of poisonous certainties fed us by our parents, our Sunday and day school teachers, our politicians, our priests, our newspapers, and others with vested interests in controlling us. The reinterpretation and eventual eradication of the concept of right and wrong which has been the basis of child training, the substitution of intelligent and rational thinking for faith in the certainties of the old people, these are the belated objectives . . . for charting the changes in human behavior."[20]

Making Less More

Epperson postulates, "In addition to destroying man's basic loyalties to family, nation and religion, the nation must be conditioned to the belief that less is better than more. The standard of living of those in the affluent nations must be reduced. This will be done by a slow, gradual process of conditioning the citizens of the rich nations to survive on less than they produce."[21]

The president of the Rockefeller Foundation, John Knowles, made this position very clear in its annual report for 1975:

I am sure of only one thing — more is not necessarily better. The web of interdependence is tightening. We are one world, and there will be one future — for better or for worse — for us all. Central to a new ethic of making less more is controlled economic growth which conserves scarce resources, provides more equitable distribution of income and wealth.

When people in the more productive nations have been conditioned to live with less, they can then be conditioned to share their excess wealth with less productive nations.

This sharing of the wealth, the exact position proposed in the Communist Manifesto, is called the New International Economic Order, a phrase that was defined by Council on Foreign Relations member Senator Charles Percy: "The philosophy behind the new international economic order is based on the fact that the developed wealthier nations use a substantially greater share of the earth's resources . . . than do the less developed poor nations. The new order calls for a more equitable distribution of the earth's resources among the earth's people and redistribution of wealth among rich and poor nations."[22]

In keeping with this program, on March 30, 1979, CFR member and former Secretary of State Cyrus Vance promised that the United States would step up its economic aid to developing nations in order to hasten "progress toward a more equitable and healthy new international economic order."

Ralph Epperson points out, "The progress towards this world government has been steady, not because the people of the richer countries have freely chosen it after hearing the arguments on both sides, but because they have been lied to. A good case in point is the article written by Richard Gardner, a top advisor to President Jimmy Carter, who was also Ambassador to Italy, in the April 1974 issue of *Foreign Affairs,* the monthly journal of the Council on Foreign Relations. He wrote that 'the house of world order will have to be built from the bottom up rather than from the top down. . . . An end run around national sovereignty, eroding it piece by piece, will accomplish more than the old fashioned frontal assault.' "[23]

U.S. Surrender to the U.N.

A United States government document published in 1961, entitled "Freedom From War" (State Department Publication 7277), was apparently a blueprint for the transfer of America's military forces to the New World Order. It proposed the gradual surrender of all the American forces to a world police force in a three-phase program:

> The first stage would significantly reduce the capabilities of nations to wage war by reducing the armed forces of the nations; the nuclear capabilities would be reduced by treaties; and U.N. 'peace-keeping' powers would be strengthened. The second stage would provide further substantial reductions in the armed forces; and the establishment of a permanent international peace force within the United Nations. The third stage would have the nations retaining only those forces required for maintaining internal order, but the United States would provide manpower for the United Nations Peace Force.

This means the Secretary General of the United Nations would become the Commander-In-Chief of the armed forces of the United States — a violation of the U.S. Constitution. We obviously finished "stage one" just before the invasion of Kuwait by Iraq. The United States is now caught in the beginning of stage two!

The World Affairs Council, on January 30, 1976, announced the next step in this program by releasing their "Declaration of Interdependence." It read, in part:

> Two centuries ago, our forefathers brought forth a new nation; now we must join with others to bring forth a new world order. To establish a new world order . . . it is essential that mankind free itself from limitations of national prejudice. . . . We affirm that the economy of all nations is a seamless web, and that no one nation can any longer effectively maintain its processes of production and monetary systems without recognizing the necessity of collaborative regulation by international authorities. We call upon all nations to strengthen the United Nations . . . and other institutions of world order.

Epperson reports that, at the time of its release, Congresswoman Marjorie Holt said this about the Declaration: "It calls for the surrender of our national sovereignty to international organizations. It declares that our economy should be regulated by international authorities. It proposes that we enter a 'New World Order' that would redistribute the wealth created by the American people."[24]

Announcing the New Order

The United Nations released a report on June 1, 1994, setting the agenda for upcoming conferences designed to establish world government in the near future. The United Nations Human Development Program (UNDP) announced plans for two meetings. The first was an International Conference on Population and Development summit held in Cairo, Egypt, during September 1994. The second was scheduled to be held in Copenhagen, Denmark, during March 1995.

The topics at these two meetings call for the creation of:

A World Court with powers to subpoena nations.

A World Police with the militaries of all developing countries to be dismantled.

A World Central Bank which would give the International Monetary Fund sole power to enforce austerity on nations.

A World Treasury.

An Economic Security Council with a mandate to intervene in those states that do not comply with U.N. protocols for genocide or "free trade" liberalization. Demilitarization would become a new condition for any aid or loans to developing countries.

A World Trade and Production Organization that would not only regulate "free trade" but also dictate quotas for nations (and, conversely, penalties and fines for those nations that might desire to resist U.N. edicts).

Global Taxation to include taxes on pollution, savings from demilitarization, foreign exchange transactions, and a global income tax on nations whose people average an income above $10,000 per year.

James Gustave Speth, head of UNDP, was the project director for Global 2000 during the Carter administration. The group demanded that world population be reduced to 2 billion by the year 2000. The UNDP report suggested that "unchecked population growth" is the biggest threat to "human security" and, by the year 2015, world population needs to be stabilized at 7.3 billion.[25]

With the world population already above 5.423 billion and

rising, some are convinced that armed insurrections will accommodate the U.N. goal with massive exterminations. Forced abortions, planned famines, and biological warfare are other options for meeting their goal.

Furthermore, there are rumors of civilian detention camps being built within our country under the auspices of the U.N.. The Clinton administration reportedly has already turned our military establishment over to the United Nations.

Many are beginning to ask how long it will take the U.N. to implement plans to accomplish their New World Order. Their projected goal is the year 2000.

New U.S. ID Card — MARC — of the Beast?

In conjunction with the emerging New World Order, the government has proposed a new ID card to be distributed in all branches of the military and has actually named it "MARC!" Does it show a sinister disdain for the military? Is it a cruel joke to play on service men and women? Or is it the beginning of the predicted "mark of the Beast?"

MARC stands for "Multi-technology Automated Reader Card." It is an individually carried smart card that includes a standard bar code, magnetic stripe, embossed data, printed information (including a digital photograph), and an integrated circuit (IC) computer chip.

A Pentagon report states:

> The Department of Defense Information Technology Policy Board initiated the MARC project in response to a proliferation of single-use card programs throughout the Department of Defense. The MARC project's purpose is to provide a multi-functional, cross-service utility card that satisfies the Department of Defense functional requirements for both a portable updatable medium and a static medium that can be used as a key to a database. The objective of Global Command and Control System (GCCS) is to give warriors real time decision support information. The goal of the MARC program is to develop a prototype that improves commanders' ability to access the information they need when they need it. MARC will accomplish this by serving as the key to a family of databases related to personnel control. As a result, MARC will enable warfighters to improve personnel asset management by:

enhancing warriors' ability to access GCCS at all levels; giving efficiencies of decentralized data manipulation without reliance on global connectivity; giving functional process owners, including the individual, control of data processing; eliminating manual data entry. The MARC program allows for expansion of evaluation into other functional areas. Potential candidate areas for additional evaluation are casual pay; straggler control; women, infants, and children program benefits; day care; and peacetime medical applications. Further areas may be added as requested.[26]

All of this simply means that the card can be used to transact business, exchange money, and totally control the lives of the cardholders.

If you think only the military will be subject to this enslavement, *USA Today,* July 1994, published an article entitled, "National Citizen ID is Proposed." The article states:

> All U. S. citizens and legal immigrants would get the equivalent of a national ID card under an expected proposal to Congress by the Commission on Immigration Reform. Similar proposals have been embraced by Congress but vehemently opposed by some immigrant and privacy advocates as costly and prone to abuse. The new Social Security-type cards, including photo and fingerprints, would allow employers to verify work eligibility through a national database. Workers would not have to carry them at all times but would have to present them when applying for a job. The idea is to prevent illegal immigrants from getting jobs through fake documents, and reduce discrimination against citizens and legal aliens. The commission's first report is due in September.

Many government proposals have been aired in recent months concerning a possible ID card for all citizens. We first heard about it when Clinton announced his so-called "Health Card." Next, we learned that all citizens on entitlement programs, such as Social Security and welfare will be given an ID card.

Jeff Leeds, writer for the *Washington Times,* wrote an article in July 1994 on the subject, saying that a debit card would deter fraud and reduce costs. Vice President Al Gore unveiled the program to distribute a "government benefits card" that would allow electronic access to government benefits. "Using a plastic card, similar to an Automated Teller Machine (ATM) card, welfare recipients and recipients of Social Security disability benefits without bank accounts would be able to walk up to any ATM terminal and withdraw their share of the $500 billion in benefit payments that the federal government doles out annually."

Reinventing Government with "MARC"

Jeff Leeds article continued on to tell about the proposed electronic delivery systems which are part of the Clinton Administration's "reinventing government" initiative. It is projected to go on-line nationally in 1999. Nine states have already started phasing in the electronic transfer plan: Florida, Alabama, Georgia, North Carolina, South Carolina, Tennessee, Kentucky, Arkansas, and Missouri.

Gore said, "This card makes it much easier to deliver the right benefits to the right people with much less paperwork." Appearing with him were Donna Shalala, Mike Espy, and Texas Comptroller John Sharp, who is overseeing what will be the largest state electronic benefits transfer project when it is fully phased in.

Donna Shalala said that with the electronic system "there's considerable less paper. The flip side is that we'll have an electronic audit trail for every transaction, making fraud much easier to detect and prosecute."

Leeds continued, "For benefits recipients with bank accounts, having their payments deposited directly is still the most cost-effective means of delivery. But for the estimated 31 million people without bank accounts who are entitled to food stamps, unemployment payments, Social Security payments, aid to families with dependent children, or other benefits, the electronic system will bring convenience and relief from the stigma associated with receiving government aid."

Federal and state governments pay $111 billion in military and federal pensions, veterans' compensation, student loans, and general assistance to recipients without bank accounts each year. In comparison, the annual fund flow for VISA, the nation's most widely used credit card, approaches $180 billion. Food stamp recipients would use the card as a debit card at grocery stores instead of paying for their purchases with paper vouchers. The card would block recipients from buying prohibited products and allow government fraud investigators to track transactions.

Meanwhile, the telephone company has cooked up the idea of having a personal telephone number that would follow you wherever you go in the world. It is called a personal communication service (PCS). Most phones are attached to a location. What's missing is a personal phone number. If each person had a personal number, a sender could use any one of a variety of devices to send information to a personal identifier rather than a physical location or device. Of course, this would require a personal identification number (PIN) different from any other of the 5 billion people in the world.

The Post Office is also working on a personal ID card and has suggested that government personnel put their heads together and come up with a single card to serve every need. Eventually, all cards will be reduced to only one card. It will be used for transfer of funds as well as other information accumulated on U.S. citizens.

I suggest that the ID card that will win over all the others will be a card that can be used in every type of reading device presently in use. In other words, it will have a magnetic strip for use in all credit card machines. It will have a bar code for use in laser reading devices such as those in grocery stores. It will have a computer chip for future use in a computerized cashless economy. It will have a digitized picture and identification number for the user.

If you haven't guessed it yet, I'm talking about the Multi-technology Automated Reader Card — MARC for short!

A New United States Currency

The time-honored U.S. Currency, revered by the rest of the world for many years, is destined to become part of this blossoming international economic system.

According to the July 1994 issue of *USA Today,* "A major plan to redesign greenbacks starting with the $100 bill . . . is expected by year's end. . . . Details remain under wraps to keep counterfeiters in the dark and consumers from being spooked by a make-over."

Some years ago, I suggested that a new "rainbow-colored" currency might have a blank spot on the face of it comparing to all the other currencies in the world. The international banking cartel could eventually use that blank area for an overprint, making all currencies of equal value. The new U.S. currency may soon provide that blank spot with a watermark.

Some day, in an unprecedented move, an announcement could be made that all currencies will be of equal value. The £10 English note will become equal to the $10 U.S. note, the 10 Francs note of France, the 10 Yen note of Japan, etc. — just with an overprint on the blank spot by the International Monetary Fund. I expect this to happen during the Tribulation Period — leading up to the "mark of the beast."

This new money has been in the works for several years, but complaints from grassroots America kept the Federal Reserve from bringing it out. Cries of conspiracy and the Reagan White House kept the Fed at arm's length. Now with a Democratic President, they are ready to introduce their program!

Back in 1989, I noticed that our currency was beginning to look worn out. I then suspected that the predicted new currency was imminent. I had a friend call the Treasury Department and ask why our bills were continuing to be circulated long after they were ready for shredding. He was told that the Bureau of Printing and Engraving had received a "bad batch of black ink." That was their lame excuse for not printing replacement currency.

We reported this and suggested that their story was a cover-up. Sure enough, a few months later, the Fed began an elaborate ad campaign about how they had to issue a new currency with microprinting and an embedded thread. But, they said, not to fear — the currency would remain essentially the same design; the greenback would remain green.

I felt that they resorted to the 1991 design because they had received such a hue and cry from grassroots America. But I suggested that someday they would conform to the design of all the other countries and convert our currency to a rainbow design, complete with a blank spot on the bill. Recently, I noticed ragged currency again, and, once again, my suspicion was correct.

Creating a Counterfeit "Crisis"

In the early 1970s, Congressman Ron Paul and others began to warn about the threat of a new currency. They stirred up such a commotion, the Fed ran for cover! It has been a long time coming, but it is now almost upon us.

The *USA Today* article says:

> Far bigger changes are now being considered, such as:
>
> Moving engraved portraits from the center to the

right or left and making them bigger.

Making greenbacks multicolored so two colors, when copied, become a third color.

Adding a watermark that can't easily be duplicated.

The Fed still claims that counterfeiting is the main reason for its proposed design changes. But that was the tale the Fed was telling almost a decade ago. The 1992 currency design changes were supposed to remedy this "counterfeiting crisis." In a *Readers' Digest* article entitled, "Do-It-Yourself Counterfeiting" which originally appeared in *Discover* magazine, author Michael Skoler wrote: "Until now, counterfeiting has been big business — estimated at $89 million in 1984."

Please note the article said the amount of $89 million was "estimated." But the article goes on to say, "Of the more than $7.5 million of bad money actually passed during 1984, only $1 million was good enough to fool bank tellers." Now that's a long way from $7.5 to $89 million. Out of an estimated $89 million, only $7.5 million was passed and confiscated by Treasury agents. And of that, only $1 million was good enough to make it past bank tellers.

In my opinion, this whole story is bogus — counterfeiting being the number-one problem which necessitates the expense of creating a new money design! No vote was taken in the Congress to approve or disapprove the currency design, though the constitution of the United States declares that Congress and Congress alone has the authority to create money and regulate the value of it.

In 1991, when Iran was accused of counterfeiting, this brought about the microprinting and embedded thread. Now, Iran is once again the bad boy in all this. It is accused of counterfeiting and distributing more millions of dollars. I call such propaganda "crisis management." The Fed created the crisis, then they propose a solution; and we end up with new currency.

An article in the May,1994 issue of *Coinage* magazine reported on the problem governments seem to be having with counterfeiting. Tom Toolen, reporter for the magazine, wrote, "The war between governments and counterfeiters has become extremely high-tech as bogus money continues to flood into the United States and other nations, both large and small, around the world." He reported that "color photocopiers are so widespread that it takes but a few seconds to turn out a $20 Federal Reserve note of high quality."

Frankly, I think color copiers, with their waxy look, would be one of the poorest ways of trying to counterfeit money! If the counterfeiter is going to spend big bucks for a color copier, he should buy the computer equipment to make negatives used in printing. You can't beat a printing press for excellent quality. An expensive color copier is no match for a nice printing press! In my opinion, the story coming from the Federal Reserve is flawed.

The three-page article in *Coinage* reported that sophisticated counterfeits of $100 Federal Reserve notes are turning up routinely in the United States as well as in other countries. Federal agents say they are being printed in Iran. The story from the Fed said that the "fake notes are virtually undetectable."

This is the same story used in 1989-91 to convince the American public that the Fed needed to change the currency by placing an embedded thread in the bill and adding microprinting around the picture. Iran was printing millions of dollars and distributing them around the world! Now, lo and behold, Iran is back in business again!

The article continued, "Many other governments throughout the world are equally concerned about the spread of counterfeiting technology to unfriendly nations — such as Iran — and to drug cartels. Both could flood the world currency markets with fake bills and notes — very sophisticated counterfeits that could cause chaos and even topple shaky governments."

I agree that it is possible for Iran to produce good-quality counterfeit Federal Reserve notes. But Iran did not use color photo-copiers. They would have used high-tech printing presses bought from the U.S. by the Shah of Iran before he was toppled.

The Coming One-World Currency

I have a large book entitled *The Art of Paper Currency*[27] in which color reproductions of all currencies used by all nations are displayed. I was amazed when I looked through the book and noticed that virtually all currencies had blank spaces over a watermark on each bill. Furthermore, all nations sported a rainbow of colors — all but the U.S. Federal Reserve note. It seems that the rest of the world is just waiting for the Fed to join the system and prepare for a one-world currency.

Most of these currencies are printed in the United States and shipped to other countries. The various designs in the currencies are so similar, it appears obvious they were all designed by the same group of artists. The colors may vary from country to country, but all the inks used are pastel and similar in appearance. The pictures of each country's heroes appear on the bills, but the technique used to draw each picture is the same. It matters not whether the currency represents a democracy or a communist country, the bills look similar in design.

The Russian ruble (or should we say rubble) sports a blank spot. The currencies of Israel and Syria look similar enough to have been printed on the same press — yet the two nations have been enemies for many years. This is true of all of the Mid-East nations. Even Iraq's currency is printed by the same people on the same presses.

It is obvious that an international banking cartel is in control of all central banks in all nations. They are the ones who have conspired to create a one-world government. They financed the United Nations. They are the members of the CFR (Council on Foreign Relations), the Bildebergers, the Trilateral Commission, the Club of Rome, the G10 (group of ten industrialized nations), the G7 (group of seven industrialized nations), etc.

Why should the Federal Reserve want to redesign the currency so soon after the 1991 design changes? I think it needs to have that blank space for the coming one-world currency.

Let No Man Deceive You

The United States is a sovereign nation. For some 200 years it has been an example to the world for freedom and prosperity. Our standard of living is higher than any other nation in this generation or at any time in history. For this reason, the poor and oppressed of all nations have desired to come here to live. In spite of all our problems, we are indeed blessed to be citizens of the United States.

There are some, however, who are determined to enslave our nation and its people — to pull down our economy and destroy the freedom of the individual. They would have us poor and hungry if they could. They would use the resources of our people for their own profit if they could. They would make America and the world one big slave labor camp if they could. Where they have gained control, they have starved the poor, killed the educated and religious, and enslaved the masses. They have "nationalized" industry and made serfs of the farmers. And they would do that here if they could.

Their master is Lucifer. He gives them power and authority to deceive the masses. Many of their spokesmen are handsome, rich, and friendly. They rise to political power with promises of freedom from tyranny. Yet theirs is a tyranny far more suppressive than the leaders they oppose.

In Matthew 24:5-6, our Saviour warned against these people, saying that they will "deceive many." In verses 24 and 25, Jesus repeated His admonition with emphasis. He said, "For there shall arise false Christs, and false prophets, and shall shew great signs and wonders; insomuch that, if it were possible, they shall deceive the very elect. Behold, I have told you before."

Jesus wanted us to remember that He had prophesied this. He warned that those who advocate world government would be so persuasive and convincing the average gullible citizen would believe them. The apostle Paul also spoke of their abilities to convince the uninformed. He wrote: "Let no man deceive you by any means: for that day shall not come, except there come a falling away first, and that man of sin be revealed, the son of perdition" (2 Thess. 2:3).

Again the emphasis was upon deception. "Let no man deceive you."

Why would both Jesus and Paul remark that many would be deceived, and that we should be careful not to be deceived? Even the apostle John described the Antichrist in those very terms: "And deceiveth them that dwell on the earth by the means of those miracles which he had power to do in the sight of the beast; saying to them that dwell on the earth, that they should make an image to the beast, which had the wound by a sword, and did live" (Rev. 13:14).

The politicians who cry for world government are trying to deceive people into accepting a Luciferian attempt to exclude God from this planet. He is trying to replace the Sovereign of the universe with himself. He is trying to keep Jesus Christ from sitting upon the throne of a world kingdom of His own. Instead of the Kingdom of heaven established upon earth, Satan wants to establish the kingdom of hell.

"Let no man deceive you," said Jesus and Paul and John. Feel good, Mr. Average Citizen, while a new currency is slipped into your billfold. Put your faith in paper money while a Judas goat is leading you down the primrose path to slavery.

Why should I accuse the average citizen of being gullible? Why should I be critical of the powers that be over their control of America's pocketbook? After all, aren't the politicians in Washington only concerned about the public good? Aren't they only trying to solve the problem of a $4 trillion national debt?

Will the shake-up of the powers-that-be in Congress that took place November 8, 1994, really constitute a change that will return power to the citizenry of the United States?

Jesus said, "Take heed that no man deceive you."

Paul wrote, "Let no man deceive you."

And John wrote that when the Antichrist appears upon the world scene, he will "deceive" the nations into accepting a world system of monetary exchange — but eventually will demand a mark in the right hand or the forehead in order to participate in the marketplace.

Return to a Gold Standard?

Is the world being deceived today? Consider a clipping sent to me which appeared in the *New York Times,* written by a conservative republican, Lewis E. Lehrman, who ran for governor of New York in 1982. He is a businessman who heads "Citizens for America," a so-called "conservative public-policy organization."

Mr. Lehrman wants us to return to a gold standard. Sounds good, doesn't it? That would mean the paper currency in your billfold would be worth a specific amount of gold. Gold certificates in the 1920s stated on them that the bearer could exchange that paper for gold upon demand.

He went on to say that an "overvalued dollar has demonstrated that free trade without stable exchange rates is a fantasy." He's tired of floating exchange rates. He wants a stable dollar. He said that "during 1985, almost 200,000 jobs, mostly in manufacturing, disappeared." He said, "Another 200,000 farms disappeared from the economic landscape."

Lehrman explained that a floating exchange rate for the dollar is like "a board of directors setting the length of a yard at 36 inches, then in a few days setting it at 30 inches, only to be changed again after a few more days to 40 inches."

However, here's the kicker: This so-called conservative politician says that our government doesn't have enough sense to regulate our own money under a gold standard. He said, "A lasting and just solution to the dilemma of the world paper dollar standard would require the leading nations to share a common monetary standard, a reserve currency independent of any national currency and not controlled by any self-interested sovereign government."

Mr. Lehrman would have you to believe that our government has been in control of our currency and that it has done a poor job. He suggests that we turn our sovereignty over to a world central bank. It will do a better job.

What he doesn't tell us is that our government has not been in control of our currency; a central bank has been doing that poor job. Now he wants to merge the Federal Reserve Bank with the Bank of England, claiming that they will do a better job when, in fact, they are the very ones who have been doing that bad job down through the years.

And he is a conservative Republican? It's time we try to understand that not all people who call themselves conservative or Republican really are. Some of them are wolves in sheep's clothing.

Mr. Conservative continues: "We could create a World Central Bank, whose independent credit would serve as neutral reserves for all national central banks — a system proposed by John Maynard Keynes in 1944 at Bretton Woods." What this so-called conservative Republican does not tell us is that John Maynard Keynes is considered by conservatives as a rank liberal socialist.

How would this plan for a world currency based upon an international gold standard be established?

First, Mr. Lehrman suggests that the president "should arrange for the Treasury and the Federal Reserve to cooperate with the Group of Five to stabilize the value of key currencies."

Second, the president should "send legislation to Congress establishing a gold dollar coin as this country's constitutional monetary standard. Convertibility would take effect in May 1987, one year from the Tokyo meeting." He said, "The price of gold must be set at a level that will cover the cost of producing the gold that goes into the monetary standard — approximately $400 to $500 per ounce."

Third, the president should "convene an international monetary conference to agree upon the reciprocal value of all major currencies and to abolish official reserve currencies."

Such a concept should not come from a conservative Republican. He is suggesting a move toward world government. He wants the United States to cease to exist as a sovereign nation. He wants the international banking cartel to totally control the economy of every nation in the world. It already directs policy in every major nation.

Through the World Bank, the cartel is loaning money to third-world countries, thus creating national debts that are impossible to pay back. Its purpose is to eventually control its currencies as well.

Mr. Lehrman went on to write, "One must emphasize that the

new international monetary system could accommodate generous social policies in every country."

Once a nation has yielded its sovereignty, new and "generous social policies" can be established. This may sound good to those who receive the benefits from social programs, but what he does not tell us is that these programs will be strapped to the backs of those who pay the taxes.

Why should we want to return to a gold standard anyway? Over the years, the international banking cartel has been buying up the gold. If we return to a gold standard, the international bankers will become entrenched in their control.

And control is the name of their game. Their goal is to enslave every man, woman, and child on the planet.

The Mark of the Beast

According to Bible prophecy, a loosely knit world government will demand a mark in the right hand or forehead of every person before he or she can participate in the market place. The mark will constitute their medium of exchange: "And he causeth all, both small and great, rich and poor, free and bond, to receive a mark in their right hand, or in their foreheads: And that no man might buy or sell, save he that had the mark, or the name of the beast, or the number of his name" (Rev. 13:16-17).

With the use of symbolic language, the writer of Revelation predicts a time when all the world will wonder after Satan and worship him:

> And they worshipped the dragon which gave power unto the beast: and they worshipped the beast, saying, Who is like unto the beast? who is able to make war with him? And there was given unto him a mouth speaking great things and blasphemies; and power was given unto him to continue forty and two months (Rev. 13:4-5).

John describes the 10-nation confederated world empire and its leader as having a mouth speaking great things. This is the same terminology used by the prophet Daniel in his description of this same beast with seven heads and 10 horns: "I considered the horns, and, behold there came up among them another little horn, before whom there were three of the first horns plucked up by the roots: and, behold, in this horn were eyes like the eyes of man, and a mouth speaking great things" (Dan. 7:8).

Again we are told that he had a mouth speaking great things. Here is the source of this leader's ability to deceive. He will be able to control the media. It will sing his praises. He will offer a solution to every economic problem. He will tell people that separate governments cannot control their balance of trade. He will say that every national government should put its faith in a global currency in order to stabilize prices.

Bought and paid-for politicians will agree. They will swing the vote in his favor. When the time is right, he will go to Jerusalem and declare the city to be internationalized — under his control. He will make Jerusalem his capital for world government. The Bible refers to it as "the abomination of desolation."

Watch out for such politicians who tell you that a global currency is the answer to our problems. Watch out for them, even if they pretend to be conservatives, or even conservative Republicans. Watch out for them, even if they are the highest and best-loved officials in our nation.

13

Planet Earth in Crisis: Overview and Update

by Dave Breese

The Man with a Plan

The pavilion of the nations was an awesome place that day
With the throb of martial music 'neath a fiery display,
With the flags of all the nations lifted upward to the stars,
With kings and queens and princes stepping from their stately cars.

The peoples of the planet were represented there,
For the world had been invited to come and think and share.
In the midst of global crises of a hundred separate kinds,
They came for new solutions, for a meeting of the minds.

"We must have all new answers," said the leaders of the day.
"We come from starving peoples, bankrupt countries, disarray.
Ugly wars are raging 'round us, rivers flood, and cities burn,
Murder, arson, rape, and pillage — death awaits at every turn."

"We sense," they said, "that we have been in every way betrayed.
Our dreams are now in ruins and our people are dismayed.
Our hope, once placed in state, in church, in God, in love, in race,
Is gone, along with faith itself. What now shall take its place?"

Then a man stepped to the platform, to the circle of the light,
Who with words of warmest greeting said, "We welcome you tonight.
You have come from every nation of this sad and troubled earth
To seek a fresh beginning, yes, a new and nobler birth."

"I can tell you," said the speaker, "in this time of hate and fear,
Though problems seem unsolvable, frustration's end is near.
The turning point of history could be this very day,
For there is one who shall soon come to sweep your fears away."

With these and many other words he promised all things new
To all the peoples of the world, the Gentile and the Jew,
To red and yellow, black and white, the miracle would come.
The new and golden age would dawn, the old must now succumb.

He spoke of possibilities, of challenges, of goals.
How man, believing in himself, the universe controls.
"You are the gods of this New Age," he said to that great throng,
Which then, transported by his words, broke forth in gladsome song.

A thunderous ovation roared from that adoring crowd.
With cheers of acclamation both loud and still more loud.
Ah, how the crowd exulted, holding high each little son
To see him who would tell them of the world that can be won.

Bathed in that light and clothed in white he welcomed their applause.
Then he, impassioned, spoke of things beyond all human laws.
How shifting in the paradigm was making all things new.
The awe-struck crowd saw in his words the beautiful, the true.

The throng was hushed, *How could,* they thought, *we live to hear this
   voice*
Which calls us to this bright design and offers us the choice?
We can now step up to greatness, affirm the spacious plan,
Give ourselves in privileged service to this dear and cosmic man.

Then he, as if divining that crowd's emergent mind,
How they would make of him the man to guide the new mankind
Then escalate him to a throne, with scepter, crown, and ring
Where he in wisdom, power, and love would rule everything.

He said, "Now you must listen and hear me in this hour.
There is one much more endowed than I with wisdom, force, and
    power.
He is himself the one who forged this wide, colossal plan.
He is himself the greatest mind yet given to mortal man."

"He has the power to move the world, to set the nations free,
To bring upon our suffering earth its long-sought liberty,
To be the final stanza of the anthem mankind sings.
And — Ah, the joy! — he even now is waiting in the wings!"

With this the crowd was plunged into silence, stunned and still,
"What could this mean — A man who now would all our hopes fulfill?"
"Yes!" said the white-clothed figure as he gestured toward the gate,
Where an entourage moved slowly as if neither soon nor late.

Each eye transfixed upon that group then focused on a man,
Who by his sheer demeanor seemed all social gulfs to span.
"He truly is majestic," thought the throng which stood and stared
As he rode astride a charger white, whose crimson nostrils flared.

He ascended to the dias, more widely to be seen,
Then stood before that trembling throng with strong and stately main.
His impact on that multitude was wondrous to behold.
They then stood still as gifted words upon them he bestowed.

"My dear and noble comrades, co-citizens of fate,
This day begins upon this earth an era new and great.
For now the gods have chosen that this must be the time
When all that is newly made — when all shall be sublime."

"We gather here from myriad scenes, from every hemisphere,
Our homes, our farms, our children are the reason we are here.
We seek the unity of earth where faction is no more.
The ship of state must anchor on a new and peaceful shore."

"When men of earth must join as one, yes e'en the stars o'erhead,
The masters of the universe, together they have said,
'The ages past and those to come conjoin this very day
To now transport us to the realm where gods alone hold sway.' "

"My promise is eternal peace, the gods of war deposed,
We'll see the age of verdant green, the fig tree and the rose.
Earth will become a garden fair which blooms from sea to sea.
The parliament of nations ordains these things to be."

The man (But was this just a man?) spoke on that fateful eve,
His flashing eyes, his golden voice, his words without reprieve
Moved from his mighty master-mind to every waiting era
To capture for the glorious cause each soul, both far and near.

But wait — the speaker lifts his hands, a roar sounds loud and high,
Then — Could it be? — cascading fire falls from the flaming sky.
The raging conflagration for a moment sweeps the tier
Before the lighted faces now aghast with living fear.

It swept upon that orator, before that wide-eyed crowd,
He still stepped out majestically unhurried and uncowed.
"The fire," he said, "has in myself now cleansed the souls of men.
The limits on humanity shall never be again."

From that moment of all moments one could never be the same.
The nations of the world became the clients of his fame.
The rulers and the ruled of earth, with tears of ecstasy,
Enrolled to join the legions of that man of destiny.

The next vortex of history was forged on earth that hour.
A cryptic new compulsion would seize men with its power.
Certain now of greatness, they would stand in glory's ray.
The pavilion of the nations was an awesome place that day.[1]

History's Most Provocative Hours

The most remarkable days in history!

Yes, by any standard, it can truly be said that we live in one of history's most provocative hours.

One glance across the culture in the world of the 1990s would remind us that a set of events is totally upon us, so provocative and so high an impact that, for many, it becomes difficult to understand the tide of our times. This, however, we must endeavor to do because the Christian is the most strategic person on the face of the earth. He is the salt, he is the light, he is a part of a city that is set on a hill.

In fact, because the Church is the bride of Christ, we can certainly argue convincingly that the presence and witness of the Church is the reason the world still holds together. The necessary judgment of God upon the violations of His moral law in our time is only withheld because the Church is still in the world. We can, therefore, derive great benefit and assurance by examining the tide of our times in the light of the teaching of the prophetic Scriptures. A knowledge of the Word of God, along with an awareness of our times, is a necessary combination in these remarkable days.

Therefore, let's all take a trip together! We shall charter a 747 jet and travel to a number of places in our world so as to take to ourselves a "first-hand" awareness of a set of developments that could have significant prophetic import. An update as to the circumstances of time and a comparison with Holy Scripture are, therefore, a valuable enterprise.

Europe's Plan for Unity

We shall then take off from New York's Kennedy Airport on a 090 heading and make our first stop the continent of Europe. Coming in on a long approach to London's Heathrow Airport causes us to think about Europe and its present circumstances.

In the late 1970s, the leaders of Europe began speaking tentatively about some kind of an economic union. Europe had been rather passive since the humiliating days of World War II and by that time appeared to be doing some new thinking about the future. Europe's leaders could not fail to recognize the fact that the major power in the world was the United States of America. They saw the beginning of coalitions coming together in both the Americas and also in Asia and calculated that these would have significant import for the future.

Following this observation, they correctly reasoned that Europe, unless it did something special, would be a collection of individual nations that would be little more than banana republics. No nations in the world believe more in the power of combined efforts than do the nations of Europe. So they announced that it would be the intention of Europe to create the EEC, the European Economic Community.

Month by month, the possibilities of a combined economic situation in Europe became the object of the study and mounting anticipation of the nations that comprise the European community. First, a half-dozen nations came together, then seven, eight, nine. Finally, Greece became the tenth nation of the new European Economic Community.

The promise was that goods would flow rather freely from one nation to another and export capability would be increased. More boldly then, Europe began to announce that it would put together a combination of 325 million people, and they would comprise a gross national product larger than that of the United States. Larger, therefore, than would be the case with any other nation or combination of nations on earth.

The promise of the possibilities of economic unity began to be announced to an onlooking and understandably concerned world. The announcement of the plans for such a union was not empty, for Europe represents massive economic capability.

In the meantime, the picture became complicated by the near-dissolution of the Soviet Union. In the late 1980s, the nations of eastern Europe suddenly were able to disconnect themselves from the massive and controlling interest of Communist power stemming from Moscow.

For this and a number of other reasons, the conviction grew in Europe that economic union would not work as a stand-alone possibility. It appeared necessary to plan a second kind of union that would work in conjoinment with economic union. This was, as the nations of Europe quickly agreed, political union.

Consequently, there emerged the oft-repeated call for an organization of European states — a political union that would work in conjunction with the efforts toward economic union. As a consequence, we have listened to ever more animated discussions from Europe as to how to put together the nations of Europe into strong economic unity.

In fact, Germany seemed to be one of the early illustrations of the possibilities of economic union. With the new independence of the eastern European states, East Germany became a country unto itself. The magnetism of nationalism was very great at this time, and so, with Helmut Kohl taking the lead, West and East Germany found themselves walking hand in hand again.

This gigantic step of unity within Europe then began what most leaders of Europe hoped would be a step toward European political unity. This program of economic and political unity has moved from then until now in a most interesting fashion. It has been drawn together by a mysterious magnetism, but it is not without its problems.

Calling for a "Man with a Plan"

These problems began to be represented by a new expression in

Europe, namely, "the bumpy road to European unity." Unity as an abstraction seemed desirable and possible.

Unity, however, in the concrete sense, embraces a thousand details that are not easily resolved. These include central banks, forms of currency, new communications, business practices, airline schedules, and dozens of other things. Even the standardization of diverse railroad tracking has become an issue. Considering these details in particular, the road to unity in Europe continues to be bumpy.

The difficulties of unity have also created a new mindset in Europe. More and more of the peoples of these nations are recognizing the fact that a new and more powerful mucilage must come to the fore in order to make unity a reality. The emergence call has since been raised in Europe, saying "we must have a leader, someone to draw us together to produce in fact the unity that we desire." The call is for a great European leader as a successor to Jacque Delors. That call is coming on strong as of now.

It is of interest that the theologian Paul Johnson has called our generation "a world without leaders." He traces every country of the world and declares that there is no leader who has the prestige or the personal strength to, by the magnetism of his life, pull together new alliances.

With this in mind, Europe must see the emergence of a leader the like of which does not really exist today. Such a leader must be able to present a vision for the future that would be a marvelous thing indeed. Yes, Europe is, even now — as it travels the bumpy road to unity — looking for "the man with a plan." The road to unity appears to be at a standstill until such a man appears.

Seeing this crossroads in the history of Europe, we remember a most interesting prophetic forecast given to us in the Word of God. "Know therefore and understand, that from the going forth of the commandment to restore and to build Jerusalem unto the Messiah the Prince shall be seven weeks, and threescore and two weeks: the street shall be built again, and the wall, even in troublous times. And after threescore and two weeks shall Messiah be cut off, but not for himself: and the people of the prince that shall come shall destroy the city and the sanctuary; and the end thereof shall be with a flood, and unto the end of the war desolations are determined" (Dan. 9:25-26).

Here we have a most telling prophecy in the Word of God. It is the advanced statement that the people who destroyed the city and the sanctuary shall produce "the prince that shall come." We believe that the Antichrist will come from a complex that is generally the revived Roman Empire.

The Roman Empire embraced a good part of the world of that day and was headquartered in Europe, Rome to be exact. From the European complex, therefore, will emerge this princely, capable man who will be able to convince the people of Europe that he is their human savior, their great leader for the days to come.

Yes, Europe will produce "the man with a plan." The call in Europe is even now for such a person who will draw together Europe's many divergencies and guarantee a future that includes global influence.

In fact, let us remind ourselves that the Antichrist will present himself to the world from his original base of power, a united Europe. From thence, he will move on to the place where finally he is the political master of earth.

He will even make a covenant with the people of Israel, which he will break in the midst of that period of time called the Tribulation. The breaking of that covenant will institute the Great Tribulation, a day so terrible that Christ spoke of it, saying, "And except those days should be shortened, there should no flesh be saved . . ." (Matt. 24:22).

Europe continues to move in a direction that will make necessary the emergence of "the man with a plan."

Russia's Destiny

Let us continue our air sojourn and fly further east and north to the land of Russia. What a scene lies before us. Central Russia, with its still large land dimensions, represents 160 million people and the remaining, massive military power.

Many books could be written about the recent changes and the present situation in Russia. The primary book dealing with Russia's destiny, however, is the Word of God.

Ezekiel, the prophet, says, "And the word of the Lord came unto me, saying, Son of man, set thy face against Gog, of the land of Magog, the chief prince of Meshech and Tubal, and prophesy against him, And say, Thus saith the Lord God; Behold, I am against thee, O Gog, the chief prince of Meshech and Tubal: And I will turn thee back, and put hooks into thy jaws, and I will bring thee forth, and all thine army, horses, and horsemen, all of them clothed with all sorts of armour, even a great company with bucklers and shields, all of them handling swords" (Ezek. 38:1-4).

This graphic description in the Word of God is the opening lines of two chapters given to us by the prophet Ezekiel. These two chapters, Ezekiel 38 and 39, provide one of the most dramatic pictures in the entire Bible of a massive war. They tell of the great army from the north — the Prince of Rosh — moving down upon the land of unwalled villages and attempting to conquer and control the nation of Israel. Bible scholars, with virtual universality, have long believed that here we have the picture of Russia attacking the state of Israel and the Middle East.

The result, of course, will be devastation coming upon the invading army. The Lord says, "And I will call for a sword against him throughout all my mountains, saith the Lord God: every man's sword shall be against his brother. And I will plead against him with pestilence and with blood; and I will rain upon him, and upon his bands, and upon the many people that are with him, an overflowing rain, and great hailstones, fire, and brimstone. Thus will I magnify myself, and sanctify myself; and I will be known in the eyes of many nations, and they shall know that I am the Lord" (Ezek. 38:21-23).

Out of this battle will come devastating consequences for the invading army. Out of it also the scene will be set for a covenant to emerge between Israel and the ruler of Europe — the Antichrist. The loss by Russia of its army will put this nation into political obscurity for a thousand years.

Never Underestimate the Power of a Tyrant

What, then, do we see in contemporary Russia which leads us to be thoughtful about the emergent prophetic picture? First we see the form of its aspiring ruler.

The world looked on with interest as Mikhail Gorbachev came to the place of the premiership of Russia. As general-secretary of the Communist party, he ruled the nation, but he brought it in a new direction. He advocated the now well-known words, *glasnost* and *perestroika*. In his writings and in his preachments, he advocated the program of "openness and restructuring." The fresh air of at least the possibility of freedom began to blow in and over the steppes of Russia.

Not strangely, this program instituted by Gorbachev led to an attempted coup in Russia. Few of us will forget that August day in 1989 when the coup attempt took place. The nation listened with fear and fascination as the story of those days unfolded. Finally, however, Gorbachev was not imprisoned or executed, but was able to go free.

Out of the event, however, came a change in the government of the Soviet Union and the emergence of a new general-secretary, Boris

Yeltsin. He stood atop a Russian tank and, by the force of his personality, thwarted an attack on the government buildings. This escalated him to power and won him the leadership of Russia in the first democratic election to have taken place in hundreds of years. Having achieved the mastery, Yeltsin has continued to hold power. Popular in the other nations of the world, he has visited the United States and the countries of Europe and has provoked the response of great acclaim.

A new force, however, moves in Russia today. It is led by one of the most colorful, clever, and provocative politicians that the world has seen come from the Soviet Union. His name is Vladimir Zhirinovsky. He appears to be totally committed to the future of Russia, but very unpredictable in his behavior.

He ran for the leadership of the Soviet Union in the last election and ended up with 26 percent of the vote. He is, therefore, 26 percent away from political mastery in Russia, a fact which he continues to announce to all who will listen.

The interesting part about this man is what he promises to do: make the Soviet Union bigger and more powerful than ever before, re-subjugate all of the nations that once were a part of Soviet power, and add to that circle of nations. In addition, he says he intends to demand that the U.S. return Alaska to the Soviet Union.

He has also promised that he will move south with the Red Army and take the land of Israel and a major portion of the Arab world. He says that he will push all the way to the Indian Ocean, thereby guaranteeing a warm-water port for his beloved Russia.

New elections are coming up in Russia within the next two years. What would happen if Zhirinovsky were elected premier of a new Soviet Union? We can only assume that he would endeavor to carry out the absurd goals that he has announced.

We have learned from Hitler that it's never smart to underestimate the intentions and the power of a tyrant. If Zhirinovsky were to take to himself all of the power that the Red Army could give, only the Lord knows how much of this he would carry out. But the potential emergence of a new ruler in Russia — the Soviet Union — is worth deep consideration on the part of the thinking student of the Word of God.

Another consideration that relates to Russia is its retained massive nuclear arsenal. The United States is now de-commissioning its Minuteman missiles and destroying the silos that housed them. We have insufficient evidence that any such corresponding reduction in arms is taking place in Russia today. Promises are one thing, performance is another.

Russia possesses 30,000 nuclear warheads and has 11,000 of them pointed at the United States. Even though the promise is that targets have been changed, missiles can be re-targeted in very short order. The retained nuclear capability of Russia makes it still the second most formidable military force in the world. The United States may not continue to be the first if her program of nuclear disarmament continues.

Ethnic Cleansing in Yugoslavia

While we continue to think about this, let us fly south, where we will look at the situation in southern Yugoslavia.

Here the war continues between the Serbs, the Croatians, and the Bosnians. So convoluted is this warfare that it is difficult to interpret on a day-to-day basis.

What we should notice about this is that the Serbs, in the process of conquering 70 percent of Bosnia, have announced their program, which they call "ethnic cleansing." Ethnic cleansing is a sanitary word that really means the extermination of a whole race of people.

The pictures and the accounts that have come to us from the terrible wars in southern Yugoslavia are heart-rending indeed. Concentration camps have been set up, and every form of cruelty has been instituted in the process of the Serbian conquest. It even became necessary for the Pope to cancel his visit to Sarejevo because of the perils of sniper fire and even an all-out attack.

This expression, "ethnic cleansing," leaves us very thoughtful.

Christ spoke about a particular time in history when He said, "For nation shall rise against nation, and kingdom against kingdom: and there shall be famines, and pestilences, and earthquakes, in divers places. All these are the beginning of sorrows" (Matt. 24:7-8).

Christ, on this occasion, spoke about this period of time called, "the beginning of sorrows." What time might this be? The beginning of sorrows is certainly the time that brings us out of the age of the Church and into the time of the Tribulation.

The Tribulation will bring upon the world the ultimate sorrow, the worst that it shall ever know. Of this Christ spoke when He said, "For then shall be great tribulation, such as was not since the beginning of the world to this time, no, nor ever shall be" (Matt. 24:21). The Tribulation will be a very terrible time indeed.

Speaking then about the beginning of sorrows, a characteristic of that time which ought not to be forgotten when we hear about Bosnia is found in Christ's statement: "For nation shall rise against nation."

Here, the word used for nation is "ethnos," which means race. Therefore, Christ is predicting severe racial warfare during that time of "the beginning of sorrows."

In that the word "ethnos" is used in this connection, we note the similarity between this expression and "ethnic cleansing." Shouldn't we sit up and take notice when we find occurring in our present time a dreadful activity that uses the same word that Christ used to characterize the beginning of sorrows?

A further note should be sounded in this regard. Looking at the condition of our time and remembering this prediction from the Word of God, shall we not expect more racial warfare to come? Some even predict a racial civil war in the United States in the very near future.

Racial conflict is most difficult to resolve, for it is hardly subject to negotiation. After all the talk, a race is a race, and nothing can change that. The war in Rwanda is essentially racial and has already consumed the lives of 500,000.

Africa — Land of Cruelty and Vengeance

The grievous outpouring of stunning news from Rwanda has brought many of us to tears. The conflict is essentially between two tribes of similar racial characteristics.

The rebels, in their successful attempt to take over the government, have presided over a massacre of a half-million people. We will not forget the grisly accounts of bodies by the hundreds lying along roadsides, in fields, or drifting down the river into Tanzania.

What human explanation can there be for such cruelty between man and man? It is almost as if a new and demonic motivation has settled upon certain peoples of the world, leaving them to indulge in unspeakable cruelties.

Notable from a prophetic point of view is the quick explosion of the disease of cholera among these people. During the height of the migration, 15,000 people per day were dying from this dreadful malady. Exposure plus lack of nutrition plus lack of pure water is a deadly combination. Reports also indicate that cholera was able to take hold quickly because a high percentage, perhaps 50 percent, of the people were already afflicted by the AIDS virus.

HIV is a very common and always fatal disease in Africa. This, along with the unspeakable conditions of Rwanda, has produced pestilence and carnage beyond description. We note that "pestilence" is one of the characteristics of this period of time called "the beginning of sorrows."

Thinking further about Africa, we look for just a moment at South Africa, where President Nelson Mandela, leader of the black majority, is now firmly in power. The question, "What will this man do?" is being asked by everyone.

The future of the resolvement of apartheid in South Africa is yet in question because Mandela has recently announced that "apartheid crimes will now be investigated." He promises that all — especially whites — who participated in one and another presumptuous crimes during the years of apartheid will be investigated and properly judged.

One reads of the plans with a certain degree of chill because a program of retribution on cruelties in the past can only trigger more retribution and further cruelties today. How well-profited would the world be if it simply read and believed the statement of Scripture in which God says, ". . . Vengeance belongeth unto me, I will recompense" (Heb. 10:30).

Yes, there will be a day of vengeance of our God. When man, however, takes into his own hands that vengeance, then the cycle of suffering and death continues. Look for this continuing cycle in South Africa today.

The Middle East: Peace Among Enemies?

In our quick trip to Africa, we have flown over the most prophetically strategic area of the world — the Middle East. The Middle East is where it all began, and the Middle East is where it is all going to end. To keep an eye on this convoluted area of the world is to keep one prophetically thoughtful.

In September of 1993, Yassar Arafat (the world's leading terrorist) and Yitzak Rabin of Israel signed a peace accord (which was professed to be the fruition of a number of months of secret negotiations) at the White House in the United States. In the accord, Israel agreed to cede limited sovereignty to the Palestinians of two areas of the world: the Gaza Strip and the Jericho area. The world applauded this accord and promised that it would be the beginning of a great program of peace that would benefit all of mankind.

The months to follow brought small and relatively insignificant results of that conference. Limited autonomy has indeed come to the Gaza Strip, and autonomy with an even greater limitation to the area of Gaza. Significant financial help to back these accords has come from the United States. (One wonders why the United States is having such a large piece of the action in these programs.)

Suspicion continues, however, with reference to the PLO because the Palestinians have only Arafat as a leader. They have no government, no constitution, no police force, and no significant military infrastructure. The PLO is reputed everywhere to be a horde of bloodthirsty thugs. It is certainly unrealistic to believe that the results of this accord will be satisfactory in the name of peace.

We note that a second conference was conducted by Yitzak Rabin, and a second accord signed in Washington, DC. This accord was not with the PLO, but with King Hussein of Jordan and, to the rejoicing of the world, ended an official state of war between Israel and Jordan. The announcement was made in Israel, and in the world, that a major second step had now been taken toward peace in the Middle East.

One of the possible prophetic implications of this second accord is the situation of Jordan with reference to Petra.

The Scripture teaches that, during the days of the Tribulation, there will be a gigantic exodus, a time of escape for Israel. During the Tribulation, Israel will be converted to Christ the King and will be the object of fearful persecution by the Antichrist. Indeed, the period of the Tribulation will not only be a time of fearful judgment coming upon the world, it will also be a time of evangelism — perhaps the greatest in all of history.

It will be during the Tribulation that Israel is converted and brought to faith in Jesus Christ as the Messiah. The result of this will be serious, dreadful persecution upon the nation of Israel by the Antichrist.

Speaking of this, the Scripture says, "And when the dragon [Satan] saw that he was cast unto the earth, he persecuted the woman [Israel] which brought forth the man child. And to the woman were given two wings of a great eagle, that she might fly into the wilderness, into her place, where she is nourished for a time, and times, and half a time, from the face of the serpent" (Rev. 12:13-14).

Finally, the Scripture says, "And the dragon was wroth with the woman, and went to make war with the remnant of her seed, which keep the commandments of God, and have the testimony of Jesus Christ" (Rev. 12:17).

Where will be Israel's hiding place? What will be the manner in which Israel is protected from the persecution of the Antichrist during those days?

In answer to this question, it is interesting that there is a rose-red city in the south of Jordan, deep in the wilderness. This city, protected by a very narrow entrance, is the city of Petra.

Many Christians have visited this city and remember it to this day with great interest. Bible scholars to a great extent have suggested that this city has been prepared by God as the hiding place, the fortress of protection for the nation of Israel during the Tribulation.

The problem is that Petra has been inaccessible to the nation of Israel for most of the last 2,000 years. But things have changed because an accord of peace has been signed between Jordan and Israel!

What are the implications of this? We suggest that it is possible that now a corridor of escape has been opened for the nation of Israel to flee from the Antichrist. This corridor, made possible by the new accord with the nation of Jordan, could well be the way that God uses to make possible the deliverance of Israel during the Tribulation. Agreeing to this possibility, we suggest, therefore, that the recent accord between Israel and King Hussein may turn out to produce results far more significant than the current expectations.

Peacekeepers on the Golan Heights

Continuing to think about Israel, we must remember that there is an element of danger in this new accord. Israel is now being pressed to come to some kind of peace agreement with the land of Syria. As such, the pressure is that Israel shall retreat from the Golan Heights. The heights above the plains of Galilee would then again be occupied by the soldiers of Syria.

In order to neutralize their effect, the suggestion is now being made that a peacekeeping force, even including Americans, occupy the Golan Heights. Such a force would be expected to put down hostilities on either side, from the Syrians or from the Israelis.

We recently spoke to a young Israeli who said, "Please do not consent to a peacekeeping force in the nation of Israel! Please remember that if Israel gives up the Golan Heights, Israel is finished."

It seems that the people of Israel know this, but its leaders do not. Therefore, what possible pressures are being put upon Rabin and his cabinet now in order to acquiesce to the ridiculous course of no longer occupying the Golan Heights? This will bear some deep thinking as we consider how the activities of the nations are developing in our time.

The Bible, we will remember, gives some very severe warnings about trusting too deeply in programs to bring human peace. Again and again we are warned as to the impossibility of peace so long as people are not related to God properly. In fact, the Scripture says, "There is no peace, saith the Lord, unto the wicked" (Isa. 48:22).

Still, we are promised in the Word of God that there will be great movements toward peace as we move to the end of the age. Speaking of this, the apostle Paul says, "But of the times and the seasons, brethren, ye have no need that I write unto you. For yourselves know perfectly that the day of the Lord so cometh as a thief in the night. For when they shall say, Peace and safety; then sudden destruction cometh upon them, as travail upon a woman with child; and they shall not escape" (1 Thess. 5:1-3).

This verse tells us that the call to peace will become very strong at the end of the age. The cry will be "peace and safety," and this will be the promise of those in power. It also tells us that this program will become an utter failure. For in the midst of a great peace movement, destruction will come upon the people of the world. They shall not escape the devastating war which is to come.

We Christians may note that we are given in this a word of assurance, "But ye, brethren, are not in darkness, that day should overtake you as a thief" (1 Thess. 5:4).

What a wonderful promise! Christians, having given attention to the Word of God, are not to be caught unaware. So we do not walk in darkness because we have availed ourselves of the marvelous message found in the prophetic Scriptures. Considering the prophetic import of the Word of God, those Scriptures become a great source of solace and comfort in our time.

A Mighty Asian Alliance

It is a long flight from the Middle East to the Far East, but we must take it. Why? Because the Far East appears to be on a program of highly accelerated growth and great emergence into global significance. The most highly populated sector of the world is Asia, with billions of people who are slowly becoming aware of the world situation and their possible participation in great events.

Watching the other coalitions of the world develop, the Asian nations have elected to do the same. Japan, South Korea, Taiwan, the Philippines, Singapore — all of the significant nations of free Asia — are coming together in a mighty Asian alliance.

This area now represents billions of people, large industrial potential, economic power, and many other potential assets that promise to be a part of the great Asian cooperative venture. The dramatic transformation in an upward direction that is taking place in Asia since World War II is a wondrous thing to behold. Under the general leadership of Japan, the Asian alliance is now being forged. It represents the potential of world influence.

In the Bible, the nations of the Far East and their leaders are called "the kings of the East." The Scripture also announces that these masses of people will respond one day to a great war call.

"And the sixth angel sounded, and I heard a voice from the four horns of the golden altar which is before God, Saying to the sixth angel which had the trumpet, Loose the four angels which are bound in the great river Euphrates. And the four angels were loosed, which were prepared for an hour, and a day, and a month, and a year, for to slay the third part of men. And the number of the army of the horsemen were two hundred thousand thousand: and I heard the number of them" (Rev. 9:13-16).

Later in the Book of Revelation, Scripture expands upon this same quote. "And the sixth angel poured out his vial upon the great river Euphrates; and the water was dried up, that the way of the kings of the east might be prepared" (Rev. 16:12). Later the Scripture notes, "And he gathered them together into a place called in the Hebrew tongue Armageddon" (Rev. 16:16).

So the Word of God duly informs us that one of the large participants in that final battle of this dispensation, Armageddon, the kings of the East will play a significant part. It is announced that they will move into that cauldron of conflict with an army of 200 million.

What an army! Never has history known such a body of men to move into a military confrontation. But the Scripture announces that two hundred thousand thousand will participate — that's 200 million. With a combined population of China and the other countries of Asia, this figure becomes possible.

Some will recall that Mao Tse Tung, before he passed to his eternal non-reward, promised such a battle. Earlier he had said, "In the battle for the world, China will field an army of 50 million men." The world was staggered at this figure, but that was not the end of it.

Before he died, Mao Tse Tung promised that China would field an army of 200 million in the conquest of earth. So we have one of the kings of the East on record as promising to produce an army of the very size predicted in the Word of God.

This figure gains significance when we remember that China is one of the nuclear powers of the world and is developing delivery systems — intercontinental ballistics missiles — for what it sees to be the inevitable coming battle.

Up until nearly this time, the Asian nations have considered themselves somewhat inferior in world politics. The defeat of Japan by the United States in World War II enhanced that spirit of defeatism.

Now this is changing! The peoples of Asia see themselves as superior in numbers, higher in purpose and, in fact, richer than the nations of the West. They note that the largest net-creditor nation in the world is Japan. They see this as a contrast to the United States which is the net-debtor of the world.

Never before has the fielding of an army of 200 million seemed a likelihood to the military planners of the world. Now the likelihood grows with the burgeoning masses of Asia.

We note in the Word of God that the River Euphrates will be dried up to make way for the kings of the East. One wonders how this could happen, but we note that it has already been done.

The Turks have built large dams across the River Euphrates and have been able to cut off the flowing waters, making the river bed dry. Having already done this, they have proved that it can be done at will.

The River Euphrates has been the traditional dividing line between the Mid-East and the Far East — the beginning of the continent of Asia. The drying up of the Euphrates, therefore, can also be seen symbolically as the shrinking of the nations of the world and the vanishing of the barriers between them.

So, when thinking about the Battle of Armageddon, we must remember that the participating nations already have the mobility — and increasingly the attitude — that will bring them there.

The United States: A Nation in Revolution

We must quickly fly back to the United States, again a long journey across the Pacific Ocean in our jumbo jet. Since the beginning of the '90s, America has witnessed a series of prophetically provocative events.

First of all, we have seen the largest hurricane in history sweep across south Florida. That mighty wind left more devastation in its wake than in any one storm on record. High-impact storms such as this can certainly be thought of as "signs upon the earth" (Luke 21:25).

We also saw the most devastating earthquake that America has known when southern California was badly shaken with damage that exceeded all previous costs.

Several times, the Book of Revelation presents earthquakes as a sign of the judgment of God. "And I beheld when he had opened the sixth seal, and, lo, there was a great earthquake; and the sun became black as sackcloth of hair, and the moon became as blood; And the stars of heaven fell unto the earth, even as a fig tree casteth her untimely figs, when she is shaken of a mighty wind. And the heaven departed as a scroll when it is rolled together; and every mountain and island were moved out of their places" (Rev. 6:12-14).

One person who had just been in an earthquake told me, "When the ground begins to shake beneath your feet, you lose faith in everything!"

I was able to say, "Perhaps that's the way God intended." Losing faith in everything — that is certainly the product of an earthquake that looks and feels like it will shake everything to pieces.

We also have seen record low temperatures in the northern part of the United States. The fact is that more individuals have died from the cold than perished in the earthquake. It seems as if a thermometer hit bottom and then planned to stay there indefinitely.

In another form of natural phenomena, we have seen the largest flood on record in the United States. The Mississippi River overran her banks for hundreds of miles. The loss in land, houses, and agricultural business was phenomenal.

As we think of these developments in the United States, we may be confident in one thing. By comparison, the loss of life was minimal despite the fact that the phenomena were very large. We have heard of floods in places like Bangladesh that produced 110,000 dead. Nothing like this has occurred in the United States.

One person has suggested that "perhaps God is allowing us to see this with our eyes but is still sparing America." America, with its commitment to the gospel and its friendship with the nation of Israel, is perhaps still being especially protected by God.

How long can this last? In answering this, let us remember that America "endured" a cultural revolution in this decade. Suddenly the blessed land of America has become openly permissive concerning homosexuals, the practice of abortion, and many other remarkable evils.

The new administration in Washington has been more of a friend to the promoters of this kind of wickedness than we have seen in the history of the nation. How long can these things continue? Not forever, because the Scripture says, "The wicked shall be turned into hell, and all of the nations that forget God" (Ps. 9:17).

As a consequence of this turning from spiritual things, the rise of crime and related wickedness has become endemic in our nation. This has happened to the extent that the Congress of the United States has just passed a crime-plus-pork bill, which commits $32 billion to take away the problem of crime in the streets.

Someday, someone in Washington will open a dusty Bible and discover the real cause of crime. In the process, he will discover how impotent government really is to do anything about it.

Yes, there is no doubt that America has seen a moral revolution in just a couple of years — or about the time when the new administration took over.

So endemic has become the rise of evil within the United States that even former Vice President Dan Quayle is found to receive an attentive audience as he extends a call to family values. He correctly decided that the basis of life is moral and that constitutes the missing element in American life.

That moral descendency has created what many are now calling "a crisis of the spirit in the United States."

Light in a Dark World

Our quick look across the world reminds us that the now-entrenched immorality is not in America alone, but has become the condition of the whole world.

With the world progressively losing its moral sensibilities, we can expect the growth of anarchy, revolution, violence, and every other kind of wickedness. This can produce a frustration in the minds and hearts of people that could be very dangerous.

The danger is that the world will call for a human savior. One can almost hear the frustrated people of earth saying, "Send us a man with a great plan. We need a ruler who can show us a way out of our problems. We need new hope for a distraught civilization and answers to problems that are better answers than we have heard before. We have been betrayed and now we look for a leader who can show us the light at the end of the trail."

With these and many other words, the distraught nations of earth could put themselves in a position whereby they find that they are demanding the rise of Antichrist. The ascendancy of the man of sin will be easier than most of us can imagine.

We have no indication in Scripture that the Antichrist will have to bulldoze his way into power. Rather, he will be thought of as the Messiah for which the nations have longed. The current conditions of our world could bring his ascendancy to pass.

How wonderful that, as we look into the conditions of our time, we have a great source of reassurance. The Scripture says to every believer, "We have also a more sure word of prophecy; whereunto ye do well that ye take heed, as unto a light that shineth in a dark place, until the day dawn, and the day star arise in your hearts" (2 Pet. 1:19).

This passage gives us knowledge that can be most reassuring. It tells us first of all that, as we move into the future, the world will become a progressively dark place. But it then reassures us that we have "a light that shines upon our path" as we move through the darkness of the world. That light is the Word of God, and especially, the prophetic Word.

But, finally, we are taught by that same passage that one day a new day will dawn "and the day star will arise in our hearts." Here we have a reminder that Jesus Christ is coming again.

"He then shall reign where'er the sun doth its successive journeys run." The King of kings and the Lord of lords will come with ten thousands of His saints and shall rule all of the nations of earth. Looking at the scene of our present world, our hearts cry, ". . . Amen. Even so, come, Lord Jesus" (Rev. 22:20).

14

The Great Physician's Rx for Mankind

by John Wesley White

When I was at Oxford, I had the opportunity to hear C.S. Lewis, who used to come back from Cambridge to give lectures.

In one of his talks, he said that a person may be about to be married, but before the wedding takes place, Christ may come and call His responding bride to the Marriage Supper of the Lord. So, he said, make your first priority a preparation for that event.

He went on to say that one may be a scientist on the verge of a society-changing invention, but, before he reaches his goal, Christ may come. So get ready now for that event. That way, instructed Lewis, you live in a constant state of meaningful expectation. Further-more, every time the coming of the Lord is mentioned in the Scrip-tures, it is used as a basis for the Creator to say to His created, "Prepare to meet thy God."

More and more it appears to me that nearly everyone expects to have a showdown of some kind with God, somewhere, sometime.

At the time of his death in 1983, Gordon Sinclair was the most outspoken agnostic in Canada. I was listening to his strong disap-proval of the prima donna treatment a Toronto Maple Leaf hockey star was getting from the press. Sinclair stormed, "You'd think it was the second coming of Christ!" Calming down, he relented that he didn't know why he referred to the second coming of Christ because he didn't believe in it. But many of his listeners, myself included, were not convinced.

Instinctively man has always somehow expected, whether in dread or welcome, an ultimate confrontation with God — a time when "... every knee shall bow ... and every tongue shall confess, that Jesus Christ is Lord, to the glory of God the Father" (Rom. 14:11). If he confesses here and now, it spells salvation forever with Christ. If he remains impenitent, it spells eventual submission, yes, but simultaneously a sentencing to the doom of the damned.

Readiness — the Key Word

Two days before Jesus' trial and crucifixion, His disciples asked Him the fateful question. "What will be the sign of thy coming, and of the end of the world? . . ." (Matt. 24:3). Jesus' answer was a 94-verse résumé of signs which, when fulfilled, would constitute the signal for His return to this earth to set up His kingdom. The whole treatise turns on Matthew 24:44: "Therefore be ye also ready: for in such an hour as ye think not the Son of man cometh."

Readiness — that's the key word; and it occurs several times in the New Testament with regard to the Lord's coming again.

Christ himself is ready at any moment to return. As St. Peter puts it, He ". . . stands ready to pass judgment on the living and the dead" (1 Pet. 4:5; NEB). With His wondrous gift of eternal life, He is "already at the door!"(James 5:8-9; Phillips).

Being the most festive event in history, the Second Coming is often compared in the Scriptures to a marriage, our Lord having gone to prepare a place for us and assuring us that "the wedding is ready," or again, "All things are now ready."

Believers are to expect the return of Christ at any moment. In short, we are to live in a state of perpetual readiness for His return. This was His message in the parable of the 10 virgins: ". . . They that were ready went . . ." (Matt. 25:10).

St. Paul begins his last chapter to Timothy with the "charge . . . before God, and the Lord Jesus Christ, who shall judge the quick and the dead at his appearing and his kingdom" (2 Tim. 4:1), and concludes: "Now the prize awaits me, the garland of righteousness which the Lord, the all-just Judge, will award me on that great day; and it is not for me alone, but for all who have set their hearts on his coming appearance" (2 Tim. 4:8; NEB). Sandwiched between is the avowal: "I am ready."

Gwen Beck, a school teacher in Cody, Wyoming, where I was holding a crusade, informed me that four years earlier her life had been constant confusion. A concerned sister on the East Coast sent her a copy of the first edition of my book, *Re-entry*.

When Gwen read it, the warning of Jesus that we are to "be ready" for the coming again of Christ especially touched her. Gwen said, "I simply was not a Christian. This led me to confess on my knees that I was a sinner, and I asked Christ to come into my life, and to be filled with the Holy Spirit." Jesus did just that, and with this new hope, Gwen's has been a life of unceasing fellowship and service to Christ.

Latching On to Anything

The coming again of Jesus Christ is imperative. Man is so fast degenerating within and so inevitably being dashed headlong toward destruction from without that, apart from the intervention of God, he simply cannot save himself.

Lewis Thomas, in his 1984 best seller, *The Unforgettable Fire,* laments that his experiences both as a physician and a philosopher have assured him that we earthlings face "epidemic disease, meteorite collisions, volcanoes, atmospheric shifts in the levels of carbon dioxide, earthquakes, excessive warming or chilling of the earth's surface." But we will not be done in by these. We will do it to ourselves by warfare with thermonuclear weaponry, and it will happen.[1] So reasons the secular humanist.

Jesus foresaw this with divine precision when He replied to His disciples, who had inquired about the signs of His coming: "For then shall be great tribulation, such as was not since the beginning of the world to this time, no, nor ever shall be. And except those days should be shortened, there should no flesh be saved: but for the elect's sake those days shall be shortened" (Matt. 24:21-22). So our Lord Jesus Christ will come again.

Out in front of our church, there was a sheet of ice, and my lovely wife and I were obliged to cross it to get to our car. Kathleen, who is from Ireland and not born with skates on her feet as Canadians have been thought to be, was gingerly looking down and cautiously picking every step. She thought that I was just ahead of her on her right; but someone had waylaid me, and I had dropped a few paces behind.

Into the place I should have been strode a man with a clerical black coat like mine, also on his way to his car. Reaching out and seizing his arm, my wife, without looking up, implored, "Darling, let me hang on to you or I will fall on this ice!"

Overhearing her request, I accelerated briskly, calling from behind, "Kathleen!" She thought at first that she was hearing stereo or something. Listening to our embarrassed apologies, the startled gentleman generously commiserated, "Anyone will latch on to anything on this slippery surface!"

Recuperating from the incident, it struck me: Anyone will latch on to anything to keep from falling on the slippery surface which is the world today. And that is just what people are doing. Those who do not choose Christ and go to be with Him when He comes again are going to be reaching out in every direction as conditions in the world worsen.

St. John, in the Revelation of Jesus Christ, foresaw this: "Then the kings of the earth, magnates and marshals, the rich and the powerful, and all men, slave or free, hid themselves in caves and mountain crags; and they called out to the mountains and the crags, 'Fall on us and hide us from the face of the One who sits on the throne and from the vengeance of the Lamb.' For the great day of their vengeance has come, and who will be able to stand?" (Rev. 6:15-17; NEB).

Man's Fragile Future

Winston Churchill wept in the House of Commons as he reviewed "the awful unfolding scene of the future."

Syndicated columnist Ellen Goodman asked of thinking people, "With Armageddon around the corner what are intelligent people to do? Wrap ourselves in mourning sheets and wait for the end? [We] are not talking about death, but extinction. Not talking about our future but about any future. This, while we see that nuclear sword of Damocles hung over us like some apocalypse without the promise of redemption." The last lament is what's wrong with the secularist.

Jesus urged us that when the apocalypse approached, ". . . look up, and lift up your heads; for your redemption draweth nigh" (Luke 21:28). That's our hope: redemption!

Only the Christian can stand up and be genuinely jubilant, for as St. Paul wrote to the Philippians, "Of one thing I am certain: the One who started the good work in you will bring it to completion by the day of Christ Jesus" (Phil. 1:6 NEB).

St. Paul was certain of the day of Christ because the coming again of the Lord Jesus is immutable: it is a changeless fact. Affirmed the writer to the Hebrews, "Wherein God, willing more abundantly to shew unto the heirs of promise the immutability of his counsel, confirmed it by an oath: That by two immutable things, in which it was impossible for God to lie, we might have a strong consolation . . ." (Heb. 6:17-18). "This is a powerful encouragement to us, who have claimed his protection by grasping the hope set before us. That hope we hold. It is like an anchor for our lives, an anchor safe and sure" (Heb. 6:18-19; NEB).

I realize that some people find the facts of Christ's coming again unbelievable. We have been told by NASA that by A.D. 2000 some people will have moved to the moon, where they'll live in air-conditioned modules growing, among other things, tomatoes as large as watermelons. They'll be surrounded by serving robots who'll mine the moon as well as cook the food and make the beds. But there's a problem.[2]

It's astonishing the number of people who believed that the moon landing was a staged hoax. Why? Because the physics of space travel were beyond them. They were not prepared to take by faith what they couldn't understand.

The fact that we can't understand the astrophysics of Christ's coming again does not alter the fact that He is coming.

Everybody wonders about the future, but no one knows exactly what the future holds. Alvin Toffler, author of *Future Shock* and *The Third Wave*, came out in 1985 with his *Previews and Premises*, assuring us that without a transformation of our social institutions, man's future is more fragile than at any time in human history.

Actually, it's the spiritual transformation of individuals by Jesus Christ that provides hope for the future.

Yet another Soviet leader takes over. Surveying his task, he assesses: "The revolutionary transformation of society is impossible without changing man himself."

Exactly! But there is only One who can change many and, through transformed people, transform society. It is Jesus Christ! He does so by providing salvation for us in the present and hope for the future.

Believers in Christ know who holds the future. And it is this confidence that the future is in Christ's hands that gives us true hope in the present.

St. Paul wrote to the Romans, "Hope maketh not ashamed . . ." (Rom. 5:5), and to Timothy he wrote, ". . . I am not ashamed: for I know whom I have believed, and am persuaded that he is able to keep that which I have committed unto him against that day" (2 Tim. 1:12).

When God Shows His Face

St. Paul was certain of one thing: the Day of Christ!

Dean W. R. Matthews of St. Paul's Cathedral in London is right in saying that the world is living on a volcano, not a rock. But the Christian's hope rests, ultimately, not on military defenses but on the coming again of Christ.

St. Paul wrote in 1 Corinthians 3:11, "For other foundation can no man lay than that is laid, which is Jesus Christ." The superstructure the believer builds on this foundation will be manifest at the coming of Christ.

The late Chief Justice Earl Warren claimed he always read the sports section first in his newspaper because it at least had some cheerful news. "The front page has nothing but man's failures," he wrote.

In a world of gloom, man can turn to the Bible for the good news of Christ's coming again.

A university student who was a star football player came forward in a crusade meeting one night to commit his life to Christ, explaining, "I got tired of playing the game without being able to see the goal posts." Without a goal, life has no direction.

A compass, wherever it is, always points north. So a believer's life should always point in the direction of Christ's coming again.

"To me the Second Coming is the perpetual light on the path which makes the present bearable," reasoned G. Campbell Morgan. "I never lay my head on the pillow without thinking that perhaps before I awake, the final morning may have dawned. I never begin my work without thinking that He may interrupt it and begin His own."

"Though He tarry past our time," reasoned Matthew Henry, "He will not tarry past the 'due time.' " There is a time, an exact time, on God's blueprinted schedule of events when Jesus Christ is due to return.

The coming again of Jesus Christ is Immanuel, that is, "God with us." Both in rapture and revelation, the return of our Lord will be personal.

"If God is so wonderful," mused the little Italian girl, "why doesn't He show His face?" That is precisely what He did do in the person of Jesus Christ and will do again at Christ's second coming.

"Look, he is coming . . ." exulted John in Revelation 1, and "every eye will see him, even those who pierced him; and all the peoples of the earth will mourn because of him. So shall it be! Amen.

'I am the Alpha and the Omega,' says the Lord God, 'who is and who was and who is to come, the Almighty' " (Rev. 1:7-8; NIV).

Perhaps John was thinking of that unforgettable moment when Jesus stood before the Sanhedrin in the house of Caiaphas, about to be condemned. Cross-examined by these green-eyed earthlings, our wonderful Lord burst forth in solitary assurance: that, one day, they would ". . . see the Son of Man sitting at the right hand of the Mighty One and coming on the clouds of heaven" (Mark 14:62; NIV).

"The Lord himself shall descend," St. Paul assured the Thessalonians. On ascension day, on the Mount of Olives, the disciples made the point that "This same Jesus, who has been taken from you into heaven, will come back in the same way you have seen him go into heaven" (Acts 1:11; NIV).

The theologian Bengel exegetes that the Greek present participle used here implies that the Second Advent, as the first, will be a bodily return of Jesus Christ.

A little girl from the farm was with her parents riding an elevator to the top of a high skyscraper. A Christian, she asked at the eighty-sixth floor, "Mommy, does Jesus know we're coming?"

One thing among others is certain in the Bible, and that is that Jesus Christ knows we're going up to be with Him forever — because He is personally coming to get us.

The historian Massilon wrote, "In the days of primitive Christianity, it would have been apostasy not to sigh for the return of the Lord."

Every time the true Christian goes to the holy communion table to celebrate the Lord's Supper, he must focus on the return of Christ to derive meaning, "This do in remembrance . . . till He come." Every time he goes to work, he ideally hears his Lord's words in his ears, ". . . occupy till I come" (Luke 19:13), for "Blessed are those servants, whom the Lord when he cometh shall find watching" (Luke 12:37).

From Gloom to Glory

The coming again of Jesus Christ is immense: the most glorious "trip" man will ever have taken.

St. Paul inspired the young preacher Titus with the ecstatic aspiration, "Looking for that blessed hope, and the glorious appearing of the great God and our Saviour Jesus Christ" (Titus 2:13).

Just when it appears that the world is going up in smoke and man has reached his perigee, Jesus said, look to the apogee: "At that time they will see the Son of Man coming in a cloud with power and great glory" (Luke 21:27; NIV).

Queen Victoria left us a beautiful portrayal of the apogee. She was barely 18 when she ascended the throne of the British empire upon which the sun never set. Officially attending Handel's *The Messiah* for the first time, she was instructed: "The point at which the 'Hallelujah Chorus' is sung, the entire audience will rise, as has been the custom since the days of George the First. But you are the queen. You alone remain seated."

When the glorious chorus was reached, all stood with military punctuality. Her Majesty alone remained seated. But when that thrilling, transcendent passage "King of kings and Lord of lords" was reached, the queen rose and bowed, and not a member of the grand audience missed the significance.

Oh, what a day! "When Christ, who is your life, appears, then you also will appear with him in glory," rejoiced St. Paul (Col. 3:4; NIV).

St. Peter exulted, "And when the Chief Shepherd appears, you will receive the crown of glory that will never fade away" (1 Pet. 5:4; NIV).

"Eternal Glory to the Heroes" was Izvestia's prepared headline for the reentry of the Soyuz II trio. But glory was turned into gloom when the hatch door was opened and the cosmonauts were found strapped in their seats without any signs of life. This tragedy is in direct contrast to the coming of Christ, when death will be turned to life and gloom to glory.

"To him who is able to keep you from falling ," pronounced St. Jude in his benediction, is the One who on the day of His coming will "present you before his glorious presence without fault and with great joy" (Jude 24; NIV).

Looking For His Appearing

The second coming of Jesus Christ is indeed the perpetual light on the path of the believer, which makes the present delightful. If Jesus Christ is not coming again, we should close our Bibles and our churches.

If we believe that He is indeed coming, the accusation of being cruel for remaining silent is not a strong enough indictment. We ought to study about His coming, sing about it, preach it, talk about it, write about it, and spread the precious word of hope everywhere.

Said our Lord, "If anyone is ashamed of me and my words in this adulterous and sinful generation, the Son of Man will be ashamed of him when he comes in his Father's glory with the holy angels" (Mark 8:38; NIV).

Eddie Fisher remarked on a radio program that during the course of the day he had discussed everything from ingrown toenails to the second coming of Jesus Christ. If ingrown toenails might be thought of as the low point of his conversation, certainly the high point was the second coming of Jesus Christ.

The coming again of Jesus Christ is imminent. No prophetic event or events await fulfillment prior to His coming for His church. All of the New Testament writers exhort us to be "watching for," "waiting for," "looking for," "praying for," "hastening unto," and "expecting at any moment" the return of Christ.

As Martin Luther said, "Christ deigned that the day of His coming should be hid from us, that being in suspense, we might be, as it were, on the watch."

The signs to which reference has been made refer primarily to Christ's coming to this earth to set up His kingdom. But His "appearing" to His own in the air to withdraw His church is referred to comparably often and always in the sense of its occurring at any moment. We are to be looking for that blessed hope, for he will not appear to everyone: ". . . unto them that look for him shall he appear the second time without sin unto salvation" (Heb. 9:28).

St. Paul wrote to the Thessalonians that "God hath not appointed us to wrath, but to obtain salvation by our Lord Jesus Christ (1 Thess. 5:9). He defined Christians as those who "turned to God from idols to serve the living and true God; And to wait for his Son from heaven, whom he raised from the dead, even Jesus, which delivered us from the wrath to come" (1 Thess. 1:9-10).

I feel sure that Paul was here referring to what would happen on earth to those who did not turn to Christ and so would be left to endure the consequent apocalyptic judgments. This same idea is to be found in the Revelation of Jesus Christ, where our Lord assures, "Because thou hast kept the word of my patience, I also will keep thee from the hour of temptation, which shall come upon all the world, to try them that dwell upon the earth" (Rev. 3:10).

No Countdown

To the Philippians, St. Paul admonished, "Let your magnanimity be manifest to all" for "the Lord is at hand" (Phil. 1:13). To the Corinthians, "So that ye come behind in no gift; waiting for the coming of our Lord Jesus Christ: Who shall also confirm you unto the end, that ye may be blameless in the day of our Lord Jesus Christ" (1 Cor. 1:7-8).

To Timothy, Paul admonished, "In the sight of God, who gives life to everything, and of Christ Jesus, who while testifying before Pontius Pilate made the good confession, I charge you to keep this command without spot or blame until the appearing of our Lord Jesus Christ" (1 Tim. 6:13-14;NIV).

The church father Cyril wrote 1,640 years ago, "Look thou for the Son of God to judge the quick and dead. Venture not to declare when, nor on the other hand slumber, for He saith, 'Watch.' We are looking for Christ."

Adjudged the historian Gibbon, "As long as this error was permitted in the church, it was productive of most salutary effects on the practice of Christians."

Dwight L. Moody, like Luther and Wesley, preached constantly that Christ's coming was imminent, declaring, "Nowhere am I told to watch for the millennium but for the coming of the Lord."

Since Christ's coming is imminent, each of us must at all times be at our best.

A Soviet premier assures the world that "Communism is the wave of the future."

The wave of our coming Lord is the expectation of every watching Christian, the wave of welcome which will greet the faithful with "Well done, good and faithful servant . . . enter into the joy of your master" (Matt. 25:21;RSV).

The coming again of Jesus Christ is immediate. There will be no countdown for the coming down of our Lord to take us home.

One Greek scholar calculates that the familiar "in the twinkling of an eye" of 1 Corinthians 15:52, which is read at nearly every Christian burial service, refers, as close as one can humanly conceive, to no time at all. That leaves no opportunity for the thief to repent or the prodigal to come home.

Jesus did not say that His coming would be a clap of thunder, but ". . . as lightning . . ." (Matt. 24:27). We can with some accuracy time thunder bursts by the lightning flash because sound travels 86,000 miles per second.

But lightning comes without a precursor.

Declared our Lord in His revelation to John, "Behold, I come quickly: hold that fast which thou hast that no man take thy crown.

Him that overcometh will I make a pillar in the Temple of my God . . ." (Rev. 3:11-12).

George Washington had a cook who was as prompt as the first U.S. president was truthful. "Gentlemen," said Washington to his guests, "I have a cook who never asks whether the company has come, but whether the hour has come!"

". . . A time is coming," said Jesus to His disciples, ". . . when the dead will hear the voice of the Son of God: and those who hear will live" (John 5:25;NIV). All of His disciples of that time fell into that category. Others, Jesus said later, will ". . . tarry till I come . . ." (John 21:22). These could include you.

Insanity or Repentance?

A United States senator reasons, "The hands of the clock are moving on toward midnight of the brief day left to us."

"Whom the gods would destroy," goes an ancient Greek proverb, "they first make mad."

"If other planets are inhabited, they must be using this earth as a lunatic asylum," mused George Bernard Shaw.

I do not believe that a compassionate Jesus will permit the pressures of an age, for which our minds were not designed, to continue to build up until there is mass insanity. Instead He invites, ". . . Repent, for the kingdom of heaven is at hand" (Matt. 4:17).

Some years ago I received a letter from Paul Shields. He had been converted through the reading of my first edition of *Re-entry*. He wrote:

> I was born the son of missionary parents while they were serving the Lord in Nigeria. While a teenager in Toronto, I rebelled. I began to smoke tobacco — then pot — to drink heavily, and after many violent confrontations with my parents, I moved out. I became a drug addict, got married, had a kid, and moved to the West coast. My life turned from bad to worse.
>
> In Vancouver my drug addiction became chronic: soft drugs, hard drugs — and hard liquor. Finally, out of work, no money, heavily in debt, and my wife planning to separate from me, I was at the bottom. I knew it. I couldn't help myself at all.
>
> Disenchanted by my addiction, one Sunday night I remembered a book that had been put in my hand by some

goody-two-shoes. It was *Re-entry*. I pulled it out and started to read. I couldn't put it down. The more I read, the more paralyzed with terror I became. Soon I fell under the conviction of the Holy Spirit.

There I was alone at 3 a.m., crying my eyes out. I knew what I had to do. I had to give my heart to the Lord Jesus Christ and ask Him to give me the peace and security I so desperately needed. I was instantly delivered and have been ever since. My wife came to know the Lord. My life has been turned around.

I first met Paul in Toronto at the Central Baptist Seminary, from which he graduated and was later ordained into the ministry to serve as a Baptist pastor.

A World that Groans

When does one become a citizen of the kingdom of heaven? When that person is born again!

Wrote St. Paul to the Philippians, "We are citizens of heaven, and from heaven we expect our deliverer to come, the Lord Jesus Christ. He will transfigure the body belonging to our humble state, and give it a form like that of his own resplendent body, by the very power which enables him to make all things subject to himself" (Phil. 3:20-21; NEB).

For this reason, as the Apostle wrote to the Corinthians: "Therefore we are always confident and know that as long as we are at home in the body we are away from the Lord. . . . We are confident, I say, and would prefer to be away from the body and at home with the Lord" (2 Cor. 5:6,8; NIV).

"Now we know that if the earthly tent we live in is destroyed, we have a building from God, an eternal house in heaven, not built by human hands. Meanwhile we groan, longing to be clothed with our heavenly dwelling, because when we are clothed, we will not be found naked. For while we are in this tent, we groan and are burdened, because we do not wish to be unclothed but to be clothed with our heavenly dwelling, so that what is mortal may be swallowed up by life. Now it is God who has made us for this very purpose and has given us the Spirit as a deposit, guaranteeing what is to come" (2 Cor. 5:1-5; NIV).

Ours is a world that groans, as St. Paul wrote to the Romans — groans for the redemption of the physical order, groans for freedom, groans for wholeness.

David Lawrence expressed in *U.S. News & World Report,* "A climax of some kind seems to be approaching the world over."

God's climax is the coming of Jesus Christ.

Omar Bradley, the late American military general, observed incisively: "We know more about war than about peace, more about killing than about living. This is our twentieth century's claim to progress. Knowledge of science outstrips capacity for control. We have too many men of science; too few men of God. . . . The world has achieved brilliance without wisdom, power without conscience — a world of nuclear giants and ethical infants."

Will the world get ethically and spiritually better? Yes, but not until it gets worse, and Christ comes.

"The facts," says *Intelligence Digest,* "show that the forces in the world struggle are grouping themselves for a decisive show-down."

Man simply cannot better himself. Before his death, elder statesman Konrad Adenauer remarked, "Security and quiet have disappeared from the lives of men."

The only answer is emigration to be with Christ for those who entrust themselves to Him.

When the tyrannies of the Old World in Europe grew too great, the freedom lovers immigrated to a New World of freedom and challenge. Ruptured by a world of escalating pressures, one of these days Christians are going to be raptured to the glories of heaven.

The Quest for Immortality

What is eternally gratifying is that the coming again of Jesus Christ brings immortality. Jesus Christ came "to bring life and immortality to light through the gospel."

When someone repents of sin and receives Christ as Saviour and Lord, Jesus says, "And I give unto them eternal life; and they shall never perish . . ." (John 10:28).

Jesus Christ gives us "eternal life" with a body of immortality. "Lay hold on eternal life," exhorted St. Paul (1 Tim. 6:19).

Pop songs reveal how people yearn for a life and a relationship which will last. "Love Me a Million Years," sings one; and another, "Forever and a Day"; and another "From Here to Eternity."

Arthur Clark, author of *2001: A Space Odyssey,* said to Walter Cronkite on CBS that he craves to live another 20 years, and then he might be able to go on living forever.

"The moon-walk goal is really a quest to live forever," observed that peerless science fiction writer Ray Bradbury on the same CBS program, adding, "This has been the quest of religion, politics, and science — to escape death."

We are living in a sad world.

"If I were God," ruminated Goethe, "this world of sin and suffering would break my heart!"

Jesus said to His disciples that, previous to His coming, there would be "the beginning of sorrows" that would then sharply increase. I saw the actual headline, "The Beginning of Sorrows," in a paper recently. The World Health Organization says that in our world there are 11 million lepers; 50 million people with onchocerciasis; 190 million with filariasis; and 200 million with schistosomiasis.

We have already identified Jesus' forecast of famines as a harbinger of His return to earth. Annually, 62 million earthlings, deprived of food, wither away in famines and die from starvation.

Who cares? Jesus does!

And He's coming back surely and suddenly, sometime, to feed sumptuously and clothe lavishly those who otherwise would have perished in hunger. Meanwhile, the highest motivation for us to live selflessly is the anticipation of Jesus Christ's coming again.

The president of the Lutheran Church in America noted the obscenity of *Time* magazine having on one page pathetic, tragic pictures of starving people in Ethiopia, and alongside it an advertisement: "For the woman who has everything, think of gold this Christmas" (1984).

In Pope John Paul II's Christmas homily, he picked up on St. John's ancient exhortation to the Laodiceans to prepare for Christ's coming again. The pope drew the contrast, "Are there not people rich in material goods, power, fame, and yet who are tragically poor? Poor by reason of the great emptiness of the human heart which has not opened itself to God. And are there not poor people who are materially disadvantaged, persecuted, oppressed, discriminated against who are rich? Rich with that inner wealth that flows directly from the heart of the God-Man Jesus Christ."

"If there is a God, why doesn't He show up?" snaps the agnostic. He has already: 2,000 years ago in His incarnation. And He will show up again.

Jesus Christ is coming and as His Revelation previews, ". . . Behold, the tabernacle of God is with men, and he will dwell with them, and they shall be his people, and God himself shall be with them, and be their God" (Rev. 21:3). "And God shall wipe every tear from their eyes; there shall be an end to death, and to mourning and crying and pain; for the old order has passed away" (Rev. 21:4; NEB).

The Christian's Incentive

The coming again of Jesus Christ is implicational. "Behold, I am coming soon!" stressed our Lord in the final chapter of the Bible. "My reward is with me, and I will give to everyone according to what he has done" (Rev. 22:12;NIV).

Throughout the New Testament, it is clearly taught that when Christ appears for His church, the first item on the agenda will be the review of believers' works. Thereupon prizes, crowns, and rewards will be distributed, and status in the life hereafter conferred according to our faithfulness.

"For we must all appear before the Judgment seat of Christ," St. Paul apprised the Corinthians, "that each one may receive what is due him for the things done while in the body, whether good or bad" (2 Cor. 5:10;NIV). On this basis, he admonished: "Therefore judge nothing before the appointed time; wait till the Lord comes. He will bring to light what is hidden in darkness and will expose the motives of men's hearts. At that time each will receive his praise from God" (1 Cor. 4:5;NIV).

It is understandable then that St. Paul should bring to a climax that chapter devoted to the coming again of Christ, 1 Corinthians 15, with "Therefore, my dear brothers, stand firm. Always give yourselves fully to the work of the Lord, because you know that your labor in the Lord is not in vain" (1 Cor. 15:58;NIV).

Similarly, 1 Thessalonians, which St. Paul devoted to the denouement events, is brought to a climax with the aspiration, "May God himself, the God of peace, sanctify you through and through. May your whole spirit, soul and body be kept blameless at the coming of our Lord Jesus Christ" (1 Thess. 5:23;NIV).

St. Peter shared the same ultimate concern: "Since everything will be destroyed in this way, what kind of people ought you to be? You ought to live holy and godly lives as you look forward to the day of God . . ." (2 Pet. 3:11-12;NIV).

Added the aged St. John: "And now, dear children, continue in him, so that when he appears we may be confident and unashamed before him at his coming" (1 John 2:28;NIV). Going on to give a vivid account of the coming again of Christ, St. John sums up, "Everyone who has this hope in him purifies himself, just as he is pure" (1 John 3:3;NIV).

A very vigorous controversy in American government for many years has been how much of the GNP should be spent on exploration of space. Currently the estimate is 1 percent.

Frank Borman, currently president of Eastern Airlines, is a potent protagonist of the concept that an escalated emphasis on space exploration will assist rather than diminish the solution of the problems of poverty and pollution here on earth.

For example, the Discovery and Challenger spaceships were able to monitor the movement of the Sahara southward into the central Africa greenbelt, which thereby escalated famine in places like Niger and Chad; solutions could then be prescribed. They were also able to spot mineral distribution and wealth deep in the earth by the highly sophisticated equipment aboard.

If man could invent equipment to discover treasure on (and under) the earth from the heavens, how much more can Jesus' exhortation to lay up treasures in heaven be realized by faithful believers on earth!

Asked what the greatest thought that ever crossed his mind was, Daniel Webster replied, "My accountability to the Almighty God."

"There is no such incentive to evangelism," reckoned D. L. Moody, "as the pre-millennial coming of our Lord. Emphasize what God hath emphasized."

In the Presbyterian Confession of 1967, it is pointed out that "the life, death, resurrection, and promised coming of Jesus Christ have set the pattern for Church missions."

Think of what a congregation like the Peoples Church of Toronto does to evangelize the world. In addition to the hundreds of workers who have gone forth from the congregation through the years, a million and a half dollars are being given annually for foreign missions to get the gospel out to the ends of the earth. What rewards will be forthcoming at Christ's return to those who pray, give, or go forth to evangelize the world!

Christ is coming. What an incentive to evangelize!

The First Step Toward Heaven

Finally, the coming again of Jesus Christ is impending. Whether the Scriptures are referring to the appearance of Christ for His church or His coming to earth to set up His kingdom, reference to His return always has attached to it the urgent exhortation to be ready.

Oh, the drama and import of Jesus' words! "Even thus shall it be in the day when the Son of man is revealed. . . . Two women shall be grinding together; the one shall be taken, and the other left. Two men shall be in the field; the one shall be taken, and the other left" (Luke 17:30,35-36).

"Watch ye therefore," warned our Lord, "for ye know not when the master of the house cometh, at even, or at midnight, or at the cockcrowing, or in the morning: Lest coming suddenly he find you sleeping. And what I say unto you I say unto all, Watch" (Mark 13:35-37.

Christian, never let the realization fully escape your consciousness that at any moment Christ may come again. Be always, and do always, those things that would please your Lord were He to come this minute.

In Joel's ancient prophecy we read, "Multitudes, multitudes in the valley of decision. For the day of the Lord is near in the valley of decision" (Joel 3:14).

In the light of the Lord's coming, Joel gave us that gospel promise which has been quoted wherever heralds of salvation have gone. "And it shall come to pass, that whosoever shall call upon the name of the Lord shall be delivered . . ." (Joel 2:32). To be rightly related to Jesus Christ is to be ready for His coming again.

As Neil Armstrong stepped on to the moon, he declared, "One small step for man; one giant leap for mankind!"

The Chinese have an old proverb: "The journey of a thousand miles begins with the first step."

Certainly the journey to heaven begins with one step: the step of faith that puts our foot down on the promise of the Word of Christ that He will take to His celestial and eternal home all who on this earth place their firm belief in Him as Saviour and Lord. Only that person can join in the final aspiration of Scripture, "Even so, come, Lord Jesus!"

Preaching the Christ of the Second Coming

There is one teaching that is more important than the preaching of the second coming of Christ. It is the preaching of the Christ of the second coming. The two are inseparable, of course.

From ancient times, the proclamation of the former has turned millions of people to seek the latter. St. Paul wrote to the Corinthians in his first epistle, at the end of the fifteenth chapter, that magnificent account of the second coming of Jesus Christ!

But the magnificent account of that passage is matched by the first four verses which express in essence and comprehension the clear plan of salvation, "Moreover, brethren, I declare unto you the gospel which I preached unto you, which also ye have received, and wherein ye stand; By which also ye are saved, if ye keep in memory what I preached unto you, unless ye have believed in vain. For I delivered unto you first of all that which I also received, how that Christ died for our sins according to the scriptures; And that he was buried, and that he rose again the third day according to the scriptures" (1 Cor. 15:1-4).

That, my friend, is the good news, the gospel, God's plan for you to be forever saved, to be ready to go when Christ comes again.

On September 5, 1953, during a month-long crusade in Britain, I preached a message on the second coming of Christ. I was recently informed that in the packed crowd in the large tent that night was Constable Baird, his gracious wife, and his three sons — Trevor, 19; Neville, 14; and Clifford, 8.

At the end of the address and in response to the invitation of Jesus to do so, many people came forward and gave their lives to Christ. Among those confessing Christ were Constable and Mrs. Baird and a very decisive and determined Clifford. He was forever changed.

On the way home that night, the father asked Neville and Trevor, "Should the Lord come again tonight, would you go to be with Him?" They didn't think they would. After a grave spiritual struggle, 14-year-old Neville made his response on September 22, and about a week later, Trevor did so.

They were completely changed by giving their lives to Christ. Today Clifford is a psychologist and university instructor living a life of enthusiastic service for Christ, as is his brother Neville and their families in Wheaton, Illinois.

Trevor served for a dozen years as minister of one of Canada's great churches, where it was my privilege to preach. He asked me to speak there on the second coming of Christ, which I did. That night his son Stephen, 19, came forward to surrender his life to Jesus. Trevor exclaimed, "That's three generations of my family — my parents, the three of us brothers, and now my son — all coming to the Lord through your preaching the message of the second coming of Christ."

Friend, before you put this book down, ask yourself, "Am I a total believer in the Lord Jesus Christ as my personal Saviour and

Lord? If Jesus were to come this moment, is my life entirely His?"

If you have the slightest doubt, pray this prayer to Christ, who actually is on the doorstep of your life, "Lord Jesus Christ, come into my life in all Your fullness, cleanse me by Your shed blood from all of my sins, and fill me with Your Holy Spirit. Help me to read Your Word each day. And help me always to be ready for Your coming again by daily prayer and the determination to share my faith with others in the worship and fellowship of Your church. I thank You, Lord Jesus Christ."

Editor's note: Questions regarding specific source references should be directed to John Wesley White, P.O. Box 120, Markham, Ontario L3P 7R5.

Conclusion

Free from Fear in Fearful Times

by William T. James

Humanity, intoxicated on the heady, high-minded wine of willful self-sufficiency, staggers toward the wrath and judgment prophesied for the generation of earth's final days. Mankind cannot find peace, although we continue to struggle in the search, always reformulating the same elements. Time after time, we use the unchanging ingredients in a fatally flawed process that brings only greater wars and more death.

Man's rebellion has led him to the precipice of world societal collapse — a chasm across which no bridge can be built because the building materials have long since been burned up in the fires of human vanities.

Ours is a generation that has expended its future of hope in an orgy of lusting after the pleasures of the moment. Yet, this generation continues to delude itself that a new world order will emerge and ultimately produce a violence-free planetary community — one in which all people are selfless, giving brothers and sisters. Heaven on earth!

Beneath this self-delusion, however, stalks a demon of fear that whispers a message that something other than utopia lurks in the not-too-far distance — an unknown era, month, week, day, hour, minute, and second when all hell will break loose.

Jesus himself predicted that incendiary moment, first when He, as the pre-incarnate Word, gave the prophecy to Jeremiah, who wrote: "Alas! for that day is great, so that none is like it: it is even the time of Jacob's trouble; but he shall be saved out of it" (Jer. 30:7).

The Lord repeated the warning on the Mount of Olives a few hundred years later. "For then shall be great tribulation, such as was not since the beginning of the world to this time, no, nor ever shall be" (Matt. 24:21).

Terrified of the Future

Apprehension about the future more and more frequently pushes men, women, and even children to acts of desperation that only a few decades ago would have been considered aberrant by the behavioral scientists. Today, newscasts and newspapers routinely report such activity, which scarcely raises the eyebrows of the viewers, hearers, and readers. That is, until these horrors invade the communities where we live.

Routine then melts into fear-spawned urgency; we no longer are insulated from the violence by the televisions, radios, and newspapers while we sit in our comfortable homes. We sense that the circle of lawlessness closes ever more tightly, more and more restricting our ability to freely move about our neighborhoods and cities as we please. Increasingly, we are becoming prisoners behind the locked and bolted doors of our homes while the human predators remain at liberty to pick and choose their victims.

There is a much deeper fear than that caused by the explosive growth of crime in our day. It is a visceral terror that haunts every human being who chooses to remain separated from God. It is a constant searching for peace.

To be truly at peace is to be secure, that is, free from uncertainty, about the safety of one's life for both the present and the future. Peace is the absolute assurance that we cannot be harmed regardless of the war-making malefactors that rage all around us.

The essays in this book tell the disturbing truth about this, the most violence-filled of the post-antediluvian world. That reality, by itself, presents enough threat to our hearts with dread of what the future might hold.

But the essayists within this volume have consistently addressed a much deeper source of fear than that generated by the intensification of violence that threatens to consume civilization in a firestorm of anarchy. It is the terrible, nagging emptiness — that cold, black void within the soul of each person who does not know God the Father in a personal, eternal relationship, that gnaws incessantly at the thought processes.

It is the chilling inner realization that when all is said and done, when friends and family are no longer gathered around, when the parties are over and the ringing of laughter and the toasts have died, there remains only the aching emptiness of isolation.

A person who does not know the true God of heaven, you see, according to God's Word, is dead, even while he or she yet walks the earth. Such a lost soul must fearfully confront an eternity of solitary confinement — forever alone in the flames and agony of outer darkness that God's Holy Word terms hell.

Preparing for a Bright Future

A glorious future beyond anything ever conceived by the human mind awaits the true child of God, whose inheritance is assured at the moment of new birth into that heavenly family.

Fear of the future will fade into forgetfulness, and the peace that surpasses understanding will grow mightily within the spirit. Joyous certainty about life in the present — and the future — will overflow and touch the lives of others with the love God has for men, women, and children. This happens naturally as the child of God surrenders to the Father's will.

How can this Father-child relationship come about? How are people reconciled to God, thus allowing the Father to snatch the walking dead from the pathway that leads to hell and give them abundant life with Him for eternity?

The answer is found in the person of Jesus Christ.

". . . There is none other name . . . bwhereby we must be saved" (Acts 4:12).

Jesus himself said, "For the Son of man is come to seek and to save that which was lost" (Luke 19:10).

The way to salvation — that is, to redemption and the reconciliation to God the Father — is found in John 6:40: ". . . every one which seeth the Son, and believeth on him, may have everlasting life: and I will raise him up at the last day."

Again, Jesus said, ". . . I am the way, the truth, and the life: no man cometh unto the Father, but by me" (John 14:6).

Your future is indeed bright beyond imagination if you have prayed the simple prayer: "Come into my heart, Lord Jesus." From that moment, you are the child of the King, a joint heir of Christ. You will reign and rule with the Lord of creation for all eternity!

Earth's Final Generation?

This generation gives every appearance of being the final generation of this earth's age. Jesus Christ's return for His own seems imminent.

When the Lord spoke of His return, he said: ". . . I go to prepare a place for you. And if I go and prepare a place for you, I will come again, and receive you unto myself; that where I am, there ye may be also" (John 14:2-3).

Jesus again says in Revelation 22:7: "Behold, I come quickly [suddenly]. . . ."

When the rapture of God's children occurs, and millions of people suddenly vanish, planet Earth will convulse with tremendous geopolitical and socioeconomic upheaval. Such chaos will demand violently austere measures by panicked governments frantically searching for a way to restore a degree of normality.

The coming of the Antichrist will follow very closely on the heels of the true Christ coming for the redeemed. Whether we are living as part of the generation of earth's final days, or God delays Christ's coming for a generation yet unborn, the reality common to all of us — called "death" — makes our rendezvous with eternity certain.

There will be one generation of believers — those living during the generation of earth's final days — who will not suffer the sting of death.

"O death, where is thy sting? O grave, where is thy victory?" (1 Cor. 15:55).

". . . We shall not all sleep [die], but we shall all be changed, In a moment, in the twinkling of an eye . . ." (1 Cor. 15:51-52).

Even so, come Lord Jesus!

Notes

Chapter One

[1] Stanley J. Grenz, *The Millennial Maze: Sorting Out Evangelical Options* (Downers Grove, IL: InterVarsity Press, 1992), page 14.

[2] Dick Teresi and Judith Hooper, "The Last Laugh?" *Omni,* January 1990, page 44.

[3] Teresi and Hooper, "The Last Laugh?" pages 43-45.

[4] Charles Trombley, "Growth of Major World Religions," *Rhema Sword of the Spirit,* May/June 1986.

[5] Robert A. Morey, *Truth Seekers with Bob Morey,* August 1994, page 1.

[6] Christopher Farley, "Moslem Faithful in USA Tackle Misconceptions," *USA Today,* August 31, 1989, page D5.

[7] Dr. Walter Martin, "Introduction to the Cults" audiotape, Christian Research Institute, 1980.

[8] Ron Rhodes, *The Culting of America* (Eugene, OR: Harvest House, 1994), page 13.

[9] "The Gods of the New Age," Jeremiah Films, 1984.

[10] *New York Times,* April 25, 1982.

[11] Johanna Michaelson, *Like Lambs to the Slaughter* (Eugene OR: Harvest House, 1989), page 11.

[12] Rhodes, *The Culting of America,* page 13.

[13] Rhodes, *The Culting of America,* page 13.

[14] Rhodes, *The Culting of America,* page 28-29.

[15] Dr. Martin, "Introduction to the Cults."

[16] Rhodes, *The Culting of America,* page 17.

[17] David A. Reed and John R. Farkas, *Mormons Answered Verse by Verse* (Grand Rapids, MI: Baker Book House, 1992), page 12.

[18] Rhodes, *The Culting of America,* page 15-16.

[19] John Ankerberg and John Weldon, *The Facts on the New Age Movement* (Eugene, OR: Harvest House, 1988), page 16.

[20] Michaelson, *Like Lambs to the Slaughter,* page 11.

[21] Laird Wilcox, *Guide to the American Occult* (Olathe, KS: Laird Wilcox, 1988), page 82.

[22] "The Gods of the New Age," Jeremiah Films.

[23] Dave Hunt, "The Impact of New Age Concepts on the Church" audiotape, John Ankerberg seminar, 1991.

[24] Dr. Walter Martin, "The Cult of Self-Esteem" audiotape, Christian Research Institute, 1980.

[25] "Shuller Goes Hollywood: Plans to Bring Services to Movies," *Expression,* September 1994, page 7.

[26] Dr. Martin, "The Cult of Self-Esteem."

[27] Dave Hunt and T.A. McMahon, *The Seduction of Christianity* (Eugene, OR: Harvest House, 1986), page 15.

[28] Dr. Martin, "The Cult of Self-Esteem."

[29] Jerald and Sandra Tanner, *Mormonism — Shadow or Reality?* (Salt Lake City, UT: Utah Lighthouse Ministry, 1982), page 187.

[30] Joseph Smith, *The Doctrine and Covenants* (Salt Lake City, UT: The Church of Jesus Christ of Latter-Day Saints, 1986), Sec. 84: 2-5.

[31] Wallace D. Slattery, *Are Seventh-Day Adventists False Prophets?* (Phillipsburg, NJ: Presbyterian & Reformed Publishing Co., 1990), page 50.

[32] Lori MacGregor, "Armstrongism — A Strange Mixture," *News and Views,* January/March, 1988, page 5.

[33] Rhodes, *The Culting of America,* page 210.

[34] *USA Today,* October 20, 1991.

[35] Dave Hunt, "Q & A," *The Berean Call,* July 1994, page 4.

[36] G. Richard Fisher, "Will Jesus Return in 1994?" *The Quarterly Journal,* January/March 1993, page 13 and 1.

[37] Dr. Martin, "Introduction to the Cults."

Chapter Two

[1] "From the Editors," *World Press Review,* October 1993, page 3.

[2] John Lloyd, "New World Wars," *World Press Review,* October 1993, page 8.

[3] Ryszard Malik, "The Federation's Shaky Center," *World Press Review,* October 1993, page 9-10.

[4] Barry Shelby, "Early Warning," *World Press Review,* April 1994, page 5.

[5] Bill Sutton, "Zhirinovsky's . . . Visions," Hal Lindsey's *International Intelligence Briefing,* April 1994, page 8.

[6] Hal Lindsey, "Strategic Forecasts," *International Intelligence Briefing,* April 1994, page 7.

[7] *Arkansas Democrat-Gazette,* April 7, 1994, page 6A.

[8] Hal Lindsey, "Hal Lindsey's Perspective," *International Intelligence Briefing,* September 1994, page 2.

[9] The Prescott Group, "Military Hot Spots Update," *International Intelligence Briefing,* September 1994, page 6.

[10] Hal Lindsey, "Global Watch," *International Intelligence Briefing,* October 1994, page 4.

Chapter Three

[1] Andreas Landwehr, "Headless Dragon? China May Splinter if Deng Dies," Deutsche Presse Agentur, 2/6/95.

Chapter Four

[1] William Cowper, "There Is a Fountain."

Chapter Five

[1] Joseph S. Exell and H.D.M. Spence, editors, *The Pulpit Commentary* (Grand Rapids, MI: William B. Eerdmans Co., 1958), volume 1, "Genesis," by Thomas Whitelaw, page 102-103.

[2] F. Pelitzsch and C.F. Keil, editors, *Commentary on the Old Testament* (Grand Rapids, MI: William B. Eerdmans Co., 1986) volume 1, "The Pentateuch," James Martin, page 141.

[3] Exell and Spence, *The Pulpit Commentary,* page 103.

[4] Pelitzsch and Keil, *Commentary on the Old Testament,* page 137.

[5] Exell and Spence, *The Pulpit Commentary,* page 103.

[6] Exell and Spence, *The Pulpit Commentary,* page 104.

[7] Exell and Spence, *The Pulpit Commentary,* page 246-247.

[8] Exell and Spence, *The Pulpit Commentary,* page 262.

[9] Steven Roberts, *U.S. News & World Report,* August 1, 1994.

[10] Phillip Elmer-Dewitt, *Time,* Fall 1990 Special Issue.

[11] *U.S. News & World Report,* August 29/September 5, 1994.

[12] Michel Marriott, *Newsweek,* December 26/January 2, 1995.

[13] *Newsweek,* December 26/January 2, 1995.

Chapter Six

[1] Philip Robinson and Nancy Tamosalitis, *The Joy of Cybersex: An Underground Guide to Electronic Erotica* (New York, NY: Brady Publishing, 1993).

[2] Robinson and Tamosalitis, *The Joy of Cybersex: An Underground Guide to Electronic Erotica.*

[3] Eugene C. Roehlkepartain, *Youth Ministries Resource Book* (Loveland, CO: Tom Schultz Publications and Group Books, 1988).

Chapter Seven

[1] William J. Bennett, *The Index of Leading Cultural Indicators — Facts and Figures on the State of American Society* (New York, NY: Simon and Schuster, 1994).

[2] Bennett, *The Index of Leading Cultural Indicators,* page 23-36.

[3] Bennett, *The Index of Leading Cultural Indicators,* page 37.

[4] Bennett, *The Index of Leading Cultural Indicators,* page 37.

[5] Richard Nixon, *Beyond Peace* (New York, NY: Random House, 1994).

[6] *Christian Crusade Newspaper,* November 1994, quoting the *Joplin Globe,* 4/30/94.

[7] Stanley Rothman, S. Robert Lichter, and Linda Lichter, *Elites in Conflict: Social Change in America Today* (New York, NY: Praeger, 1992).

[8] William J. Bennett, *The Devaluing of America, The Fight for Our Culture and Our Children* (New York, NY: Simon and Schuster, 1994).

[9] "The Government Waste and Fraud Index," Special White Paper Report for U.S. Taxpayers by the National Taxpayers Union.

[10] Special White Paper Report for U.S. Taxpayers by the National Taxpayers Union.

[11] Texe Marrs, *Big Sister Is Watching You* (Austin, TX: Living Truth Publishers, 1993).

Chapter Eight

[1] Thomas K. Burke, *Moving Toward One World Religion* (Richmond, IN: Endtime, 1993).

[2] Ken Klein, "Catholicsm, Jerusalem, and the United Nations," *Storm Warning,* April 1994.

[3] *This Week in Bible Prophecy,* vol. 1, issue 6, page 5.

[4] *Canada's Western Report,* July 12, 1993.

[5] "Spirit in the Hills," *Houston Chronicle,* May 30, 1993.

[6] "Radiance: A Village that Practices T.M.," *Houston Chronicle,* May 30, 1993.

[7] William F. Jasper, *Global Tyranny . . . Step by Step* (Appleton, WI: Western Islands, 1992), page 4.

[8] Jasper, *Global Tyranny . . . Step by Step,* page 212-213.

Chapter Nine

[1] Carroll Quigley, *Tragedy and Hope* (Hollywood, CA: Angris Press, 1975).

Chapter Ten

[1] John J. Medina, *Uncovering the Mystery of AIDS* (Nashville, TN: Thomas Nelson Publishers, 1993), page 2.

[2] Moody Adams, *AIDS: You Just Think You're Safe* (Los Angeles, CA: Dalton Moody Publishers, Inc., 1986), page 101.

[3] Adams, *AIDS: You Just Think You're Safe,* page 121.

[4] Dr. Peter Duesberg, PhD., spokesman, *Rethinking AIDS,* Monthly publication dedicated to the reappraisal of the HIV/AIDS hypothesis. (415) 775-1884.

[5] *Press Enterprise,* Riverside, CA, 1/31/95.

[6] Dr. Robert Strecker, "Mega Murder," tape, 1993. (213) 344-8038.

[7] Dr. Judith A. Reisman and Edward W. Eichel, *Kinsey, Sex and Fraud* (Lafayette, LA: Huntington House Publishers, 1990), page 119.

[8] David Webber, "AIDS and the Club of Rome," tape. David Webber Ministries, (405) 524-1199.

[9] Robert Harris and Jeremy Paxman, *A Higher Form of Killing* (New York, NY: The Noonday Press, 1982).

[10] Dixy Lee Ray, *Environmental Overkill* (Washington, DC: Regnery Gateway, 1993).

[11] Ray, *Environmental Overkill,* page 77-78, 80, 204.

[12] Adams, *AIDS: You Just Think You're Safe,* page 138-139.

[13] Adams, *AIDS: You Just Think You're Safe,* page 146, 182.

[14] Larry Kramer, "We Have Lost the War Against AIDS," *USA Today,* May 1992.

[15] Mike McManus, *Hemet News,* January 30, 1993.

[16] Adams, *AIDS: You Just Think You're Safe,* page 188-189.

[17] Randy Shilts, *And the Band Played On* (New York, NY: Penguin Books, 1987), page 39.

[18] Lorraine Day, M.D., *AIDS: What the Government Isn't Telling You* (Palm Desert, CA: Rockford Press, 1991), page 122.

[19] Shilts, *And the Band Played On,* page 19.

[20] *Hemet News,* July 9, 1994.

[21] Colonel Ronald D. Ray, USMCR, *Military Necessity & Homosexuality,* (Louisville, KY: First Principles, Inc., 1993), page 40.

[22] James Antonio, *The AIDS Cover-Up* (San Francisco, CA: Ignatius Press, 1987), page 170.

[23] *Lambda Report,* published by the *Report,* June/July 1993.

[24] William H. Masters, M.D., Virginia E. Johnson, and Robert C. Kolodny, *Crisis Heterosexual Behavior in the Age of AIDS* (New York, NY: Grove Press, 1988), page 28-29.

[25] *San Francisco Chronicle,* June 1989, information from the *New England Journal of Medicine,* page 1458.

[26] Day, *AIDS: What the Government Isn't Telling You,* page 30.

[27] Stanley Monteith, M.D., *AIDS: The Unnecessary Epidemic* (Sevierville, TN: Covenant House Books, 1991), page 309.

[28] Day, *AIDS: What the Government Isn't Telling You,* page 84.

[29] Medina, *Uncovering the Mystery of AIDS,* page 106.

[30] "Do Insects Transmit AIDS?" Office of Technology, September 1987, page 15.

[31] Lawrence J. McNamee, M.D., and Brian F. McNamee, M.D., *AIDS* (La Habra, CA: National Medical Legal Publishing House, 1988), page 76.

[32] Keith Stone, "Forced AIDS Tests Gaining Support," *Press Enterprise,* Riverside, CA, March 20, 1994.

[33] Christine Gorman, "Opening the Border to AIDS," *Time,* February 22, 1993.

[34] *Memphis Commercial Appeal,* October 5, 1993.

[35] Adams, *AIDS: You Just Think You're Safe,* page 182.

[36] Monteith, *AIDS: The Unnecessary Epidemic,* page 203, 308.

[37] Ray, *Military Necessity & Homosexuality,* page 171.

[38] *Press Interprise,* August 10, 1994.

[39] "Sex Ed: A Matter of Life and Death," *Redbook,* March 1993, page 50.

[40] Richard D. Glasow, PhD., *School Based Clinics, The Abortion Connection* (Washington, DC: National Right to Life Educational Trust Fund, 1988).

[41] *Insight,* January 31, 1994.

[42] James S. Morre, PhD. and Dorsett D. Smith, M.D., "FACT," FCCP Publication Education Committee, Seattle, WA.

[43] Monteith, *AIDS: The Unncessary Epidemic,* page 47.

Chapter Eleven

[1] Ken Ham, *Genesis and the Decay of the Nations* (El Cajon, CA: Master Book Publishers, 1991), page 2.

[2] Dr. Henry Morris, *The Long War Against God* (Grand Rapids, MI: Baker Book House, 1989), page 145.

[3] Morris, *The Long War Against God,* foreword.

[4] W.R. Bird, *The Origin of Species Revisited* (New York, NY: Philosophical Library, 1987), volume 1, page 5.

[5] Morris, *The Long War Against God,* page 52.

[6] Neil Postman, *The Disappearance of Childhood* (New York, NY: Delacorte Press, 1982), page 151.

[7] Marie Winn, *Children without Childhood* (New York, NY: Pantheon Books, 1981), page 18.

[8] Charles L. Wallis, editor, *Our American Heritage* (New York, NY: Harper & Row, 1970), page 192.

[9] Postman, *The Disappearnace of Childhood.*

[10] Berit Kjos, *Your Child and the New Age* (Wheaton, IL: Victor Books, 1990), page 25.

Chapter Twelve

[1] J.R. Church, *Guardians of the Grail and the Men Who Plan to Rule the World* (Oklahoma City, OK: Prophecy Publications, 1989), page 11.

[2] Albert Pike, *Morals and Dogma of the Ancient and Accepted Scottish Rite of Freema sonry* (Washington, DC: House of the Temple, 1966), page 819. Originally published in 1871 in Charleston, SC.

[3] Gary H. Kah, *Enroute to Global Occupation* (Lafayette, LA: Huntington House Publishers, 1992), page 101, 112, 124.

[4] Kah, *Enroute to Global Occupation,* page 145.

[5] Kah, *Enroute to Global Occupation,* page 28.

[6] Kah, *Enroute to Global Occupation.*

[7] Col. Edward Mandell House, *Philip Dru: Administrator* (Reedy, WV: Liberty Bell Publications, 1912), page 222.

[8] Kah, *Enroute to Global Occupation,* page 20.

[9] Kah, *Enroute to Global Occupation.*

[10] Kah, *Enroute to Global Occupation,* page 45.

[11] *New York Times,* September 12, 1990, page 1.

[12] Gary Allan, *None Dare Call it Conspiracy* (Rossmoor, CA: Concord Press, 1971), page 35.

[13] Kah, *Enroute to Global Occupation,* page 33.

[14] Paul Kurtz, *Humanist Manifestos I and II* (Buffalo, NY: Prometheus Books, 1973), page 21.

[15] Tal Brooke, *When the World Will Be as One* (Eugene, OR: Harvest House Publishers, 1989), page 271.

[16] Ralph Epperson, *The Unseen Hand* (Westlake Village, CA: American Media, 1985), page 368.

[17] James P. Warburg, *The West in Crisis* (Garden City, NY: Doubleday, 1939), page 30.

[18] Epperson, *The Unseen Hand,* page 368.

[19] Kah, *Enroute to Global Occupation,* page 33.

[20] Epperson, *The Unseen Hand,* page 368.

[21] Epperson, *The Unseen Hand,* page 369.

[22] Epperson, *The Unseen Hand,* page 369.

[23] Epperson, *The Unseen Hand,* page 369-370.

[24] Epperson, *The Unseen Hand,* page 370.

[25] United Nations Human Development Report, June 1, 1994.

[26] Pentagon Report on MARC, June 1994.

[27] Martin Monestier, *The Art of Paper Currency* (London, Quartet Books, Ltd., 1983).

Chapter Thirteen

[1] Dave Breese, "The Man with a Plan."

Chapter Fourteen

[1] Lewis Thomas, *The Unforgettable Fire.*

[2] *Toronto Star,* December 26, 1984.

William T. James

William T. James, "Terry," as he is addressed by those who know him, prefers to be thought of as an intensely interested observer of historical and contemporary human affairs, always attempting to analyze that conduct and those issues and events in the light of God's Holy Word, the Bible. He is frequently interviewed in broadcasts throughout the nation.

James has authored, compiled, and extensively edited two previous books, *Storming Toward Armageddon: Essays In Apocalypse* and *The Triumphant Return of Christ: Essays in Apocalypse II*. Each book presents a series of in-depth essays by well-known prophecy scholars, writers, and broadcasters.

As public relations director for several companies, he has written and edited all forms of business communications, both in print and electronic media. Prior to that he worked as creative director for advertising agencies and did extensive political and corporate speech writing as well as formulated position papers on various issues for the clients he served. In addition to writing, he worked closely with clients and broadcast media in putting together and conducting press conferences and other forums.

As with all his books, Terry James' overriding desire for this book is that Jesus Christ be magnified before the world so that all people might be drawn to the Saviour, that the lost might be redeemed, and that the child of God might be persuaded to faithfully work to sow the gospel message while expectantly watching for the soon return of the Lord.

Bob Anderson

Bob Anderson, former radio and TV sports broadcaster and TV station manager, heads Take Heed Ministries, a Christian apologetics ministry dedicated to bringing people involved in cults out of bondage and into a relationship with Jesus Christ. His sensitive and scripturally sound presentations have edified and informed churches around the world on the teachings and pitfalls of modern day cults, including the New Age movement. His teachings explore various theological and sociological problems found in the cults, and provide information that will equip his listeners/viewers with the answers they need for effective witnessing.

Anderson is a graduate of Youngstown State University with a B.A. in telecommunications. He has participated in courses on the cults, world religions, and evangelism at Elim Bible College in Lima, New York, and at East Coast Bible College in Charlotte, North Carolina. He has also taught apologetics at Greater Works School of Ministry in Monroeville, Pennsylvania.

Anderson hosts a satellite television broadcast dealing in a wide range of religious topics.

Phil Arms

Phil Arms is a nationally known evangelist from Houston, Texas, where he recently started the Houston Church and Worship Center, one of the fastest growing churches in America.

As founder and president of Phil Arms Ministries, he conducts city-wide and area-wide crusades, which are recorded for broadcast over his national television and radio programs.

His reputation as a young, dynamic minister with ability to communicate the truths of God as they relate to God's Word generated many invitations to speak from churches and interested groups around the nation. The ministry continues to expand on a nationwide basis.

Phil Arms' television program is now broadcast weekly, and his radio program can be heard daily in most major cities across America. Additionally, he often appears as a guest on both Christian and secular talk shows across the nation, addressing a wide spectrum of topics.

Phil Arms has authored two books on success in life for the Christian, *Wet Flies Can't Fly or (The Keys to the Victorious Christian Life)* and *The Winner in You.*

He and his wife, Suzanne, an accomplished author, recording artist, and speaker in her own right, have two daughters, Britanny, twelve, and Lindsey, eight, and a son, Phillip William, two years old.

The stated goal of Phil Arms Ministries is to reach vast cross sections of the American population with a clarion call to return to the moral and spiritual principles that made this nation great.

Converted as a young man who had grown up going to church regularly but who had rebelliously gone in a direction opposite to God's way, Phil Arms is known for his straight-forward, no-nonsense approach to presenting the uncompromising message of the marvelous, saving gospel of Jesus Christ.

John Barela

John Barela is busily in-volved in one of the most active Bible-centered ministries in America today. As founder and president of Today, the Bible, and You Ministry, his efforts are directed toward disseminating the gospel of Jesus Christ on a daily basis through radio and televi-sion programming, originating from the Tulsa, Oklahoma, area. Also, the ministry's newspaper, *Frontpage,* provides valuable, in-depth insights into issues as ana-lyzed in light of prophecy.

He has pastored churches in Nevada, Wyoming, and Oklahoma, where he currently serves as pastor for Christ Community Church.

John Barela is at the center of a dynamic higher Christian education movement both in his home area of Tulsa and abroad. He is president of Tyndale Bible Institute, which offers an extension program for Bible study, including the establishment of the Bible Institute of St. Petersburg in St. Petersberg, Russia. This exciting, vital program has more than 400 students enrolled at present.

John, who received his theological training at BIOLA (Bible Institute of Los Angeles), has authored a number of books that have generated considerable interest. His most recent books are *The Coming Holocaust in the Middle East, Desert Storm, Phase 2,* and *The New Covenant of Bill Clinton and Al Gore.*

He is a well-known national and international conference and seminar speaker, focusing on Russia, Israel, Korea, South and Central America, and Africa. Additionally, he is frequently sought out for radio, television, and print media interviews on matters of biblical importance, particularly as they pertain to God's prophetic Word.

He is past vice president of Independent Fundamentalist Churches of America.

John and his wife, Sharon, have three children, Scott, John, and Coral. They have nine grandchildren.

Dave Breese

David Breese is an internationally-known author, lecturer, radio broadcaster, and Christian minister. He ministers in church and area-wide evangelistic crusades, leadership conferences, student gatherings, and related preaching missions.

He is president of Christian Destiny, Inc., of Hillsboro, Kansas, a national organization committed to the advancement of Christianity through evangelistic crusades, literature distribution, university gatherings, and the use of radio and television.

Dr. Breese is active in a ministry to college and university students, speaking to them from a background of theology and philosophy. He graduated from Judson College and Northern Seminary and has taught philosophy, apologetics, and Church history. He is frequently involved in lectures, debates, and rap sessions on university campuses.

Breese travels more than 100,000 miles a year and has spoken to crowds across North America, Europe, Asia, the Caribbean, and Latin America. His lectures and debates at universities in the United States and overseas center on the confrontation of Christianity and modern thought.

Breese is also the author of a number of books, including *Discover Your Destiny, His Infernal Majesty, Know the Marks of Cults, Living for Eternity,* and the latest, *Seven Men Who Rule from the Grave.* His books, booklets, and magazine articles have enjoyed wide readership across the world. He also publishes *Destiny Newsletter,* a widely-circulated periodical presenting the Christian view of current events.

Steve Butler

As Life Support Ministries Director for Central Baptist Association, Stephen A. Butler, pastor of Highland Heights Baptist Church in Benton, Arkansas, coordinates Christ-centered support groups sponsored by area Southern Baptist churches for individuals who are dealing with unresolved spiritual and emotional issues in their lives.

A dedicated Southern Baptist, he has pastored churches in Arkansas and Texas, and also has been involved in language missions work among Laotian and Hispanic church groups in Texas. He is currently president of the Saline County Ministerial Alliance, an association of ministers that seeks to promote inter-church cooperation in benevolence work in their community.

Butler holds degrees in history and political science from the University of Central Arkansas at Conway as well as a Master of Divinity degree from Southwestern Baptist Theological Seminary in Fort Worth.

Steve and his wife, Barbara, an elementary school teacher, have two children: Lori, an eleventh-grader, and Brian, a tenth-grader. Both Lori and Brian know Jesus Christ as their personal Saviour and are active in their church's youth ministry.

Steve Butler's desire is to proclaim Jesus Christ as the Saviour of the world and to see this generation prepared for His second coming.

J.R. Church

J.R. Church is widely recognized as among the foremost prophecy teachers in America. He has authored numerous books on the subject, among them, *Hidden Prophecies in the Song of Moses, Hidden Prophecies in the Psalms,* and *Guardians of the Grail,* which tells of European political intrigue and the move toward a New World Order. His books have sold hundreds of thousands of copies worldwide, having been translated into a number of languages.

In 1964, he organized a church in Lubbock, Texas, where he pastored for over 17 years, building a large bus ministry and a Christian school. He moved to Oklahoma City in 1979, and over the years has developed the ministry, Prophecy in the News.

The ministry publishes a monthly newspaper on prophetic research entitled *Prophecy in the News* and presents a syndicated television broadcast by the same name, which airs on stations across the country and by satellite network to the entire western hemisphere.

Converted at age seven, he set out with one main goal in life — to win people to Jesus Christ. He and his wife, Linda, have been married 35 years. They have two children, a daughter, Teri, and a son, Jerry, Jr.

J.R. Church is in wide demand as a speaker and lecturer on matters pertaining to biblical prophecy, appearing at national and international prophecy conferences and seminars. In addition, he is often seen and heard on various television and radio shows throughout the nation.

His latest books include *They Pierced the Veil,* a commentary on the 12 minor prophets, and *The Mystery of the Menorah.*

Don S. McAlvany

Donald S. McAlvany is the editor of the *McAlvany Intelligence Advisor,* a monthly geopolitical/financial intelligence newsletter analyzing global economic, social, political, and monetary developments, free enterprise system, families, and personal finances for today and the future of America.

His hard-hitting approach has made him a favorite on such radio talk shows as Marlin Maddoux's "Point of View," Moody Network's "Prime Time America," South Africa's 15-million viewer prime time Network, and many more. In 1990, he launched his own radio show that quickly gained acceptance throughout the U.S.

McAlvany, a featured speaker at Christian, political, monetary, and investment conferences all over the world, has met with South Africa's most influential political, business, and military leaders.

A member of the Counsel on National Policy, McAlvany serves on the board of the Conservative Caucus, is chairman of the Council on Southern Africa, was founder of the Industry Council on Tangible Assets, and is one of the founding directors of the Fellowship of Christian Financial Advisors.

With a background in under-cover intelligence work, he remains closely connected with the international intelligence community. President and owner of International Collectors Associates, a securities, precious metals brokerage, and consultation firm, Don and his wife have four children and currently reside in Durango, Colorado.

To order the McAlvany Intelligence Advisor, contact:
McAlvany Intelligence Advisor
PO Box 84904
Phoenix, AZ 85071
One year (12 issues) $115; Two years (24 issues) $185
Foreign Airmail: One year (12 issues) $145; Two years (24 issues) $241

D.A. Miller

D.A. Miller is an author, researcher, and in-demand lecturer for conferences on AIDS and other topics of interest to Christian and secular audiences alike. She has co-produced a video, works as a consultant on made-for-TV movies, and written two prophecy best-sellers, including *Forbidden Knowledge*. Miller also collaborates on books with other Christian authors and has had numerous articles published in Christian periodicals such as *Power for Living, Seek, War Cry,* and *Songs from the Heart.* Her 25 years as a nursing home volunteer prompted her to write two books on volunteerism in nursing homes as well.

God's preparation has given occasion for Dorothy to speak on a number of television programs as well as hundreds of radio programs. It was her work with Jeremiah Films on some of its outstanding documentaries that laid the groundwork for her interest in and knowledge of the vital subject of AIDS. As a conference speaker in Vail, Colorado, with Hal Lindsey, Chuck Missler, and Don McAlvany, Miller's perceptive presentation about the AIDS epidemic prompted a standing ovation. People appreciated hearing the truth about AIDS.

Dorothy has been active in Christian service since she accepted Christ as her personal Saviour at the age of nine. She and her husband, Tom, who works as a volunteer-director in a mercy-ship ministry, have established a number of businesses, including a nationally recognized equestrian center.

Chuck Missler

As an expert on Russia, Israel, Europe, and the Middle East, Chuck Missler gives intriguing behind-the-scenes insight to his audiences. His more than 30 years in the corporate world as CEO of four public corporations contracting with the U.S. Department of Defense has left him with an extensive network of overseas contacts. With affiliates and associates in nine countries, Missler is a major contributor to several international intelligence newsletters. He has also negotiated joint ventures in Russia, Israel, Malaysia, Japan, Algeria, and Europe.  In addition, Missler is an authority on advanced weapons and strategic resources and has participated in projects with SAMCOM-USSR, DSL, JCS, USACADA, DOJ, CCIA, and SDI. A member of the International Press Association, he is an honors graduate from the U.S. Naval Academy.

For 20 years, Chuck Missler taught a Bible study in southern California that grew to more than 2,000 attendees. In 1992, he moved to Coeur d'Alene, Idaho, where he founded Koinonia House to distribute his books, lectures, and tapes. His dynamic style, conservative values, and adherence to biblical principles have made him a highly acclaimed speaker and critic.

His newsletter, *Personal UPDATE,* a Christian prophecy and intelligence newsletter, has grown to reach more than 45,000 monthly subscribers and he has more than 8 million tapes in circulation worldwide.

If you wish to receive a 12-month complimentary subscription, call 1-800-UPDATE-1.

Lester Sumrall

Sixty-five years ago, God gave a sickly young man the choice to either die, or live and preach the uncompromised Word of God. The choice was simple. Since that day, Lester Sumrall has never relented in his desire to fulfill his calling.

Respected throughout the world as a missionary statesman, Lester Sumrall has founded churches from Australia to Alaska. His travels to over 100 countries and visits with various world leaders have given him invaluable insight in his study of biblical prophecy.

He traveled through turbulent China during the mid-30s. He traveled across the Soviet Union while Josef Stalin was in control. He preached in Berlin while Adolph Hitler was in power. He saw the rebirth of the nation of Israel, and even lived in Jerusalem during the 1956 Sinai War.

His love for Israel and respect for its place in God's heart has driven him to study biblical prophecy intently. He has visited Israel over 50 times to research and study biblical events on the very spots where they took place.

Lester Sumrall continues to travel widely in championing the cause of Christ, often journeying overseas to pioneer new projects and to supervise those which he has already established.

David F. Webber

Dr. David Webber, a speaker for more than 35 years on Southwest Radio Church, a long-running radio broadcast ministry founded by his father, E. F. Webber, in the 1930s, is a well-known author of a number of significant books on prophecy. He has conducted tours to Israel and to other regions of interest to Christians. He is an internationally-known conference speaker and publishes a monthly newsletter, *David Webber Reports*. David Webber Ministries produces a daily radio broadcast and a weekly shortwave radio program heard worldwide.

During his many years of Christian broadcast work, David has interviewed most every prophetic scholar of note from around the world. Additionally, he himself is often sought out for interviews on biblically prophetic matters as they relate to current events and issues.

Dr. Webber attended Oklahoma City University, where he obtained a B.A. in theology, and Belen Memorial University in Chillicothe, Missouri, where he received an honorary doctorate.

His published books include *The Image of the Ages* and *The Mark is Ready,* which is scheduled to be released in early 1995.

John Wesley White

As an associate evangelist in the Billy Graham Evangelistic Association, Dr. John Wesley White is one of the team of men selected by Dr. Billy Graham to assist him in the worldwide work of evangelism. Along with responsibilities in the crusade services, Dr. White addresses the School of Evangelism, speaks at universities, civic clubs, professional sports team chapels, churches, and prisons during a crusade period. Dr. White also holds area-wide, as well as occasional single-church evangelistic crusades, speaks at conventions and special meetings, and presents the gospel on radio and television.

John Wesley White, a native of Saskatchewan, Canada, has a B.A. degree from Wheaton College, Wheaton, Illinois and a Ph.D in the Origins and Development of the Modern Ecumenical movement from Oxford University, Oxford England. He did extensive research work in Europe at Queens University, Belfast, Ireland, and Trinity College (Dublin University) in the field of ecclesiastical history.

Dr. White initially became interested in the work of Billy Graham in November, 1949, when he first heard him in Chicago. Dr. Graham asked him to become associate evangelist in June 1961.

In recent years, he has been the speaker on "Agape" and "Join the Family" television programs. He currently is the speaker on "The White Paper," a news/prophecy television program seen coast to coast in Canada and the United States. He has authored 20 books.

Dr. White most recently served 16 years as chancellor of Richmond College in Toronto. He believes scripturally-based presentation of the gospel of Jesus Christ, set in the current events of the times in which we live, is the only solution to the problems our world faces today.

During his first European tour, he met Kathleen Calderwood in Belfast, Ireland. They were married in 1952 and are the parents of four sons. Dr. and Mrs. White reside in Ontario, Canada.

i.e.
issues and events
from prophetic perspectives

The William T. James monthly briefing paper that presents analysis of current issues and events in the words of the world's best-known writers, speakers, and broadcasters

For a free issue of "i.e." simply fill in, then clip the coupon below and send to:

James Informarketing
P.O. Box 1108
Benton, AR 72018-1108

Please include with the coupon a self-addressed, business-sized envelope stamped with first-class postage.

Please send me a free issue of "i.e." I have enclosed, along with this coupon, a business-sized envelope stamped with first-class postage.

Name _____

Address _____
     (Street)

_____
  (City)   (State)   (Zip)
